ISIS

A HISTORY

ISIS

FAWAZ A. GERGES

WITH A NEW PREFACE BY THE AUTHOR

PRINCETON UNIVERSITY PRESS

PRINCETON AND OXFORD

Copyright © 2016 by Princeton University Press
Preface to the paperback edition copyright © 2017 by Princeton University Press
Published by Princeton University Press,
41 William Street, Princeton,
New Jersey 08540
In the United Kingdom: Princeton University Press,
6 Oxford Street, Woodstock, Oxfordshire OX20 1TR

press.princeton.edu

Cover design by Jason Alejandro

Fifth printing, and first paperback printing, 2017
Paperback ISBN 978-0-691-17579-9
Cloth ISBN 978-0-691-17000-8

The Library of cataloged the cloth edition of this book as follows:
Library of Congress Control Number: 2015956950

British Library Cataloging-in-Publication Data is available

This book has been composed in Sabon Next LT Pro

Printed on acid-free paper. ∞

Printed in the United States of America

10 9 8 7 6 5

To the Yazidi women who have suffered the brunt of ISIS's "culture cleansing" with such fortitude. Their courage in the midst of a sea of savagery is living testament to the resilience of the human spirit.

CONTENTS

PREFACE TO THE PAPERBACK EDITION

Since publication of the book a year ago, a series of dramatic events continue to keep ISIS atop headlines around the world. Despite relentless bombings and ground offensives by the US-led coalition and other local forces against ISIS targets in Iraq, Syria, and Libya, ISIS has shown resilience, creativity, and organizational depth and has carried out spectacular terrorist operations worldwide. Even with dramatic and developing current events and a shifting landscape, the book's findings and conclusions continue to resonate. The social and political crisis in the Middle East that has given rise to ISIS and other jihadist groups will not be resolved for the foreseeable future.

Broken state institutions and ungovernable spaces in Syria, Iraq, Libya, Yemen and elsewhere continue to provide ISIS and Al Qaeda Central (AQ) with refuge. Jihadism is nourished in conflict zones, and the raging wars in the Greater Middle East have been and remain a fertile breeding ground for jihadists. ISIS and other sectarian-based militias receive further sustenance from deepening sectarian tensions between Sunni Muslims and Shia Muslims, coupled with a fierce geostrategic and geosectarian rivalry between Saudi Arabia and Iran.

What all this means is that even if ISIS is overrun militarily in the coming year or so as seems likely, the jihadist group will revert to its original type—urban guerrilla warfare and counterinsurgency in the Middle East, and terrorism worldwide.

Increasing evidence shows that ISIS has already begun to brace itself for the morning after the violent storm demolishes its "caliphate" in Iraq and Syria and Libya, and expels the group from major cities and towns under its rule. While ISIS is losing territories in Iraq and Syria and Libya, it is spreading its tentacles near and far, setting up transnational networks, bases, and sleeping cells in many countries, including Yemen, Egypt, and beyond. ISIS's planners and ideologues have made it clear that the fight will go on even if the "caliphate" is militarily crushed.

In May 2016, in one of his last messages before he was killed by a US airstrike in Syria in September, Abu Mohammad al-Adnani, the second most powerful man after the top leader, Abu Bakr al-Baghdadi, prepared ISIS's followers for future battles:

> Do you, O America consider defeat to be the loss of a city or the loss of land? Were we defeated when we lost the cities in Iraq and were in the desert without any city or land [2006–2010]? And would we be defeated and you be victorious if you were to take Mosul or Sirte or Raqqa or even take all the cities and we were to return to our initial condition? Certainly not!

Adnani's defiance carries within it two messages: a threat to attack America and its allies and a reminder of the dynamism, adaptability, and resilience of jihadist groups like ISIS. Time and again, despite the frequent announcement of prominent jihadists, many around the world overlook ISIS's ability for self-renewal and regeneration. Al Qaeda in Iraq (AQI) is a case in point. After suffering a crippling blow by Iraqi Sunnis who got fed up with AQI's extremism between 2006 and 2010, ISIS's progenitor bided its time until circumstances in Iraq facilitated its spectacular rebirth.

Even if the "caliphate" in Iraq and Syria collapses militarily, ISIS will return to its "initial condition," which in Adnani's words means carrying out terrorist operations and biding its time. A more alarming long-term prognosis is that the "caliphate" model set up by Baghdadi, Adnani, and their associates, which has survived for a few years, will provide motivation and inspiration for the next jihadist wave. Long after Baghdadi disappears from the scene, his "caliphate" legacy will continue to haunt the imagination of fellow jihadists.

Indeed, ISIS faces reckoning. It is on the defensive and bleeding, losing territories in Iraq, Syria, Libya, and losing top leaders, field commanders, and thousands of skilled combatants. The loss of skilled fighters, in particular, is hampering ISIS's capacity to defend its urban centers. It is showing fatigue, corrosion, and cracks within its ranks, no longer capable of replacing seasoned fighters who are killed on the battlefields. Foreign fighters, who represent the backbone of ISIS's military apparatus, have almost dried up, especially after Turkey's August 2016 military incursion into Syria and the "cleansing" of the border.

The group's financial empire has been systemically dismantled by the US-led coalition, exacting a heavy toll on its ability to pay the salaries of its fighters and the costs of providing minimal services to the inhabitants under its rule. Residents say life under ISIS has become more hellish, living precariously at the mercy of the group's severe rules and the danger of constant airstrikes. Pressed hard to either militarily join the ISIS fight or pay more taxation, many peoples in Mosul, Iraq's second most populous city, and Raqqa, the group's nominal capital in Syria, attempt to flee with their families, risking their lives.

ISIS's aura of invincibility and legitimacy, resulting from its earlier military success, appears to be shattered beyond repair. In the eyes of Sunni Muslims who initially welcomed ISIS as liberators and protectors, Baghdadi, Adnani, and their associates had promised heaven but have delivered only dust: a utopia has turned into a nightmare. As the group suffers more military setbacks in Iraq and Syria and Libya, popular anger and despair have not turned into a floodgate of revolt yet. There are few credible reports of armed resistance by residents in Mosul and Raqqa against ISIS. Ghastly videos of executions of alleged "traitors" and "collaborators" with the Iraqi government are likely pre-emptive measures. Unlike Fallujah, which was swiftly re-captured by Iraqi forces in June 2016 after an extended siege, Mosul is a much tougher battle. As ordered by Abu Bakr al-Baghdadi in an audiotape, ISIS combatants are putting up stiff and creative resistance, and fighting to the last breath.

Although the US says it has killed 50,000 ISIS fighters, these losses do not mark the beginning of the end of the Islamic State. Far from it. As the battle for Mosul shows, ISIS's dedicated followers will not give up that easily. As long as ISIS occupies Mosul and, more importantly, Raqqa, its self-declared capital, there will be no closure. The group is hunkering down and digging trenches in both cities, bracing itself for a long, bloodied and a costly fight. One of the lessons learned since the US led a global coalition against ISIS in 2014 is that the group will not collapse quickly. The most core ISIS members fight to the bitter end, to the last man, as Baghdadi put it in an early pronouncement. Despite the high attrition rate of skilled combatants removed from the battlefields, ISIS has plenty of die-hard fanatics who wage a protracted battle and die for the cause, leaving cities and towns in ruins.

Another complicating factor is that Al Qaeda is positioning itself to inherit the spoils of the Islamic State in Syria and Iraq and beyond. Sensing an opportune moment with the accumulation of ISIS's military losses, Ayman al-Zawahiri reiterated criticism of ISIS's shortsightedness and recklessness while also calling on Iraqis to wage a guerrilla war against the Shia based regime in Baghdad. In Syria, Zawahiri has guided Al Qaeda's affiliate, Jabhat al-Nusra, which has changed its name to Jabhat Fatah al-Sham, to blend with other moderate rebels, thus securing a jihadist base in Belad al-Sham (Greater Syria or the Levant). Moreover, the war in Yemen, fuelled mainly by a rivalry between Saudi Arabia and Iran, has empowered Zawahiri's more important outfit in the country, Al Qaeda in the Arabian Peninsula (AQAP), allowing it to control huge swaths of territory and important financial assets, such as ports and banks.

As the dust settles on the battlefield in the Middle East in the coming years, the challenge facing war-torn societies will be not only physical reconstruction but also state building and social and political development. Both AQ and ISIS are creatures of fragile and broken state institutions. Although the "caliphate" in Iraq and Syria will ultimately be forced to surrender the major cities it controls, the movement will persist as long as Sunni communities feel excluded from the existing order and as long as regional and great powers instrumetalize radical groups to achieve political ends. Inclusive governance is key to addressing the multi-faceted organic crisis that has shaken the very foundation of the Middle Eastern state system, fuelling large scale social protests, revolutions, armed insurgencies, and the rise of tribal, parochial and sectarian tendencies.

ACKNOWLEDGMENTS

It is easy to dismiss the Salafi-jihadists of the so-called Islamic State—also known as ISIS, ISIL, or by its Arabic acronym, *Da'esh*—as monsters, savages, and killers. It is also tempting to belittle their religious fanaticism and messianism as un-Islamic. This type of moral and ethical condemnation overlooks a painful truth: that an important Sunni constituency believes in the group's utopian and romantic vision of building an Islamic state, even though many might not condone its gruesome violence. Other Sunnis have lent a helping hand to ISIS because they see it as an effective bulwark against the Shia- and Alawite-dominated governments in Baghdad and Damascus respectively, as well as their Iranian patrons. Through its rapid emergence in the aftermath of the civil strife that has gripped the Middle East since 2011, ISIS has managed to effectively tap into a crisis of Sunni Arab identity in Iraq, Syria, and beyond.

ISIS's planners and ideologues are not wild madmen who parachuted into Iraq and Syria from nowhere. The group is a proud member of a Salafi-jihadist family that has given birth to similar offspring, including Egyptian Islamic Jihad, Al Qaeda Central (AQC), Al Qaeda in Iraq (AQI), and Al Qaeda in the Arabian Peninsula (AQAP) over the past three decades. ISIS does not differ either from its predecessors or its current jihadist rivals except by its extreme violence, a spectacle staged to deter enemies and inspire young recruits. It is worth mentioning that ISIS's progenitor, AQI, pioneered the practice of staging displays of flamboyant violence, including beheadings.

Salafi-jihadism might not be a mass movement but it is surely a social movement with transnational networks and an expanding social base, especially among the youth. Across all age groups, the young seem to be drawn to ISIS's message of salvation, military triumph, and domination over the enemies of Islam, defined mainly as the infidels and heretics—in particular, the Shia minority. Regardless of what happens to ISIS, the ideology of Salafi-jihadism is here to stay and likely to gain more converts, particularly after the derailment of the Arab Spring uprisings, when doors to peaceful political change have been closed. The ISIS narrative has greater appeal due to the absence of credible alternatives.

This fact calls for critical deliberation and investigation of the forces behind this complex modern phenomenon as well as its resilience and durability. This book does precisely that by focusing on the social and political factors that fueled ISIS's rebirth and its current and long-term strengths and weaknesses. It examines ISIS in comparative perspective by contrasting the group with like-minded Salafi-jihadists of the Al Qaeda variety. Taking ISIS's Salafi-jihadist ideology seriously, the book explores its appeal among local and foreign recruits as well as its narrative of ritualized violence. The journey of Abu Bakr al-Baghdadi, ISIS's leader, is pieced together in this book from the recollections of contemporary witnesses in order to make sense of this "mysterious" man, but, more importantly, in order to assess his role and influence within the group.

ISIS's story is complex and it cannot be derived from its propaganda narrative, a narrative that some scholars take for granted at their own peril. By relying, for the most part, on primary Arabic sources, this book critically engages with ISIS's pronouncements and literature as well as the writings of protagonists within the larger Islamist and Salafi-jihadist movement; these protagonists sometimes attack and sometimes support one another, varying in respect to particular issues related to ISIS's conduct and goals. In a way, this book is a dialogue in Islamist politics, shedding further light on the inner workings of the global jihadist movement and the shifting loyalties and alliances among its lieutenants and chiefs. It is an extension of field research that I have conducted on radical religious activists over the past two decades.

Given the near impossibility of conducting interviews with ISIS's members (any claim otherwise would be bogus), I have relied on hundreds of firsthand articles and reports by Arab journalists, activists, and observers inside Iraq, Syria, and elsewhere. My narrative has been enriched by their meticulous coverage of ISIS and the conflicts raging in the Arab heartland. There is not enough space here to list all of these contributors who report from the field and the region. Above all, though, I am indebted to the reportage of Wael Essam, Ra'id al-Hamed, Omar al-Jabouri, and Bassam al-Badareen at *al-Quds al-Arabi*, a pan-Arab newspaper; Ali al-Sibai, Alaa Yussef, Ahmed al-Anbari, Yasir al-Za'atirah, and Hisham al-Hashimi at AlJazeera.net, a popular online news site; Mohamed Abu Rumman, a specialist on Salafis and Salafi-jihadists, at *Al Ghad*, a Jordanian-based newspaper; Abdullah Suleiman Ali at *Assafir*, a Lebanese-based newspaper; Kamil al-Taweel and Hazem Amin at *Al Hayat*, a pan-Arab newspaper; and Saheeb Anjarini and Firas al-Hakkar at *al-Akhbar*, a Lebanese-based newspaper. I have also benefited from the writing of Abdel-Bari Atwan, a Palestinian journalist and author, and Hassan Abu Haniyeh, a Jordanian researcher, both specialists on Salafi-jihadists. In addition, I have widely consulted articles and studies by Western journalists and writers as well as reports by the Syrian Observatory for Human Rights, the International Crisis Group, Amnesty International, and Human Rights Watch.

I have been extremely fortunate to have a group of sharp doctoral candidates at the London School of Economics who assisted me in my research and writing of the book. I am particularly appreciative of the great skill and invaluable input of my research assistant, Ms. Anissa Haddadi, who saw the project

through from inception to conclusion. I owe special thanks
to Mr. Andrew Delatolla, who edited, synthesized, and organized most of the chapters. My thanks go to Mr. Ranj Alaaldin
for critiquing chapters 3 and 5 on Iraq. Ms. Magdalena C.
Delgado was kind to edit chapter 3.

Mr. Moustafa Menshawy, a doctoral candidate at the University of Westminster, and Ms. Sherifa Abdel-Razek, an MSc
student at LSE, researched Salafi-jihadist websites and helped
access valuable primary material. My thanks also go to Ms.
Noor Al-Bazzaz, consultant and researcher on Syria and Iraq
and a promising young scholar, who edited, critiqued, and organized chapters 3, 6, and 7 and the conclusion.

Of the many senior scholars whose feedback helped
improve the book, I owe special thanks to Professor Nader
Hashemi, director of the Center for Middle East Studies at the
University of Denver. Nader promptly and critically read
every chapter and offered substantive comments. I also want to
thank Emile A. Nakhleh, research professor at the University
of New Mexico, who read chapters 1, 2, and 8 and the conclusion. His critique forced me to sharpen my arguments.

The chapters on Iraq were strengthened considerably as a
result of several conversations I had with Professors Kamil
Mahdi, political economist, and Saad Jawad, sociologist. Kamil
and Saad challenged the dominant discourse on Iraq and drew
my attention to major gaps in the literature on the war-torn
country. Similarly, the chapter on Syria greatly benefited from
critical feedback by Professor David W. Lesch of Trinity University, Professor Jasmine Gani of St. Andrews University, and
Dr. Linda Matar, a research fellow at the National University
of Singapore. Kamran Bokhari, an author and a specialist on
Islamism and Muslim geopolitics, provided substantive feedback on chapter 8 and the conclusion. I am deeply appreciative of these scholars' time and effort.

I could not have asked for a more informed and gentler edi-
tor than Eric Crahan at Princeton University Press. A historian
at heart, Eric was supportive of my attempt to move beyond

journalistic and securitization accounts toward a more empirically rich and analytically rigorous narrative. I owe appreciation to Jennifer Lyons, a friend and my book agent; without her prodding me to write this book, it would never have come to fruition.

Last but not least, I could not have written this book without the support and sacrifice of my family. For more than a year and a half, I labored hard to complete the manuscript, often at the expense of being with Nora and the children. The beauty and the burden of writing books is that they become a family affair. A loving critic and a lifelong inspiration, Nora gave me the necessary time and space to write. Whenever I reached a hurdle, I called my eldest son, Bassam, who is finishing his law degree at Yale University, to brainstorm. My daughter, Annie-Marie, who is completing an undergraduate degree in Middle Eastern studies at Manchester University, often pointed out missing links and connections in my story. Hannah, seventeen, frequently asked: How could an extreme organization like ISIS exist in the twenty-first century? And why does the world not do more to confront the group? Laith, fourteen, regularly engaged in heated discussions with Hannah about the deep divisions in our world, and the need to understand the soil from which ISIS has sprung.

Fawaz A. Gerges
London School of Economics
January 7, 2016

ISIS

INTRODUCTION:

DOWN THE RABBIT HOLE AND

INTO THE HISTORY OF ISIS

Following a rapid rise and concomitant territorial conquests, the so-called Islamic State, also known as ISIS (Islamic State of Iraq and Syria), ISIL (Islamic State of Iraq and wa-Sham or Levant), or by its Arabic abbreviation, *Da'esh*, has for now, by default, taken operational command and leadership of the global jihadist movement, eclipsing Al Qaeda Central (AQC), which attacked the US homeland on September 11, 2001. At the time of writing, ISIS controls a wide swath of territory in Iraq and Syria, as large as the United Kingdom, with a population estimated at roughly between six million and nine million people. Additionally, ISIS controls a sectarian army numbering more than thirty thousand combatants, in part through an amalgamation of local armed insurgencies in Iraq and Syria and foreign recruits.

ISIS's military surge in Syria and Iraq in 2013 and 2014 was a rude awakening for regional and global powers. Despite being trained by the United States and costing anywhere between $8 billion and $25 billion,[1] the Iraqi security forces were shattered like a house of glass in the summer of 2014 by ISIS's blitzkrieg, which was carried out by a force numbering only in the hundreds or at most the low thousands, catching neighboring states and the great powers off guard. According to the *New York Times*, an army that once counted 280,000 active-duty personnel, one of the largest in the Middle East, was now believed to have as few as 50,000 men by some estimates.[2] In June 2014, a few weeks before ISIS captured Mosul, Iraq's second largest city, with a population of almost two million people, US president Barack Obama derisively dismissed the organization as amateurish and said that it did not represent a serious threat to America's regional allies or interests: "The analogy we use around here sometimes, and I think is accurate, is if a 'j.v.' team puts on Lakers uniforms that doesn't make them Kobe Bryant. . . . I think there is a distinction between the capacity and reach of bin Laden and a network that is actively planning major terrorist plots against the homeland versus jihadists who are engaged in various local power struggles and disputes, often sectarian."[3] Although Obama is correct to say that ISIS did not pose an immediate or a strategic menace to the US homeland, critics seized on his comment as evidence of the Administration's underestimation of ISIS's strength.

From 2013 until the summer of 2014, ISIS overran Iraqi, Syrian, and Kurdish security forces and rival Islamists as well. The group's prowess was confirmed by the seizure of al-Raqqa and Deir al-Zour provinces in Syria in 2014 and the expeditious collapse of four Iraqi divisions overnight in Mosul and elsewhere in northern Iraq under the determined assault of outnumbered fighters in summer 2014.[4] ISIS's sweep of the so-called Sunni Triangle—an area of central Iraq to the west and north of Baghdad mostly populated by Sunni Muslims—and the threat to the Kurdish regional capital of Irbil alarmed the governments across the Middle East and the Western powers. US officials feared that Saudi Arabia and Jordan might be the next ISIS targets.[5]

By the end of 2014 ISIS had captured approximately a third of Syrian and Iraqi territories and had edged closer to the Iraqi–

Jordanian–Saudi Arabian frontiers, with significant networks of supporters in both Jordan and Saudi Arabia. In Lebanon, ISIS is purported to possess a few hundred fighters on the Syrian-Lebanese border at Lebanon's eastern and northern front. ISIS and its network of like-minded militants have carried out spectacular suicide bombings and made multiple deadly incursions into Lebanese territory, capturing dozens of Lebanese security forces and traumatizing a society already polarized along social and sectarian lines. In addition, the organization's tentacles have spread to Egypt, Libya, Yemen, North Africa, Afghanistan, Nigeria, and beyond, exposing the fragility of the Arab state system and the existence of profound ideological and communal cleavages within Middle Eastern and Islamic societies.[6] To maintain their interests and prevent the collapse of the Iraqi and Syrian regimes, the United States and Russia are leading two different coalitions and waging sustained airstrikes against ISIS and other affiliated armed groups in both countries. At the time of writing, at the end of 2015, the effectiveness of the US and Russian coalitions has been limited due to the fierce rivalry between the global and regional powers. This might change, as in November 2015 ISIS allegedly exploited a security loophole at Sharm al-Sheikh Airport in Egypt and smuggled a homemade bomb on board a Russian jet, which killed 224 passengers. The group also carried out a massive operation in Paris with seven suicide bombers that killed and injured hundreds of civilians on November 13, 2015. A day earlier ISIS struck a crowded neighborhood in Beirut, Lebanon, with two suicide bombers leaving a trail of blood and destruction. On December 2, 2015, two "supporters" of the group, a husband, Syed Rizwan Farook, twenty-eight, and a wife, Tashfeen Malik, twenty-nine, attacked a social services center in San Bernardino, California, in the United States, killing at least fourteen people and wounding twenty-one. Russia and the Western powers, particularly France, have begun to indirectly coordinate with one another, ratcheting up attacks against areas held by ISIS in Syria, though this coordination is still in its infancy.

President Obama said he was open to cooperating with Russia in the campaign against ISIS if President Vladimir V. Putin begins targeting the group, though the two great powers have divergent interests in Syria.[7]

ISIS represents a new step, a new wave, in jihadism. In contrast to ISIS's stunning rise, Al Qaeda Central, the previous leading group of global jihadism or Salafi-jihadism (the two terms are used interchangeably to refer to militant religious activists of the Al Qaeda variety), seems small by comparison. It possessed fewer than three thousand fighters and no territories of its own, a borderless, stateless, transnational social movement during the height of its power in the late 1990s. Osama bin Laden, Al Qaeda's emir, was under the protection of the Taliban in Afghanistan, swearing fealty to its leader, Mullah Omar (pronounced dead of natural causes in 2015). In sharp contrast, ISIS's chief, Ibrahim ibn Awwad Ibrahim Ali al-Badri al-Samarrai, better known under his nom de guerre, Abu Bakr al-Baghdadi, anointed himself the new caliph, or supreme ruler of Muslims worldwide, thus challenging Omar's claim to the same title. ISIS's blatant challenge of the Al Qaeda leadership and its imperial ambitions show an organization determined to impose its will as a new major player in the region and as a de facto state as well.

ISIS marks a new peril to the regional security order at a time of fierce social and political struggle within Arab societies and creeping sectarianism fueled mainly by the geostrategic rivalry between Shia-dominated Iran and Sunni-dominated Saudi Arabia. ISIS not only threatens the survival of civil-war-stricken Syria and the Iraqi state that was set up after the US-led invasion and occupation in 2003, but also the stability of neighboring Arab countries. Its ability to do so stems more from the fragility of the Arab state system than its own strength as a strategic actor. Baghdadi and his planners have recently devoted more resources and effort to local divisions that pledged their loyalty to ISIS. For example, ISIS's Egyptian affiliate, Wilayet Sinai (Sinai Province), which is active in the north Sinai region, has waged economic warfare against the state. Carrying out deadly operations against the Egyptian security forces and foreign targets in the capital and beyond, Wilayet Sinai threatens the tourist sector, a lifeline of the Egyptian economy. With its role in the crash of a Russian passenger jet in Sinai in October 2015 that killed all 224 people on board, ISIS's chapter in Egypt has shown organizational capacity and potency. United Nations and Western officials with access to intelligence reports say that of the eight affiliate groups that pledged allegiance to ISIS worldwide, they are most worried about the Libyan arm based in Surt, a port city on the Mediterranean about four hundred miles southeast of Sicily. According to a November 2015 report by a UN monitoring group examining terrorist groups in Libya, it is the only affiliate now operating under the direct centralized control of ISIS with as many as three thousand fighters, half of whom are based in Surt, and many clustered to the east, around Nawfaliya. As military pressure intensified against ISIS in Syria and Iraq, Baghdadi has dispatched scores of his lieutenants to Surt as a rearguard base to fall back to if the organization is forced out of Syria.[8]

Arab countries, however, are in part responsible for the growth of armed nonstate actors such as ISIS. If the chaos in both Iraq and Syria provided ISIS with a fertile ground to implant, expand, and consolidate itself, the failure of Arab states to represent the interests of their citizens and to construct an inclusive national identity strong enough to generate social cohesion also contributed to its growth. The reliance of Arab regimes on tyranny, widespread corruption, and coercion led to the breakdown of the state-society relationship. Groups such as ISIS exploit this political tyranny and these dismal social and economic conditions by both challenging the ideology of the state and, at a practical level, presenting a subversive alternative through the reestablishment of the caliphate or the "Islamic State."

One of the defining features of ISIS's strategy that contrasts with that of Al Qaeda Central is that it, along with its predecessor, Al Qaeda in Iraq (AQI), has so far consistently focused on the Shia and the "near enemy" of the Iraqi and Syrian regimes and their Persian ally, rather than the "far enemy" of the United States, Israel, or other global actors. Baghdadi, like AQI leader Abu Musab al-Zarqawi before him, has a genocidal worldview, according to which Shias are viewed as infidels, a fifth column in the heart of Islam who must either convert or be exterminated. AQI and ISIS view the struggle against America, Europe, and even Israel as a distant secondary goal that must be deferred until a Sunni Islamic state is built in the heart of Arabia and ISIS consolidates its grip on the Iraqi and Syrian territories it occupies. However, as the group suffered military setbacks in Syria and Iraq in 2015, it began to target the far enemy by relying on its far-flung affiliate groups in Egypt, Libya, and limited networks of followers and stay-at-home groupies in Europe and North America. These attacks against the far enemy divert attention from ISIS's military losses in Syria and Iraq and also reinforce its narrative of invincibility and triumphalism. Despite this tactical shift in ISIS's modus operandi in attacking Western targets, Riyadh, Baghdad, and Damascus are ISIS's immediate strategic targets, not Rome, Paris, London, and Washington.[9] This disproportionate media attention to the massive attacks in Paris and California and the conspiracies in Belgium, fueled by ISIS's actions, has created widespread confusion regarding ISIS's strategy; those gruesome acts account for a tiny percentage of the deaths ISIS has perpetrated. That ISIS is much more interested in the near enemy underpins the relationships between ISIS and members of the global jihadist network, including Al Qaeda Central.[10]

Although ISIS is an extension of the global jihadist movement in its ideology and worldview, its social origins are rooted in a specific Iraqi context, and, to a lesser extent, the Syrian war that has raged since 2011. Its strategic use of sectarian clashes between Sunni Muslims and Shia Muslims in Iraq and Syria greatly benefited the group and shaped its activities. While most Salafi-jihadists are nourished on an anti-Shia, anti-Iranian propaganda diet, Al Qaeda Central prioritized the far enemy, specifically America and its European allies. From the mid-1990s until the present, Al Qaeda Central has waged a transnational jihad against the United States, trying to bog it down in a total war against the Islamic world.[11] Only afterward would bin Laden and Ayman al-Zawahiri, AQC's current leader, level the playing field with the near enemy (local rulers) and then seize power in their native lands, a strategy that has certainly failed.[12] In contrast, ISIS's primary strategic target is the consolidation and expansion of the lands and authority of the Islamic State in Iraq and Syria and other neighboring Muslim countries. ISIS wants to destroy the colonial borders in the Fertile Crescent, or Levant, which were drawn by the European powers at the end of World War One. In doing so, the group seeks to replace the "apostate" regimes with an Islamic state, a caliphate. Baghdadi, who anointed himself as the new caliph, invested his local political ambitions with transnational symbolism and utopia. The formal entrance of the United States into the war against ISIS in August 2014, and Russia's entrance, together with other Western powers at the end of 2015, partially collapsed these distinctions between the near enemy and the far enemy. In a way, ISIS turned the tables on Al Qaeda Central, laying claim to the leadership of the global jihadist movement. Nonetheless, it would be foolish to lose sight of ISIS's core strategy of statehood in the Levant, a factor that continues to affect the group's activities and actions.

The rise of ISIS shows the urgent need to understand what has happened within Arab societies and the international relations of the Middle East. ISIS is a symptom of the broken politics of the Middle East, of the fraying and delegitimization of state institutions as well as of the spreading of civil wars in Iraq, Syria, and beyond. The cause of the group's development and rise is located in the severe social and political conditions in Arab societies as well as in regional and global rivalries. The sustained crisis of governance and the political economy, decades old, is a key factor. This book will thus trace the journey of this *takfiri*[13] organization from inception and consolidation to the military surge that allowed it to settle and expand, first in Iraq, then in Syria and beyond. The text focuses on four key factors in ISIS's rebirth. The first is that ISIS can be seen as an extension of AQI, which was itself a creature of the 2003 US-led invasion of Iraq and its aftermath. By destroying state institutions, the invasion reinforced popular divisions along ethnic and religious rather than national lines, creating an environment that was particularly favorable for the implantation and expansion of groups such as AQI and ISIS. Second, the fragmentation of the post–Saddam Hussein political establishment and its incapacity to articulate policies that emphasized the country's national identity further nourished intercommunal distrust, thus deepening and widening the Sunni-Shia divide. Thirdly, the breakdown of state institutions in Syria and the country's descent into a full-blown war is a significant factor in the revitalization of ISIS. Finally, ISIS could not have consolidated the gains it made with the Syrian war without the derailment of the Arab Spring uprisings and the consequent spreading fires in neighboring Arab countries.

THE US-LED INVASION AND OCCUPATION OF IRAQ: REPERCUSSIONS

The US-led invasion and occupation of Iraq in 2003, combined with the subsequent social turmoil and prolonged and costly armed resistance, led to the dismantling of state institutions and the establishment of a political system based on *muhasasa*, or the distribution of the spoils of power along communal, ethnic, and tribal lines.[14] Iraqi national identity has been in flux, gradually transformed as local sectarian and ethnic identities supersede the collective identity adopted by the Baath ruling party, one premised on Arabism and nationalism. By exposing the failure of the postindependence, postcolonial state to build an inclusive national identity, the 2003 US-led invasion of Iraq caused a social rupture. The present sectarian-based political system and the dominant forces within it are largely a product of the US occupation and the destruction of the state. Separate sectarian identities do not and cannot represent a viable alternative for a new Iraq. ISIS succeeded in trading on the political system's failure, but doing so does not make it a repository of Sunni aspirations. Nevertheless, the US-led invasion and occupation of Iraq and the Syrian civil war were a defining moment in the reconstruction of a potent pan-Sunni identity in both countries and the wider region. Even though ISIS would not have done as well as it has without backing by an important Sunni segment, it is doubtful whether this pan-Islamism sentiment can now be seen as an enduring identity for Iraqi and Syrian Sunnis.

We know very little about the complex relationship between ISIS and the population under its control, and most of the reports are fragmentary and offer contradictory synopses of life under the caliphate. On balance and for their own separate reasons, the Shias and Kurds felt that the supra-state identity endorsed by the Iraqi regime favored Sunni Arabs at their own expense. In this sense, the dismantling of state institutions in 2003 and the setting up of a sectarian-based system triggered and intensified a clash of identities, a struggle that has almost wrecked modern Iraq.[15]

ISIS's viciousness reflects the bitter inheritance of decades of Baathist rule that tore apart Iraq's social fabric and left deep wounds that are still festering. In a sense, ISIS internalized the brutal tactics of the Baathist regime and Iraq's blood-drenched modern history. Although Baghdadi and Hussein come from two different ideological poles, both sought to build a tyrannical regime that tolerates no dissent and uses terror to silence the opposition. Baghdadi surrounds himself with junior and senior officers of Hussein's army and police, many of them former enforcers of Baathism's brutal rule. This does not imply that ISIS's Salafi-jihadism is synonymous with Baathism, a relatively secular nationalist ideology, as some observes claim. (Chapter 5 fleshes out this argument further.) Former Baathists did not hijack ISIS but, rather, the latter converted many Baathists to its cause. It is important to distinguish between

ISIS's vicious tactics, which resemble those of the old Baath ruling party, and revolutionary Islamist ideology and those of the Baath's nationalism. This has also been a point of contention between ISIS and Jabhat al-Nusra—another Salafi-jihadist armed group in Syria and the official arm of Al Qaeda Central there, formally established in the war-torn country in 2012—as members of each group often accuse their rivals of having been former Baathists, attempting to delegitimize them in the eyes of the Islamist base. For example, a prominent scholar of Salafi-jihadism, Abu Mohammed al-Maqdisi, who backs al-Nusra against ISIS, explained the brutal ways of Baghdadi and his associates by asserting that "they have just discovered Islam, and were until recently Baathists slaughtering Muslims."[16] Of course, Maqdisi's blame of Baathists is designed to absolve Salafi-jihadists, his cohorts, of responsibility for the massive shedding of civilian blood.

The causes of ISIS's unrestrained violence lie in (1) its origins in AQI and its founder, Abu Musab al-Zarqawi, who represents a post–Al Qaeda generation of Salafi-jihadism focusing on identity and communal politics; (2) its Iraqization through the instrumentalization of Baathist tools of repression as well as the country's bitter legacy of violence; and (3) the ruralization of ISIS's rank and file.[17]

Whereas the two previous jihadist waves of the 1970s–1990s had leaders from the social elite and their bases were mainly composed of middle-class and lower-middle-class university graduates, ISIS's cadre is rural and agrarian, lacking in both theological and intellectual accomplishment. While the majority of ISIS's combatants tend to be poor, the leadership is solidly middle class and lower middle class; this might spell trouble for the group if and when its military fortunes decline, because the foot soldiers are not as versed in or even committed to the Salafi-jihadist ideology as the top echelons are. These poor combatants could easily shed their ISIS affiliation and be reintegrated into their communities.[18] The current wave of Salafi-jihadists is facilitated by its rural and tribal social origins, providing a deep sense of victimhood and religious inevitability of victory as well as of *isti'la'* (superiority) over Shia Muslims, who are, historically, a marginalized community in Iraq and neighboring Arab countries. Social profiles of mid-level commanders of ISIS and its Islamist rival, al-Nusra, show a background of manual labor and blue-collar jobs as mechanics, vegetable and fruit vendors, farmers, construction workers, shopkeepers, and low-level workers in restaurants. ISIS thrives among poor, disenfranchised Sunni communities, including those in the Fallujah, Tikrit, and Anbar regions in Iraq; the al-Raqqa province and Deir al-Zour in Syria; Akkar, Tripoli, and the Bekka Valley in Lebanon; and Maan and Zarqa in Jordan. The lower-class background of ISIS's combatants explains why the organization justifies its actions as a defense of the poor and disfranchised as well as why it targets areas with natural and raw resources.[19] In contrast to the typical recruits joining ISIS from within the Middle East, many of the foreign fighters who have migrated to ISIS from around the world, especially those from Europe and North America, are reportedly educated and middle class, an inconsistency that calls for further exploration.

By 2010, AQI, the forerunner of ISIS, suffered military defeat and was socially besieged; yet, in less than four years, it has reconstituted its cells and has expanded far beyond the Iraqi Sunni Triangle, threatening the state system in the Fertile Crescent. Although objective material conditions in Iraq and Syria fueled ISIS's emergence, its ideology appealed to radicalized religious activists and a small segment of young men and women worldwide; these volunteers and recruits want to be part of the resurrection of the caliphate—a romantic, utopian metanarrative that has increasing allure in a broken Middle East dominated by repressive, illegitimate, minority-based regimes.

IRAQ'S BROKEN POLITICAL SYSTEM

The social turmoil caused by the US-led invasion, particularly the destruction of state institutions, triggered a deep sectarian divide between Sunni Muslims and Shia Muslims and propelled the rise of ISIS from an inconsequential nonstate actor to an Islamic state. Filling an ideational and institutional void, ISIS stepped in and offered aggrieved Sunnis a potent pan-Sunni (sectarian-Islamist) identity that transcends nationality, ethnicity, and borders. Baghdadi and his cohorts attempt to reconstruct Iraq's supra-state identity (Arabism and nationalism) along sectarian terms (pan-Sunni), challenging the very foundation of the separate nation-state as well as the norms and rules that underpin international society. Sectarianism is the fuel that powers ISIS, and it is fueled by ISIS in return, an essential dynamic at work that requires further exploration of the reconstruction and redefinition of Sunni Arab identity and should not be assumed to be a fait accompli. Since 2003 Iraq has descended into a sustained crisis, inflaming the grievances of the Sunni population over their disempowerment under the new Shia ascendancy and preponderant Iranian influence (for developments in Iraq after 2003, see chapter 3). Although Sunnis have protested the discrimination they face for some time, their protests fell on deaf ears in Baghdad and Washington. The disintegration of the social fabric in this manner created an opening for ISIS to step in and take advantage of the wrongs felt by Iraq's Sunnis and depict itself as their "defender" and "protector." In addition to its strategic manipulation of sectarian divisions, ISIS and its predecessors, AQI and the Islamic State of Iraq (ISI), managed to gain support through their anti-US rhetoric, which appealed to the Sunni youth who felt that the country had been humiliated and colonized by the United States with Iran's backing. Iraq's dysfunctional and broken political system, which suffered from increasing factionalism, provided ISIS with ideological nourishment.

Like their predecessors, the Baathists, the new ruling elite in Iraq failed to construct an inclusive national identity and rebuild state institutions on more solid legal foundations. The post-Hussein elite are accountable for the misfortunes that have befallen Iraq after 2003. Although the US-led invasion is responsible for causing a rupture in state and society, Iraq's new leaders could have ameliorated dismal social conditions and strengthened national unity. For most of the eight years of Nuri al-Maliki's premiership (May 20, 2006–September 8, 2014), Sunnis felt disenfranchised by what they viewed as sectarian-based policies, leading to their decision to organize themselves communally. Maliki's reluctance to support the Sahwa forces, tribal Sunni councils organized and financed by the US occupation authorities, only further deepened the rift with the Sunni community, and the intensification of identity politics led to a vicious cycle of polarization between Sunnis and Shias. Also, his conflicted relationship with some high-profile Shia figures, combined with the inefficiency of the government and its widespread corruption, left the Shia community divided. From 2010 on, Maliki's increasing hold over the state apparatus and its institutions did not foster confidence in the government, and his heavy repression of the Arab Spring protests provoked anger and resistance. As armed groups infiltrated the sit-ins, it became more and more difficult to distinguish peaceful protesters from violent militias. Social and ideological cleavages weakened Iraq, thus enabling Baghdadi and his planners to infiltrate the country's fragile body politic.

Baghdadi presented ISIS as the sole defender of *Ahl al-Sunna* (the Sunni community), the voice and champion of Sunni Arabs who feel excluded and persecuted by the Shia-dominated regime in Baghdad and the Alawite-led regime in Damascus.[20] Unlike his notorious predecessor and the founder of AQI, Zarqawi, Baghdadi cultivated a powerful social constituency that provided ISIS with a steady supply of skilled fighters as well as a territorial and political safe haven. This point requires further explanation: thousands of embittered Iraqi and Syrian Sunnis fight under ISIS's banner, even though many do not subscribe to its extremist Islamist ideology. The group has successfully inserted itself in an unfolding mini civil war in Iraq and blended with the local Sunni community. In a way, there is nothing mysterious about the spectacular rise of ISIS. It is worth stressing that there is no credible evidence to show that ISIS's ideology of Sunni pan-Islamism is the adopted identity in Sunni areas in Iraq and Syria, though this hypothesis is presented by writers with little empirical evidence to substantiate it. According to Sunni Iraqis in Mosul, Tikrit, and other Iraqi cities to whom I talked, Sunni rebels and tribes played a pivotal role in facilitating ISIS's takeover of the Sunni Triangle only to have the group turn against them after the cities had fallen. Additionally, during conversations I have had with Iraqi tribal leaders, many acknowledged that their sons initially joined the ISIS caravan not because of its Islamist ideology but as a means of resistance against the sectarian-based central authority in Baghdad and its regional patron, Iran. Increasing evidence now shows that Iraqi Sunnis are divided between those who back ISIS as an effective weapon against their Shia tormentors and others who express regrets about having supported the organization and are turning against it because of its brutal tactics and tyrannical rule.

According to reports from the Sunni Triangle, more and more tribes are distancing themselves from ISIS and denying taking part in its mass crimes,[21] though the tide has not turned against the group yet. For the moment, ISIS still maintains *hadanah sha'biyya* (a social base), which has allowed it to withstand punishing attacks by the US-led coalition and the Iraqi and Syrian armies and Kurdish and Shia militias. The group greatly benefited from abuses and violations of Sunnis by Shia militias in Iraq and Syria as well as a widespread perception among Sunnis that airstrikes by the United States and its allies unjustly target their coreligionists while turning a blind eye to Shia radicals. However, ISIS has not offered Iraqi and Syrian Sunnis a positive political and socioeconomic vision that addresses the severe challenges facing their community. Jihadists of all colors and stripes, past and present, lack a political imagination, the result of a structurally flawed decision-making process, argued a well-known Al Qaeda theorist, Abdullah Bin Mohamed, in a recent memo called "The Problem in the Jihadist Decision Making." As long as clerics and preachers dominate the jihadist movement, Bin Mohamed concludes, jihadists will be unable to translate their military gains on the battlefield into political capital.[22]

THE SYRIAN CIVIL WAR

Another key factor in the resurgence of ISIS is the breakdown of state institutions in Syria and the country's descent into all-out war after 2011. Not unlike Arab protesters in Tunisia, Egypt, Libya, Bahrain, and Yemen, tens of thousands of Syrians revolted against *al-istibdad* (repression) and *al-tahmeesh* (exclusion). Bread, freedom, social justice, and *al-karama* (human dignity) were the rallying cries that echoed from Syria's *mayadeen* (squares), reflecting political and economic vulnerabilities, not sectarian and parochial concerns. Only later did the uprising become militarized, taking on a sectarian façade. The nature of civil-military relations in Syria was radically different from that of relations in Tunisia and Egypt, other sites of Arab Spring uprisings; the Syrian security forces recognized that their survival in their current form depended heavily on the survival of the Assad regime. As Bashar al-Assad's security services violently clamped down on peaceful protesters and depicted antiregime social mobilization in sectarian terms, the revolt rapidly mutated, militarized, and eventually radicalized. Nationalist-based protests increasingly acquired religious symbols and references, with armed Islamist groups and militias in rural villages taking advantage of the tumult to advance their ultraconservative Salafist ideology and agenda.

What started as a progressive call for social and political reforms turned into a sectarian clash and war of all against all. In a repeat of the Iraqi scenario, Islamist armed groups and the Islamist rhetoric of jihad were empowered, their existence becoming somewhat justified in the eyes of a significant proportion of Syrians due to the regime's violent crackdown on civilians. Islamist groups in Syria portrayed themselves, and were often perceived, as the defenders of the persecuted Sunni community. Similar to the case of Iraq, where the Islamic Republic of Iran's support of the Shia community increased sectarian tensions, Iran's unwavering support of the House of Assad reinforces the sectarian narrative. In late 2011 Baghdadi and his commanders had the political foresight to send a contingent of their men led by two trusted lieutenants, Abu Mohammed al-Joulani and Mullah Fawzi al-Dulaimi, to supposedly battle the Assad regime and establish an operational base in the country.[23] In less than a year Joulani's al-Nusra, as an extension of the Islamic State of Iraq, built an effective network in Syria that included thousands of local and foreign fighters who gained notoriety on the battlefield against Assad's forces. According to subsequent testimonies by top jihadists, from the start a decision was made to keep the real identity of al-Nusra secret and blend in with the local population in a bid to avoid alerting the Americans to Al Qaeda's presence in Syria.[24] This move allowed al-Nusra to expand and build coalitions with various Islamist factions. By the time Baghdadi publicly divulged the connection between the Islamic State of Iraq and al-Nusra in April 2013, stating that al-Nusra's strategic goal was to establish an Islamic state in Syria,[25] he had already gained strategic depth and baptized his fighters with blood and fire, a stroke of evil genius. (For context and analysis about the ISI–al-Nusra connection, see chapter 5 on Syria.) Unilaterally dissolving both the Islamic State of Iraq and al-Nusra, Baghdadi announced a merger, a new entity called the Islamic State of Iraq and wa-Sham,[26] an initiative swiftly rejected by Joulani, which triggered an internal jihadist civil war.[27] Although al-Nusra, together with other armed groups, launched a preemptive strike against ISIS, in the end the group prevailed over al-Nusra and its allies and captured major cities, including al-Raqqa, which became the seat of its capital.

Feeding upon each other, Iraq and Syria were vital to the resurgence of ISIS, which defined the struggle in both countries through the framework of identity. It developed a distinct pan-Sunni sectarian identity, a deliberate contrast to the pan-Shia identity represented by the sectarian-dominated, Iran-backed regimes in Damascus and Baghdad. Of all variables empowering ISIS, the anti-Shia, anti-Iranian factor tops the list. ISIS has developed a narrative—rooted in a pan-Sunni identity that is intrinsically opposed to what it portrays as a pan-Shia, aggressive, expansionist ideology—that has infiltrated and is taking over the Islamic world. ISIS's anti-Shia, anti-Iranian program is the most effective card it has played in Iraq and Syria, and it has so far proved to be a powerful recruiting tool. The organization has tapped into the communal rift that grew after the US-led invasion of Iraq in 2003. This dispute spiraled out of control after the Arab Spring was aborted and after Syria and Iraq descended into war and chaos. It is this clash of sub-Islamic identities, a mini intra-Islamic war, that has fueled ISIS's spectacular growth. After the fall of Mosul in June 2014 and the declaration of the Islamic State, time and again the organization's spokespeople have asserted their leadership of the *umma* (the global Muslim community) and Ahl al-Sunna and dismissed existing and potential rivals to this honor as pretenders.

Although Iraq is ISIS's original home, its expansion to neighboring Syria provided it with strategic depth and significant economic resources. Syria is the location of ISIS's capital, al-Raqqa, and its major sources of income, including the oil trade, taxation, wheat and fertile agricultural lands, and criminal activities, and, according to US intelligence officials, more than two-thirds of its fighters are deployed in the country (though this might be changing for operational reasons as military pressure takes its toll on ISIS in Syria). In addition, the disintegration of the country's social fabric and political system and its transformation into a battlefield for regional wars by proxies also offer motivation and inspiration for potential recruits to ISIS and similar groups like al-Nusra. As long as Syria's conflicts rage, ISIS will continue to entrench itself in the midst of the chaos that defines the war-torn country today. However, at the time of writing, at the end of 2015, ISIS is squeezed by Syrian Kurdish insurgents backed by the United States, and other opposition factions, prodded by their regional patrons, which have also pressurized ISIS, diminishing the group's prospects considerably in Syria. ISIS's grip on Syria is not as strong as that of Iraq. Nevertheless, ISIS's successful comeback in Iraq was greatly bolstered by its power consolidation in Syria. Following its takeover of important Syrian cities in 2014, ISIS dissolved the international border that separated the two countries. By doing so, it affirmed its supremacy at the head of the global jihadist network, proving that its tactic of *kasr al-hudud* (breaking down borders) had worked. ISIS used its achievements in Iraq and Syria to taunt other neighboring countries, which in turn only increased its popularity across the region.

THE ARAB SPRING

Finally, ISIS could not have surged without the derailment of the Arab Spring uprisings and the sabotage of the aspirations of millions of citizens who called for a more just social contract and a bill of rights. The Arab Spring did not occur in a vacuum. Millions of Arabs reached a breaking point because of decades of developmental failure and repressive rule. It was an emancipatory moment that could have progressively transformed the Arab Middle East had it not been derailed by an unholy alliance of internal and external counterrevolutionary forces. This included a multitude of actors, such as autocratic rulers backed by regional allies, the military-security apparatus, *al-fulul* (elements of the old regime), and ISIS, whose interests converged in blocking peaceful political change. (Chapter 7 develops this argument further.) ISIS could not have surged without the grand collusion between authoritarian Arab rulers and their regional and global patrons to maintain the status quo at all costs. Although bitter regional rivals, both Saudi Arabia and Iran acted as counterrevolutionary powers, trying to stem the tide of political change at home and in the neighborhood and to consolidate their influence.

As the Arab uprisings gathered steam, Saudi Arabia spent more than US$100 billion at home in an effort to keep domestic peace and buy the loyalty of its citizens. The Saudi kingdom also invested billions of dollars in Bahrain, Egypt, Oman, Yemen,

Morocco, and Jordan to prevent revolutionary change and keep its conservative Arab allies in control.[28] Saudi Arabia, together with the United Arab Emirates, even deployed two thousand troops to Bahrain to allow its Gulf ally to crush the opposition. Although initially the United States did not accept the official Saudi and Bahraini claims that Iran had fomented the protests in the tiny Gulf sheikdom, it reversed course and implicitly acquiesced to Saudi military intervention, suggesting that pro-Iranian elements might attempt to hijack the popular will. Bahrain became a flash point, a casualty of the US-Iranian rivalry and American economic and strategic interests with Gulf Arab countries.[29] While US policy makers backed regulated change in Tunisia, Egypt, Libya, Yemen, and Syria, they were reluctant to do so in the Gulf because the stakes were much higher for American national interests there.

Similarly, the Islamic Republic of Iran, which prides itself as a revolutionary state, has fought tooth and nail to sustain the Assad regime. Iran also backed Maliki, whose divisive sectarian policies brought ruin to Iraq, and did not distance itself from Maliki until after the powerful Iraqi Shia religious establishment had done so. Ironically, at the beginning of the Arab uprisings in February 2011 and before the storm had wrecked Syria, Iranian leaders sought to take credit for events in their neighborhood. The Iranian supreme leader, Ayatollah Khamenei, called the Arab Spring a "natural enlargement of Iran's Islamic revolution of 1979" and credited his country for being the catalyst of this "Islamic awakening."[30] But as the "Islamic awakening" reached Syria and Iraq, the premature jubilation of Iranian leaders darkened and their closest Arab partners, Maliki and Assad, fought for their political future and literally their political lives. Iran threw a lifeline to rescue the two drowning men, pouring gasoline on a raging sectarian fire in Iraq, Syria, and beyond. In its efforts to prevent the collapse of the Assad regime, Iran found a natural ally in Russia. In September 2015 President Putin intervened directly in the Syrian conflict and launched airstrikes in support of the Assad regime. In a way, Syria has also become the location of a global war by proxy between the Western powers and Russia, which has invested considerable diplomatic and military capital to thwart Western intervention in the war-torn country.

This new cold war between the leader of Arabian Sunni Islam, Saudi Arabia, and the leader of Shia Islam, (Persian) Iran, has played out on the streets of weaker and more tumultuous Arab countries, particularly Iraq, Syria, and Yemen. It diverted the struggle from social and political emancipation in Arab countries and toward geostrategic and sectarian rivalry. Syria and Iraq, together with other countries, have become battle-grounds for regional wars by proxies in which Saudi Arabia and Iran, together with Turkey and Qatar and others, vie for influence and hegemony by arming and financing warring camps. Firmly rooted in power politics as well as the politics of identity (Sunni versus Shia) and the construction of rival national identities (Arab versus Persian), this regional war by proxy is a godsend for ISIS and other Al Qaeda local factions in general. At the beginning of hostilities in Syria and Iraq, al-Nusra and ISIS obtained funds, arms, and a religious cover from neighboring Sunni states, precious social and material capital that proved decisive. ISIS's rebirth was facilitated by this geostrategic and geosectarian rivalry between Sunni-dominated states and Shia-led Iran. The fragility of the Arab state system triggered a free-for-all struggle for competitive advantage by pivotal regional powers. As a nonstate actor, ISIS initially climbed on the shoulders of key regional states that battled each other for influence and supremacy in the heart of Arabia. Not unlike Al Qaeda Central, which emerged out of the US-Soviet violent rivalry over Afghanistan in the 1980s, ISIS is also a creature of the geostrategic and geosectarian conflict, as well as of the foreign intervention in the Arab Middle East.

ISIS AND THE STORY OF BAGHDADI

As this book explores the history of ISIS through the framework of identity and sectarian politics, chapter 4 provides a portrait of Baghdadi by reconstructing his journey from invisibility to infamy. His story is pieced together from recollections of contemporary witnesses who had known him before he joined AQI, as well as others who spent time with him before and after he was detained by the Americans in Camp Bucca, near Umm Qasr in southern Iraq, in February 2004 on charges of being a Sunni "foot-soldier."[31] When he assumed the leadership of AQI in 2010, the group was on the brink of collapse, bereft of its social and territorial base in the Sunni Triangle. This was mainly due to an internal civil war between AQI and the Sunni community in Iraq, which had initially provided refuge to the group. Baghdadi and his inner circle patiently and systemically rebuilt their social network and expanded its constituency among disfranchised Sunnis in Iraq and then Syria after the political uprising there escalated into all-out war. At the time, Baghdadi cleverly reorganized AQI's military apparatus, relying on the operational expertise of former Iraqi army and police officers and skilled Chechen trainers in Syria, turning it into a professional fighting force capable of waging urban and conventional warfare. With years of combat experience and training and a long history of fighting that included participation in the Iran-Iraq war in the 1980s, Kuwait in 1990–1991, the counterinsurgency in the 1980s and 1990s, and resistance against the Americans from 2003 until 2010, these skilled Sunni officers of the disbanded army transformed Baghdadi's ragtag bands and networks into a potent guerrilla force, likened to a mini sectarian army, capable of carrying out large-scale offensives and vanquishing Iraqi and Syrian military brigades.

Concerning ISIS's rapid surge, many questions surrounding Baghdadi still have yet to be answered. Specifically, how did Baghdadi, a man with no previous military background who is neither a political theorist nor a religious preacher, transform ISIS into the world's leading Salafi-jihadist organization, which controls a contiguous "nation" across the Syrian-Iraqi border with a force of more than thirty thousand fighters? How did he manage to fill its coffers with up to $2 billion annually (by 2015 ISIS's annual budget has plummeted to about $1 billion) and turn it into one of the wealthiest nonstate actors, now a proto-state with the aspiration of being a state, through a diversified war economy? To what extent is Baghdadi helped by the fraying state institutions in Iraq and Syria and by rival regional powers' fostering of sectarian mobilization and polarization? We cannot be confined to Baghdadi's personal experiences or a focused study in leadership or the great man himself. Baghdadi's rise to power coincided with increasing political and communal tensions in Iraq, where central government policies were widely seen as marginalizing and undermining the Sunni community. The chaos in Iraq and then Syria has inadvertently empowered Baghdadi's jihadist caravan.

ISIS is tied to the raging sectarian fires in Iraq and Syria and the clash of identities that is ravaging Arab countries, and, should ISIS be defeated, there is always the risk of another like-minded militant group, such as al-Nusra, filling a power vacuum in the region. If ISIS is a manifestation of the breakdown of state institutions, then the fragile authoritarian state system must be rebuilt on a more solid, legitimate foundation. This requires a transparent, inclusive, and representative government that delivers public goods, including jobs, and gives millions of young men and women, who feel forsaken, a stake in the future of their countries. A more complex challenge is to confront ISIS's Salafi-jihadist ideology and worldview. By portraying itself as the only alternative to a broken and corrupt political system, ISIS is trying to hijack agency from the people, yet in many ways, it uses the same tactics of the authoritarian regimes that it seeks to replace. The challenge is to provide hope to the millions of men and women who called for justice, freedom, and a life with dignity, as we saw during the Arab Spring uprisings, while simultaneously convincing them that there are nonviolent options that can bring about meaningful and substantive political change. Until we do, the menace of the "Islamic State" and similar Salafi-jihadist groups will remain a problem both for the Arab-Islamic world and for the international community.

THE WORLD ACCORDING TO ISIS

Although the spectacular surge of ISIS must be contextualized within the social and material circumstances and conditions that exist in Iraq and Syria and beyond, its worldview and ideology must also be taken seriously. Ideology is a super-glue that binds Salafi-jihadist activists and combatants to each other and allows the movement to renew and revitalize itself after suffering setbacks. A traveling and expanding ideology, Salafi-jihadism has gained new converts and has taken hold of the imagination of small Sunni communities worldwide; it has developed its own rituals and references and produced its own iconic figures and theorists who provide intellectual guidance and theological sustenance. Historically a fringe social move-ment, now Salafi-jihadism vies for public influence and offers an alternative for both mainstream and radical Islamists. The movement's propagandists and preachers openly proselytize and boast that the tide of history has shifted in their favor. Whether it is on the cusp of victory or not, the ideology is here to stay and the challenge is to shine light on it and make sense of it. Researchers underestimate the power of the Salafi-jihadist ideology at their own peril. ISIS is first and foremost an extension of the global Salafi-jihadist movement. Baghdadi and his cohorts represent another wave, a new generation, of

Salafi-jihadists or revolutionary religious activists. (Chapters 2 and 8 examine in depth ISIS's ideological references and mindset as well as the similarities and differences between it and other Salafi-jihadist groups.) At present, ISIS—its ideology, as well as its state and security status—has successfully tapped into a fierce clash of identities between Sunni Muslims and Shia Muslims in the Middle East and beyond. Although ISIS is a Salafi-jihadist organization, it is fundamentally oriented toward a genocidal anti-Shia campaign conducted in the name of the romantic idea of resurrecting the caliphate.

In comparing the emergence of Al Qaeda's central organization to that of ISIS, it is possible to distinguish ideological threads that have provided ISIS with an advantage. Al Qaeda's central organization emerged from an alliance between ultraconservative Saudi Salafism (or Wahhabism) and radical Egyptian Islamism known as Salafi-jihadism. ISIS was born of a marriage between an Iraq-based AQI (Salafi-jihadism) and an identity frame of politics. The group's ideological lineage of Salafi-jihadism forms part of the ideological impetus; the other part of its ideological nature is a hyper-Sunni identity driven by an intrinsic and even genocidal anti-Shia ideology. The US-led invasion and occupation of Iraq in 2003 caused a rupture in an already fractured Iraqi society. America's destruction of Iraqi institutions, particularly its dismantling of the army and the Baathist ruling party, unleashed a fierce power struggle, mainly along sectarian lines, creating fissures in society. These growing ruptures provided the room necessary for non-state actors and armed insurgent militias, including Al Qaeda, to infiltrate the fragile body politic in post-2003 Iraq. The strategy of ISIS's planners is designed to exploit the Arab state identity crisis by claiming that they aim to implement a socioeconomic framework that can rival that of Western modernity. Despite ISIS's insistence that it operates within a different value system from that promulgated by Western liberalism, the group's rhetoric is anchored not in novelty but in identity politics whose main articulating pole is religious. Religion can act as a potent framework for social identity, especially in war environments where insecurity runs high, and cultivates group loyalty by projecting itself as the truth and the right path to follow.[1] By providing a clear structure through strict sets of rules and beliefs and a worldview that encompasses life on earth and in the afterlife, ISIS presents individuals with the promise of an eternal group membership, which can prove particularly attractive for people prone to existential anxiety. Moreover, scholars point out that several factors feed into (Abrahamic) fundamentalist ideology, including dualism (absolute evaluations of good versus evil), authority (of a sacred book or leader), selectivity (choosing certain beliefs or practices over others), and millennialism (confidence in eschatology as God's will). Of all factors, however, one facet is thought to be vital: "reactivity,"[2] which takes the form of a hostility toward secular modernity that is directed not only toward people outside of the fundamentalists' religious in-group but also toward members of their own religious group who are not viewed as "true believers."

In this light, ISIS's development of a pure ideology can be seen as part of a strategy to feed its members' fundamentalism by emphasizing their exclusivity while projecting a universalist vision. For example, the widespread use of suicide bombers by Salafi-jihadist groups such as ISIS constitutes a recent modus operandi in Islam rather than a return to the roots. A convincing argument can be made that Muslims are currently entangled in a war of subjectivities that stems from a series of ruptures that started with the Enlightenment and that takes the form of an Islamic-Islamic civil war over the Muslim identity itself.[3] Meanwhile, Arabs are also involved in an interpretative dispute about their being-in-the-world in which both the Arab world and the world at large are being questioned and contested. The current rise of Salafi-jihadism and terrorism represented by groups such as ISIS is the result of not only creeping sectarianism or a crisis of the modern state, but also a growing nihilism that signals the collapse of peace and progressive values in its conception of humanity.[4]

Nevertheless, far from being sui generis, genealogically and ideologically ISIS belongs to the Salafi-jihadist family, or global jihadism, although it marks another stage in the evolution or, rather, mutation of the ideological gene pool. Its leader, Abu Bakr al-Baghdadi, not only inherited the bloody legacy of his predecessor, Abu Musab al-Zarqawi, the founder of Al Qaeda in Iraq, but also models himself on Osama bin Laden, who is for Salafi-jihadists a "martyr" and remains the undisputed, charismatic leader of the global jihadist movement. Over the past half century, the global jihadist movement has developed a repertoire of ideas, a frame of reference, theorists, thousands of followers, and "martyrs" who provide inspiration for new volunteers and ensure the movement's survival. ISIS has been able to draw from this repertoire, rearticulating old concepts and presenting them as new or revolutionary. Its rhetoric makes use of religious ideology to articulate identity politics. Indeed, religion has for some time been the glue that maintains the coherence, if not the unity, of various factions and divisions, and the rationale for vicious and flamboyant violence. Time and again, Salafi-jihadists from various movements have cited verses from Qur'anic scripture to portray their offensive jihad as blessed.

The world according to ISIS is frozen in time and space, incorporating the rules and laws of seventh-century Arabia into the twenty-first century. Baghdadi and his associates depict themselves as battling the "antichrist" and paving the way for the ultimate triumph of the "Mahdi" and Islam (in Arabic, the Mahdi means "the Guided One," the central crowning element of all Islamic end-time narratives, or an expected spiritual and temporal ruler destined to establish a reign of righteousness throughout the world). This millenarian thinking is at the heart of ISIS's caliphate ideology and the global jihadist movement in general. The problem is not to know whether ISIS is Islamic—of course it is, though Muslims worldwide disavow it and distance themselves from its actions—but rather to understand how this organization borrows heavily but selectively from the Islamic canon and imposes the past on the present wholesale. Baghdadi and his propagandists overlook centuries of Islamic interpretations and counterinterpretations and rely on a narrow, strict, and obsolete textualist reading of the Islamic doctrine, a move that is very controversial and deeply contested by the religious community and *al-Islam al-Sha'bi* (lived Islam). Despite its sound and fury, ISIS remains a fringe phenomenon that is too extreme for mainstream Muslim opinion but sounds like a sweet melody to the ears of its social base. This base continues to replenish the ranks of ISIS and similar organizations with willing combatants and suicide bombers. Time and again politicians and observers have penned the obituary of the global jihadist movement only to be shocked by its resilience and capacity for self-renewal. Ideology is a significant factor in this process of regeneration, and it confers legitimacy on ISIS's actions. By tracing ISIS's social and ideological origins and comparing it with the first two jihadist waves of the 1970s–1990s, we can gauge the extent of continuity and change and account for the group's notorious savagery.

Under ISIS, there is no breathing space for social mobilization and political organization, including by like-minded Salafi-jihadist activism. ISIS possesses a totalitarian, millenarian worldview that eschews political pluralism, competition, and diversity of thought. Baghdadi and his associates criminalize and excommunicate free thought, and the idea of the "other" is alien to their messianic ideology. Any Muslim or co-jihadist who doesn't accept ISIS's interpretation of the Islamic doctrine is an apostate who deserves death. In the same vein, any Muslim or co-jihadist who refuses to submit to the will of the new caliphate faces either expulsion from the land or death. One here needs to recall the words uttered by ISIS's chief propagandist and official spokesman, Abu Mohammed al-Adnani, following the establishment of the Islamic State. In a communiqué, Adnani, whose real name is Taha Sobhi Falaha, demanded that all jihadist factions everywhere pledge allegiance to the new caliph, Baghdadi, as the legality of all emirates, groups, states, and organizations was now null and void. He said, "The land now submits to his order and authority from Aleppo to Diyala."⁵ Adnani made it clear that there is only one Islamic state and one caliphate, with no room for dissent: "Indeed, it is the state. Indeed, it is the *khilafah* [caliphate]. It is time for you to end this abhorrent partisanship, dispersion, and division, for this condition is not from the religion of Allah at all. And if you forsake the State or wage war against it, you will not harm it. You will harm yourselves."⁶ He also warned that all Muslims must obey the commander of the faithful, including former and current aspirants to the title, and ordered his fighters to "split the head" and "strike the neck" of anyone who breaks the ranks and does not submit to the will of the new caliphate.⁷

In ISIS's worldview, then, the caliphate is not just a political entity but also a collective religious obligation (*wajib kifa'i*), a means to salvation: Muslims have sinned since they abandoned the obligation of the caliphate, and, ever since, the umma has not tasted "honor" or "triumph." ISIS's repeated message to Muslims is that they must pledge allegiance to a valid caliph, Baghdadi, and honor that oath and live a fully Islamic life.

Behind the romantic idea of the caliphate, however, lies identity politics, as the core of ISIS's ideological framework is the affirmation of its "Sunni Islamic" identity and its redefinition of true Islam. Adnani's orders might have given the illusion that the establishment of the Islamic State entails a real rupture from the present state system, but, just like under Saddam Hussein, under ISIS, the Islamic State in Iraq is headed by an absolute leader who tolerates no dissent. In fact ISIS's conception of sovereignty does not break away from the autocratic mode of governance that has plagued Arab countries for decades: for example, both Hussein in Iraq and the Assads in Syria have used identity politics as a pillar for their policies—albeit an ethnic rather than a religious version.

ISIS has used its messianic ideology to brutally suppress both Islamists and nationalists (Baathists) in areas under its domination. Its raison d'être is to convert everyone to its cause, including rival jihadists who share a similar vision. For example, in a severe rebuttal, Adnani harshly criticized Ayman al-Zawahiri, the leader of Al Qaeda Central and the most senior living jihadist, for daring to side with the chief of Jabhat al-Nusra, Abu Mohammed al-Joulani, against Baghdadi in the power struggle for Syria. ISIS's chief spokesman bluntly reminded Zawahiri that should he make it to the territories of the Islamic State, he would have to swear *baiya* (fealty) to Baghdadi and serve as one of his foot soldiers. As Baghdadi pledged allegiance to Zawahiri in 2010, this open attack represents the ultimate insult.[8] ISIS's hard-line stance has caused much havoc within the global jihadist movement, even leading to a split between ISIS and al-Nusra, which was originally constituted on Baghdadi's orders. A key cause of the rift between the two organizations was that Joulani rejected an order by Baghdadi in April 2013 to annex his front to ISIS. Baghdadi considered Joulani's snub treacherous and ever since has waged all-out war against al-Nusra and its Islamist and nationalist Syrian allies. The intra-jihadist confrontation in Syria has killed thousands of skilled fighters from both camps and has seen atrocities committed by each side, including wholesale rape, beheadings, and crucifixions. The war within the jihadist tribe is as savage as the war with outsiders. Islamic State followers and those of Al Qaeda Central excommunicate one another and marshal religious discourse to show that they are the real jihadist vanguard, while their rivals are pretenders. In Syria ISIS could not coexist with al-Nusra or any other Islamist group because that would have challenged its monopoly on the scared and on the global jihadist project as well. As a totalitarian-religious movement, ISIS will ultimately self-destruct, not because it commits evil deeds, but because it lacks a political imagination and its ideology is deeply at odds with the values and ways of life of local communities (more on this point in the conclusion). In addition to mastering the art of making enemies of all regional and global powers, ISIS eliminates politics altogether and aspires to organize society along puritanical lines of seventh-century Arabia, a worldview that imposes the distant past on the present.

It is no wonder, then, that ISIS engages in cultural cleansing, purifying the Islamic lands of all alien and infidel influences, including traditional Sunni practices that clash with its fundamentalist and timeless interpretation of the Islamic doctrine. The idea of purifying the Islamic lands is deeply ingrained in the imagination of radical religious activists, but ISIS is the first social movement to attempt to operationalize this ideology. As Islamic State militants swept across Syria and Iraq, they destroyed, damaged, or looted numerous cultural sites and sculptures, condemning them as idolatry. Celebrating their cultural cleansing in spectacular propaganda displays, Islamic State fighters show by deeds, not words, their intent to purify the lands and resurrect the caliphate. While ISIS's propaganda is abhorrent to the outside world, it is greedily devoured by its social base. Its slickly produced recruitment films about cultural cleansing not only reinforce its strategic message of triumph and expansion but also divert attention from battlefield setbacks.[9]

For an authentic Islamic state to be erected, the Sunni militants of ISIS feel that the Islamic lands must be cleansed of apostasy and heretics, regardless of the human or civilizational costs. In fact ISIS's fighters are keen on displaying an ideological zeal and purity. For example, in an attempt to cleanse Sunni society of other cultural influences, ISIS has sought to dismantle the diverse social fabric made up of Sunnis, Shias, Kurds, Yazidis, and Christians that has developed and persevered since the ancient civilization of Mesopotamia, today's Iraq. Broadly, their wrath is directed at minorities whom they view as infidels without human rights. A case that illustrates ISIS's ideology of ethnic cleansing is its extraordinary punishment of the Yazidis, a tiny religious minority, representing less than 1.5 percent of Iraq's estimated population of thirty-four million, whom ISIS considers heretics. After the capture of Mosul and its outlying towns in summer 2014, including Sinjar, near the Syrian border, home to tens of thousands of Yazidis, ISIS engaged in systemic cultural cleansing, forcing hundreds of thousands of minorities from their homes and using sexual violence as a weapon by indiscriminately raping Yazidi girls and women. ISIS viciously attacked the Yazidis, killing men and boys of fighting age and abducting a total of 5,270 Yazidi girls and women (at least 3,144 of whom are still being held at the time of writing), who were subsequently forced into sexual slavery, according to human rights organizations, United Nations figures, and community leaders. To handle the modern sex trade, ISIS has set up a Department of "War Spoils" and a detailed bureaucracy of sex slavery, including sales contracts notarized by its Islamic courts, according to a cache of documents seized by US Special Operations Forces in a May 2015 raid in Syria that killed top ISIS financial official Aby Sayyaf.[10] And systemic rape has become an established and increasingly powerful recruiting tool for ISIS to lure men from deeply conservative Muslim societies, where casual sex is taboo and dating is forbidden.[11] According to the Human Rights Watch, Amnesty International, and investigative reports by the media, ISIS has destroyed hundreds of Yazidi women's lives.[12] Donatella Rovera, Amnesty International's senior crisis response adviser, spoke to forty Yazidi women who had managed to escape from ISIS captivity, and said that what ISIS had done to them amounted to war crimes. "Hundreds of Yezidi women and girls have had their lives shattered by the horrors of sexual violence and sexual slavery in IS captivity," she said.[13] Zainab Bangura, a UN envoy investigating sexual violence in the conflict, has confirmed that an ISIS pamphlet that gives prices for the purchase of women is real and that "the girls get peddled like barrels of petrol." Bangura notes that prices for boys and girls aged one to nine are about $165. Adolescent girls cost about $124, and it's less for women over twenty. "They have a machinery, they have a program," she told *Bloomberg News*. "They have a manual on how you treat these women."[14] According to ISIS's ideology, Yazidis are seen as polytheists and, worse, devil worshipers, and they are not even entitled to be treated like "People of the Book," Christians and Jews, who can atone for their sins by paying a tax known as *jizya* to be set free. In contrast, ISIS either kills or coverts Yazidis by force and enslaves their women, a punishment sanctioned, they say, by their experts of Islamic jurisprudence. ISIS's involvement in the sex trade and its enslavement of girls and women from the tiny Yazidi religious community are driven not only by power and male (patriarchal) domination but also by ideological zealousness. Baghdadi and his *shura* council (cabinet) want to distinguish themselves from Islamist rivals by attempting to revive traditions, rituals, and practices that have been dormant for over a thousand years in Muslim history. They have made emulation of the Prophet Mohammed a strict duty, a tool to display their religious purity and authenticity.[15] For example, citing sayings of the Prophet, a booklet entitled "From Creator's Rulings on Capturing Prisoners and Enslavement" calls for both kindness and cruelty to captives by ISIS. Enslaved women should not be separated from their children, the booklet says, but the rules allow the group's combatants to have sex with female slaves.[16] ISIS has also publicly boasted about its enslavement of Yazidi women in their magazine called *Dabiq* and in their propaganda videos. ISIS has justified its actions on religious grounds by juxtaposing the distant past with the present and selectively citing verses from the scripture or the Sunna (the traditions based on the sayings and deeds of the Prophet Mohammed) to justify their sex slavery. In an October 2014 article titled "The Revival of Slavery before the Hour," the group argues that the Yazidi women "could be enslaved unlike female apostates [the Shia], who the majority of the *fuqahā'* [experts in Islamic jurisprudence] say cannot be enslaved and can only be given an ultimatum to repent or face the sword. . . . After capture, the Yazidi women and children were then divided according to the *Sharī'ah* [Islamic law] amongst the fighters of the Islamic State who participated in the Sinjar operations, after one fifth of the slaves were transferred to the Islamic State's authority to be divided as *khums* [the one-fifth of booty or spoils that goes to the state]."[17]

Christians do not fare much better. After capturing Mosul and other cities in Iraq and Syria, ISIS presented Christians in both countries with a stark choice: convert to Islam, pay a special tax (jizya), or get out immediately and be disinherited from everything you own. Recent evidence shows that despite paying the special tax, Christian girls and women have been victims of ISIS's practice of systemic rape. In light of this ultimatum, the ISIS surge has triggered another wave of exodus by Christians, an exodus that began in earnest when its forerunner, Al Qaeda in Mesopotamia, also commonly known as Al Qaeda in Iraq, forced 1 million of Iraq's surviving 1.5 million Christians to flee the country between 2003 and 2010. There is a real danger that Baghdadi could finish the job of his predecessor, Zarqawi, who was killed in 2006 by the United States— a job that would entail ridding Iraq of its ancient Assyrian community, nearly two thousand years old. Moreover, ISIS's totalitarian ideology also openly targets Muslims. Trying to distinguish themselves theologically from like-minded Islamist radicals, including Al Qaeda Central, Baghdadi and his cohorts are super *takfiri* who have no qualms about excommunicating Muslims at will. ISIS considers Shia Muslims to be apostates, sanctioning the shedding of their blood as well as that of Sunnis who oppose their vision (more on this later). While it can be argued that Arab authoritarian rulers such as President Bashar al-Assad and former Iraqi prime minister Nuri al-Maliki have not done enough to protect the region's minorities against ISIS, these sectarian-based regimes created fertile conditions that allowed Salafi-jihadist groups like ISIS to build a popular base of support among Sunnis and surge. Indeed, ISIS is the main beneficiary of the divisive and destructive policies of the central governments of Iraq and Syria and the breakdown of state institutions in the Arab arena in general. From the beginning Baghdadi and his cohorts depicted themselves as the sole defenders of excluded and aggrieved Sunni communities against Shia-dominated regimes, first in Baghdad and then in Damascus. As explained in the introduction, ISIS is a near-enemy revolutionary movement, focusing on the Arab-Islamic world, not a far-enemy organization targeting the Western powers, even though it has recently devoted more resources to carrying out attacks against the far enemy, including Russia, Europe, North America, and Southeast Asia. It is an ideational, hyper-Sunni movement that harbors a genocidal ideology against the Shia, which means that roughly 120 Shias are marked for death. After it burst out of its original home in Iraq, ISIS expanded to Syria in 2012, with grand ambitions to spread to neighboring countries. In his second address to the world in November 2014, Baghdadi confirmed that his imperial ambitions were not limited to Iraq and Syria but also included Libya, Saudi Arabia, Egypt, Yemen, Algeria, Tunisia, Morocco, and beyond.[18]

THEORIST ENABLERS OF ISIS

Although ISIS does not have its own scholars or theorists, it has mined Salafi-jihadists' repertoire of ideas and selectively borrowed whatever fits its unique worldview. At times, the organization has even been accused of falsely appropriating the works of extremist Salafi theorists. For example, a prominent Salafi-jihadist scholar, Abu Mohammed al-Maqdisi, lashed out angrily against Baghdadi's cohorts for stealing his writings and claiming them as their own. Maqdisi, however, is not a major inspiration for ISIS, as the organization is nourished on a bloodier and deadlier diet. Baghdadi and his inner circle rely particularly on three Salafi-jihadist manifestos to rationalize and justify what they do.[19] The most well-known of the three is *The Management of Savagery*. Circulated in PDF format under the pseudonym Abu Bakr al-Najji in the early 2000s, the manifesto provides a strategic road map of how to create an Islamic caliphate that differs dramatically from similar efforts by Salafi-jihadists in earlier decades. The second book is *Introduction to the Jurisprudence of Jihad* by Abu Abdullah al-Muhajjer, which calls on Salafi-jihadists to do whatever it takes to establish a purely unified Islamic state. The final book is *The Essentials of Making Ready [for Jihad]* by Sayyid Imam al-Sharif, aka Abdel-Qader Ibn Abdel-Aziz or Dr. Fadl. This massive work focuses on the theological and practical meanings of jihad in Islam, and it has become a central text in jihadi training. Dr. Fadl admitted that he wrote the book in 1987–1988 in order for it to be a manual for training camps of what subsequently became known as Al Qaeda.[20]

While Najji's identity remains unconfirmed, both Muhajjer and Dr. Fadl were close associates of Zawahiri. Muhajjer is an Egyptian national who fought in Afghanistan alongside Osama bin Laden and Zawahiri. After graduating from the Islamic University in Islamabad and teaching at jihadist camps in Kabul, Muhajjer mentored fighters at Zarqawi's camp in Herat, and he was seriously considered as a candidate for the scientific and scholarly committee of Al Qaeda Central.[21] After the collapse of the Taliban rule in 2001, he escaped to Iran and was held by the authorities there till his release to Egypt just after the January 25, 2011, revolution. Dr. Fadl was an early associate of Zawahiri. The two first met in the late 1960s in Cairo, where they both attended Cairo University's medical school. In the early 1980s their paths crossed again in Pakistan-Afghanistan, where they worked together to rebuild Egyptian Islamic Jihad, a Salafi-jihadist group. After September 11, 2001, Dr. Fadl and Zawahiri parted ways, engaging in a public feud over ideology and the future direction of the global jihadist movement. While serving a life sentence in an Egyptian prison, Dr. Fadl subsequently disowned his ideas and called for the demilitarization and deradicalization of the Salafi-jihadist camp. The story and journey of the three theorists show the enduring intellectual impact of the pioneers or the first generation of Salafi-jihadists on the movement as a whole. As a traveling ideology, Salafi-jihadism is nourished on ideas that can be tailored to fit the predilections and whims of every wave, providing nourishment, sustenance, and motivation to new coverts and adherents.

The three manifestos represent the most extreme thinking within the movement and the degeneration of the Salafi-jihadist ideology into *Fiqh al-Damaa* (the jurisprudence of blood). Although most analysts focus mainly on *The Management of Savagery*, the other two manifestos are as important in providing intellectual and ideological motivation and inspiration for Baghdadi and his ideologues. Despite differences, there are common conceptual threads among the three manifestos that offer theoretical guidance for ISIS's actions. First, the three books call for all-out war and advocate offensive jihad as opposed to defensive jihad in order to bleed the *kuffar* (infidels) or the enemies of Islam, thus creating chaos and fear. At the heart of this rationalization lies the belief that Salafi-jihadists must rid themselves of the illusion that the establishment of an Islamic state is possible through gradual electoral means or the political process. The authors poke fun at fellow Islamists who call for a reformist approach, arguing that it is impossible to build the institutions of an Islamic state under a system of apostasy. Second, although this total war should target both the near enemy and the far enemy, they prioritize the fight against tyrannical Muslim rulers who do not apply *shariah* (Qur'anic law). Finally, all three manifestos call on the movement's planners and lieutenants to kill with impunity, to observe no limits and follow in the footsteps of the Prophet's companions, who, in their opinion, brutally punished dissenters and rivals. They cite selective cases of early Islamic history to prove their claim that excessive violence produces the desired effect: submission. According to their logic, viciousness is the secret to success and victory, while softheartedness is a recipe for failure and defeat. They also argue that the ends—reclaiming Islam's golden age and establishing the Islamic state—justify the means—viciousness and savagery.

TOTAL WAR = VICTORY

Although all three Salafi-jihadist theorists advocate offensive jihad rather than defensive jihad, Najji explicitly makes the case for all-out war. According to Najji, in the past Salafi-jihadists lacked a strategic blueprint and carried out isolated acts of violence with no comprehensive "military strategy" or master plan. He harshly criticizes fellow Islamists for squandering precious time and effort on "preaching" jihad rather than doing jihad.[22] Instead, Najji offers an expansive plan with three stages in which violence would be escalated qualitatively and strategically rather than in an ad hoc and random way. In the first stage, *al-Nikaya wal-Tamkeen* (vexation and empowerment), the will of the enemy must be broken by carrying out attacks against vital economic and strategic targets such as oil facilities and the tourism infrastructure. As security forces would rush in and mobilize resources to protect these sensitive targets, the state would be weakened and its powers would wither away, a condition conducive to "savagery and chaos." Salafi-jihadists would then take advantage of this security vacuum, notes Najji, by launching an all-out battle on the thinly dispersed security forces.[23] Once the rulers are overthrown, a second phase would commence, *Idrarat al-Tawhush* (the administration or management of savagery), and the third and final stage, *Shawkat al-Tamkeen* (empowerment), would see the establishment of the Islamic state. This Islamic state, Najji explains, should be ruled by a single leader who would then unify diffuse and scattered groups and regions of "savagery" in a caliphate.[24] According to Najji, this third stage employs a mixture of persuasion and coercion to win hearts and minds and gain legitimacy and recognition for the Islamic rule.

Although Najji does not directly acknowledge the influence of Sayyid Qutb, the master theorist of contemporary revolutionary Islamism, he borrows some of his terminology and Islamist references, such as *al-Qilla al-Mumtaza* (the vanguard) and *Zulm al-Jahiliyya* (the darkness of ignorance of divine guidance).[25] However, he explicitly professes inspiration from an influential fourteenth-century radical Islamic scholar and theologian called Ibn Taymiyya, whose fatwas (religious edicts) have provided motivation for multiple waves of Salafi-jihadists, including ISIS. Unsurprisingly, Najji emphasizes the significance of the media and propaganda as an ideological tool to mobilize and recruit the Muslim masses to the side of

Salafi-jihadists during the first and second stages of the long war, and then to control them and pacify them during the final stage under a centralized Islamic rule.

TARGETING THE NEAR AND THE FAR ENEMIES

In *The Management of Savagery* Najji's sole preoccupation is with the near enemy, secular and renegade Muslim rulers. He lists a few countries as a potentially fertile ground, mainly Jordan, Saudi Arabia, Yemen, North Africa, Nigeria, and Pakistan. However, Najji qualifies his shopping list by saying that it is temporary and that it would be more effective to apply his master plan to two or three countries before targeting the other cases.[26] Similarly, in *The Essentials of Making Ready [for Jihad]*, Dr. Fadl contends that although jihad should target both the far enemy and the near enemy, the latter should take precedence. According to Dr. Fadl, the near enemy is those "infidel rulers" who "apply infidel laws and infidel democracy."[27] He argues that attacking these rulers, whom he called *Murtadeen* (apostates), should even take priority over the other "jihad against Jews," because they "are closer to us and they have abandoned and renounced Islamic beliefs."[28] He depicts these Muslim rulers as more dangerous than kuffar—Christians and Jews.[29] Like Najji and Muhajjer, Dr. Fadl draws on Ibn Taymiyya's fatwas to justify war against the near enemy, claiming that jihad against "apostate leaders" is *Fard Ayn* (an obligation) of every Muslim who has reached the age of fifteen.[30] Citing Ibn Taymiyya and being inspired by Qutb without naming him, he expands the list of apostates to "include anyone who rules by positivist [secular] laws."[31] During this phase of jihad, Muslims should "display animosity and hatred towards those living infidels," "disavow their infidel principles such as communism and democracy," and "isolate themselves even by migration from the infidels' land."[32] Dr. Fadl even argues that jihad against the enemy in its homeland should take place "at least once a year," although he cites other Muslim scholars who argued that "there are no time limits to this Jihad."[33] The Muslim umma, he notes, must prioritize this offensive jihad, and both its internal and external policies, including agriculture, industry, commerce, and housing, must be geared to support this sacred mission.[34] He warns Muslims that anyone who avoids "jihad for the sake of God" would "betray Allah, his prophet and the religion itself."[35] The key goal, notes Dr. Fadl, is to create *Hakimiyya* (the rule of God) on earth; this would occur "when Muslims defeat their enemies and apply Islam's rules in the conquered lands."[36] The concept of the vanguard is essential to the success of Dr. Fadl's jihadist project, and he first and foremost calls on Salafi-jihadists to "form a Jama'a Muslima [Muslim group]" whose task is to recruit others to join the mission described in the manual.[37] The significance of Dr. Fadl's manual is that it provides doctrinal justification in the fight against the near enemy, which ISIS prioritizes over that against the far enemy— the Western powers.[38]

Prioritizing the fight against the far enemy, Muhajjer calls on Salafi-jihadists to launch war on kuffar. In *Introduction to the Jurisprudence of Jihad*, he opposes the consensus among jurisprudents over the centuries and asserts that "killing *kuffar* and fighting them in their homeland is a necessity even if they do not harm Muslims."[39] Muhajjer does not distinguish between "civilians" and "combatants" among non-Muslims because he bluntly confesses that the main reason for "killing them and confiscating their property" is the fact that "they are not Muslims."[40] Moreover, the writer who earned the pseudonym Faqih al-Damaa (jurisprudent of blood) expanded the definition of *Dar al-Kuffr* (land of apostasy) to include countries inhabited by a majority of Muslims; these states do not apply shariah or Islamic law and thus are legitimate targets for attacks by Salafi-jihadists.[41]

SAVAGERY: A MEANS TO AN END

Whether they prioritize the fight against the near enemy, as Najji does, or insist that attention should be paid to both the near enemy and the far enemy, as Dr. Fadl and Muhajjer (to a lesser extent) do, all three authors argue that the existing system of *Kufr* (apostasy) must be overthrown, incinerated, regardless of the inherent cost or sacrifice. In fact, the authors' key argument is that Salafi-jihadists must hasten social and institutional disintegration of the state system and induce mayhem and be prepared to manage this cataclysm. The goal is to kill and terrorize not for the sake of killing or terrorism but for a higher moral purpose: cultural cleansing and the imposition of God's laws on kuffar. For example, in *The Management of Savagery*, Najji points out that "the worst chaotic condition is by far preferable to stability under the system of apostasy,"[42] thus turning the received wisdom of the mainstream religious establishment on its head. He depicts Salafi-jihadists as the vanguard best equipped to trigger an apocalypse or an end to apostasy, an end to the world as we know it, and a religious rebirth. "We must drag all the people to battle and bring the temple down on the heads of everyone," Najji states. Even "if the whole umma perishes, they would all be martyrs," he adds, justifying the death of millions of Muslims as for a worthy cause.[43]

As to their favorite methods of violence, it seems that the authors have a preference for beheading and burning, which they see as effective in instilling fear and deterring others from resisting. Such vicious methods, they insist, can also be used to attack economic targets, particularly petroleum. Requiring sacrifice and pain, this confrontation must use shock-and-awe tactics to overwhelm the enemy, make him "think one thousand times before attacking us . . . and keep him on the defensive and off balance."[44] Najji advocates attacking the population and infrastructure in order to terrorize the enemy and maximize levels of savagery.[45] In a similar vein, Muhajjer advocates the use of gruesome methods such as beheading, a favorite tactic of his. In *Introduction to the Jurisprudence of Jihad*, he devotes a whole chapter to beheading, arguing that it will "convey a gory picture" by "strengthening the hearts of Muslims and terrorizing the apostates" by deterring them.[46] Muhajjer even provides theological justification for grotesque forms of punishment such as transporting and displaying the heads of those non-Muslims killed in battle from one country to another in order to boost the deterrence power of Salafi-jihadists.[47] He dedicates another chapter to suicide bombings, claiming that killing oneself is theologically legal because it is designed to boost religion. Going beyond Najji's guidelines, Muhajjer advises Salafi-jihadists to obtain weapons of mass destruction, which he sees as a "necessity" in this total war.[48] Although he says that weapons of mass destruction must only be used in defense against an invasion by kuffar, he qualifies this by insisting on other measures of punishment if that would benefit Muslims.[49]

There is a sober, realist, cold-bloodedness to the guidelines offered by Najji, Muhajjer, and Dr. Fadl, a businesslike attitude that belies the dark, sinister, and vile ideological message. Their point of departure is that the Islamic State can only be nourished on "blood" and erected on "skeletons and human remains"; the whole society must be transformed into a war society prepared to wage a prolonged battle that will produce historical leaders. Although these leaders, caution the authors, will sustain deep wounds and suffer great personal losses, they are necessary to build a jihadist generation, a Qur'anic generation baptized by blood and fire.[50] Theirs is an existential fight between faith and Kufr, Islam and apostasy, and only total war against enemies near and far will bring about the Islamist utopia.

ISIS BEYOND IDEOLOGY: STATE, GOVERNANCE, AND MILITARY CAPABILITIES

While ISIS's repeated displays of brutality point to a movement that rules by force and terror, it has steadily built its capacity to govern through the introduction of services such as policing, a shariah-based justice system, identity cards for residents, consumer watch programs, garbage collection, and day care centers.[51] Local residents in al-Raqqa, Mosul, and other cities say that ISIS is acting like a rudimentary functioning state and providing security, a precious commodity in short supply in war-torn Iraq and Syria. Residents are left alone if they obey ISIS's rules and commands and its severe and narrow interpretation of shariah. Like the Taliban in Afghanistan in the 1990s, ISIS is welcomed and feared by Sunni communities who have lived through decades of repression, tyranny, corruption, and violence. Baghdadi and his foot soldiers are not seen as monstrous and evil, as they are seen from the outside, a testament to the breakdown of state institutions and the fraying of the social fabric in Iraq and Syria. Like the Taliban, if ISIS retains control over territory and populations and delivers services, it will likely consolidate its hegemony and gain the implicit acquiescence of the governed. This makes ISIS radically different from and more dangerous than Al Qaeda Central, which never controlled territory or people or had immediate designs to create a state of its own. In contrast, ISIS is building a rump state in both countries and offers a subversive vision that dates back to seventh-century Arabia. Given the breakdown of Middle Eastern politics and raging civil wars, the organization threatens the foundation of the Arab state system in a more fundamental way than other nonstate actors have done before.

The rise of ISIS has triggered an intense public debate about the disintegration of the Arab state system and the bitter legacy of Sykes-Picot, a secret agreement made in 1916 between the French and British that divided the spoils of the defeated Ottoman Empire between them. That secret deal drew a new set of borders for the former Arab provinces of the empire that more or less have survived till now. Baghdadi and his cohorts made it clear that they want to tear down the "colonialist" borders that divide the Arab-Islamic world into separate states and replace them with a caliphate, a pan-Islamist state. To show their resolve after they seized Mosul in June 2014, ISIS's fighters bulldozed the official border between Syrian and Iraq after seizing contiguous territories in both countries, an act designed to display their revolutionary credentials and appeal to an Arab constituency that still views the Sykes-Picot agreement as illegitimate, a Western plot to divide, weaken, and conquer the

Arab world. In contrast to existing nonstate actors in the region, ISIS is more ambitious and revolutionary, presenting itself as a more authentic, identity-driven alternative to the Middle Eastern state system. Its propagandists go further by comparing their nascent state to that of the Prophet in seventh-century Arabia and by imposing the past on the present as a means to invest their state project with religious legitimation. What sets ISIS apart from other nonstate actors, including Al Qaeda Central, is its possession of material capability, willpower, and ideological capital, which it has combined to deadly effect. Ideology, masquerading as radical theology, has been used to rationalize and justify ISIS's violent deeds, with Baghdadi reminding Muslims that their "Prophet . . . was dispatched with the sword" to made God's laws supreme. ISIS's enduring threat lies in its combination of lethal military force with a totalitarian ideology that observes no limits.[52] Thus, the capabilities and resources of Baghdadi and his cohorts are effective and their numbers larger than any other insurgency group in the greater Middle East, though the group has monstrously miscalculated by overextending itself and turning the entire world against it. By the end of 2015, ISIS appears to be losing territory in Iraq and Syria and bleeding.

FOREIGN FIGHTERS AND THE SECURITY DILEMMA

Western governments worry that ISIS's swift conquests in the Arab heartland, an arena of strategic and economic significance, represent a threat to the security of their Arab allies. They also fear the potential spillover effects of the expansion of ISIS's power on their own national security. The images of ISIS's beheadings of American, British, Japanese, and Egyptian hostages as well as its deadly attacks in Beirut, Paris, and San Bernardino, California, heightened anxieties in Western capitals. Particularly alarming is the fact that, as stated by Nick Rasmussen—director of the US National Counterterrorism Center—during testimony for a hearing of the House of

Representatives Committee on Homeland Security in February 2015, more than 20,000 foreign fighters from more than ninety countries have traveled to Syria, with at least 3,400 of them coming from Western countries.[53] The number of foreign fighters has increased steadily, reaching 36,500 foreign fighters, including at least 6,600 from Western countries, at the beginning of 2016, according to James Clapper, the director of National Intelligence, and UN sources.[54] Not since the Afghan jihad against the Soviet occupation in the 1980s have so many foreign religious activists traveled to fight in distant lands. In fact, today Syria and Iraq attract many more Western recruits than did either Afghanistan or Iraq after the US-led invasion of the country in 2003, a phenomenon that deserves critical scrutiny. "The rate of foreign terrorist fighter travel to Syria ... exceeded the rate of foreign fighters who travelled to Afghanistan and Pakistan, Iraq, Yemen or Somalia at any point in the last 20 years," concluded the State Department's annual terrorism report in 2015.[55]

European and American leaders are particularly anxious that the foreign fighters radicalized and militarized in Iraq and Syria could return home and carry out terrorist attacks, a nightmarish scenario that security officials say keeps them awake at night. Abdelhamid Abaaoud is a case in point. A foot soldier turned lieutenant in ISIS's platoons in Syria, Abaaoud, a twenty-eight-year-old Belgian, was sent back to Belgium where he organized a network of nine militants who carried out massive suicide bombings in Paris in November 2015, the deadliest terrorist assaults in France in fifty years.[56] The anxieties of Western governments had already been heightened after a terrorist attack in Paris that targeted the satirical magazine *Charlie Hebdo* on January 7, 2015, killing twelve people; it was followed by a related attack on a kosher supermarket in east Paris two days later, resulting in four more deaths. The terrorist network in Paris included three suspects: two brothers, Said Kouachi, thirty-four, and Cherif Kouachi, thirty-two, who allegedly belonged to an offshoot of Al Qaeda Central in Yemen called Al Qaeda in the Arabian Peninsula (AQAP); and Amedy Coulibaly, thirty-two, a self-proclaimed ISIS foot soldier. The trauma caused by the Paris attacks in January and November 2015 not only affected the French nation; its reverberations were felt on every European street. The significance of these attacks led to an increasing recognition that the recruitment of young men in the West creates security risks across Europe and North America. This point was driven home when in February 2015 a copycat attack took place in Copenhagen, Denmark, where two individuals were killed. A climate of fear and panic has taken hold of the European and American imagination. The terrorist threat, though real, has been blown up out of proportion with British Prime Minister saying that ISIS poses an "existential" threat to his country, a statement that mischaracterizes a limited menace with a strategic.[57] In the US, in an attempt to reduce the danger to the homeland, Republican presidential candidates have called for banning Muslims from entering the country and for bombing civilians in Iraq and Syria, a recipe that aides Salafi-jihadists like ISIS.[58]

Although the phenomena of foreign fighters, wannabe jihadists, and lone wolves are not new, ISIS's counternarrative has had a wider appeal than that of its co-jihadists, including Al Qaeda Central. In July 2015, FBI director James B. Comey told the Aspen Security Forum in Colorado that ISIS poses a more challenging threat within the US homeland than Al Qaeda Central. It is much more effective at recruiting impressionable and "troubled souls" through social media than other groups, Comey said, adding, "It's currently the threat that we're worrying about in the homeland most of all."[59] The White House is also increasingly alarmed by what Lisa Monaco, Obama's homeland security and counterterrorism adviser, recently called ISIS's "unique threat" to the United States. In contrast, the US national security establishment, led by the Pentagon, intelligence agencies, and the National Counterterrorism Center, is more anxious about Al Qaeda Central overseas. These agencies warn that Al Qaeda operatives in Yemen and Syria are capitalizing on the turmoil in those countries to plot much larger "mass-casualty" attacks, including bringing down airliners carrying hundreds of passengers.[60] As the *New York Times* implicitly cautioned, the debate within US government agencies is not academic; it will influence how the Obama administration allocates about $15 billion in counterterrorism funds, and how it will assign thousands of officers to combat evolving and shifting threats to national security.[61] The debate on terrorism in the US cannot be separated from the business side of "selling" counterterrorism which is a big business in Washington. According to a report by the Center for Strategic and International Studies (CSIS), the US spends $124.9 billion a year on the overall fight against terrorism, a massive sum that reflects panic, opportunism, and gross overreaction to the threat.[62]

ISIS's efficacy in attracting young recruits from around the world lies in its sophisticated outreach campaign and strategy. The group appeals to disaffected and disadvantaged Sunni youths around the world, who are often dealing with issues concerning their identities. More than its like-minded predecessors, ISIS is a youth movement. By presenting the group as a powerful vanguard movement capable of delivering victory and salvation, ISIS's propagandists offer alienated Muslim youths a utopian worldview and a political project: resurrecting the lost caliphate.[63] The idea of the caliphate, a political institution that was disposed of in the 1920s with the emergence of the Republic of Turkey, has taken hold of the imagination of many Sunni Islamists who see it as redemptive, a means to salvation, and a worthy cause to do jihad for. At the heart of this utopian longing for the imagined caliphate is the feeling of some Muslims that the modern nation-state has failed to build a just and inclusive order.

In addition to targeting individuals who feel disaffected and playing on the desire for a more inclusive political system, ISIS also capitalizes on each of its territorial gains in Iraq and Syria. With their seizure of Mosul and their growing military momentum in the summer of 2014, Baghdadi's battalions seemed unstoppable and unbeatable, fired with a "faithful ideology."

More than any other factor, ISIS's swift expansion attracts recruits from near and far. As a victorious vanguard, ISIS appeals to politicized Sunnis who feel disfranchised by Shia-led regimes and who aspire to regain power and implement a cultural renewal. ISIS's ideologues and propagandists used this impetus to strike fear and terror in the hearts of their enemies and "scar their consciousness," as they put it, and to encourage euphoria and a feeling of inevitability among their supporters, which allowed ISIS to defeat bigger formations of the Iraqi and Syrian armies and recruit thousands of foreign fighters. The group seemed to be on a roll in Iraq and Syria, with neighboring Arab countries like Jordan, Lebanon, and Saudi Arabia feeling anxious about the potential security reverberations of ISIS's spectacular expansion. The Obama administration faced pressure at home and in the region to intervene and stop the ISIS blitzkrieg.

Initially, to blunt ISIS's swift advances, Obama ordered "limited" airstrikes to protect Americans in Irbil and to help thousands of civilians, mainly Yazidis, trapped on Mount Sinjar after an ISIS offensive. Within days, the US mission broadened, with Obama saying that it would now "provide military assistance and advice to the Iraqi government and Kurdish forces as they battle these terrorists, so that the terrorists cannot establish a permanent safe haven." After ISIS beheaded two American hostages in September 2014, Obama again expanded the airstrikes beyond Iraq to targets in Syria. The brutal murder of two American citizens, combined with the near collapse of the Iraqi armed forces and a lackluster performance by the Kurdish Peshmerga, forced Obama's hand. He vowed to "degrade and ultimately destroy" the organization, marking a turning point in US policy regarding ISIS. As the threat emanating from ISIS continued to grow, reaching Western capitals, including the US homeland at the end of 2015, Obama authorized the deployment of Special Operations contingents in Iraq and Syria and deepened American involvement in the war in Iraq and Syria. To reassure a nervous nation and anxious allies abroad, the US president vowed to "destroy" ISIS through relentless airstrikes and building up local forces to spearhead the fight against the group. Obama's basic strategy of avoiding a ground war has not changed,[64] though at the time of writing, at the beginning of 2016, his aides say the US is willing to deploy "boots on the ground" to help Iraqi and Syrian forces liberate Mosul and al-Raqqa, an important shift in tactics.

ISIS's downing of a Russian jet and its attacks in Beirut, Paris, and California brought a convergence of interests between the rival global powers of the United States and Russia; both signaled their willingness to indirectly coordinate the fight against the Islamic State in Syria, though they still differ on the future of Assad. Importantly, the United States found itself aligned with Iran on the issue of ISIS and started to coordinate with Shia militias in Iraq, which are directly under Iran's umbrella. The new alignment between Iran and the United States was formalized in a historical nuclear deal after months of intense negotiations, a deal that both Israel and the US Republican Party strongly opposed but failed to scuttle. At least for the time being, ISIS has managed to change the geostrategic environment, notably pushing the interests of the Obama administration closer in line with those of Iran.[65]

Although the United States is now leading a broad anti-ISIS coalition made up of sixty-two countries, including Saudi Arabia, Jordan, the United Arab Emirates, and Bahrain, the alliance is disunited and lacks an effective plan to defeat ISIS. Twenty-one states provide air and military support, but just thirteen have launched airstrikes. Nearly four out of five airstrikes on ISIS territories have been conducted by the United States. After carrying out more than ten thousand airstrikes (and counting) against ISIS and killing more than twenty-two thousand of its operators according to the independent monitoring group Airwars, the US-led coalition has only rolled back some of the military gains made by the group so far.[66] By the beginning of 2016, ISIS has lost approximately 40 percent of the territory they once held in Iraq and between 5 and 20 percent in Syria since the declaration of the caliphate in June 2014.[67] American officials and strategists say that ISIS is replacing its combatants in Iraq and Syria as fast as the United States and its allies are killing them there, and the CIA estimates that ISIS still maintains a mini-army of thirty-one thousand fighters. Other groups such as the Syrian Observatory for Human Rights claim that ISIS may field as many as one hundred thousand combatants.[68] ISIS remains well funded—earning close to $1 billion a year in oil revenues, taxes, and criminal activities, according to Treasury Department estimates—and has expanded to other regions, including Libya, Yemen, Afghanistan, and the Sinai Peninsula in Egypt.[69]

Senior American and British officials acknowledge that it would take years to recapture all the cities and towns seized by ISIS in Iraq, though they are more optimistic about the fight in Syria. The group does not appear to have as large of a social constituency in Syria as it does in Iraq. Critics are skeptical that Western and Middle Eastern governments have a winning "strategy" in Iraq and Syria, which, in their opinion, has only helped empower ISIS. Although the United States and its European allies say they are committed to degrading ISIS and eventually destroying the group, they are unwilling to deploy a large contingent of ground troops lest they play into the group's apocalyptic narrative and suffer casualties. For now the gap between Western objectives and means bolsters ISIS's narrative of invincibility, allowing it to draw thousands of recruits, though as the group fights for its survival by the end of 2015, it is attracting fewer recruits. Baghdadi and his planners have also exploited the regional rivalry between the Saudi-led bloc of Sunni Arab states and Shia-dominated Iran, a discord that has taken sectarian overtones and has become a zero-sum contest for influence.[70] While the fragility of the state structures in Iraq and Syria is the key cause of ISIS's swift and spectacular surge, regional and global rivalries sustain and prolong its existence. As long as these conditions and cleavages exist, it is going to be difficult to defeat ISIS and dislodge it from Iraq and Syria.

WHERE ISIS CAME FROM:
ZARQAWI TO BAGHDADI

As a social movement, ISIS must be contextualized through its origins, its journey traced from the crux of the American-led invasion and occupation of Iraq in 2003 to its expansion beyond the Iraqi borders to Syria in late 2011. Through this frame of reference, we can understand the driving forces behind the ISIS insurgency. While Arab states such as Egypt, Algeria, and Libya have experienced jihadist insurgencies, it is worth stressing that before the US military venture, Iraq had never experienced such a phenomenon, and Saddam Hussein, a staunch secular Arab nationalist, had no operational relationship with Al Qaeda Central.[1] The Hussein regime and Al Qaeda chiefs were deeply suspicious of each other. Hussein did not gamble or take risks with Salafi-jihadists, even though he projected a pious image in the last decade of his rule as a way to respond to punishing economic sanctions imposed on Iraq by the United States and the United Nations after the second Gulf War in 1991.[2]

In March 2015, President Barack Obama traced the origins of ISIS to his predecessor George W. Bush's decision to send US troops to occupy Iraq. In an interview with *Vice News*,

Obama said that the rise of the Islamic State can be directly linked to the US-led invasion of Iraq: "ISIL is a direct outgrowth of Al-Qaeda in Iraq that grew out of our invasion, which is an example of unintended consequences. Which is why we should generally aim before we shoot."[3] Obama's comments triggered a storm of protests by conservative commentators and directly contradicted much of the rhetoric that had been presented by his predecessor to justify the 2003 invasion.

Indeed, between 2001 and 2003, the US case for an attack on Iraq relied on two main assertions: that Hussein possessed weapons of mass destruction, and that he supported extremist Islamism of the Al Qaeda variety. However, US weapons experts struggled to find proof of Hussein's alleged arsenal, and the Bush administration shifted the emphasis to the Iraqi regime's alleged link with Al Qaeda's transnational jihadist network. In a speech at the United Nations Security Council in February 2003, Colin Powell, then secretary of state, said,

> Our concern is not just about these illicit weapons. It's the way that these illicit weapons can be connected to terrorists and terrorist organizations that have no compunction about using such devices against innocent people around the world. . . . But what I want to bring to your attention today is the potentially much more sinister nexus between Iraq and the al Qaeda terrorist network, a nexus that combines classic terrorist organizations and modern methods of murder. Iraq today harbors a deadly terrorist network headed by Abu Musab Zarqawi, an associate and collaborator of Osama bin Laden and his al Qaeda lieutenants.[4]

These allegations were subsequently proved to be unfounded.

In the final report, titled *The National Commission on Terrorist Attacks upon the United States* (also known as the 9/11 Commission Report), there was said to be "no credible evidence that Iraq and al Qaeda cooperated on attacks against the United States."[5] In addition to the 9/11 Commission Report, a senior Al

Qaeda military commander, Seif al-Adl, confirmed that his group had no connection with Hussein and considered him a staunch enemy. According to Adl's firsthand account, on the eve of the American-led invasion of Iraq, the challenge faced by Al Qaeda's lieutenants was how to evade Hussein's security services and reach the Sunni-dominated areas in order to establish a foothold there, store weapons, and recruit fighters for the coming war.[6] The accounts by the 9/11 Commission Report and Adl set the record straight regarding claims made by officials in George W. Bush's administration about the existence of an Al Qaeda–Hussein connection. Nevertheless, Powell's 2003 speech gained traction at home and abroad and provided the international media with a name and an address for the alleged leader of Al Qaeda in Iraq: Abu Musab al-Zarqawi. Joining Osama bin Laden and Ayman al-Zawahiri, the two senior leaders of Al Qaeda, Zarqawi was a new face of the global jihadist movement, and he subsequently became a key figure in the development of a new wave of jihadists like ISIS, a post–Al Qaeda generation.

WHO IS ZARQAWI?

Ahmad Fadeel al-Nazal al-Khalayleh was born in 1966 and later came to be known as Abu Musab al-Zarqawi, taking his surname from the town in which he was born and raised, Zarqa, Jordan. Located just seventeen miles north of the capital of Jordan, Amman, Zarqa suffers from a high unemployment rate among the youth, many people live in abject poverty, and it is home to criminal networks. Zarqawi grew up in modest means with his Bedouin family from the Bani Hassan Tribe, a semi-nomadic confederation that includes twelve main clans. These clans are not necessarily related by blood or common descent; they sometimes regroup for reasons of mutual interests, such as defense and strategy. The environments, both social and material, that Zarqawi was brought up in would shape his future worldview and decision-making process.

The first turning point in young Zarqawi's life was the death of his father in 1984. In the same year, Zarqawi, described as semiliterate and not a promising student, dropped out of school. He was not docile, often described by his contemporaries as a wild adolescent with a fiery temper, embroiled in street brawls and with no interest in religion. Zarqawi's behavior is said to have peaked following the death of his father; he became known for committing petty crimes and was driven to alcoholism. He eventually wound up in prison, charged with sexual assault and drug possession.[7] Upon his release from prison, the young Zarqawi discovered Islam, a discovery that acted as a second turning point in his life. In 1989, four years after the death of his father, Zarqawi migrated to Afghanistan to join the jihad caravan there, settling in the border town of Khost.[8] While Zarqawi dreamed of becoming a *mujahid* (a jihadist fighter) against the Soviet occupation, he never realized his dream, as the Red Army was defeated on his arrival and returned to Jordan in 1993. Notwithstanding this setback, Zarqawi remained in northern Afghanistan until 1992 or 1993, where, surprisingly, he first served not as a foot soldier but as a journalist, despite his poor literary skills, for the jihadist magazine *al-Bunyan al-Marsus* (The impenetrable edifice). While stationed in Afghanistan, Zarqawi formed ties with several jihadists, such as Salah al-Hami, a Jordanian-Palestinian and correspondent for *al-Jihad*, a magazine that disseminated the ideas of Abdullah Azzam, a prominent Palestinian Islamist theorist and preacher and military commander who was assassinated in Peshawar in 1989. Azzam was bin Laden's mentor before the two fell out over the future direction of the global jihadist movement and bin Laden's close relationship with the Egyptian Islamist Zawahiri. Hami said that he and Zarqawi became close following the former's stint in the hospital after he lost a leg to a landmine. Their friendship was sealed when Hami married one of Zarqawi's seven sisters. The wedding took place in Peshawar and, until 2006, the video of the ceremony provided the only authenticated footage of

Zarqawi.[9] After the wedding, Hami and his bride returned to Jordan. Zarqawi, on the other hand, stayed in Afghanistan and fought with the Afghan mujahideen. He was under the protection of a Pashtun warlord, Gulbuddin Hekmatyar, who later served as prime minister in Afghanistan from March 1993 to January 1994 and opposed both the Taliban and General Ahmad Shaha Massoud's Northern Alliance. Hekmatyar, a figure who will be discussed in greater detail below, would also prove to be an important link for Zarqawi in a network of contacts.

After his return to Jordan in 1993, Zarqawi's civilian life was cut short, and he would soon be drawn back into revolutionary Islamist circles. During this period, Zarqawi became a member of a prominent Jordanian-Palestinian Salafi-jihadist group led by the radical Islamist scholar Issam Mohammed Taher Barqawi, better known by the pseudonym Abu Mohammed al-Maqdisi. The two spent much of their time proselytizing, preaching *al Dawa* (the call to Islam), and criticizing the Jordanian government for its rapprochement with Israel, which culminated in a peace agreement signed by the two countries in October 1994. At this time, Maqdisi became Zarqawi's mentor, and, in the latter part of 1993, the two radical activists founded an underground militant cell called Al-Tawhid, which later became known as Bayat al-Imam. According to Mohammed Wasfi, a former jihadist who met with Zarqawi in the summer of 1993, Zarqawi directed his rage against the near enemy—the authoritarian secular Arab regimes: "He was a simple Muslim who wanted to serve Islam. He didn't stay long here, and the next day he came with another guy. We sat, and we spoke about our hopes and dreams and ambitions to establish the caliphate and raise the flag of jihad against the enemies of Islam everywhere. I disagreed with him on some strategic issues, like his view of Israel and Palestine. He didn't have an idea of making jihad against Jews and Israel. Abu Musab wanted to change Arab regimes."[10] Before Zarqawi and Maqdisi could execute their agenda, they were arrested in March 1994 and charged with possession of arms and explosives. In 1995, following a flamboyant trial during which the two suspects accused the judiciary and the king of treason for acting against the teachings of the Qur'an, they received a fifteen-year prison sentence for establishing an illegal jihadist cell. Both were jailed in the al-Suwaqah prison, where Zarqawi was recurrently subjected to torture and solitary confinement.

Zarqawi's prison experience in al-Suwaqah marks a third turning point in his life, engendering a mental and physical transformation. It is well documented that Arab prisons serve as incubators of future terrorists, and, like numerous Arab jihadists, Zarqawi was traumatized by his prison years in Jordan. According to prison inmates, Zarqawi's experience left deep scars on his character. Fu'ad Hussein, a journalist who spent time with Zarqawi in prison in the mid-1990s and who talked to his closest friends and associates, writes that Zarqawi's prison experience "was the most significant phase in the development of his personality," more important than his participation in the Afghan jihad in the late 1980s and early 1990s. It is often believed and stated by individuals who knew him before and after his experience at al-Suwaqah that it was the prison years in Jordan that turned him into a hardened killer and psychopath. Hussein states, "The prison left a clear mark on al-Zarqawi's personality, which grew more intense. In his opinion, policemen, judges, and government members of all ranks were supporters of the regimes, which he believed were *tawagheet* [tyrants] who should be fought." He also relates a story of Zarqawi's experience with torture, during which, in one instance, he was held in solitary confinement for eight and a half months. When Hussein saw Zarqawi afterward, he states that he no longer had toenails, as a result of infections caused by severe torture.[11]

According to another inmate who was with Zarqawi in jail, the prison years in Jordan reshaped his personality, making him more ruthless and, eventually, causing him to even overshadow his mentor, Maqdisi, and become one of the most feared and respected figures among the prisoners.[12] In addition to Zarqawi's mental transformation, during which he is reported to have gone from a follower to a feared commander, he also improved his physical conditioning, spending much of his time exercising and increasing his strength. In another eye-opening testimony, Abu al-Montasser Billah Mohammed, with whom Zarqawi jointly established his first jihadist group, Al-Tawhid, said that the Jordanian radical often acted recklessly and hastily: "The hastiness of brother Abu Musab was a problem for me. He wanted everything to be done quickly. He wanted to achieve all his ambitions in a matter of months, if not hours. Such haste posed one of the most dangerous threats to our call. Abu Musab made decisions unilaterally at the wrong time and place. More tragically, the majority of brothers used to agree with him."[13] His hot temper, although not a new development, led him to get embroiled in disputes with the guards, which in turn helped him make a name for himself among the prisoners. He saw the guards as protecting an illegitimate regime, a US client, and defied their authority. According to an inmate, for many prisoners, Zarqawi's arguments and defiance of the guards, including his opposition to the Jordanian state, were signs of his strength and determination.[14] It can be argued that his experience growing up in tough social conditions helped him acclimate to the prison environment and solidify his resolve against the Jordanian state and authority in general. Additionally, for struggling Islamists from rural and urban working segments, Zarqawi's poor background made him an easy figure to relate to. An important development, as a contemporary inmate points out, is that as Zarqawi gained popularity, imprisoned jihadist fighters flocked to him, and soon the inexperienced Zarqawi morphed into the leader of a group of skilled jihadists and wannabe jihadists,[15] forging lasting links with them.

While Zarqawi was becoming a natural leader within the prison environment, he was also undertaking the arduous task of memorizing the Qur'an, despite having little knowledge of classical Arabic. In undertaking such a project, Zarqawi sought out help from Faiq al-Shawih, a cellmate, who states, "I helped him, he used to recite at least ten verses a day to me. Al Zarqawi was relentless when it came to Jihad and learning."[16] Though he was described as relentless in his learning process, Zarqawi's elementary knowledge of classical Arabic meant that he must have relied on a secondhand interpretation of the Qur'an, a common challenge faced by poor and uneducated youths in Arab countries. Under normal circumstances, this may seem fine, but in the case of Zarqawi, it is possible that the secondhand interpretation made him, and others like him, more susceptible to ideological indoctrination by hard-line Salafi-jihadist interpreters.

The viciousness of the Zarqawi generation is organically linked to its social status in the hierarchy of the global jihadist movement. In a way, Zarqawi was the representative of a new wave of jihadists who came from deeply disadvantaged and marginalized social backgrounds. In contrast to the bin Laden and Zawahiri generation, Zarqawi's generation lacked the theological depth and learning of the two previous waves of the 1970s and 1990s and was influenced by many mediating factors. Some of these factors were environmental and social and reflected in his upbringing, education, and class background. Other factors were institutional, developing from his violent encounter with authority and the judicial system. However, a note of qualification is in order. This discussion of Zarqawi's biography is not intended to imply that he played a key role in the creation of the current Islamic State and the caliphate. Rather, Zarqawi was instrumental in building a base for Al Qaeda in Iraq and laying the foundation for the subsequent emergence of ISIS. His story is inextricably tied not only to the foundation of Al Qaeda in Iraq but also to the beginning of the revolt against the founding fathers of the global jihadist movement, bin Laden and Zawahiri.

ZARQAWI'S SECOND JOURNEY TO AFGHANISTAN

In May 1999, the newly crowned king of Jordan, Abdallah II, granted a general amnesty to thousands of political prisoners, including Zarqawi and Maqdisi. Upon his release, Zarqawi left Jordan for Afghanistan—a war-torn country that had become the epicenter for the transnational jihadist movement, particularly Al Qaeda Central—carrying with him his bitterness against the whole world, not just the Jordanian state that tortured him. Instead of jumping on the bin Laden caravan, Zarqawi established his own jihadist shop in Herat, a city close to the Iranian border that also provided a gateway to northern Iraq and Turkey, and preserved his autonomy. Maqdisi painted an illuminating portrait of his disciple as reckless and strongheaded, with a supersized ego that demands "absolute allegiance" from subordinates, a man who "attracts ignorant people who are not qualified for many missions and whose flaws often shocked us," a veiled reference to the catastrophic "jihadist decisions" that Zarqawi would make later on in Iraq.[17] Maqdisi even lamented that after Zarqawi left for Afghanistan in 1999, he acted true to character and did not learn from past mistakes: "He was not successful in choosing the right individuals with organizational expertise, despite the availability of financial resources."[18]

In Afghanistan there was no meeting of the minds between Zarqawi, who was in a hurry to do battle against the global forces of imperialism and injustice, and bin Laden and Zawahiri. According to testimony by Adl, when Zarqawi returned to Afghanistan in 1999, Al Qaeda Central's top leaders did not meet with him and maintained their distance from the young upstart; however, secondary accounts assert that bin Laden and Zarqawi welcomed him in Afghanistan.[19] In his firsthand testimony, Adl relates that he lobbied bin Laden and his second in command, Zawahiri, to get permission to assist Zarqawi in setting up a small training camp in Herat. According to contemporaries of Zarqawi, he was openly critical of Al Qaeda

Central for not going on the offensive against the United States and Israel, as well as "apostate" Arab regimes (obviously, he was not privy to bin Laden's active plans to attack the US homeland on September 11, 2001).

Zarqawi, who was not formally a member of Al Qaeda Central but who, despite ideological differences with the organization's leadership, shared its Salafi-jihadist worldview, had established a jihadist training camp in Herat with the help of Adl and AQC. According to contemporary witnesses, the camp was at first small and basic, with Zarqawi intent on living a simple life modeled after that of the Prophet Mohammed.[20] Recruitment was by word of mouth or through personal connections, and soon volunteers from Palestine, Jordan, Iraq, Syria, and Lebanon flocked there. As a result of the overwhelming presence of Arab fighters from the Levant, the group soon became known as Jund al-Sham (Levant Warriors). In October 2001, following the US bombing campaign on Herat, Zarqawi and his followers decided to escape to Kandahar, a journey that took four days. Iyad Tobaissi, who trained in the camp, recalls that it took almost four hundred cars to evacuate all the followers, including women and children,[21] and, to the combatants' surprise, the convoy was neither stopped nor shelled. Once they reached their destination, the women and children were reportedly ordered to leave for Turkey via Pakistan while the rest of the group stayed in the city. According to Fu'ad Hussein's investigation for LBC Television in Lebanon, Zarqawi and his men then headed to Tora Bora, a Taliban and Al Qaeda stronghold, where they reportedly participated in the Battle of Tora Bora in December 2001.[22]

Despite Zarqawi's refusal to officially join Al Qaeda Central, almost two years later his jihadist path would bring him to Iraq's killing fields and see him swearing baiya to bin Laden while acting independently against the wishes of his new emir. Iraq provided Zarqawi with a stage and a social base of support that allowed him to chart his own vision, a path that marked another radical twist in the journey of the global jihadist movement. The Zarqawi generation would ultimately over-shadow that of Al Qaeda Central and defy its authority in a serious bid to change the direction of movement.

SADDAM HUSSEIN'S INSTRUMENTALIZATION OF RELIGION IN THE 1990S

Under Hussein's reign, Iraq had never experienced a full-fledged Islamist insurgency, and in this aspect it stands out from other Arab countries such as Algeria and Egypt. A strict nationalist, Hussein did not trust or tolerate Islamist parties of the Sunni and Shia variety, though he was not averse to instrumentalizing religious symbols and references to mobilize Iraqi opinion against external threats to his rule. For example, in a speech during the 1990–1991 Gulf Crisis, he declared holy war against the "infidel regimes" of Kuwait and Saudi Arabia and their Western allies: "O Arabs, O Muslims and believers everywhere. This is your day to rise and defend Mecca, which is captured by the spears of the Americans and the Zionists. Revolt against oppression, corruption, treachery and backstabbing. . . . Your brothers in Iraq are determined to continue jihad without any hesitation or retreat and without any fear from the foreigner's power."[23] In a further bid to consolidate his religious credentials, the Iraqi president also added *Allahu Akbar* (God is greater) to the Iraqi flag, while attempting to broaden his support among Arabs in general by championing the Palestinian cause, going so far as to fire scud missiles into Israel in January 1991. Building on this appeal, Iraq hosted a Popular Islamic Conference in the same month, days before the United Nations' deadline for Iraq's withdrawal from Kuwait. Although the conference was initially a joint Saudi-Iraqi effort, Saudi Arabia convened its own Popular Islamic Conference in Mecca, held on the same dates as the conference in Iraq. The Iraqi-Saudi "Islamic confrontation" led to a split in Islamic circles. The split went deeper than the appeals made by Arab governments, and while Egypt, Syria, and Saudi Arabia condemned Iraq for its invasion of

Kuwait through their Islamic institutions, Hussein's rhetoric appealed to Islamists who were being oppressed by these same regimes.

With running inflation and almost 50 percent unemployment in Iraq, Hussein's credibility was rapidly dwindling. It was during the period following the Gulf crisis in the 1990s that socioeconomic conditions worsened and the regime's oppressive apparatus became increasingly weakened due to the punishing sanctions imposed by the United Nations at the behest of the United States. In turn, Shia and Sunni religious activism gained more converts. Hussein thus looked for new ways to broaden his domestic base of support in a bid to maintain control of Iraq by reverting to religious tactics that would provide him with the support of the religious organizations within the country. This served as an important adjustment to Iraqi society, which was traumatized and became more religiously conservative because of dismal socioeconomic conditions. In the mid-1990s, Hussein launched his Faith Campaign (*al-Hamla al-Imaniya*), which included valorizing Islamic teachings first in mosques and then in schools, freeing prisoners who could memorize the Qur'an, reintroducing the call for prayer (*al-Athan*) in the Iraqi media, reducing the hours of operation for drinking establishments, and banning the public consumption of alcohol. The Iraqi media also started to report regularly on the activities of Hezbollah, presenting the group as the national resistance movement of Lebanon. However, these steps taken by Hussein in the 1990s were more tactical and utilitarian than sincere or strategic. He remained a staunch nationalist and did not alter the ideological foundation of the Baathist ruling party. For example, on one occasion Hussein reprimanded the minister of endowment, Abdul Minem Ahmad Salih, for getting carried away in his dealings with some Islamic personalities and groups and believing that the president was genuine in his Faith Campaign.[24] Hussein did not want his rhetoric on religiosity to be taken seriously by officials in his government such as the minister of endowment.

Knowing that many Iraqi citizens were turning to the mosques in times of hardship, Hussein tried to revamp his image as that of a pious man. In 1998, construction for the Umm al-Ma'arik (Mother of All Battles) Mosque—now known as the Umm al-Qura (Mother of All Cities) Mosque—started in Baghdad at a cost of $7.5 million. In the same year, the regime also opened the Jami'at Saddam lil-'Ulum al-Islamiyya (Saddam University for Islamic Studies), which, ironically, Abu Bakr al-Baghdadi, the leader of ISIS, would later attend. In the last decade of Hussein's rule, religious symbolism and references were frequently used as a way to appeal to the public, which had been pressed by social problems. He instrumentalized religiosity for political gains,[25] and continued to support the Palestinian cause by engineering a rapprochement with Hamas, an Islamist resistance movement. Between 2000 and 2003, the Iraqi regime provided financial support for the families of Palestinian suicide bombers, including those of Hamas members, in the form of awards of up to $25,000, while relatives of Palestinians killed during Israeli military operations were given up to $10,000.

Nevertheless, Salafi-jihadism of the Al Qaeda variety did not resonate with Sunni Iraqis, whose doctrines and worldviews, in comparison to those of Al Qaeda, were cosmopolitan and religiously tolerant.[26] The mixture of repression and hostility to the jihadist project promoted by Hussein and his regime, coupled with Iraq's historically tolerant society (despite tensions, Sunnis and Shias coexisted in relative harmony), inhibited Al Qaeda from making inroads in the country. Although an increasing number of Iraqis, including members of the armed forces in the 1990s, turned to religion, partly because of Hussein's Faith Campaign and partly because of their suffering under the weight of punishing sanctions, they did not seem to shed their Baathist colors. At that stage, there existed no clear indication of any deep sectarian divide in Iraq.[27] A key point to emphasize is that despite increased religiosity among Iraqis in the 1990s, Islamism did not find fertile soil in the country.

Under Hussein's Baathist regime, Iraq was a hostile territory for radical religious activists, and it would take America's dismantling of the state apparatus to open the floodgate for Zarqawi and his cohorts. The destruction of the Iraqi state in 2003 was the most important variable in the emergence of Al Qaeda in Iraq and its subsequent rebirth as ISIS.

THE MAKING OF ZARQAWI'S NETWORK IN IRAQ

In his testimony on Zarqawi, Adl reveals that when the United States invaded Afghanistan in October 2001, Al Qaeda dispersed its lieutenants and fighters into neighboring states, including Iran, to prevent the destruction of the bin Laden network and to carry on the struggle. Adl notes that Zarqawi became Al Qaeda's point man in Iraq, "a well-studied choice." According to Zarqawi's semiofficial biographer, Fu'ad Hussein, Zarqawi had managed to escape from Tora Bora unharmed, fleeing to Pakistan and then entering Iran on foot.[28] Once in Iran, Zarqawi and his cohorts—including Tobaissi—spent a week in Zahadan being protected and fed by a group of Iranian Sunnis before moving to Tehran.[29] In Hussein's examination of this period, it was revealed that Gulbuddin Hekmatyar, the Afghan warlord who had taken Zarqawi under his wing during his first visit to Afghanistan in the early 1990s, also helped the group as they made their way through Iran. Hussein also points out that the Iranian government was aware of Zarqawi's presence and that, following US pressure on the government, the Iranian authorities started to crack down on his group, making dozens of arrests. Following the arrests by Iranian officials, the fighters from Zarqawi's cohort split into two groups. One group headed into Turkey and another, including Zarqawi, made its way into northern Iraq. Hussein's account of the events that took place in Iran is mirrored by that of Adl, who notes that Zarqawi headed to northern Iraq from Iran with only a small percentage of the men who had initially made up his cohort. Indeed, many of the operatives working for

Al Qaeda and upward of 80 percent of Zarqawi's men were arrested and extradited to their home countries after the United States pressured the Iranian government. The crackdown by the Iranian authorities on Al Qaeda operatives "put us off balance and disrupted 75 per cent of our plans," lamented Adl. For this reason, Zarqawi and his few remaining men hastily left Iran for Iraq, where, with the help of Ansar al-Islam (subsequently renamed Ansar al-Sunna), a local jihadist group whose precursor group was Jund al-Islam, Zarqawi made his way to the Sunni Triangle.

Adl's firsthand account is consistent with the personal testaments of other former associates of Zarqawi with whom he communicated after he left Iran for northern Iraq. These recollections clearly show that Zarqawi originally possessed humble resources when he reached Iraq and did not have a power base or large sums of money to finance his jihadist network. He is portrayed as a strong-willed and fanatical man, determined to engage in battle with American troops in Iraq and to build a constituency of Salafi-jihadists in the country. As a Jordanian from a respected Bedouin tribe, Zarqawi is said to have fit in quite well in Iraq. Due to the similar dialects, temperaments, and physical traits of Iraqis and the Arabs in the Levant, Zarqawi and his cohorts were able to blend in with the local population, and, because of this, he quickly built a potent social constituency and operational infrastructure in the Sunni Triangle.

Most of Zarqawi's men were said to have been trained in a camp in Khurmal, close to the Iranian border. According to one source, this arrangement developed from a meeting in 2002 between Zarqawi and leaders of Ansar al-Islam, a Sunni Islamist group that mainly operated in Iraqi Kurdistan. From this meeting Zarqawi secured access to the organization's arsenal and military bases for his own men.[30] The camp provided shelter to new arrivals, which included many Arab fighters from Afghanistan and new recruits from the Levant. However, following the US invasion in 2003, the coalition forces led an extensive bombing campaign against Islamist strongholds in Iraqi Kurdistan, including that of Ansar al-Islam. Most members fled to Iran or to the Sunni Triangle, northwest of Bagdad. By September of the same year, despite having lost many of its members, Ansar al-Islam reorganized in Iraq, and by March 2003 the group had renamed itself Ansar al-Sunna. The new environment in which Ansar al-Sunna found itself forced it to mainly operate within the Sunni Triangle, and, despite the operational and geographic limitations, it provided a way in for Zarqawi and his men. While Zarqawi's links with Ansar al-Sunna provided an opportunity for the expansion of his own group, which in 2004 he initially called al-Tawhid wa al-Jihad, in 2003–2004 Zarqawi's band of fighters was only one among many local insurgent groups.

In their book *Zarqawi: The New Face of al-Qaeda*, Jean-Charles Brisard and Damien Martinez provide a list of members of Zarqawi's inner circle in Iraq, which reportedly includes Abu Anas al-Shami, also known as Omar Yussef Jumah, a Jordanian cleric who was, like Zarqawi, a disciple of Maqdisi; Khaled Mustafa Khalifa al-Aruri, whose aliases are Abu al-Qassam and Abu Ashraf, a Jordanian national who is also Zarqawi's brother-in-law; Abdel Haadi Ahmad Mahmoud Daghlas, also known as Abu Ubaydab and Abu Muhammad al-Sham, who helped run the Herat camp in Afghanistan; Nidal Mohammad al-Arabi, alias Abu Hamza Mohammed, who is known for coordinating most of the attacks for which the group took credit; Abu Mohammed al-Lubnani, a former Lebanese soldier and a specialist in explosives; Abu Ali al-Iraqi, an Iraqi who specialized in explosives; and Hassan Ibrahim, who was one of three personnel in charge of the group's propaganda. In addition, the higher echelons of the organization reportedly included ten Jordanians who were believed to be around thirty years old.[31] The book also notes that Tawhid wa al-Jihad's activities in the Sunni Triangle were divided into nine autonomous operational bases, each under the orders of a commander. The group's main headquarters were in Fallujah and contained a force of 500 fighters. The Baghdad sector had 50 fighters and the province of Anbar maintained 60 fighters. Up to 400 fighters were also reportedly stationed in Mosul, 50 in the city of Samarra, and 80 in the province of Diyala, and the northern region also included men from the group. Moreover, up to 150 fighters were also in al-Qaim, a city close to the Syrian border.[32]

As is evident from the figures reported by Brisard and Martinez, Zarqawi's power base was growing quickly, and his men focused their efforts on recruiting fighters from Bilad al-Sham (the Fertile Crescent and the surrounding areas, including Syria, Jordan, Palestine, Lebanon, Iraq, Saudi Arabia, and North Africa). As the recruitment process veered in the direction of Syria, so did Zarqawi's reliance on Syrian jihadists. His reliance on native Syrians or expats was a consequence of the deaths of many of his trusted Jordanian lieutenants. The Syrian jihadists who rose in the ranks had joined his training camp in Herat, which was primarily supported by wealthy Syrian businessmen in Europe. One of the central members of the Iraq-Syria connection, who is believed to have been an important financier of Zarqawi's network, is Sulayman Khalid Darwish, better known as Abu al-Ghadiya, a Syrian allegedly from Damascus who left for Afghanistan in the 1990s after graduating as a dentist in the Syrian capital. It is believed that Ghadiya and Zarqawi met in Afghanistan during Ghadiya's time at the Herat camp, where Zarqawi trained him in the use of arms and explosives.[33] Reunited with Zarqawi in Iraq, in the aftermath of the US invasion, Ghadiya was put in charge of moving fighters from Syria into Iraq, where the porous border between the two countries facilitated infiltration. After Zarqawi's death in 2006, Baghdadi is also said to have worked closely with Ghadiya in Syria.[34]

In addition to recruiting Syrians and raising funds from Syrian expats in Europe, there was a great emphasis on recruiting suicide bombers. Mullah Fuad, an Iraqi Kurd and alleged member of Ansar al-Islam, acted as a key connection between European recruits for potential suicide bombings and the Zarqawi network in Iraq. Although Mullah Fuad was arrested in June 2005 in Syria, his operational base, he played an important role in the recruitment of suicide bombers—a key component of Zarqawi's arsenal. Suicide bombers came from Syria and neighboring countries, including Kuwait, Saudi Arabia, Libya, Tunisia, Palestine, and Jordan, as well as Europe.

According to Fu'ad Hussein, although Zarqawi started with fewer than thirty fighters at the beginning of the US-led invasion of Iraq, he quickly amassed at least five thousand full-time fighters, bolstered by twenty thousand homegrown supporters,[35] a testament to the rapid radicalization and militarization of Iraqi society and Al Qaeda's ability to infiltrate the country's fragile body politic. Although there is no credible way to know the precise number of foreign recruits who joined Zarqawi's jihadist caravan (the American and Iraqi authorities estimated the number of Arab fighters under Zarqawi at about one thousand), homegrown radicalized Iraqis gradually came to dominate Al Qaeda and shape its identity and modus operandi. For example, to deflect criticism that most suicide bombers in Iraq were foreign fighters, Al Qaeda in Iraq posted a statement on a jihadist website known for carrying its messages, announcing that it had formed an exclusively Iraqi suicide squad.[36] Regardless of Zarqawi's real strength, he was a trailblazer for Al Qaeda in Iraq and built it a home in a deeply scarred country, one that would survive his death by American forces in 2006.

Nonetheless, Zarqawi's variety of revolutionary Islamism was a tiny minority if not a rarity among the plethora of local insurgents in Iraq, an environment that was far from homogenous. Differences among these armed groups mostly involved their ideological agendas. As we will see in the following section, at the outset of the US occupation of Iraq, the bulk of armed resistance can be typified as religious-nationalist, secular Baathist, or Salafi-jihadist. Initially, the odds were against the jihadists, but when the United States prioritized the fight against them, the environment created by the US occupation and subsequent developments provided an impetus for the Islamist insurgency. Groups such as Ansar al-Sunna used the US occupation to recruit fighters, increase their sphere of action and influence, and implant themselves in the Sunni Triangle, the heart of the Sunni opposition to coalition rule, by calling for jihad against US forces.

The narrative of anti-American sentiment that characterizes this period was bolstered by images of dead US soldiers. Ansar al-Sunna was not an exception, and in 2004 the group placed a video of the killing of a twenty-six-year-old American, Nicholas Berg, on the Muntada al-Ansar website. Filmed on April 9, 2004, just west of Baghdad, the video had a worldwide impact and was a harbinger of the increasing savagery that was soon to tear Iraq apart. The video shows five masked men standing behind the kneeling and bound hostage. One of them reads a statement warning the United States against the mistreatment of prisoners in Abu Ghraib and calls for jihad before killing Berg. The executioner is believed to be Zarqawi, and the execution marks the beginning of a long series of other similarly brutal crimes. With the video propagating online and the murder making the media headlines, Zarqawi's name became more prominent. The media coverage only made him more popular among militant Islamist circles in both the Arab world and the West, and, in turn, it facilitated the recruitment of jihadists from abroad.

THE ARMED RESISTANCE AND ZARQAWI'S FIGHT FOR DOMINANCE

By destroying state institutions and establishing a sectarian-based political system, the 2003 US-led invasion polarized the country along Sunni-Shia lines and set the stage for a fierce, prolonged struggle driven by identity politics. Anger against the United States was also fueled by the humiliating disbandment of the Iraqi army and the de-Baathification law, which was first introduced as a provision and then turned into a permanent article of the constitution. In addition to these measures, the use of torture by US and British forces, and a summary of executions and war crimes revealed by the WikiLeaks website, increased disdain and hatred of the US-led coalition. While many Sunni Arabs did not mourn Hussein's downfall after his reckless and costly wars against Iran and Kuwait, which turned the country into a pariah state, they chafed at America's dissolution of the nationalist army. The dissolution of the army, which had stood at three hundred thousand strong, coupled with the de-Baathification campaign, which dismissed people based on rank and affiliation, not behavior, and which was mainly seen as a punitive and discriminatory policy against Sunnis by Iraq's newly installed Shia rulers, left widespread feelings of injustice and bitterness within the Sunni community. As a result, many Iraqis sought retribution by taking up arms in the name of resistance to the American occupation of their country.

The US and British governments increasingly portrayed Iraq as a country divided into Shias, Sunnis, Kurds, Turkmens, Assyrians, and other ethno-religious communities, emphasizing sectarianism rather than a national Iraqi identity. In 2004, for example, the US-appointed Governing Council of Iraq, which worked on a confessional-style basis, continued to place sectarianism and not national governance at the center of Iraq's new political system. Profiting from growing sectarianism, Al Qaeda swiftly moved in and blended in with local Sunnis, who felt that the new order erected by the Americans empowered the Shias at their own expense and crowned Iran as their master. As a counterresponse, the United States tried to build a wedge between the Sunni and Shia communities, both integral parts of the Iraqi resistance against the United States, while Al Qaeda swiftly took advantage of the generalized and rapidly spreading anti-US sentiment. As a conflict zone in the heart of the Arab world, and with growing resentment against the coalition forces and the Iraqi government, Iraq provided bin Laden and Zawahiri with a "golden and unique opportunity" to expand global jihad to the Arabian heartland of Iraq, Syria, Lebanon, Jordan, and Palestine. In their words, the war in Iraq marked the second most important development since September 11,

2001, and a "historic opportunity" to establish the long-awaited Islamic state in the region, which only a few years earlier had been a far-off possibility.[37]

Despite the attention often given to the Sunni side of the resistance, the Iraqi revolt against the US-led coalition forces and the Iraqi government had first taken root in Sadr City. Calls for resistance against the American occupation were prompted by Muqtada al-Sadr, who called on the Shia majority to stand up for their rights during a time when many were disillusioned with the transitional government, and insecurity, looting, and abject living conditions had become the norm.[38] Sadr, a young cleric, was the only surviving son of the prominent Shia leader Ayatollah Mohammed Sadeq al-Sadr, who had been killed, along with two of his sons, on February 18, 1999, allegedly by the Baathist regime. Muqtada al-Sadr's aim was first to consolidate his leadership of the Shia insurgency, which led to an internal struggle with moderate Shia leaders. In 2003, Sadr's militia, Jayish al-Mahdi (Army of the Mahdi), was created, and within months violent attacks and kidnappings against coalition forces were taking place. As Sadr's popularity among the Shia community grew, so did the violence. A Shia resistance was now spreading across Iraq, with Sadr's strongholds in Sadr City, Najaf, and Karbala. In May 2003, a Sunni resistance, mainly within the Sunni Triangle, also emerged and solidified, particularly after the United States disbanded the military and carried out its systematic campaign to purge the country of Baathists, a policy that, as mentioned, was seen to disproportionally discriminate against the Sunni community. As the country spiraled into chaos following Hussein's fall, the mood soon darkened.

The Sunni resistance was multifaceted, made up of Islamic nationalists, secularists, and tribal leaders. In addition to their different religious backgrounds, the Shia and Sunni resistances also had different visions and motivations. While the Shia fight was framed as a fight against decades of inequalities that they believed the transitional government had failed to overturn, the

Sunni fight was framed as one against foreign invaders, based on a widespread perception that the occupiers had handed Iraq to Shia-dominated Iran on a silver platter.

The Shia and the Sunni poles, although both driven by the American invasion, soon diverged and began to come into direct conflict with each other. In summer 2003, Zarqawi's network repeatedly targeted the Shia population during its gatherings in pilgrimages, weddings, funerals, markets, and mosques. The Shias responded by forming vigilante groups and militias, which only added to communal polarization. In addition to his attacks on the Shia community, Zarqawi targeted Sunnis who did not convert to his cause, leaving behind a trail of blood and grievances. On August 7, 2003, Zarqawi's network targeted his native, Sunni country with the car bombing of the Jordanian embassy in Baghdad, which killed at least eleven people and wounded at least sixty-five.[39] A few days later, on August 29, 2003, the Zarqawi network attacked the Imam Ali ibn Abi Talib Mosque in Najaf, killing up to ninety-five Shias, including Ayatollah Muhammad Baqer al-Hakim, the founder of the Supreme Council of the Islamic Revolution in Iraq (SCIRI). In this specific case, Yassin Jarad, the father of Zarqawi's second wife, had driven a car loaded with explosives into the mosque.

By September 2003, Zarqawi's calls for attacks against the Shias did not receive widespread support, as both Sunnis and Shias were focusing their resistance against the coalition forces. Each community defined the enemy as the foreign invaders, not the group's local rivals. Nevertheless, Zarqawi launched a relentless anti-Shia propaganda campaign. He first linked the US-led invasion to the Mongols' invasion of the Muslim world, including Iraq, and the destruction of Baghdad in the thirteenth century. In his first declaration of war against the United States in 1996, bin Laden had also used the same analogy. Zarqawi then framed the Shia in similar terms to those uttered by Hussein in April 2003. In an article published in *al-Quds al-Arabi*, a pan-Arab, London-based newspaper, immediately after the US-led invasion, Hussein accused Bush of having

invaded the country with the help of Ibn al-Alqami, a refer-
ence to the vizier of Baghdad who had cooperated with the
Mongols. For Zarqawi, then, the Shia represented a new
Alqami, and, just like him, they had helped the invaders.

ZARQAWI'S PLEDGE OF ALLEGIANCE TO AL QAEDA: A MARRIAGE OF CONVENIENCE

Al Qaeda had suffered crippling setbacks in Afghanistan, Pakistan, Yemen, and Saudi Arabia, with a diminished operational
capacity and constant bleeding. Scattered in many theaters and
besieged by the end of 2002 and the beginning of 2003, as an
organization Al Qaeda was near its breaking point. Bush's war
in Iraq resuscitated it and gave it a new lease on life. In the
meantime, as Zarqawi's network gained momentum in Iraq,
pressure was put on him by operatives to formally join Al
Qaeda Central and swear baiya to bin Laden.[40] In a policy
memo to bin Laden and Zawahiri that was intercepted by Iraqi
Kurds and published by the US State Department in 2004, Zarqawi spends much time legitimizing his anti-Shia stance—
one of his points of contention with Al Qaeda Central—and
explains his plan of action, narrowing down the enemies to
four groups:

1) The Americans: "These, as you know, are the most cow-
   ardly of God's creatures. They are an easy quarry, praise
   be to God. We ask God to enable us to kill and capture
   them to sow panic among those behind them and to
   trade them for our detained shaykhs and brothers."

2) The Kurds: "These are a lump [in the throat] and a thorn
   whose time to be clipped has yet to come. They are last
   on the list, even though we are making efforts to harm
   some of their symbolic figures, God willing."

3) The Iraq security forces: "These are the eyes, ears, and
   hands of the occupier, through which he sees, hears,

and delivers violent blows. God willing, we are determined to target them strongly in the coming period
before the situation is consolidated and they control
arrest[s]."

4) The Shias: "These in our opinion are the key to change.
I mean that targeting and hitting them in [their] religious, political, and military depth will provoke them to
show the Sunnis their rabies and bare the teeth of the
hidden rancor working in their breasts. If we succeed in
dragging them into the arena of sectarian war, it will become possible to awaken the inattentive Sunnis as they
feel imminent danger and annihilating death at the
hands of these Sabeans."[41]

In concluding the brief, Zarqawi clearly expresses a desire to
formally join the global jihadist network: "This is our vision,
and we have explained it. This is our path, and we have made
it clear. If you agree with us on it, if you adopt it as a program
and road, and if you are convinced of the idea of fighting the
sects of apostasy, we will be your readied soldiers, working
under your banner, complying with your orders, and indeed
swearing fealty to you publicly and in the news media, vexing
the infidels and gladdening those who preach the oneness of
God."[42] However, the document attests to Zarqawi's unwillingness to collaborate with Al Qaeda at all costs: an alliance could
only be made if bin Laden and Zawahiri agreed to Zarqawi's
road map, which prioritizes the war against the Shia, not that
against the far enemy—the US coalition.

In an Internet statement in October 2004, Zarqawi announced
that he was changing the name of his group—al-Tawhid
wa al-Jihad—to Al Qaeda in the Land of the Two Rivers or Al
Qaeda in Iraq, and declared his allegiance to bin Laden, saying that he considered him "the best leader for Islam's armies
against all infidels and apostates." The statement noted that
the two had communicated and agreed to unite against "the
enemies of Islam." Two months later, in an audiotape broadcast

by Al Jazeera satellite television, bin Laden accepted Zarqa-wi's baiya and appointed him the emir of AQI. Bin Laden praised Zarqawi's "gallant operations" against the Americans, saying that he and his followers were fighting for God's sake: "We have been pleased that they responded to God's and his Prophet's order for unity, and we in Al Qaeda welcome their unity with us."[43] The unholy alliance between Zarqawi's al-Tawhid wa al-Jihad and bin Laden's Al Qaeda should not obscure the existence of fundamental differences between the two jihadist groups, though, in their opinion, the advantages of joining ranks outweighed the costs.

In contrast to Zarqawi, although intrinsically hostile to the Shia, bin Laden and Zawahiri prioritized the struggle against the far enemy (the United States). It is worth noting that the two Al Qaeda leaders did not publicly condemn Iran and they never attacked Iranian Shias in Afghanistan or the Shias in Saudi Arabia. Scores of Al Qaeda lieutenants, together with their families, were under house arrest in Iran, and bin Laden and Zawahiri did not want to trigger a confrontation with Tehran because the interests of both sides converged in the fight against the Americans. Their aim was to attack the far enemy first and postpone the confrontation with the near enemy. Following the US-led invasion of Iraq, they called on Muslim Iraqis and non-Iraqis of all ethnic and linguistic backgrounds to unite and resist the nascent order installed by the Americans in Baghdad. Bin Laden also demonstrated a similar disregard for ethnic, sectarian, and ideological differences in issuing condemnations of Iraqis who collaborated with the American-led coalition, including Sunni Arabs, whom he saw as equally guilty parties. He said, "I call on Muslims, in general, and on the Iraqi people, in particular, to not support the Crusader US forces and their allies. Those who cooperate with the United States or its off-shoots, regardless of names and titles, are infidels and so are those who support infidel parties such as the Arab Socialist Baath Party, and the democratic Kurdish parties and their like."[44] Bin Laden reportedly was not in favor of Sunni-Shia civil strife, lest it distract from the focal confrontation against the American occupiers. It is no wonder that bin Laden was initially reluctant to agree to a merger between al-Tawhid wa al-Jihad and Al Qaeda, because Zarqawi's unbounded sectarianism and bloodletting were seen as a liability. In fact, the merger came only after a number of radical religious figures supported Zarqawi's call to jihad in Iraq and his use of suicide bombers. On August 23, 2004, *al-Quds al-Arabi* published an appeal by ninety-three clerics, including the prominent Sunni cleric Youssef al-Qaradawi, to support the Islamic resistance in Iraq against the "US-Zionist colonising campaign."[45]

Yet, as mentioned previously, by the end of 2004 and despite their disagreements, bin Laden and Zarqawi put their apparent differences aside and joined ranks. They needed each other to sustain their organizations and expand into "the heart of the Islamic world." For bin Laden and Zawahiri, Iraq had become "the place for the greatest battle of Islam in this era" against "the head of apostasy" (the United States), and Zarqawi was a trailblazer, dominating news headlines and gaining popularity within the Salafi-jihadist movement and beyond. The unruly and fearless Jordanian was stealing the limelight from the charismatic Saudi leader, who was on the run and being hunted by American forces.

Although troublesome, Zarqawi's swift rise provided bin Laden and Zawahiri with a lifeline—proximity and access to Islam's holiest places and its political epicenter and fault line (the Israel-Palestine conflict)—and an opportunity to expand their confrontation against the United States. Bin Laden reportedly enlisted Zarqawi to attack American targets.[46] By appointing Zarqawi as emir of AQI, bin Laden could take credit for military successes there, rejuvenate his battered base, and broaden his group's appeal to Arab and Muslim masses who strongly opposed the American occupation of Islamic territories. It was a win-win move for the Saudi, who hoped to reverse the negative attitudes that many Muslims had toward his transnational jihadist project. He also used the move to depict himself as a defender of the rights of the Palestinians. In fact, Zarqawi's rapid rise in popularity among jihadist circles in Arab countries contrasted with the suspicion and distrust that had accompanied news of Zarqawi's merger with bin Laden's Al Qaeda.[47] Unlike Zawahiri and bin Laden, Zarqawi was not from a wealthy background but from a poor family. He also was not a well-educated man or even a great theologian, but just a Jordanian whose route toward radicalization started in his own country, against his own regime, a fact that resonated with many youths who had turned to Salafism in the Arab world and that facilitated his claim to be emulating the example of the Prophet Mohammed. His unlikely rise to the heart of the jihadist movement made him an inspiring figure for wannabe jihadists from the poorest sections of Arab societies. His Bedouin roots also provided him with cultural and ethnic ties in the Arab crescent that bin Laden had always lacked. For bin Laden and Zawahiri, the advantages of a merger with Zarqawi's al-Tawhid wa al-Jihad outweighed the disadvantages, as they believed that they could tame the shrew after the union had been consummated.

In a similar vein, according to Fu'ad Hussein, a formal association with Al Qaeda finally conferred revolutionary legitimacy on Zarqawi and transformed him from a mere field commander in Iraq into a global jihadist leader on par with the original founding fathers of the Salafi-jihadist movement, such as Abdullah Azzam, bin Laden, and Zawahiri. Despite Zarqawi's initial reluctance to join with Al Qaeda, its masterminding of the 9/11 attacks and the placement of bin Laden's and Zawahiri's names on Bush's list of the most wanted terrorists helped the organization consolidate its legitimacy and spread its ideology within Islamist circles, thereby only further enhancing Zarqawi's legitimacy and authority. In addition, the merger brought Zarqawi a steady supply of new recruits and money, which he badly needed in order to solidify his plan to dominate the jihadist movement and take ownership of the Sunni resistance in Iraq.

While his ethnic ties helped in the Levant, his rapprochement with Al Qaeda led to an important increase of pro–Al Qaeda fighters in his ranks before the union was even finalized. Many came from the Arabian Peninsula and North Africa, and wealthy Arab businessmen donated generously to his cause, which greatly strengthened his network. This windfall, more than any other factor, prompted Zarqawi to pledge his "full allegiance to bin Laden."[48]

The story of the bin Laden–Zarqawi marriage of convenience clearly shows that as political actors, jihadists are driven by interests rather than by pure ideology and theology. On the other hand, personality clashes and pride can be real obstacles to the formation of certain alliances. Time and again, jihadists have fought each other as fiercely as they did their enemies, exposing the poverty of their lofty rhetoric and sacrificing unity at the altar of narrow political ambition and self-interest. As will be shown later, the jihadist universe is fraught with political and regional rivalries, egoism, and fragmentation. The utopian worldview of the global jihadist movement is a myth, one that masks earthly concerns of power and domination.

In this sense, although Zarqawi formally established a base for bin Laden and Al Qaeda in Iraq, a chasm persisted between their two worldviews over the best means to expel the Americans from Iraq and establish an Islamic emirate there. The merger between al-Tawhid wa al-Jihad and Al Qaeda did not usher in a shift in Zarqawi's conduct, as he persisted in his vicious ways and continued to act independently of his senior partners. Zarqawi's spectacular rise could partially be attributed to his flamboyant use of suicide bombers, particularly against the Shia, and the deepening sectarianization of Iraqi society. As could be seen in Zarqawi's road map for bin Laden and Zawahiri, he clearly prioritized the fight against the Shia, and he offered Al Qaeda's leaders the choice to either agree with him and formally ally or disagree. Despite Zarqawi's pledge of allegiance to Al Qaeda, the merger between al-Tawhid wa al-Jihad and bin Laden's group was on his terms, and, despite the baiya, Zarqawi retained his own agency.

An important letter from bin Laden's deputy, Zawahiri, addressed to Zarqawi was intercepted by the United States when, in the summer of 2005, they got hold of an envoy of Zawahiri's. The document, dated July 9, 2005, helps shed further light on the thinking of bin Laden and Zawahiri and highlights the major differences and disagreements between Al Qaeda Central and Zarqawi's branch. It is worth highlighting its major points. At first, Zawahiri showers Zarqawi with praise for his courage, his willingness to stand up to Islam's enemies, and his two-pronged strategy—removing the Americans from Iraq and establishing an Islamic emirate in Iraq, or a caliphate, if possible. The tone changes, however, when he reminds the Jordanian chief that "the strongest weapon" in the jihadists' arsenal "is popular support from the Muslim masses in Iraq, and the surrounding Muslim countries. So, we must maintain this support as best we can, and we should strive to increase it." In the absence of popular support, Zawahiri argues, the jihadist movement would be crushed; therefore, the challenge is to co-opt the Muslim masses and not alienate them, an implicit criticism of Zarqawi's actions: "And it doesn't appear that the Mujahedeen, much less the al-Qaida in the Land of Two Rivers, will lay claim to governance without the Iraqi people. Therefore, I stress again to you and to all your brothers the need to direct the political action equally with the military action, by the alliance, cooperation and gathering of all leaders of opinion and influence in the Iraqi arena. I repeat the warning against separating from the masses, whatever the danger."[49]

The crux of Zawahiri's letter unpacks Zarqawi's sectarian road map, which is, in Zawahiri's opinion, highly counterproductive for gaining the hearts and minds of the umma. Although Zawahiri says he agrees with Zarqawi's vision of the Shia as enemies, he warns him that the majority of Muslims do not comprehend this inevitable confrontation and could not even imagine it. He cautions Zarqawi that ordinary Muslims who admire his jihad in Iraq oppose the attacks on the Shia, particularly their mosques and especially the mausoleum of the Imam Ali ibn Abi Talib Mosque. Zawahiri also urges his junior partner to desist from attacking the Shia and Iranian interests, because scores of jihadists and their families were either in detention in Iran or under house arrest after they escaped to Iran following the US invasion of Afghanistan in 2001. The implication is that Zarqawi's confrontation with the Shias and Shia-dominated Iran would trigger a counterresponse by Iran against the jihadists, a point that shows a policy of coexistence between Al Qaeda and Iran. Instead of directly confronting Zarqawi and ordering him to desist from attacking the Shias, he poses a series of questions that he says are being asked by jihadists and their supporters about the correctness of Zarqawi's conflict with the Shias:

Is it something that is unavoidable? Or, is it something that can be put off until the force of the mujahed movement in Iraq gets stronger? And if some of the operations were necessary for self-defense, were all of the operations necessary? Or, were there some operations that weren't called for? And is the opening of another front now in addition to the front against the Americans and the government a wise decision? Or, does this conflict with the Shia lift the burden from the Americans by diverting the mujahedeen to the Shia, while the Americans continue to control matters from afar? And if the attacks on Shia leaders were necessary to put a stop to their plans, then why were there attacks on ordinary Shia? Won't this lead to reinforcing false ideas in their minds, even as it is incumbent on us to preach the call of Islam to them and explain and communicate to guide them to the truth? And can the mujahedeen kill all of the Shia in Iraq? Has any Islamic state in history ever tried that? And why kill ordinary Shia considering that they are forgiven because of their ignorance? And what loss will befall us if we did not attack the Shia? And do the brothers forget that we have more than one hundred prisoners—many of whom are from the leadership who are wanted in their countries—in the custody of the Iranians? And even if we attack the Shia out of necessity, then why do you announce this matter and make it public, which compels the Iranians to take counter measures? And do the brothers forget that both we and the Iranians need to refrain from harming each other at this time in which the Americans are targeting us?[50]

To lessen the blow, Zawahiri concludes on a personal note, saying that he had himself learned the hard way to avoid reaction and to keep focused on the key target: "And this is a lifetime's experience, and I will not conceal from you the fact that we suffered a lot through following this policy of reaction, then we suffered a lot another time because we tried to return to the original line."[51] Zawahiri also warns Zarqawi that his beheading and slaughtering of hostages is bad propaganda that only plays into the hands of their enemies. He reminds him that the propaganda battleground is as important as the military battlefield and that the jihadist movement is in a race for the hearts and minds of the umma: "And we can kill the captives by bullet. That would achieve that which is sought after without exposing ourselves to the questions and answering to doubts. We don't need this."[52] Ironically, Zawahiri concludes his letter by imploring Zarqawi to provide Al Qaeda Central with a payment of $100,000 because the United States had cut off many of its sources of income, a request that shows an important shift in the balance of power between the parent organization and the Zarqawi group.

The correspondence between the leaders of the two groups, along with leaks and public statements by their respective supporters, exposed a conceptual and operational rift between the two camps that they had carefully tried to keep under wraps. But with Zarqawi's continuous escalation of violence and savagery, the signs of estrangement and discord became hard to dissimulate. Zarqawi's formal response to bin Laden and Zawahiri's pleas came in an audiotape speech a few months later in which he declared "total war" not only against the Shias but also against the Sunnis who took part in the newly reconstituted Iraqi government.[53] His declaration only formalized what his suicide squads had been doing through the shedding of blood. In his brazen speech in September 2005, Zarqawi stated that his "organization has decided to declare a total war against the Rafidite [rejectionist, a derisive term for the Shia] Shi'ites throughout Iraq, wherever they may be," and "whoever is proven to belong to the Pagan [National] Guard, to the police, or to the army, or whoever is proven to be a Crusader collaborator or spy—he shall be killed. Furthermore, his house shall either be destroyed or burned down, after the women and children are taken out of it." He even threatened to slaughter Sunni tribes if they collaborated with the US-led coalition or the nascent Iraqi regime. "There are only two camps—the camp of truth and its followers, and the camp of falsehood and its Shi'ites. You must choose in which of the two trenches you lie," Zarqawi concluded.[54]

ZARQAWI'S GENOCIDAL ANTI-SHIA IDEOLOGY

Zarqawi was a sectarian psychopath who harbored a genocidal worldview against the Shias. In a policy memo to bin Laden and Zawahiri intercepted by Kurdish forces and published by the US State Department in February 2004, Zarqawi depicts the Shias as an existential enemy and calls on religion and history to validate his claim: "The Qur'an has told us that the machinations of the hypocrites, the deceit of the fifth column, and the cunning of those of our fellow countrymen whose tongues speak honeyed words but whose hearts are those of devils in the bodies of men—these are where the disease lies, these are the secret of our distress, these are the rat of the dike. 'They are the enemy. Beware of them. Fight them. Shaykh al-Islam Ibn Taymiyya spoke with truth and honesty when he said this."[55] He continues by calling the Shias "the insurmountable obstacle, the lurking snake, the crafty and malicious scorpion, the spying enemy, and the penetrating venom."[56] Zarqawi belonged to a new wave of Salafi-jihadists who are obsessed with identity politics and the struggle to purify Islam and Islamic lands of apostasy. The Shias top their list of real and imagined enemies.

In the memo Zarqawi explains that he relies on "Orientalists" to indict Shia Muslims for treachery, a fifth column within the Muslim body politic that allegedly impeded the emancipation of Europe by Muslim armies. It is useful to quote Zarqawi at length here to give the reader a glimpse of his thinking:

> One of the Orientalists spoke truth when he said that had the [Shia] Safavid state not existed we in Europe would today be reading the Qur'an just as the Algerian Berber does. Yes, the hosts of the Ottoman state stopped at the gates of Vienna, and those fortifications almost collapsed before them [to permit] Islam to spread under the auspices of the sword of glory and jihad all across Europe. But these armies were forced to return and withdraw to the rear because the army of the Safavid state had occupied Baghdad, demolished its mosques, killed its people, and captured its women and wealth. The armies returned to defend the sanctuaries and people of Islam. Fierce fighting raged for about two centuries and did not end until the strength and reach of the Islamic state had waned and the [Islamic] nation had been put to sleep, then to wake up to the drums of the invading Westerner.[57]

From the beginning, Zarqawi's strategic goal was to trigger all-out Sunni-Shia Islamic war and mobilize and co-opt Sunni opinion. In the policy brief, Zarqawi clearly reiterated that he prioritized the fight against the Shias and pledged to savagely attack civilian and religious targets, thus provoking the Shias to retaliate against the Sunnis. This, he added, would wake the Sunnis from their slumber and force them to join the war: "The solution that we see . . . is for us to drag the Shias into the

battle because this is the only way to prolong the fighting between us and the infidels."[58] Although the Americans represented an archenemy, the Shias, according to Zarqawi, posed a
greater and a more destructive threat to the umma: "They have
befriended and supported the Americans and stood in their
ranks against the mujahidin. They have spared and are still
sparing no effort to put an end to the jihad and the mujahidin."[59] Zarqawi excommunicated not only the Shias and minorities in general but also rival Sunnis, and he justified collateral killing of Muslims "in order to ward off a greater evil,
namely, the evil of suspending jihad," according to a statement
by his group.[60]

It is worth stressing that Baghdadi's perception of the Shias
is an extension of al-Tawhid wa al-Jihad's vision; ISIS and
al-Tawhid wa al-Jihad or AQI share a similar worldview. Both
belong to the generation of jihadists who consider the Shias
not only heretics but also a "dagger" in the heart of the Islamic world, and both go as far as to blame the Shias for the
decline of Islamic civilization, drawing heavily on the inflammatory statements and edicts by the controversial radical cleric
Shaykh al-Islam Ibn Taymiyya, a twelfth-century ultraconservative Islamic scholar who advocated a puritanical interpretation of Sunni Islam and had significant influence on contemporary Wahhabism, Salafism, and jihadism. Ibn Taymiyya
is known to have depicted the Shias as "more evil than the
sectarians and more deserving of being fought than the Khari-
jis," an indication of an irrational and visceral hatred.[61]

Zarqawi sent waves of suicide bombings that targeted Shia
civilians and their holy places, triggering violent reactions by
Shia militias. His strategy only increased the chasm that prevented a potential Sunni-Shia alliance, an alliance that would
have put the nationalist fight at the forefront, pushing Islamists
into the background of the struggle for the future of Iraq. Indeed, an entente along those lines had already taken place in
the country in 1920 during the Iraqi national uprising against
the British.[62] In a way, then, it seems that Zarqawi's struggle

against the Shias in Iraq is rooted in his aspirations to power as well as a worldview driven by identity politics.

AQI'S SAVAGERY: A ROAD MAP FOR A POST-AL QAEDA GENERATION

An alarming and prophetic report by the National Intelligence Council (NIC) in 2005, which included analyses by one thousand US and foreign specialists, concluded that Sunni Iraqis will supply the next generation of "professionalized" jihadists, a generation that would replace the previous wave trained in Afghanistan.[63] Echoing the findings by its US ally in a major study, the foreign affairs committee of the British House of Commons said, "Iraq has become 'a battleground' for al Qaeda with appalling consequences for the Iraqi people."[64] Ironically, US intelligence and security heads also subsequently understood the effects of the American-led occupation and the war in Iraq on radicalization inside and outside the country—albeit too late. "Our policies in the Middle East fuel Islamic resentment," US vice admiral Lowell E. Jacoby, director of the Defense Intelligence Agency (DIA), told the Senate Select Committee on Intelligence in 2005.[65] Similarly, a classified assessment by the Central Intelligence Agency noted that Iraq might prove to be an even more effective training ground for militants than Afghanistan was in Al Qaeda's early days, because it provides a real-world laboratory for urban combat. President Bush's former heads of intelligence, Porter J. Goss and George Tenet, told Congress that the war in Iraq had given birth to a "next wave" of terrorism that will endure "for the foreseeable future with or without Al Qaeda in the picture."[66] While Iraqi and US-run prisons in Iraq acted as incubators for radicalization, the endemic marginalization of Sunnis and the sectarian-led policies of the Iraqi governments in the aftermath of the 2003 invasion contributed to the resurgence of Al Qaeda in Iraq in a more extreme form. Agency matters, however. The systemic problems facing post-Hussein Iraq could have been overcome if the new governing elite had put national interests ahead of their own parochial concerns and had learned the lessons of the old regime. The new ruling elite have failed the Iraqi people, who have suffered an endless cycle of reckless and devastating wars and punishing economic sanctions. Nevertheless, few had predicted the long-lasting consequences of Zarqawi's brutal methods on the next generation of Salafi-jihadists, which would leave a trail of terror that extended well beyond Iraq.

In *Al-Dawla al-Islamiyya: Bayna al-Haqiqa wa al-Wahm* (The Islamic State: Disentangling Myth from Reality), Abu Abdullah Mohamed al-Mansour al-Issawi—the leader of Jayish al-Mujahideen (Mujahideen Army), a Salafi-jihadist (Iraqi) armed group—discusses in great detail the methods used by Zarqawi and his successors. Issawi was one of Zarqawi's close theological mentors in Iraq, and he also knew the men who took command of Zarqawi's network after his death, namely, Abu Hamza al-Muhajjer, Abu Omar al-Baghdadi, and Abu Bakr al-Baghdadi. In the book, the author recollects that Zarqawi and his cohorts used takfir as a weapon. They were takfiri par-excellence and instrumentalized takfir to serve a deviant ideological agenda, notes Issawi, who frequently hosted Zarqawi and his successors at his private residence. Issawi also spent time with Abu Bakr al-Baghdadi and senior lieutenants of ISIS in Camp Bucca, the infamous US-run prison near Umm Qasr in southern Iraq, in 2005.[67] Although Issawi showers Zarqawi with praise, he draws a portrait of an ultra-extremist man who, for example, excommunicated all policemen who "wear blue uniforms," including traffic cops. When pressed by his mentor to explain his reasoning, Zarqawi retorted, "If a policeman is tasked by the Crusaders [the Americans and their allies] to fight the mujahideen, he would," thus, killing them is justified. Issawi relates how he told Zarqawi that his logic was flawed, stating that "you cannot ex-communicate people based on suspicions and intentions."[68] Issawi concludes that Zarqawi was much less deviant in his worldview than his successors and a better person than Abu Bakr al-Baghdadi,[69] a deadly indictment of Al Qaeda in

Iraq and its successor by a radical Islamist and a mentor of its chiefs.

Despite the fact that Issawi states that Zarqawi is a better person and less extreme than his three successors, he concludes that the Jordanian sanctioned the killing of Muslims based on false grounds and an overzealous twisting of the Islamic doctrine, legitimizing his reign of terror in Iraq through a distorted interpretation of the Sunna. Worse still, from Issawi's viewpoint, was that Zarqawi, his companions, and his successors refused to listen to highly respected religious scholars and went as far as to repeatedly and openly criticize such scholars, excommunicating some of them in the process. For Issawi, this proved that they behaved like the Khawarji, an extremist group in early Islam that excommunicated Muslims at will. In fact, throughout his book, Issawi, who taught Zarqawi and his associates religious lessons, describes their thinking and actions as more Khawarji than Islamic, and he blames their indiscriminate violence against Iraqis for the loss of popular support for the Salafi-jihadists. He makes it clear that he backs "martyrdom operations" and refuses to call them "suicide operations," but he decries the liberal and un-Islamic use of suicide operations by AQI, which, he says, has poisoned peoples' attitudes toward the jihadist movement. He reveals that the group assassinated scores of rival jihadists and Sunni tribal and religious leaders who supported the armed resistance against AQI. As we will see in the next chapter, despite initially working with AQI against the US-led coalition, following disagreements over strategy and Al Qaeda's hegemonic designs in the Sunni Triangle, Sunni tribal leaders soon switched alliances and cooperated with the coalition.[70]

Issawi's insider account sheds lights on the root causes of the Sunni revolt against Al Qaeda in Iraq, a revolt fueled by opposition to Zarqawi's brutal tactics and terrorism that bled the community and dragged it into sectarian strife, with catastrophic repercussions. While some Iraqis supported the armed resistance against the US-led coalition, they initially opposed attacks against civilians, despite sectarian divisions. The bombing of Sunni resistance strongholds by the coalition forces, such as that of Fallujah in late 2004, led to large communities being forced out of their homes and cities. As a result, tens of thousands of Sunnis in need of new housing fled to Baghdad, creating a growing humanitarian crisis. As the number of internally displaced Sunnis increased, armed Sunni groups in the capital started to systematically turn against the Shia community, many angered by the Shia-dominated government troops that were sent to help the Americans in Fallujah and other Sunni cities.

From intimidation campaigns to forced expulsions, the Shias were repeatedly targeted, with many heading either to the already overcrowded Sadr City or to other Shia-dominated cities. The conflict continued to heighten, and, in January 2006, Sunni jihadists bombed the Golden Dome in Samarra. This event marked the beginning of an increased and widespread Shia retaliation against Sunni violence. The escalation was so intense that in Baghdad, Shia-armed militias turned into death squads, while suicide bombers were used by each camp against the other, turning the capital into a theater of macabre internal civil war.[71]

In 2004, Zarqawi's gruesome plans might have seemed to be coming to fruition, but his vision clashed with the silent majority and the local Salafis who prioritized the fight against the occupation. Unaware that his actions were leading to increasing resentment in his base of operation—the Sunni Triangle—Zarqawi violated a cardinal rule of armed insurgencies: he gradually alienated popular support. From afar, bin Laden and Zawahiri observed Zarqawi's self-destructive conduct with alarm, powerless to reverse the disastrous trend he had started. The truth is that Zarqawi was consistent with his own belief system and, importantly, he belonged to a new wave of jihadists with strategic priorities that were different from those of Al Qaeda Central. He had no inhibitions about engaging in mass bloodletting, including that of his fellow Muslims, and expanding beyond the borders of Iraq. Zarqawi's vicious tactics (which the public has now become accustomed to through their routine usage by ISIS) earned him much ire from bin Laden and Zawahiri. Pioneering the beheading of captives, Zarqawi was eventually anointed with the name "the sheikh of the slaughterers," reflecting his indulgence in the slaughtering of hostages.[72]

Subsequently, in 2005, Zarqawi provoked widespread uproar in Jordan when, reportedly under his order, suicide bombers attacked three US-owned hotels in Amman.[73] Following the attack, protesters gathered in the capital, some carrying placards that read, "Why?" Many sympathizers wondered why Zarqawi would target their country, where so many people had supported his jihad in Iraq.[74] The bombings also had dire consequences for Al Qaeda, with many Jordanians now openly considering it a terrorist organization.[75] By 2007, this strategy had turned the Iraqi public in general against Al Qaeda in Iraq. Zarqawi's attacks on Sunni religious, tribal, and armed resistance figures and groups such as Jayish al-Islam (the Islamic Army) and other Islamist battalions triggered widespread local opposition to his brutal tactics and the blanket takfiri ideology that guided them. These attacks on Sunni communities can be seen as the crux of a Sunni-Sunni civil war that had raged long before and continued long after Zarqawi's death. The civil war degraded his organization and severed its ties with the local community. Although the Americans co-opted many Sunnis in 2006–2008 to fight Al Qaeda in Iraq with money and arms, the so-called Sons of Iraq or Sahawat (Awakening Councils), which first started in the Sunni Anbar province, represented a collective public desire to expel Zarqawi's network from Sunni-dominated areas. AQI met its Waterloo at the hands of Sunnis who had initially welcomed Zarqawi and his men with open arms as part of the resistance against the US-led occupiers. However, as time passed and Zarqawi's activities became clear, popular support for Zarqawi's transnationalist jihadist project and his sectarian path or vision eroded. It quickly became evident that Zarqawi's views and actions clashed with the political aspirations of the silent Sunni majority. The backlash was not contained within the Sunni strongholds of Iraq, and it reverberated across the Arab world.

In addition to the loss of public support, bin Laden also had to contend with public criticism from some of his closest mentors, who blamed Al Qaeda for transforming a generation of disenfranchised youth into walking bombs and questioned his authority to speak in the name of Islam. With few options at their disposal, bin Laden and Zawahiri used gentle means to persuade Zarqawi to change his dangerous ways and fall in line with Al Qaeda Central. Bin Laden and Zawahiri pleaded with Zarqawi to keep in mind that, by pursuing a genocidal strategy, he was losing the battle for Muslim hearts and minds and discarding popular support at his own peril. Revisiting that dark period between 2004 and 2006 (Zarqawi was killed on June 8, 2006), one finds striking similarities between the worldview and conduct of Zarqawi's AQI and those of Abu Bakr al-Baghdadi's Islamic State. Having inherited the blood-drenched legacy of Al Qaeda in Iraq, the Islamic State is an extension of Zarqawi's organization. The two groups can be viewed as two sides of the same coin, with the only difference being of degree, not tactics or vision. Both revel in theatrical exhibitions of savagery and viciousness, both consider the Shias heretics, both seek to exterminate them, and both have an expansive interpretation of takfir that goes far beyond that of bin Laden and Zawahiri.

In addition to the clash of personalities between Al Qaeda Central's old guard and the likes of Zarqawi and ISIS's current leader, Baghdadi, there is an ideological divide that has played out publicly in the aftermath of bin Laden's death in May 2011. While the new generation of jihadists shares Al Qaeda's overall worldview, it has a distinctive identity and does not feel beholden to its parent organization. For example, although Zarqawi swore baiya to bin Laden, he did not carry out his orders; similarly, Zarqawi's successor, Baghdadi, carried out a coup against his former emir, Zawahiri, and has labored hard to convince Al Qaeda Central's factions to switch loyalty and join the Islamic State. Some have in fact already done so. This post–Al Qaeda wave or generation is more about action and shock and awe than theory and theology. For them, shock value, slaughter, and blood speak louder than words. Zarqawi, Baghdadi, and their companions wage total war with no limits. In contrast to the founding fathers of the jihadist movement, the Qutbians (disciples of the Egyptian master theorist Sayyid Qutb), and the first generation, Zarqawi and Baghdadi are theologically illiterate and have shown little interest in co-opting prominent preachers or theorists to their camp. What distinguishes the post–Al Qaeda wave from its predecessors is its poverty of ideas. In fact, the jihadist clerical community vehemently criticizes the extremism of the new wave as subversion of the faith, as well as of the Salafi-jihadist ideology, a verdict that speaks volumes about the rift among jihadists. Zawahiri and other heavyweights now agree with Issawi and label Baghdadi and his associates Khawarji, in a way excommunicating their co-jihadists.[76] In response, the post–Al Qaeda generation denounces its elders as cowards who are losing heart and faith in the jihadist cause. They depict themselves as the real vanguard of the Sunni umma, struggling to purify the Islamic lands of the kuffar and moral corruption and resurrect the caliphate.[77]

As long as bin Laden was alive, Zarqawi and others felt obliged to pay homage to him, though on their own terms. They took action into their own hands and pursued an independent local agenda that served their interests and overzealous, fanatical convictions without severing the umbilical cord with their elders. With bin Laden's death, Al Qaeda Central was orphaned, losing its charismatic leader, anchor, and equilibrium. Seen as divisive and weak, Zawahiri, bin Laden's successor, did not inspire confidence or loyalty among jihadists like bin Laden. For example, Baghdadi has challenged Zawahiri's leadership by anointing himself as the caliph of the Islamic State. Baghdadi and his inner circle have shown contempt for

Zawahiri and derogatively refer to his organization as Zawahiri's Al Qaeda, a direct disputation of his moral and political authority.[78]

ZARQAWI'S DEATH AND THE TRANSITIONAL PERIOD FROM 2006 TO 2010

When the Americans killed Zarqawi in June 2006, he had already lost the hearts and minds of many Arabs and especially Iraqis, sealing the fate of his organization. Zarqawi's fall from grace happened quite close to the time of his death. By 2005 the hundreds of suicide bombings, kidnappings, and beheadings had turned the vast majority of Iraqis and Muslims against Al Qaeda in Iraq and Al Qaeda Central in general. While the Sunni revolt against AQI had gained momentum, many Sunni scholars across the Arab world, including Zarqawi's spiritual mentor, Maqdisi, openly criticized his brutal methods and blanket takfiri ideology. In summer 2005, Maqdisi, who had groomed Zarqawi while both were in prison in Jordan in the 1990s, publicly reprimanded his former pupil for his terrorism against civilians. In several interviews, including an appearance on Al Jazeera satellite television station, a widely watched Arabic news channel, Maqdisi said that violence against civilians is wrong because it harms the interests of the umma and tarnishes the image of Islam. He reminded Zarqawi that so-called martyrdom operations should be carried out only under specific and exceptional conditions. He warned him against alienating Iraqis by losing sight of the nature of the struggle in Iraq and forgetting that Iraqis knew what was best for their country.[79] Maqdisi's public criticism elicited an angry public rebuttal by Zarqawi, who challenged his former mentor's authority and accused him of wavering and losing heart.[80]

As was feared by bin Laden and Zawahiri, Zarqawi's attacks and slaughter of civilians prompted other radical Islamist scholars to blame Al Qaeda Central for allowing his actions to take place. In an open letter written to bin Laden in 2007,

Salman al-Oudah, an influential radical Saudi preacher and scholar who spent years in prison, asked, "How many innocent children, elderly people, and women were killed in the name of Al Qaeda?"[81] Oudah pointed an accusatory finger at bin Laden:

> You are responsible—brother Osama—for spreading *takfiri* ideology and fostering a culture of suicide bombings that has caused bloodshed and suffering and brought ruin to entire Muslim communities and families.... To what end, even if your plan succeeds by marching over the corpses of hundreds of thousands of people? ... Is Islam only about guns and war? Have your means become the end themselves? ... Many of your brethren in Egypt, Algeria and elsewhere have come to see the end road for al-Qaeda's ideology. They now realize how destructive and dangerous it is.[82]

Like Oudah, Dr. Fadl, one of bin Laden's top theorists, also condemned the killing of civilians and the selection of targets based on religion and nationality.[83] For many, the incessant use of suicide bombers, most of them young and inexperienced, showed that the organization had little value for the lives of those who joined the Salafi-jihadist cause. In October 2007, in an audiotape aired by Al Jazeera, bin Laden was forced to recognize that his fighters in Iraq "had made mistakes," and he called for the unity of the umma before national, tribal, or party loyalty. In this tape, bin Laden quoted the Prophet Mohammed: "The prophet, peace be upon him, said once: no one is perfect. We all make mistakes and we should seek forgiveness of these mistakes. Human beings commit wrongs, and wrongs always lead to conflict and dispute. Having acknowledged that we have made mistakes ... we can now seek to rectify these mistakes."[84] As Al Qaeda's leaders usually did not air their dirty laundry in public, bin Laden's public acknowledgment of "mistakes" was unusual, proving that the organization was fully aware that it had made a monumental strategic error by agreeing to the merger with Zarqawi, a decision now threatening to erode the standing of Al Qaeda Central in the eyes of Muslim opinion as well as of its own base.

Far from bringing reconciliation, Zarqawi's death intensified clashes between his successors and local communities. A few days after Zarqawi's death, the Mujahideen Shura Council (*Majlis Shura al-Mujahidin*), an umbrella organization that includes Al Qaeda in Iraq and seven like-minded factions, named Abu Omar al-Baghdadi and Abu Hamza al-Muhajjer (also known as Abu Ayyub al-Masri), two of Zarqawi's closet aides, as the new emir and defense minister, respectively.[85] Although Muhajjer, born in Sohaj, Upper Egypt, was secretive and mysterious, he and Zarqawi belonged to the same jihadist generation and possessed a similar worldview that defined the universe in binary terms: the camp of belief versus the camp of the kuffar. Similarly, Abu Omar al-Baghdadi was an Iraqi who preceded Abu Bakr al-Baghdadi as emir of AQI. Like their predecessors, Zarqawi, Baghdadi, and Muhajjer excommunicated all the Shias as well as the ordinary Sunnis who worked for the Iraqi authorities. Their arrival at the head of the organization did not calm critics or bring about a moderating shift in AQI's modus operandi. For many, Abu Omar al-Baghdadi's succession constituted an attempt at reimagining the group as Iraqi, rather than Sunni. Despite initial skepticism about the real identity of Baghdadi and even that of Muhajjer,[86] they controlled the remnants of Al Qaeda in Iraq until both were killed in a joint American-Iraqi raid near Tikrit on April 18, 2010.[87] After Baghdadi's and Muhajjer's deaths, AQI acknowledged their identities as the leader of the believers and his first minister of war, respectively.[88]

In an attempt to rebrand AQI, the Mujahideen Shura Council merged the group with like-minded local insurgents and militias and declared, on October 13, 2006, the establishment of the Islamic State of Iraq (ISI). Despite the rebranding, the group continued to be known and referred to as AQI. The central command of Al Qaeda Central and its two top leaders, bin Laden and Zawahiri, were not consulted prior to the pronouncement of the Islamic State of Iraq. After the establishment of ISI, Muhajjer sent a letter to bin Laden stating that the consultative council had witnessed the new leader, Abu Omar al-Baghdadi, swearing baiya to bin Laden, thus confirming ISI's allegiance to Al Qaeda Central.[89]

Despite Muhajjer's assurances to bin Laden, the Islamic State of Iraq was acting independently from Al Qaeda Central. As discussed previously, the relationship between the two groups was voluntary, not mandatory, based on the willingness of AQI's commanders to acknowledge an organizational-institutional link. The period between Zarqawi's death in June 2006 and the deaths of his first two successors in April 2010 expanded the cleavage between the two groups, even though both sides displayed solidarity in public and kept their differences under wraps. However, this was a transitional period in which internal bleeding and hemorrhaging intensified and threatened to crush ISI. With hindsight, ISIS's followers have attempted to rewrite history by painting a rosy picture of the transitional period after Zarqawi's death and portraying the Mujahideen Shura Council and the so-called Mutayabeen Front, a loose jihadist alliance, as representative of the collective will of the Sunni Iraqi resistance. We are told that the two groups were pioneers in establishing an Islamic state in Iraq and paving the way for the coming caliphate.[90] In reality, the transitional period, marked by the leadership of Muhajjer and Abu Omar al-Baghdadi and their declaration of an Islamic state in Iraq, is better characterized as a mafia-like network, carrying out hit-and-run assassinations and attacks against both Sunni and Shia enemies. Top Al Qaeda leaders such as bin Laden, Zawahiri, and Atiya Allah al-Liby, a senior commander, called ISI "blessed" and backed it against other Islamist armed groups in Iraq. In 2008, during an open forum on the Al Qaeda media outlet, al-Sahab, Zawahiri praised ISI as "a legitimate emirate founded on a righteous foundation and established by *shura* [that has] gained *baiya* of most mujahideen and tribes in Iraq."[91] With hindsight, Zawahiri subsequently conceded that he and bin Laden had not been consulted before ISI had been declared and that they had privately opposed it. Zawahiri's public acknowledgment shows clearly how little control Al Qaeda Central exercised over its division in Iraq. In a conversation online with his supporters after the rupture of relations between Abu Bakr al-Baghdadi and Zawahiri in 2013–2014, the latter revealed that he and other top leaders of Al Qaeda Central had argued in vain that the disadvantages of declaring an Islamic state outweighed any potential advantages. For instance, in a letter to his supporters written in 2010, less than a year before his death, that was found in a cache of documents seized from his hideaway and recently released by American authorities, bin Laden warned them against the rush to create Islamic emirates, because experience has shown that the United States would crush them, and he cited the Taliban, Hamas, and the Islamic State of Iraq as examples. Bin Laden advised his followers first to wage a war of attrition against the United States and weaken its ability to topple future Islamic states. Otherwise, bin Laden concluded, the declaration of Islamic states would be like "putting the cart before the horse."[92]

Zawahiri's public endorsement of ISI would come to haunt him after the violent break between Al Qaeda Central and ISI, ISIS's predecessor, in late 2013. He was subsequently reproached by prominent Iraqi Islamists for ignoring their earlier warnings and siding with ISI, and they explicitly accused him of putting the interests of his organization before those of the community and righteousness.[93] Indeed, and contrary to Zawahiri's endorsement of ISI, Abu Omar al-Baghdadi and Muhajjer were sectarian psychopaths as much as Zarqawi was. Issawi points out that Muhajjer was a strange character and much more extremist than his predecessor. The jihadist leader and author explains that after the declaration of the Islamic State of Iraq, Muhajjer boasted that they had built a "podium" for the Mahdi and went on to show Issawi's deputy "a picture of the podium."[94] In the conversation, the ISI leader also referred to his foot soldiers as the "the Mahdi's knights." Issawi notes sarcastically that Muhajjer insisted he had chosen Abu Omar al-Baghdadi as *Emir al-Mu'minin* (commander of the faithful) because "he was married to two wives!"[95]

Far from remodeling and restrengthening the organization, Zarqawi's successors, Muhajjer and Abu Omar al-Baghdadi, steered it onto rocky shores. Zarqawi, Muhajjer, and Abu Omar al-Baghdadi alienated their hadanah sha'biyya (social base) and risked expulsion. According to Issawi, his disciples killed "a long list" of Sunnis, including preachers, civil society leaders, activists, jihadists, and ordinary people, because they suspected them of disagreeing with their extremist vision. Issawi also states that in one conversation with an AQI lieutenant in Camp Bucca prison, the lieutenant revealed that his superiors in Iraq sanctioned the killing of Zarqawi's spiritual guide, Maqdisi, because he criticized some of their tactics and misinterpreted Islamic doctrine.[96] According to Abu Ali al-Anbari, an Iraqi insurgent leader, AQI, in addition to kidnapping women and looting property, killed about 1,500 Sunnis in the Anbar province alone.[97] The Sunni-Sunni rift deepened, with many locals joining Sahawat militias in taking up arms against AQI and its successor, ISI, pushing their fighters from major cities to the Iraq-Syria border.

It is no wonder, then, that the killing of Muhajjer and Abu Omar al-Baghdadi in April 2010 by a joint American-Iraqi raid was hailed as a tipping point in the struggle to rid Iraq of AQI and ISI. For example, US vice president Joe Biden said that "their deaths are potentially devastating blows to al Qaeda in Iraq," adding that the operation "demonstrates the improved security strength and capacity of Iraqi security forces."[98] US forces commander general Raymond Odierno went even further by stating, "The death of these terrorists is potentially the most significant blow to al-Qaeda in Iraq since the beginning of the insurgency."[99] He added, "There is still work to do but this is a significant step forward in ridding Iraq of terrorists." Iraq's prime minister at the time, Nuri al-Maliki, explained, "The attack was carried out by ground forces which surrounded the house, and also through the use of missiles." He added, "During the operation computers were seized with e-mails and messages to the two biggest terrorists, Osama bin Laden and Ayman al-Zawahiri."[100] Despite the celebratory tone of these pronouncements, between 2010 and 2014, a new captain named Abu Bakr al-Baghdadi begin rebuilding the organization, turning it into a lethal weapon capable of controlling a large part of Iraq and Syria. Baghdadi's hold on the organization would soon threaten the very foundation of the state system in the heart of the Arab world.

3

HOW BROKEN IRAQI POLITICS
FUELED THE REVIVAL OF ISIS

In May 2010, when Abu Bakr al-Baghdadi replaced Abu Omar al-Baghdadi as commander of the faithful after the latter's death, the Islamic State of Iraq was internally besieged and bleeding. It faced a two-pronged battle in Iraq: one against the predominately Shia government and the Shia population in general; another against fellow Sunnis who opposed its dark vision and takfiri ideology. The issues facing ISI in 2010 were due to a slow buildup of pressure. Since 2003, relations between Al Qaeda in Iraq and the Sunni tribes had become increasingly confrontational, with AQI targeting local sheikhs and tribal leaders. In addition to the clash of interests between Sunni tribes and AQI, insurgent groups, including one of the most powerful, Jayish al-Islam, an Islamist Sunni armed militia, sent signals to the Americans that they might negotiate if certain conditions were met. Other Sunnis joined Sahwa (awakening councils) and fiercely battled AQI and its successor, ISI, exacting a heavy toll on Baghdadi's network. New trends and shifts in Sunni society did not bode well for ISI's worldview, which could easily be summarized as "war against all." During this period, it looked like the odds were against ISI.

It would turn out quite differently. The fall of Mosul in summer 2014 reinvigorated ISI, which grew to become the Islamic State of Iraq and Syria (ISIS). The group's renewal was a rude awakening for Middle Eastern rulers and their Western patrons, who had indirectly facilitated its revival. Although its gains may have surprised the United States and Syria and other neighboring Arab countries, ISIS neither fell from the sky nor was resurrected from the dead. Rather, the driving forces behind ISIS's resurgence were much more temporal in nature. Specifically, they stemmed from contentious social and political developments in the recent history of the Arab Fertile Crescent particularly failed developmental policies and the derailment of the Arab Spring uprisings.

From 2003 until 2005 relations between Sunni tribal leaders and the US-led coalition were either hostile or unfriendly. Despite the widely reported images of jubilant Iraqis following the toppling of Hussein's regime in 2003, many people across the country remained distrustful and suspicious of the United States. The 1991 US-led bombing campaign following Hussein's invasion of Kuwait in 1990 targeted not only civilian and military infrastructures but also the country's electrical plants and water purification and sewage treatment facilities, leading to cholera and typhoid epidemics. During the war, US president George H. W. Bush had called on the Iraqis to topple Hussein, but once uprisings against the Iraqi regime in the north and the south of the country gained momentum in February 1991, promised US support did not materialize, and Hussein's special forces quickly unleashed their full wrath against the protesters, violently putting down the rebellions. In addition, the UN sanctions regime, led by the United States and seconded by Great Britain, also further contributed to the collapse of the country's water, electricity, health care, and agriculture systems, and hyperinflation set in. As the country's economy continued its downward spiral, two-thirds of the Iraqi army were demobilized, with many facing unemployment upon their return home. Government salaries were heavily cut if even paid. With teachers leaving their jobs and chronic shortages in school supplies, the education system was also heavily affected, leading to a sharp fall in the country's literacy rates. Between Hussein's catastrophic wars and policies, the bombing campaign, and the UN embargo, Iraq's socioeconomic fabric had been torn by the time of the 2003 invasion, with the population facing high unemployment and an increase in poverty, malnutrition, and child mortality along with a collapsed housing and transportation infrastructure. The UN embargo had left the country ostracized and the population further entrenched in Hussein's grip, leaving many Iraqis feeling abandoned and disillusioned with the international community. It is in this context that the uprising against the coalition's forces in 2003 on both the Sunni and the Shia sides took place.[1]

Nonetheless, after years of costly resistance against the US-led coalition and the sectarian-dominated order in Baghdad, Sunnis were exhausted, and they were divided regarding the way forward and the most effective means for exercising more influence in post-Hussein Iraq. The brutal tactics of Abu Musab al-Zarqawi, the founder of Al Qaeda in Iraq, had fostered growing resentment among the Sunni community. With the tide turning against the Salafi-jihadist organization, influential Anbar tribal leader Sheikh Osama al-Jadaan put it bluntly: "We realized that these foreign terrorists were hiding behind the veil of the noble Iraqi resistance. They claim to be striking at the US occupation, but the reality is they are killing innocent Iraqis in the markets, in mosques, in churches, in our schools."[2]

In addition to the violent conflict that was being waged, AQI angered Sunni communities by appointing its own local emirs and monopolizing financial resources in the territories under its control, directly bypassing tribal authorities and proving to be insensitive to local beliefs and traditions. As tensions escalated, more and more Sunnis concluded that AQI's strategy was designed not to liberate them but to control their land, resources, and people. Many Sunnis also grew increasingly distrustful of the sectarian-led government in Baghdad, seeing it as a front for Iranian interests, which in turn threatened their stake in the country's political future. With the Bush administration announcing a surge of additional troops, Sunni leaders knew that it would be impossible to militarily defeat the US coalition. Increasingly, AQI was being seen as an Arab export eager to battle the United States for control of Iraq, and, by 2005, AQI faced resistance from certain Sunni communities—particularly the Albu Mahal tribe around the city of al-Qaim—who attacked Al Qaeda fighters operating in their neighborhoods. This provoked a change in the environment, and the Albu Mahal tribe began cooperating with the United States.[3]

More significantly, in 2006, Sunni fighters were defeated by Shia militias and authorities following the battle of Baghdad. This may also have influenced the growing number of individuals, tribal leaders, and Sunni Islamist groups who began to liaise with US occupying forces at this time. Although Jayish al-Islam had fought American and Iraqi government forces, in 2007 some of its fighters turned their guns against the jihadists and joined the Sunni Sahwa, with their leader warning that "Iraq faces a dual occupation, American and Iranian, and the Iranian is worse."[4]

Thus, several factors—primarily the hope to retain a measure of influence within the country—motivated and helped Sunni religious nationalists to realign their position and work with the United States against AQI. Fearing their weakening position, in January 2006 AQI established the Mujahideen Shura Council in an attempt to heal a widening rift with tribal leaders and depict the organization as indigenous. The council united at least six Sunni Islamist groups engaged in armed resistance, including Jayish al-Taiifa al-Mansoura, Katbiyan Ansar Al-Tawhid wal Sunnah, Saray al-Jihad Group, al-Ghuraba Brigades, al-Ahwal Brigades, and Jund al-Sahhaba.

In September 2006, in an attempt to salvage the relationship between ISI and the Sunni tribes, Abu Hamza al-Muhajjer, who succeeded Zarqawi as defense minister for a short while after the latter's death, offered tribal leaders amnesty on the condition that they join his organization. Muhajjer called for unity between Al Qaeda and the Sunni community, and aimed to move away from Zarqawi's confrontational strategy. In a message posted on several radical Islamist websites, Muhajjer stated, "Because Ramadan is the month of forgiveness, we offer the traitor tribal leaders amnesty, on one condition—that you announce your repenting openly in front of all your people and get the word to us."[5] Far from being acquiescent, Ahmed Naji Jibarah al-Juburi, leader of the Salahaddin Tribes Council, provided a response on behalf of the tribal chiefs: "Iraq is our Iraq. It does not belong under the leader of the Al Qaeda organization who came and entered Iraq to liberate it from occupation. He did not come to liberate Iraq from its own people. We are the people of Iraq, and he wants to liberate us, which means that he wants to eliminate us and make Iraq a wasteland void of its people and citizens. . . . Al Qaeda helps the occupiers to divide and tear Iraq to shreds."[6]

In addition to the battle between AQI and rebellious Sunni tribes, the jihadist organization suffered from internal dissension and fragmentation. Many within AQI viewed Muhajjer as a weak leader and opposed his strategy of assassinating tribal sheikhs and other Iraqis. Ultimately, they called for a change in the leadership of the organization. On October 12, 2006, one day before the announcement of the establishment of the Islamic State, a video posted on jihadist websites and attributed to an Iraqi jihadist known as Abu Osama al-Iraqi or Abu Osama al-Mujahid made waves in radical Islamist circles. In the video, Iraqi, an allegedly former officer of Hussein's army, called on Al Qaeda Central (that is, bin Laden and Zawahiri) to sever its ties with AQI. Iraqi publicly criticized Muhajjer's leadership and actions, saying that AQI's targeting of civilians, hospitals, schools, tribal leaders, imams, and religious scholars had turned the tribal community against the organization.[7] Calling for the Iraqization of the jihadist group, Iraqi put it bluntly: "Just because you don't know the men in Iraq is not a reason for you to choose anyone who makes himself visible. . . . We urge that the [leadership] be delegated to an Iraqi just as it has been delegated to an Afghan in Afghanistan. . . . We pray to God that you receive our message and that some of those surrounding you don't hide it from you, so that you can make the appropriate decision and cancel the pledge of allegiance in Iraq. We are your sons and won't fail in leading the war and jihad."[8]

Eager to play down the rift among Iraqi jihadists, the leadership of Al Qaeda Central condemned Iraqi's statement by claiming that it was false. Notwithstanding Al Qaeda Central's denials, ISI was torn apart by internal conflict and external Sunni armed resistance. According to Abu Abdullah Mohamed al-Mansour al-Issawi, the leader of Jayish al-Mujahideen, there was credible evidence of bloodletting among AQI, ISI, and likeminded jihadist groups. Issawi, who was a mentor to Zarqawi and the two Baghdadis, revealed that Zarqawi and his successors had waged a campaign of terror against anyone who disagreed with them, including other Salafi-jihadists.

Despite the internal dissension, and with the support of the six Sunni Islamist groups who joined ranks with AQI in January 2006, AQI pushed forward, and, on October 13, 2006, the Mujahideen Shura Council announced the formation of the Islamic State of Iraq. The newly formed ISI swore allegiance to a new emir, a former Iraqi military officer called Hamed Dawood Mohammed Khalil al-Zawi, better known by his nom de guerre, Abu Omar al-Baghdadi. Following the swearing of allegiance, ISI declared Baquba as its capital and included the cities of Baghdad, Anbar, Diyala, Kirkuk, Salah al-din, and Niwana and swaths of the Babel governorate as part of its state.[9]

However, the declaration did little to heal the rift between ISI and the Sunni tribes. The situation came to a head in September 2006 when tribal mobilization against ISI formalized with the creation of the al-Anbar Salvation Council (Majlis inqadh al-Anbar) by the Ramadi tribes. The al-Anbar Salvation Council was led by Abd al-Sattar al-Rishawi (also known as Abu Risha), who formalized cooperation with the occupation forces, primarily the Americans.[10] A letter discovered by coalition forces and attributed to members of the Shura Council attested to the fierce struggle unfolding between ISI and tribal leaders. The document listed a number of tribal leaders and members of the Islamic Party as targets for assassination.[11]

Other tribes soon followed suit in October, setting up *Majalis al-Sahwa* (councils) in Anbar and beyond. Across the country, Arab Sunni fighters and Islamist resistance groups also joined ranks against ISI, regrouping under a broad coalition known as Concerned Local Citizens or Sons of Iraq. By 2006–2007, Sahwa formed across the Sunni lands with preponderant backing by the Americans. The Sahwa movement gained momentum and expanded to almost eighty thousand members in less than a year while the United States provided financial and military backing for the movement.[12] Volunteers received weapons and financial support eventually formalized as monthly salaries of $300, which, although lower than the wages of the Iraqi security forces, constituted a badly needed income for pressed communities and an attractive incentive for unemployed young Sunni men to work with the coalition forces rather than against them. The responsibilities of Sahwa members included training, manning checkpoints, providing intelligence on other insurgents and jihadist-affiliated militias, and participating in direct combat against Al Qaeda. In an interview, a Sahwa member confirmed collaboration with the US-led coalition: "Yes, we did that with the support of the coalition forces when we captured some gangsters. After missions, the coalition forces used to issue letters of appreciation for us and gave us a reward. And that was good. I got $700 from the coalition forces: $300 for salary and a $400 reward for a total of $700 in one month—U.S. dollars."[13]

In less than a year the American-backed Awakening program, which paid tribesmen to switch sides and fight against Al Qaeda in Iraq or the Islamic State of Iraq, improved security conditions in Anbar and its vicinities. According to General David H. Petraeus, commander of the Multinational Force–Iraq, attacks in the area had dropped from 1,350 in October 2006 to just over 200 in August 2007. By 2007 the Awakening movement had expanded nationally and General Petraeus established the Force Strategic Engagement Cell (FSEC), which was tasked with cultivating contacts and ties between the Iraqi resistance and the central government via the Key Leader Engagement (KLE) initiative. This new structure proved effective in targeting Al Qaeda militants and driving them out of tribal territories. From 2007 to 2008, the Sahwa became a key instrument of US anti–Al Qaeda strategy, clearing the group from its strongholds in Ramadi and Fallujah. According to Riyadh al-Ogaidi, a senior lieutenant of AQI, the organization's active force in the country had fallen from 12,000 in June 2007 to about 3,500 in early 2008.[14] In the meantime, ISI continued to attack tribal leaders and Iraqi civilians. In September 2007, a few days after a meeting with President George W. Bush in Iraq, ISI took responsibility for killing Sheikh Abdul Abu Risha near his home.

In 2007 Prime Minister Nuri al-Maliki tried to replicate the Sahwa system in Shia-dominated neighborhoods, especially in southern Iraq, by establishing Isnad, or supportive councils. Similar to the Sahwa councils that were fighting ISI, the Isnad councils were established to confront rival Shia militias in the region as well as to counter the influence of Maliki's political rivals, who commanded their own militia forces, such as the Islamic Supreme Council of Iraq (ISCI). The Isnad were essentially tribal groups established in an array of provinces. They were paid for by Maliki's office, reported directly to Maliki, and were loyal only to Maliki. Because of the success of the Sunni Sahwa, both in obtaining support from the United States and by their sheer numbers, which were upward of eighty thousand members, Maliki became alarmed. He had been consistently hostile to the idea of arming the Sunnis because their success, in his opinion, could transform them into a legitimate political force and a powerful military power.[15]

Speaking at a news conference in 2006, Maliki warned, "The state is the only one that has the right to carry weapons. . . . We will deal with anybody who is outside the law. . . . Everyone now realizes that the existence of armed groups and militias harms the stability and unity of the state."[16] His statement highlights the mutual mistrust between Sunnis in general and the prime minister. However, US pressure forced Maliki's hand, and, although cooperation between former nationalist insurgents and the United States helped foster better ties with coalition forces, Maliki remained skeptical and suspicious. On the other hand, tribal leaders publicly criticized Maliki's government for its failure to restore security and improve basic services across the country. Mistrust turned into hostility in 2008 when the Iraqi authorities were put in charge of Sahwa forces, a move that tribal chiefs saw as a betrayal by the United States.[17] Although in the same year Maliki promised to incorporate a quarter of Sahwa forces within the government's security forces and other official sectors, by 2010 he had not taken concrete measures to allay the tribes' fears. Maliki justified the government's decision not to integrate Sahwa members into the Iraq security sector by accusing jihadists and former Baathists of infiltrating the Sahwa movement, and he ordered mass arrests of Sunni activists, particularly in Mosul.[18] When Sahwa members were incorporated into the government institutions, they were offered low-rank and low-paid government jobs, often on temporary contracts with wages intermittently paid, poisoning the relationship even further. In the following years the relationship between Sunni tribes and Maliki's government continued to deteriorate, reaching a point of no return at the beginning of the Arab Spring uprisings at the end of 2010 and the beginning of 2011.[19]

Tribal leaders were not the only Sunnis who worked with US occupying authorities. In 2007 Abu Azzam al-Tamimi, a senior leader of Jayish al-Islam, held a series of secret meetings with US forces in Abu Ghraib. Tamimi said he could mobilize a large force of almost seventeen thousand men to assist in the fight against ISI. Like Sunni tribal chiefs, members of Jayish al-Islam feared that the balance of power was tilting against them and that their position was growing increasingly precarious. In addition to confronting US troops, Jayish al-Islam now also had to face opposition from fellow Sunni Sahwa and Shia

militias, as well as internal jockeying for advantage. After Tamimi's militiamen successfully expelled ISI from Abu Ghraib,
Maliki's government, under pressure from the United States,
agreed to integrate his men with the Iraqi security forces. In Am-
riya, western Baghdad, another lieutenant of Jayish al-Islam
known as Abu Abed also joined the anti-ISI coalition,[20] and he
cleared the area of ISI's combatants.

While the Sahwa councils proved relatively effective, not all
Sunni resistance groups joined the US-led coalition. For exam-
ple, Jayish Rijal al-Tariq al-Naqshabandi (JRTN) and the Army
of the Men of Naqshband, a Baathist-dominated militia, con-
tinued to resist occupation forces in Mosul, Salah al-din, and
Kirkuk. In October 2007 six Sunni armed factions, including
Jayish al-Islam, Jammat Ansar al-Sunna, al-Jabha al-Islamiya lil-
Moqawama al-Iraqiya (also known as the Islamic Front for the
Iraqi Resistance), al-Fatiheen Army, and Hamas al-Iraq, established a unified command called the Political Council for the
Iraqi Resistance (PCIR).[21] The PCIR released a statement that
said, "The occupation of Iraq is an act of aggression and an act
of gross injustice which is rejected Islamically, legally and rationally, and which all laws grant the right to oppose and resist,"[22]
and warned that "laws and treaties agreed under the occupation
would be rescinded."[23] In 2010, the new grouping asserted
that it did not recognize Maliki's government, with its spokesman, Abdul Rahman al-Janabi, stating, "We in the Political
Council of the Iraqi Resistance refuse to enter into dialogue
with al-Maliki because these postinvasion governments are illegal, established under the auspices of the occupation and sought
to legitimize its existence and practices."[24] Although it refused
to join the Sahwa movement, the PCIR opposed ISI. It is apparent that the Sunni community, despite its ideological diversity, showed widespread opposition to Al Qaeda in Iraq.

Throughout this period running up to the Arab Spring
uprisings, Maliki adopted measures to co-opt the Sunni community and confront the Shia militias who challenged his
authority. Although this appeared promising at first glance,

Maliki's policies were calculated to consolidate his power and respond to US pressure. Despite his best efforts, both policy initiatives fell short of expectations because of his continued quest to maintain and increase his power. For example, in summer 2006 he launched a reconciliation initiative with a twenty-four-point plan.[25] The initiative was aimed at drawing the disenfranchised Sunni community into the political fold. Maliki even visited the Gulf States in a bid to garner support for his road map. The prime minister announced some of the measures in his reconciliation initiative, including granting amnesty to insurgents who laid down their arms and renounced violence, revising the de-Baathification program, fighting sectarianism within the government, and hosting a national reconciliation conference.[26] However, this initiative neither healed the deep wounds in Iraqi society nor bridged the communal divide.

The reconciliation initiative was viewed by Sunni leaders as an empty gesture because insurgents who had fought Iraqi and coalition forces were not granted amnesty. In a similar vein, influential Shia voices opposed Maliki's plan because they feared that freed Baathists would reorganize and attempt to regain political power, while Shia militiamen would remain in jail.[27] The Shia camp in Iraq was further antagonized in November 2006 as a result of Maliki's meeting with George W. Bush in Amman, Jordan. During that meeting, the prime minister vowed to fight Shia militias and he agreed to the US surge of troops in Iraq. The goal was to show the Sunni community that the government would now increasingly target Shia insurgents. In 2007 the central authorities launched operation Fardh al-Qanun (Imposing the Law) in Baghdad's Shia-populated neighborhoods, including Sadr City.[28] The same year also saw the execution of the Implementation and Follow-Up Committee for National Reconciliation (IFCNR), led by Bassima al-Jadri and aimed at fostering dialogue with the Sahwa and former Baathists. One of the IFCNR's recommendations was to put the Sahwa under the government's authority, a decision that, as noted previously, did little to reduce distrust with Sunni tribes. In 2008, with tensions between the government and Jayish al-Mahdi increasing, Maliki launched operation Saulat al-Fursan (Charge of the Knights) against the Sadrists in Basra.[29] The city saw fierce fighting, which eventually came to an end following a cease-fire brokered by Iran in March by which Muqtada al-Sadr agreed to withdraw his men from the streets. By the end of 2008, Maliki's government had signed an agreement with the Bush administration that stipulated that the United States would withdraw troops from Iraqi cities by June 2009 and from the entire country by the end of 2011.

Despite the twists and turns in the journey of the Sunni community after the 2003 US-led invasion and occupation of Iraq, by 2006–2007 a significant segment had turned against Al Qaeda in the war-torn territory known then as ISI. Tribal sheikhs, Sunni nationalists, and even religious insurgents confronted ISI and attempted to expel it from their cities and neighborhoods. During this period the ground shifted under Al Qaeda's feet and it lost its refuge in the Sunni heartland and faced an existential threat. By 2010 Zarqawi's successors were besieged and on the defensive; they needed a political miracle to survive, let alone revive.

THE FAILURE OF THE POLITICAL ESTABLISHMENT

The divided post-Hussein Iraqi political establishment and Maliki's growing authoritarian tendencies from 2010 onward were significant underlying factors that ripened the environment for Al Qaeda and ISI to take advantage of the situation. The political elite failed to move Iraq forward and help it escape the country's history of Baathist rule, including its legacy of war and conflict, destructive sectarian polarization, and widespread corruption. This not only antagonized the long-suffering and disillusioned population but it further marginalized sentiments of national unity. The de-Baathification and dismantlement of the army, on which tens of thousands of Arab Sunnis, if not more, depended for income, angered the Sunni community at large. The move caused large portions of not only soldiers but also former government officials, civil servants, doctors, professors, and teachers to be dismissed from their positions. Under the former regime, party membership was generally a prerequisite for employment. The postconflict reconstruction was, therefore, greatly mishandled and too radical in its aims and objectives. The destruction of the Iraqi state's institutions came before the country was stabilized and before reconciliation took place, which was particularly important because of the history of creeping sectarianism that predated the toppling of the Baath regime. For many of those disaffected professionals who felt let down by the nascent order in Baghdad, their tribal settings provided a network to fall back on. Additionally, as a result of the surge of violence during the first years of the occupation, millions of Iraqis were forced to flee their homes, with some retreating to rural areas where tribal structures could provide protection. The violence also had an impact on the government, as it became increasingly difficult for bureaucrats to reach their offices, bringing the state to its knees. The government for national unity that was elected in May 2006 was formed along ethno-sectarian lines, exacerbating further a situation that was already conducive to the aims and objectives of religious militias and Salafi-jihadist groups. Although by 2010 the Sahwa forces and the Sons of Iraq had proved themselves to be powerful against AQI, they had developed a better relationship with the coalition forces than with their own government. While Maliki and the broader Shia ruling elite remained distrustful of the Sahwa and the Sons of Iraq throughout this period, the Sunni political leadership also saw them as a political threat.

Most of the high-ranking politicians that made up the post-Hussein political landscape had spent much of their time in exile outside Iraq. In contrast, the Sahwa possessed a strong social base of support within Iraq. In fact, tribal networks were empowered from 1991 onward, after which the Hussein rule had become weaker as a result of the Shia rebellion in the south and the sanctions regime. To mitigate its circumstances, the Baath regime decentralized its grip on the country by empowering Iraqi tribes.[30] Following the US withdrawal and the transfer of control to the Iraqi government, some Sons of Iraq leaders, including former Baathist elements and Islamist militants, attempted to form a political movement. They had hoped that, following their role in the counterinsurgency, they would be allowed to play a formal role in the political future of the country.[31] As long as US troops were in Iraq, the Sahwa were protected and their actions were heralded as a triumph, even though their tactics were not always lawful. After the transfer of authority to the Iraqi government, many of their members were incriminated and placed under investigation, thus deepening the divide between local and national politics.[32] While for the Sunnis living in areas that had been purged of AQI the Sahwa and Sons of Iraq represented real local heroes, at the national level they were held responsible for the crimes they had committed before and after joining the coalition forces. By 2009, tribal leaders were targeted by both ISI and the Iraqi forces. Another key fact to highlight is that although by 2008 levels violence across the country had plummeted, in the same year, violent attacks in Nineveh province had risen, suggesting that AQI was already retreating to the area to consolidate its power base there.[33]

Soon before the March elections, the Sunni community faced another political setback when 511 individuals, most of them Sunnis, were banned from participating in the elections.[34] The move reignited sectarian tensions and, although some decried it, others warned of a Baathist plot to retake power. The decision to ban the candidates had been made by the de-Baathification committee headed by Ahmad Chalabi, a controversial politician accused of trying to eliminate the political opposition. The decision also contrasted with the general mood of the electoral campaign for the provincial elections in 2009, in which Maliki had tried to rebrand himself along national rather than sectarian lines. The prime minister also revamped the image of his administration by promising to deliver social public goods, including more jobs and increased investment in infrastructure work, health, and education. His electoral strategy worked, and his State of Law Alliance (SLA), which he established in October 2009 in a bid to distance himself from the sectarian image of his Iraqi National Alliance (INA), won a majority of seats against his rivals. The results confirmed that a plurality of voters favored nationalist-secular candidates as opposed to sectarian-based political parties. Although votes were divided along ethno-sectarian lines in that no party was able to garner votes across ethno-sectarian boundaries, there was a marked rejection of those parties that failed to espouse nationalistic and secular values. Victims of this rejection included ISCI, which was demolished in the elections. It is no wonder, then, that throughout 2009, Maliki continued to distance himself from the INA by condemning sectarian rifts and insisted that the way forward was through national unity and integration.

Following the strong nationalist mood that prevailed in the 2009 elections, most politicians also emphasized the need for national reconstruction and unity. With the planned withdrawal of US troops, political rhetoric focusing on the fight against the occupation took a backseat. In contrast to the 2005 elections, both camps put less focus on Sunni and Shia religious symbols. Instead, Maliki's opponents criticized his failed governance and economic mismanagement, particularly the lack of basic services and the deteriorating social conditions. They also accused the government of systemic corruption, pointing to the minister of trade, Faleh al-Sudani, a close ally of Maliki who allegedly used his position for personal gain. Called before a plenary session of the parliament in 2009 to answer allegations of embezzlement, the minister resigned and attempted to flee the country but was arrested.[35] Maliki's critics took him to task for his growing authoritarianism and abuse of the law by settling scores with political adversaries.[36]

On March 7, 2010, twelve million Iraqis went to the polls and delivered their verdict. Maliki's SLA, with eighty-nine seats, lost to Ayad Allawi's secular Iraqiyya coalition, which gained ninety-one seats. The INA came in third, followed by the Kurdistan Alliance. Maliki, who after the 2009 provincial elections had expected to win, dismissed the results and warned of a plot by former Baathists, terrorists, and foreign powers.[37] After insisting on a recount, which ended up confirming initial results, Maliki still came out on top when the Supreme Court ruled that the largest alliance formed after the elections could form the next government and seek parliamentary approval, as opposed to that privilege being awarded to the winning coalition. Seen widely as being influenced by Maliki, the Supreme Court's decision did not end the fierce political struggle, though it did allow the prime minister to preserve his power. The new government did not see the light of day until nine months after the elections, a period of contestation that further aggravated dismal socioeconomic conditions in the country. The long time it took to form the coalition government shows that, despite the clear message from the Iraqi population, infighting among Iraq politicians prevailed as they jostled for power and advantage, seeking to serve their ethno-religious affiliations rather than the populace. As Iraq's security continued to deteriorate, the aftermath of the elections saw the deepening of the prime minister's authoritarianism.

Maliki's grip on state institutions soon expanded, encompassing the military, the police, the courts, and the central bank. Monopolizing power, Maliki also acted as interior minister from 2010 to 2014 and retained the role of defense minister from December 2010 to August 2011, which he used to bypass the authority of the Defense Ministry by creating special brigades that reported directly to him and moving the office of commander in chief to his office.[38] Iraqis labeled his special brigades Fedayeen al-Maliki (al-Maliki's martyrs), a term reminiscent of Hussein's *Fedayeen* (martyrs), which had for years terrorized the country. Maliki surrounded himself with submissive loyalists and filled the security services with political appointees, a move that structurally weakened the capability of the armed forces to defend the homeland, as subsequently transpired when

ISIS seized a third of Iraqi territory without a fight in 2014. He also consolidated his control over the army and the police by appointing a general to supervise them. The population did not escape his authoritarian tendencies. As discontent grew over the government's inability to provide basic services, especially electricity and water, which suffered recurrent cuts, protesters mobilized across the country and demanded accountability, but they were put down by the security services. Demonstrations were soon banned, and the population was once again pushed back to the margins of the country's political life. The popular participation and government transparency that many had dreamt of when Hussein's regime was toppled had now become distant memories. In the opinion of many Iraqis, Maliki had reactivated the repressive security apparatus of Hussein's rule by establishing private militias and secret police units as well as committing widespread violations of human rights. The path taken by Maliki was designed to consolidate his power and prevent the emergence of organized opposition.[39]

Maliki's hubris is exemplified in his push to rein in the authority of the Iraqi Parliament, creating a political system that answered directly to him rather than to its constituents. With the help of the co-opted Higher Judicial Council in 2010, a ruling was proclaimed that hampered the parliament's authority by depriving it of any right to propose legislation. In an attempt to prevent parliamentarians from forcing ministers to be accountable, Maliki ended the parliament's right to summon them. His efforts continued to snowball and, following the withdrawal of US forces from Iraq in December 2011, he escalated the fight against his political nemeses by arresting scores of former Baathists in the governorates of Salah al-din, Anbar, Ninewa, and Diyala, where the Iraqiyya coalition had polled the strongest.[40] Any political opponents daring to criticize Maliki or his government also found themselves in the prime minister's line of fire. Arrest warrants for high-profile Sunni politicians whom he accused of plotting a coup were also soon issued. These targeted politicians included Deputy Vice President Tariq

Al-Hashimi, Finance Minister Rafi al-Issawi, and Deputy Prime Minister Saleh al-Mutlak, all leading members of the Iraqiyya coalition. Under Maliki, the Supreme Court, led by Chief Justice Medhat al-Mahmoud, who had until then been relatively shielded from political maneuvers, lost its independence. The increasing concentration of power in the hands of the prime minister made it increasingly difficult for the judiciary to remain neutral; Maliki's pact with Mahmoud and his close circle further ensured that the court would side with the prime minister. Independent agencies did not escape Maliki's grip and, in 2011, the head of the integrity commission, Judge Rahim al-Ugaili, was forced to resign.[41]

In January 2011, Chief Justice Mahmoud issued a ruling that expanded Maliki's domination over the country's remaining institutions, including the central bank, the Committee of Integrity, the Independent High Electoral Commission (IHEC), and the High Commission for Human Rights. In 2012, Maliki's influence in the central bank was clearly displayed, as criminal charges were filed against the bank's governor and deputy governor. By curtailing the power of the Iraqiyya coalition, Maliki's policies were blamed for undermining the Irbil Agreement, which stipulated that Iraqiyya had authority to appoint the defense minister. After rejecting several of the coalition's proposed candidates, Maliki retained the defense minister position for eight months, appointing loyalists to high-ranking positions and ensuring that his successor was an ally. In June 2011, he named one of his close advisers, Falih al-Fayyad, as a national security minister and Saadoun al-Dulaimi, minister of culture, as acting minister of defense.

A damning telegram from US ambassador Ryan C. Crocker dating back to 2007 shows that the United States was aware of Maliki's rising authoritarianism but continued to publicly support him. The document describes Maliki as "paranoid" and outlines how his decisions and policies produced "increasing centralization of power in the hands of an inner circle of Shia Islamists at the expense of the formal chain of command." It even goes as far as to warn that Maliki was following in the footsteps of Hussein.[42]

Maliki's control of the military increased sectarian tensions, with Sunnis accusing him, during his second term, of turning the security services into a Shia-led militia of up to five hundred thousand men.[43] Not to be overlooked is the enormous size of the protection forces of MPs, ministers, local councilors, high-ranking officials, and, of course, the presidency. For example, Vice President Tariq al-Hashimi did not have just a handful of bodyguards but rather a battalion of eight hundred, as did Maliki, Allawi, and Nujaifi. The president had a Kurdish brigade of six thousand, stationed primarily in the presidential zone in Baghdad. It is no wonder then that the security forces did not put up a fight against ISIS in Mosul in June 2014, where the largest army camps and concentrations of military hardware were on the left bank of the Tigris, where almost no fighting took place. The army simply melted away, with reports saying that those were some of the better-armed detachments of the army, unlike the federal police units that had been stationed on the right bank of the river.

Maliki's monopoly on, and abuse of, power poisoned the political system further and put the country on edge. After the arrests of the three leading politicians of Iraqiyya, Deputy Prime Minister Mutlak warned that the bloc would boycott the cabinet's session. "This decision is based on the deterioration of the political process, and to ensure that the country will not head towards a catastrophe if Maliki's dictatorship continues," he noted. Mutlak continued to criticize the prime minister on his Babiliyah television channel, describing him as "worse than Saddam Hussein."[44] This affront was costly to Mutlak, as the prime minister sacked him. In an op-ed on April 9, 2012, Allawi, the leader of Iraqiyya, sounded the alarm bells:

> The country is slipping back into the clutches of a dangerous new one-man rule, which inevitably will lead to full dictatorship.... Mr. Al-Maliki presides over an increasingly

Kafkaesque bureaucracy characterized by corruption and brutality, relying on the compromised judiciary as a weapon against political opponents while concealing the crimes of his cronies. The government falls short of providing basic services, including clean water, electricity and decent health care; the unemployment rate among our frustrated youth is above 30 percent, making them easy recruits for terrorists and prey for gangs; the security situation is deteriorating day by day in spite of an increase in special security forces. Unfortunately, some of these forces turn out to be part of the problem, operating torture chambers tied directly to the prime minister himself, as widely reported by international human rights organizations.[45]

Allawi's criticism of Maliki was not taken seriously because Allawi's popularity among the nationalist secular middle class in Iraq had reached a low point. Many Iraqis blamed Allawi for having joined a government that struggled to provide basic services and engaged in the repression of popular protests (more on this point later).

During a visit to Washington in April 2012, Massoud Barzani, president of the Kurdish autonomous region, seconded Allawi's warning:

Iraq is facing a serious crisis . . . it's coming towards one-man rule. . . . We have a situation in Baghdad where one man is the prime minister and at the same time he is the commander in chief of the armed forces, he is the minister of defense, he is the minister of the interior, and he is the chief of intelligence. And lately, he has been communicating to the head of the Central Bank that that should also come under the power of the prime minister. Where in the world can you find such an example?[46]

Of all the factors fueling ISIS's resurgence, the inability of the coalition and the Iraqi political establishment to put forward an inclusive national project and rebuild the political landscape tops the list. Rather than moving away from the political authoritarianism and cult of personality that epitomized the Hussein years, the political class that inherited the spoils failed to end factionalism and social fragmentation. Even those Iraqis who cooperated with the US forces and the Iraqi government against AQI were aligned along sectarian lines. Although groups like the Islamic Da'wa Party have an important social base, with the exception of the Sadrist movement and the Kurdish political parties, most of the high-ranking Iraqi politicians in post-2003 Iraq had been in exile, a fact that provoked resentment among the population. Iraqis were bitter about the lives of luxury enjoyed by the exiled politicians while they themselves suffered under Hussein's oppression. Exile essentially weakened the post-Hussein elite's connection with the Iraqi people, causing them to have an inadequate understanding of or appreciation for the very complex social and political terrain. For example the aftermath of the US-led invasion was marked by a will to de-Baathify the country. Yet the ruling elite did not undertake serious measures to fill the vacuum left by de-Baathification, particularly in terms of redefining the identity of the new Iraq. Within this vacuum of ideas and social chaos, which intensified because of the dismantling of Iraq's security institutions and armed resistance, there hardly existed a nationalist vision to replace the old regime's, no unifying symbol that would galvanize Iraqis as a whole.

Moreover, Iraq inherited severe challenges from the Hussein era—problems exacerbated further by postconflict reconstruction plans. In particular, Maliki's policies of exclusion and sectarianism led the country to the brink of an abyss. His Shia-dominated government treated Sunni Arabs like second-class citizens in the eyes of Iraq's Sunnis, and in many respects signaled to Sunnis that the Shias' numerical majority and oppression under Hussein provided a license to monopolize power. Maliki's communal shortsightedness, his perceived deference to Iran, his increasing authoritarian turn from 2010 onward, and his inability to curb corruption and human rights abuses provided the fuel that powered ISIS.

A NEW LEASE ON LIFE: NURI AL-MALIKI
AND THE ARAB SPRING UPRISINGS

A few key questions regarding the relationship between the Sunni community and ISIS deserve scrutiny: Why did ordinary Sunnis welcome ISIS's return after a majority had revolted against the parent organization a few years earlier? What were the social and political factors that provided ISIS with a new lease on life? How did an underground network besieged and on the defensive manage against great odds to dominate a third of Iraq and almost half of Syria's territory so quickly? How did it succeed in blending in with local, poor Sunni Iraqis and Syrians and establish a significant constituency?

There is no doubt that ISIS learned important lessons from its predecessors, carefully avoiding the mistakes of AQI and ISI while building bridges and social networks within the Sunni communities. ISIS, in its new form, relied initially more on co-option and commonalities than on coercion and ideological rigidity. In terms of the hierarchy of explanations, four inter-related variables help explain the spectacular resurgence of ISIS in Iraq. First, the US-backed Sahwa councils left behind a troubled legacy, sowing political rivalries among Sunni leaders in addition to corruption and financial dependence, according to Iraqis and Americans who spearheaded the program.[47] ISI subsequently exploited these rivalries and contradictions within the Sunni community and gradually co-opted disaffected Sunnis to its network.

Second, Baghdadi and his lieutenants could not have succeeded without the catastrophic mistakes of the central government in Baghdad. Prime Minister Maliki provided ISI with a new lease on life by paying lip service to the urgent task of integrating Sunnis into the social and political process and taking the Sahwa councils off the government payroll. ISI's stalled efforts in Iraq were revived by Maliki's half-hearted efforts to pacify rebellious Sunnis and tackle their legitimate grievances.

A third driving force emerged from the large-scale popular Arab uprisings in 2010–2012, which turned violent in Syria and degenerated into all-out civil war. Baghdadi and his lieutenants exploited the breakdown of state institutions in neighboring Syria to expand their social networks among local Sunni communities in the war-torn country and extract precious assets and resources. Syria is as important as Iraq to ISIS because it has given the organization strategic depth and maneuverability, which have proved decisive. ISIS received high returns on its initial investment in Syria and used the gains to surge and expand in Iraq in 2014. Now both Iraq and Syria supply ISIS with social and material sustenance, including young recruits, money, and territory.

A fourth and final factor was ISIS's ability to reconnect with the Sunni rural community by allying, for a time, with local groups and militias. Between 2011 and 2013, the country went through its own waves of protests. Although they started as peaceful demonstrations calling for reforms, the mood soon changed in Sunni areas. As government repression grew, demands turned to the resignation of Maliki and a plethora of organized political and armed groups surfaced, making it harder to distinguish peaceful from violent protesters. By then, ISIS had in its highest ranks former Baathists who had converted to its Salafi-jihadist cause, which made it easier for the group to work with such nationalist factions.

Maliki's divisive policies coincided with the Arab Spring uprisings, whose reverberations reached Iraq and provided ISIS with a greater propensity to grow. On February 12, 2011, dozens of demonstrations were organized in Iraq to protest the government's policies, particularly its widespread corruption and failure to provide basic services. In Baghdad, hundreds of Iraqis gathered in Tahrir Square, chanting "No, no to corruption" and "The government's officials are thieves." On the same day, a thirty-year-old man and father of four set himself on fire in Mosul to protest his unemployment. Despite poor Internet access in Iraq, activists and journalists also used social media such as Facebook to promote the protests. In early February, several Facebook pages were created, mostly along secular and nationalist lines, demanding better public services as well as an end to rising poverty and corruption. One banner on a protest group's page read, "Sunni, Christian, Shiite, Sabean, Yazidi ... all of this is not an identity. ... What is important is my blood is Iraqi."[48] In addition to calling for reforms, Facebook groups such as Baghdad Won't Be Kandahar also criticized government's support of the growth of religious influence, as bars and alcohol consumption in the capital were heavily curtailed.[49]

On February 25, the Day of Rage, the largest antigovernment protest occurred, with tens of thousands of Iraqis gathering in at least twelve demonstrations organized across the country, including the capital, Baghdad. Maliki prevented live media coverage of protests in which at least twenty-three people—including six in Fallujah, six in Mosul, two in Kurdistan, and three in Baghdad—died as a result of security forces opening fire.[50] In Basra, angry crowds forced the resignation of the governor and the entire city council in Fallujah and caused the governor of Mosul, who was also in Fallujah, to flee the city. A week later, despite police brutality, a "second day of rage" was organized.[51] In Baghdad, a crowd of two thousand protesters chanted "Liar, liar, Nuri al-Maliki," "Oil for the people, not for the thieves," and "Yes to democracy and the protection of freedom." In Mosul, three thousand demonstrators gathered while protests were also organized in Basra, Najaf, and Nasiriyah.

In a bid to prevent people from reaching the popular rallies, the government banned vehicles in Baghdad and other key cities. The intensity of the protests resulted in the resignation of three southern provincial governors and the mayor of Baghdad. After two weeks of demonstrations, twenty-nine people had been killed, with the government detaining up to three hundred more for their role in the protests, including journalists, poets, TV presenters, and intellectuals.[52] Although few key Shia leaders publicly supported the protests, with most calling for more reforms instead, the highest-profile Shia figure to do so was radical cleric Sadr, who warned Maliki, "Beware of the Arab Spring in Iraq."[53] In the face of popular discontent, Maliki promised a 50 percent cut of his own salary and gave his cabinet one hundred days to improve its performance and curb corruption or face dismissal. He also called for early provincial elections to meet the peoples' demands, but these did not take place until April 2013.

By 2012, the relationship between the Iraqi government and the Sunni community had not improved. Iraqis in general were angry at the failure of Maliki's regime to deliver on its promises, and the repression of the protests did not help foster a better relationship. Sunnis were also angry because of their political marginalization by both the government and the ineptitude of the Sunni political parties. At the same time, protests against the extension of the mandate of US troops in Iraq were held in cities including Mosul, where tribesmen from Ramadi, Fallujah, Najaf, and Kirkuk had traveled to support the protests.[54] In the same year, the government stepped up the execution of prisoners, killing 129 people, with human rights organizations highlighting the use of torture to force "confessions" and the lack of transparency of most death row trials.[55] The executions were criticized by the United Nations High Commission for Human Rights, with High Commissioner Navi Pillay demanding in January an immediate moratorium on the death penalty after the government carried out thirty-four executions on terrorism-related charges in one day.[56] A report by Human Rights Watch also criticized the targeting of women by the security forces; many of them were arrested because of the alleged activities of their male relatives, imprisoned, tortured, beaten, and raped.[57]

The increasing anger over the government's treatment of prisoners, especially women, within the Sunni community coincided with ISIS's operation called "Breaking Down the Walls." ISIS launched the campaign in July 2012 with a two-pronged goal: to secure the release of prisoners and to recapture territories lost in the past few years. Although Baghdadi claimed that the aim of Breaking Down the Walls was to supply the group with skilled combatants, he targeted an issue that resonated with Sunnis and was very close to their hearts. In December 2012, tensions increased following a government raid on Rafi al-Issawi, then finance minister, along with the arrest of twelve of his bodyguards, which led to more protests being organized, initially in Fallujah. While previous protests had called for better delivery of public services, this time protesters demanded the resignation of Maliki. In fact, December 2012 marked a turning point in the protests: the first wave was articulated along nationalist lines, while the second wave focused on what the Sunnis saw as the regime's deepening sectarianism.

Maliki's support of Bashar al-Assad in the unfolding civil war in Syria poured gasoline on a raging fire in Iraq and intensified Sunni misgivings and fears. Soon protests extended to Ramadi, the Anbar province, the cities of Samarra and Mosul, and neighborhoods in Baghdad. On December 30, Deputy Prime Minister Mutlak traveled to Ramadi in an attempt to engage with the protesters, but he was attacked by the crowds. By January, protests were also organized in Salah al-din and Diyala provinces. As antigovernment protests grew in intensity in Sunni-populated areas, pro-government protests were organized in southern Shia cities, thus widening communal rifts between the two communities. In the next few months, the protest movements escalated on both sides. With sectarian tensions reignited, violence spiraled out of control with bombings carried out by both Sunni and Shia groups. As Sunni-Shia hostilities intensified, ISIS's Breaking Down the Walls operation took an increasingly sectarian tone, with the group stepping up attacks against Shia civilians in a bid to trigger all-out war.

By 2013, levels of violence in Iraq mirrored the height of turmoil in 2008. In one year, ISIS took responsibility for twenty waves of devastating attacks and eight major prison breaks, which culminated with the attack on the Abu Ghraib prison in July 2013. Initially, ISIS focused on its former strongholds in northern Iraq, but soon it directed its attacks increasingly against Shia-dominated areas. By then the organization managed to gain control of territories close to the Iraqi border with

Syria, which provided an opening for its fighters in Anbar and Nineveh provinces to smuggle men and material between the two neighboring countries.

In a nutshell, protests, repression, and increasing chaos fueled the regeneration and return of previously weakened armed groups, including ISIS and nationalists of the Baathist variety. In summer 2013, tribal leaders, who had been sidelined and marginalized by the government despite their role in the Sahwa and Sons of Iraq, formed al-Majlis al-Askari al-Amm li-Thuwar al-Iraq (General Military Council for Iraqi Revolutionaries, or GMCIR); their affiliated tribal militias were organized as al-Majlis al-Askari li-Thuwar al-Asha'ir al-Iraq (Military Council of Iraqi Tribal Revolutionaries). The group formally announced its existence in January 2014, saying that it had operated in Al Anbar, Fallujah, Mosul, Salah al-din, Ta'ameem, Baghdad, Abu Ghraib, Diyala, and Dhuluiya. It described itself as a nationalist and nonsectarian movement aimed at overthrowing the Maliki regime. In addition to calling on all Iraqis to support its cause, the communiqué especially urged the Shia tribes in the south to join the movement.[58] According to GMCIR, most of its members are Sunni Arabs who come from the Sahwa or Sons of Iraq or are former Baathist officers. The group claims that protesters began to join its ranks following a government raid and the subsequent arrest of Anbari MP Abu Ahmad al-Alwani in his home in Ramadi in December 2013, in which eighteen people were killed.[59] Other sources also link the rise of ISIS in the area to this particular event.[60] Alwani had supported the protests in Anbar, which had angered the government. Maliki's decision to target Alwani provoked Sunnis in Anbar and triggered social and political chaos. Despite claiming to be aligned along secularist-nationalist lines, GMCIR also works with sociopolitical movements such as Hay'at al-Ulama al-Muslimeen (Association of Muslim Scholars) and Islamist factions such as the Islamic Army and Jayish Rijal al-Tariq al-Naqshabandi, a group led by Izzat Ibrahim al-Douri. Douri was one of Hussein's right-hand men, occupying the key positions of vice president and deputy chairman of the Iraqi Revolutionary Command Council.

From the 1980s onward, JRTN functioned as a patronage network, ensuring its members' loyalty to the regime. It included wealthy Iraqis and military families, and its membership doubled in the 1990s as a result of the Islamization campaign launched by the Iraqi government after the Second Gulf War. Although the group officially describes itself as a Sufi order, it aimed at accumulating power and influence. It kept a low public profile during the first years of the US-led occupation of Iraq and did not formally declare its armed resistance until 2006, following the hanging of Hussein. Made up mainly of former Republican Guard soldiers and military and police officers, the group's main goal is to overthrow the Iraqi government and abolish the constitution. By 2013, JRTN had re-emerged stronger than before amid continued violence, with Douri openly supporting the protests.[61] When protesters refused to go away, a massacre took place in April 2013, when fifty-three people were killed by the security services in Hawija, near Kirkuk, which only further strengthened the armed rebellion against the Maliki government.[62]

By 2013, it had become increasingly difficult to understand who was leading the protests as civilians and armed groups mixed together while security forces were trying to clamp down on dissidents and insurgents. ISIS tapped into this spiraling conflict and proclaimed its backing of Sunnis, a clever move that allowed it to blend in with the local community. Now strengthened by its success in Syria, the group orchestrated its consolidation in Iraq. Embittered by the government's exclusionary policies and disillusioned with mainstream political parties, Sunnis bolstered ISIS's infiltration and penetration efforts in the community. What further strengthened ISIS's advance was its collaboration with armed nationalist-Baathist groups such as GMCIR and JRTN, which both had strong support bases in rural areas to which ISIS had been expelled during the Sahwa counterinsurgency.

Moreover, as political economist Kamil Mahdi noted, it is clear from looking at Iraqi government reports on rural areas that AQI's strong social base included Anbar, Diyala, Salah al-din, and Nineveh; these are highly rural in comparison to most of Iraq, and their populations feel disenfranchised and disillusioned by a worsening socioeconomic and political situation. By 2012, the total rural population of those provinces was 50.7 percent, towering above the average total rural population in Iraq, 31.7 percent. Nineveh's rural population was particularly high at 40 percent, even though it includes Mosul, Iraq's second largest city.[63] According to the World Bank, Nineveh witnessed a sharp increase in poverty as levels rose to 32 percent in 2012 from 20 percent in 2007, although by 2012 most of the country's poorest provinces were still in the south, where the Shia live.[64] In addition, the total population of Iraqis living on less than $1.25 a day in the province had increased to 18 percent, meaning that more and more people were pushed to the margins, with little hope for improvement, a fertile environment for social conflict.

In 2013, these rural areas, including Nineveh, still constituted the strongest base of support for radical Islamist factions, which likely used land disputes to mobilize support for their land grabs. In the north of the country, for example, a fight over the territorial boundaries of the Kurdistan region and control of the country's hydrocarbons has raged for years among Sunni Arabs, Kurdish authorities, and the Baghdad government. While the 2004 Transitional Administrative Law (TAL) and the 2005 constitution define the territories of the Kurdistan Regional Government (KRG) as including the Dohuk, Irbil, and Sulimaniya governorates, parts of the Kirkuk, Diyala, and Nineveh governorates were considered disputed territories and subject to a mechanism under Article 140 of the constitution that would allow for settling the issue of the disputed territories. Nevertheless, the array of ethno-sectarian groups in these territories enabled the Kurds to have a significant presence, with reports pointing out that the KRG had moved Kurdish civilians and Peshmerga forces into these areas to improve its demographic and strategic advantage over other communities. These areas in Kirkuk, Salah al-din, Diyala, and northern Mosul have a significant Sunni Arab presence, from which ISIS and other Islamist factions field supporters. An interesting fact is that by 2013, ISIS, JRTN, and GMCIR all had power bases in Mosul and Salah al-din, in addition to those in Anbar. As political, territorial, sectarian, and religious tensions intensified, the government's inability to forge a common identity stood in stark contrast to the clearly defined ideologies of Salafi-jihadists, Baathists, and nationalists and the backing and solidarity within their community. Despite the ideological gulf separating the three groups, they worked together to defeat the security forces. Mosul is a case in point. Although the swift collapse of the security forces before the advancing ISIS units in Mosul in summer 2014 might be attributed to poor morale, insufficient training, lack of leadership and corruption, other factors were at play.[65] For example, the Nineveh operational commander, Lieutenant General Mahdi Gharawi, was a close ally of Maliki and had been a member of Hussein's Republican Guard. Gharawi was well known for his brutality, killings, and repeated use of torture, and he had allegedly sold Sunni prisoners to Shia militias. The United States had even tried to have him removed from his position as army commander and have him arrested for running his police brigades as a front for a Shia militia that was allegedly responsible for the murder of hundreds of Sunnis.[66] Maliki resisted the US effort, denying that Gharawi had committed crimes, and after some time he reinstated Gharawi to his post. Gharawi and his thugs had alienated the local population, using excessive force, carrying out arbitrary arrests, and killing and mistreating detainees.[67] A report by Human Rights Watch in 2013 accused Gharawi and his associates of killing five men, including a fifteen-year-old boy, during a raid in Mosul.[68] Local residents insisted that the victims were innocent, and the police offered no credible explanation for the five deaths. With the security forces out of control, the local population threw its lot in with armed groups, including ISIS. ISIS's planners played their cards right by collaborating with Baathist-nationalist armed groups that had a stronger position in Mosul than their own.[69] When Mosul fell, the Baathist presence displayed itself in the streets with photos of Hussein and Douri gracing the walls of buildings. That presence would prove to be short-lived, however. Soon after the capture of the city, ISIS quickly arrested and killed many of its former Baathist and nationalist allies. Mosul was purged not only of "deviant" Baathists but also of its cosmopolitanism and cultural diversity. The new caliph, Baghdadi, delivered his first sermon in Mosul, calling on Muslims everywhere to swear fealty to his authority and migrate to the lands of the caliphate in Iraq and Syria, portraying migration as all but a religious duty.

BAGHDADI'S EVOLUTION:
FROM INVISIBLE TO INFAMOUS

With the understanding that personalities are pivotal in jihadist groups, observers and media have searched for a villain, a hero, a sole architect, or another shadowy figure that could help explain the strategic maneuvering responsible for ISIS's spectacular surge in the summer of 2014. The premium put on absolute loyalty (*sam wa a-ta'a*) to the emir or leader helps to explain why there is so much media emphasis on trying to understand the psyche of a single individual. Seen as the custodian of the faith and the protector of the organization, the emir is invested with the authority of religious legitimation and members swear baiya to him, a binding duty. The call for obedience and the obligation of loyalty were professed as universal Islamic values, and in Baghdadi's first appearance in July 2014, he gave the order to Muslims, "Obey me."[1] By the force of a magnetic personality, a charismatic leader, such as Abdullah Azzam, Osama bin Laden, or Abu Musab al-Zarqawi, exercises considerable influence over adherents and draws new recruits to the cause. Time and again the emir sends fighters to their death, including in suicide bombings, if he sees fit. In a hierarchical, top-down movement, leadership matters greatly.

Nevertheless, the story of ISIS is bigger and more complex than that of a shadowy leader like Abu Bakr al-Baghdadi or Haji Bakr. Baghdadi's rise to power in May 2010 coincided with a highly polarized political and ideological situation in Iraq, where the central government's policies had marginalized the Sunni community further. At the time, more and more Sunnis had begun to view Prime Minister Nuri al-Maliki's sectarian-based policies as the result of a greater Iranian influence. This increasingly hostile perception among Sunnis of Maliki's government allowed Baghdadi and his inner circle to reinvigorate the weakened jihadist group and position it as the vanguard of the Sunnis against the Shia-based regime in Baghdad. Baghdadi's leadership of the Salafi-jihadist movement in Iraq, however, led to shifts in the organization's modus operandi on various levels.

The real name of Baghdadi is Ibrahim ibn Awwad Ibrahim Ali al-Badri al-Samarrai, and he is sometimes referred to as Abu Awwad or Abu Dua—Dua being the name of his eldest daughter. Baghdadi is a nom de guerre. Not much is known about Baghdadi before he assumed leadership of ISI, and it is difficult to disentangle myth from reality. Born in Samarra in the Sunni Triangle north of Baghdad in 1971, Baghdadi was raised in al-Jibriya district, a lower-middle-class neighborhood and a religiously conservative part of Iraq, dominated by the Albu Badri and Albu Baz tribes. Like the neighborhood in which he lived, Baghdadi's family was lower middle class. He went to a local school and liked sports, mainly soccer, which he played in a field near his home. "He would rarely get upset during a match, even if you crashed into him or misbehaved with him," recalls a former neighbor, Tareeq Hameed.[2] Contemporaries of Baghdadi point out that the young man was typical of his social class—religiously pious, devoted, and aloof. We are told that Baghdadi was nicknamed "The Believer," an endearing term designed to show his piety at an early age and unwavering commitment to a strict interpretation of the Islamic doctrine. This testimony must be balanced against the fact that the Iraq of the 1970s and 1980s was a relatively secular country; religious piety was not synonymous with conservative Salafism or radicalism, and, even though ISIS's propagandists and sympathizers impose the present on the past and portray Baghdadi as having been a fundamentalist since a young age, this is a doubtful proposition. It behooves us to be cautious about buying into the branding of Baghdadi as a God-fearing "Believer" who has battled the enemies of authentic Islam from childhood to manhood.

There is, nevertheless, a consensus among people who knew Baghdadi that the US-led invasion of Iraq in 2003 was a turning point in his radicalization. This was also a turning point for thousands of Sunnis who suspected the United States of offering Iraq on a silver platter to the Shia and their regional sectarian patron, Iran, consequently disinheriting the Sunni Arabs. Many individuals who held this belief, especially those of Baghdadi's social stratus, took up arms against the US-led occupation and increasingly against the Shia, who were seen as collaborators and traitors. By the time the US-led occupation had begun, Baghdadi, who was in his twenties, had already moved to Baghdad to study and lived in the Adhamiya district in a room attached to a small local mosque. The mosque was located in the poor, ramshackle neighborhood of al-Tobchi. It sat on the Western fringes of the capital and was inhabited by both Sunni and Shia Muslim residents. Acquaintances of Baghdadi from this period say that he played football with a team formed by the mosque.[3] Additionally, he concentrated on his studies of *tajweed*, the rules of recitation of the holy book, largely focusing on aesthetics rather than practicalities.

Though there is some dispute about his education, Baghdadi reportedly earned an undergraduate degree and eventually his PhD in Islamic jurisprudence at Saddam University for Islamic Sciences, whose name changed after 2003 to the Islamic University of Baghdad. After the US-led invasion Baghdadi helped found an insurgent group called Jamaat Jaish Ahl al-Sunnah wal Jamaa. This group was one of dozens that sprouted from a broad Sunni revolt. For Baghdadi, the move toward insurgency could be linked to the heavy bombing by the US coalition in 2004 of Baghdadi's birthplace, Samarra, a strategic attempt by the Western coalition to root out Sunni dissidents. At this early stage Baghdadi was not part of Zarqawi's Al Qaeda network, and the US security forces labeled him a Sunni "foot soldier" in their roundup of suspected militants in February 2004. After capturing Baghdadi, the US authorities detained him in Camp Bucca. The Pentagon says that Baghdadi, after being arrested in Fallujah in early 2004, was released that December with a large group of other prisoners deemed to be low-level threats. Other accounts estimate that Baghdadi spent one to five years in Bucca.[4] His status was that of a "civilian internee," implying that he belonged to a militant group but had not been caught actively engaged in hostilities. In either case, the exact dates of his detention and release are unclear.[5]

THE MAKING OF A SUPER TAKFIRI

If the US-led invasion of Iraq was a turning point in Baghdadi's drift toward radicalization, his incarceration in Camp Bucca was a watershed moment. Abdel-Bari Atwan, a veteran writer on Islamism, interviewed another prisoner who had been incarcerated with Baghdadi in Camp Bucca in 2004 for his 2015 book *Al-Dawla al-Islamiyya*. This unidentified co-prisoner said that Baghdadi's experience in Bucca had been imbued with feelings of "revenge." Upon his release, Baghdadi approached his American guard to speak these words: "We will find you ... anytime and anywhere ... here or New York."[6] Sunni radicals who knew Baghdadi before and after his detention state that he became "more extreme" after his release, joining Zarqawi's Islamic State of Iraq in 2006.[7] Camp Bucca turned out to be a godsend for this Sunni "foot soldier" because it advanced his jihadist career and introduced him to the big leagues, a who's who in the armed insurgency. Many of the jihadist commanders spent time in this US-run prison, providing them with access to like-minded individuals and the opportunity to expand their networks. In the case of Baghdadi, one of his contacts at Camp Bucca, Abu Mohammed al-Adnani, is ISIS's current chief propagandist, its official spokesman, and a close confidante of Baghdadi.[8]

Reinforcing this argument, former detainees compare Camp Bucca to an "Al Qaeda school," an institution that produced jihadists in a factory-like environment. Camp Bucca housed about twenty-four thousand men, many of whom were Baathist officers and nationalist fighters who worked for Saddam Hussein's regime.[9] At Camp Bucca they sat at the feet of Salafi-jihadists, who mentored them and converted them en masse to their Islamist ideology. A common denominator among many former Baathist officers who joined AQI and, later, ISI was that they had been incarcerated at Camp Bucca, Camp Cropper, or the notorious and ill-fated Abu Ghraib prison on the capital's western outskirts. In a very real sense, ISIS's command-and-control tier emerged with "made-in-US-run prisons" tags. While the prisoners did network with one another, however, their radicalization runs deeper and has much to do with their individual experiences at the hands of security forces that often employed torture. Stories regarding torture and abuse are not limited in scope, nor are they hearsay. The stories from Abu Ghraib, accompanied by photographic and video evidence, particularly come to mind. Such experiences had a radicalizing and transformative effect on detainees, who were not members of Al Qaeda in Iraq and did not believe in its Salafi-jihadist ideology. By the time they left prison, many had become hardliners and subsequently joined AQI and other militant factions. According to the Iraqi government, seventeen of the twenty-five most important ISIS leaders running the war in Iraq and Syria spent time in US-run detention facilities between 2004 and 2011.[10] In an interview, a prisoner called Adel Jassem Mohammed said that a friend who spent only two weeks in Bucca, which closed down in September 2008, recruited twenty-five out of the thirty-four inmates who were there. This fact reveals that Camp Bucca, together with other US detention centers, was an incubator of Islamist radicalization and a recruitment center for jihadists.[11] It was during this period of detention that "Baghdadi had realised that life is meaningless without killing."[12]

Camp Bucca provided the environment necessary to transform Baghdadi from an unknown, low-level "foot soldier" into an ambitious leader and a member of a larger social network of Sunni militants. According to an early mentor of Baghdadi who became a senior military commander as well, Camp Bucca brought about a radical change in Baghdadi's conduct. Abu Abdullah Mohamed al-Mansour al-Issawi, the leader of Jayish al-Mujahideen, lamented that Baghdadi "was turned upside down, a transformed man" after he left Bucca.[13] Similarly, an ISIS operator who uses the nom de guerre Abu Ahmed and who met Baghdadi at Camp Bucca told the *Guardian*, a UK newspaper, that Baghdadi honed his negotiation skills at the US-run prison. He impressed his American jailers, who saw him as a "fixer," a man who could solve fractious disputes between rival factions and keep the camp quiet. "But as time went on, every time there was a problem in the camp, he was at the centre of it," Abu Ahmed told the *Guardian*. "He wanted to be the head of the prison—and when I look back now, he was using a policy of divide and conquer to get what he wanted, which was status. And it worked," he added.[14]

Nevertheless, Baghdadi's meteoric rise to power was a surprise even to the leaders of Al Qaeda Central, a fact that displays the extent to which they were out of touch with developments on the ground in Iraq and the internal dynamics within ISI. According to a personal testament by Zawahiri, when news reached bin Laden of Baghdadi's selection as emir of ISI in 2010, Al Qaeda's leader did not know the man and requested information on Baghdadi's background and experience. Bin Laden was told by senior commanders in Iraq that Baghdadi was a temporary choice because the security situation did not permit the leadership to meet and choose a new permanent emir.[15] The point of Zawahiri's personal testament is that Baghdadi had not displayed outstanding leadership qualities and was an unknown personality in Salafi-jihadist circles before he inherited the bloody torch of Zarqawi, the founder of Al Qaeda in Iraq.

BAGHDADI'S CONTESTED BIOGRAPHY

In contrast to ISIS's ideologues, contemporaries of Baghdadi draw a dramatically different portrait of him as a run-of-the-mill militant who did not distinguish himself either in religious learning or on the battlefield. Echoed by Zawahiri, Baghdadi's contemporaries trace how he went from being a shy, unimpressive, and humble student of religion to an infamously self-anointed caliphate and reputed heir to Osama bin Laden. According to Issawi, a mentor to both Zarqawi and Baghdadi, there was nothing unique or exceptional about Baghdadi. Issawi recalls that Zarqawi stayed at his home for a long time, supposedly in 2004–2005, and Baghdadi was a familiar face. The picture that Issawi draws of Baghdadi is of an ordinary combatant who managed to climb the jihadist ladder through ambition, luck, and favorable circumstances. Issawi recalls Baghdadi taking theology lessons with him, along with a number of people, in 2003 and 2004: "Classes ended [in 2005] because I was detained [by the Americans]. I know him quite well. He has limited intelligence with no leadership skills."[16] Issawi concludes that Baghdadi was a "mediocrity," a severe indictment by a radical Islamist scholar at whose feet Baghdadi sat.[17] Rif'aat Said Ahmed, a specialist on Islamist groups, drew a similar conclusion, stating that Baghdadi "was mediocre in his Islamic studies."[18] It is also worth citing the testimony of the commander of the Islamic Army, Ahmed al-Dabash, another of Baghdadi's contemporaries, who provides a description of his early years prior to joining the jihadist movement: "I was with Baghdadi at the Islamic University. We studied the same course, but he wasn't a friend. He was quiet, and retiring. He spent time alone."[19] Later, when Dabash helped found the Islamic Army in 2003, he fought alongside insurgent leaders, including those who would later establish Al Qaeda in Iraq, but he said Baghdadi was not one of them: "I used to know all the leaders [of the resistance] personally. Zarqawi [the former leader of Al Qaeda] was closer than a brother to me. But I didn't know Baghdadi. He was insignificant. He used to lead prayer in a mosque near my area. No one really noticed him."[20]

Baghdadi appears to have been a talented insurgent who climbed on the shoulders of the Islamic State of Iraq after he joined the network in 2006. He lacked the charisma of bin Laden, the academic flair of Zawahiri, and the fierceness of Zarqawi. However, Baghdadi made up for these shortcomings by earning the trust of the top echelons of ISI, particularly his immediate predecessor, Abu Omar al-Baghdadi, who replaced Zarqawi in 2006. Abu Bakr al-Baghdadi became the "closest aide" to Abu Omar al-Baghdadi, according to an insider's account.[21] Baptized by blood and fire, Baghdadi was a fast learner and a survivor, rising from the bottom and making his way to the top in just a few short years, an impressive feat. Again, adding to the complexity of Baghdadi's story, some of his acquaintances argued that it is his "charisma" that was of importance. One of the inmates of Camp Bucca said, "If you sat in the same room and listened to him as I had done, you would find it hard not to be affected by his personality, ideas, and beliefs."[22] Indeed, this inmate likened Baghdadi to bin Laden, whom he had been in close contact with before. "He was calm, self-composed, with a usual smile on his face that reveals comfort," said this inmate, who spent two years in the camp with Baghdadi.[23] Indeed, others, including security analyst Hisham al-Hashimi, allegedly repeated this comparison between Baghdadi and bin Laden; in his book, Hashimi notes that Baghdadi was "imitating even his speeches and his quotes. He was adopting bin Laden's discourse in a copy paste manner."[24]

When his predecessor, Abu Omar al-Baghdadi, was killed in 2010 by a joint US-Iraqi military operation, Abu Bakr al-Baghdadi was put in charge. There are conflicting accounts of why Baghdadi was chosen as the leader of ISI. As mentioned above, credible evidence indicates that he was an insider candidate, a close confidant of Abu Omar al-Baghdadi, a safe bet for an organization teetering on the brink of collapse. By 2010 ISI faced a severe crisis—it was besieged internally by organized Sunni tribal resistance and externally by punishing attacks by US and Iraqi forces. The Syrian supply of foreign fighters also dried up by 2010. In this sense, Baghdadi's ascendancy to the top post did not signal a dramatic change in ISI's predicament. Survival was the name of the game for ISI in 2010, though its commanders never lost sight of their strategic goal: to dominate the Sunni areas of Iraq and to consolidate and transform their fragile existence into an Islamic state.

The few existing testimonies regarding Baghdadi by fellow radical insurgents draw contradictory sketches of the man. They range from portraits of a ruthless psychopath who created a reign of terror in Iraq to ones of a hero who singlehandedly resurrected the caliphate. Each is a black-and-white picture with no blurred or shaded edges. Despite the metaphorical mountain of paint and ink used, there exists no clear portrait of Baghdadi and no clarity about his past. On one hand, his cohorts depict him as a clerical-warrior-king who will deliver salvation and free the umma of political oppression and darkness. In further justification of Baghdadi's reign, his followers claim that he has a doctorate from the Islamic University of Baghdad, with a focus on Islamic culture, history, shariah, and jurisprudence. Baghdadi's supporters use this to portray him as a man of letters, someone who is theologically learned and amply qualified to be a caliph. For example, in announcing the establishment of the Islamic State and crowning Baghdadi as a caliph in June 2014, ISIS's chief propagandist and official spokesperson, Adnani, calls him "the sheikh, the mujahid, the scholar who practices what he preaches, the worshipper, the leader, the warrior, the reviver, descendant from the family of the Prophet."[25] Baghdadi has been actively seeking to establish this image and align himself with the caliphs of the early days of

Islam, for example by wearing clothing similar to the frocks donned by them.

Adnani is part of a propagandist circle that sought to shape public perceptions of the caliphate by portraying Baghdadi as a superhero, a savior of the Sunnis, and a descendant of the Prophet's family. He called on Muslims worldwide to pledge allegiance to Baghdadi. Additionally, Abi Hamam Abd al-Aziz Al-Athari, an ISIS propagandist, penned a manifesto with a similar title in which he heaped praise on Baghdadi, portraying him as a superhuman. ISIS's associates have distributed several pamphlets that invest Baghdadi with heroic and mystical qualities and even compare his state to the original state established by the Prophet in seventh-century Arabia, a claim treated with derision and contempt by Islamist rivals who had closely known him. Another key assertion made by ISIS's advocates is that Baghdadi has succeeded in expanding his authority to both Iraq and Syria and now "sits on the caliphate chair," while other jihadists have failed to do so. ISIS's advocates would argue that the re-creation of the caliphate and Baghdadi's accession to the position show not only that the position is rightfully his, but that there is legitimacy to his position. This is a constant theme in the ISIS lore designed to invest his leadership with religious legitimation, and Baghdadi's followers have gone so far as to attempt to trace Baghdadi's family lineage to the Prophet.[26] This claim is also disputed by authoritative Iraqi sources who keep a record of tribal and familial lineages. According to an independent guild that traces Hashemite lineage, the Albu Badri and Albu Baz tribes from which Baghdadi originates are not descendant from or related to the Prophet's family.[27] However, the arguments that seek to justify and legitimize Baghdadi's position are purely based on power calculations.

BAGHDADI'S STRATEGY OF MYSTERY

As has become apparent to the reader by now, almost every personal detail about Baghdadi is disputed. He is both controversial and shadowy, with his followers actively attempting to shape the public image of the man. There exists only a foggy sketch of Baghdadi, not a clear portrait, and with such abstraction comes a problem of simplification. One thing that his friends and foes agree on is that Baghdadi is more ruthless than his two predecessors, Zarqawi and Abu Omar al-Baghdadi. He is "the most bloodthirsty of all," according to an ISIS operator who has known Baghdadi since his prison days.[28] Issawi echoes this sentiment. He relates that although Baghdadi's predecessors were bloodthirsty, their thirst pales in comparison with that of Baghdadi. "He is a super slaughterer," concludes Issawi.[29] Commanders of insurgent groups who fought with AQI and ISI recall that Baghdadi excommunicated his insurgent rivals at will and said that the fight against Sunni dissidents should take priority over that of the Americans.[30]

ISIS's propagandists have spun Baghdadi's ruthlessness into evidence of his ability to be a caliph, including such descriptions and justifications in the few ISIS manifestos. Adnani, Athari, and others voice contempt for those Islamists who criticize the brutality of ISIS and its literal application of *hudud* (Islamic punishment); they accuse them of weakness and moral corruption for believing in universal standards of human rights. ISIS's propaganda chiefs also voice contempt for proponents of the human rights regime that, in their opinion, subverted authentic Islam and softened its defenses against decadent Western influences. Following on this notion of the increasing penetration of Western cultural influence, the ISIS narrative is pregnant with an assumption that links Islam's retreat and decline to the absence of a powerful caliphate as well as its abandonment of jihad, a sacred duty that is critical to realizing an Islamic state. Baghdadi's greatness as a decision maker lies in his enforcement of Islamic rules and his restoration of Islam's power and glory. ISIS's pamphlets and statements often remind Muslims that Baghdadi's calls to violent jihad must be heeded as the only means to arrest cultural decline and restore the Islamic golden age.

Obsessed with hard, physical power, ISIS's ideologues are crude realists who do great injustice to Islam's ethical tradition by reducing its essence to war making and acts of extreme brutality. According to Baghdadi and his cohorts, the Islamic revival is contingent on rekindling a fervor for jihad in the hearts and minds of Muslims and building an ideological army willing and ready to battle the enemies of Islam near and then far. Baghdadi, together with his propagandists, often cites verses from Qur'anic scriptures to remind Muslims that violent jihad is an obligation, not a free choice. Pledging to enforce God's laws on earth in the areas under their control, they prioritize violent jihad over all other sacred duties. In his audio statement in May 2014, Baghdadi turned the traditional narrative on its head by indirectly mocking opponents who criticize ISIS's cruelty as un-Islamic: "O Muslims, Islam was never for a day the religion of peace. Islam is the religion of war. Your Prophet . . . dispatched with the sword."[31]

In ISIS's worldview, the caliphate and the sword have always been linked together in an offensive strategy as a means to make Islam reign supreme. Baghdadi and cohorts have made it clear that jihad, as perpetual war or the institution of war, is offensive, not defensive, thus requiring permanent mobilization. In the few public statements that Baghdadi has given, he lends his voice to his definition of jihad as constant warfare, a definition that dates back to the early expansionist days of Islam. Although ISIS has limited military capability, Baghdadi says he will not stop fighting until he reaches Rome.[32] The underlying assertion is that jihad cannot be neglected or suspended until Muslims and others convert to ISIS's millenarian vision of Islam, thus pursuing a strategy of continuous conflict.

In the marketplace of ideas, ISIS offers an alternative narrative that defines the struggle with the *other* (Muslim and non-Muslim, especially Shia Muslims). They have defined this struggle in ideational religious terms, which has challenged the foundation of modern Islamic thought and dominant political discourse. The organization rejects the concept of peaceful coexistence and the nation-state as well as the norms and rules that underpin international society. More importantly, ISIS's rejection of the status quo allows it to claim that it is standing on higher moral ground than its arch enemies—both Arab regimes and rival jihadist groups. However, this is only true for as long as it continues to control territory and people. Its defiance and ritualized violence provides inspiration to many radicals who deserted Zawahiri's Al Qaeda and declared allegiance to Baghdadi. Armed with this revolutionary grand vision, ISIS's ideologues invest Baghdadi's cruelty with a divine purpose, which is to make Islam reign supreme on the global stage. In contrast, ISIS's ideologues come close to accusing Zawahiri of being a kafir, or infidel, because he did not urge former Egyptian president Mohamed Morsi to apply shariah law immediately after his ascendancy to power in 2012.[33] While ISIS's Islamist rivals are dismissed as traitors and petty warlords, Baghdadi is depicted as a tall leader who follows in the footsteps of the Prophet Mohammed and his four blessed companions.

In contrast, radical Islamist groups like al-Nusra attempt to discredit Baghdadi and delegitimize him by leaking information that links him with the former Baathist regime in Iraq. In such instances, it is argued that Baghdadi is only a front for powerful Baathists who control ISIS from behind the scenes; a network of shadowy former military and police officers that once worked for Hussein chose Baghdadi because he did not threaten their domination of the organization. Such stories are promoted not only by al-Nusra, but also by the apparent whistle-blower on Twitter, @wikibaghdady, who from December 2013 until January 2015 posted more than a thousand tweets in Arabic that collectively shatter the ISIS narrative while seeking to diminish Baghdadi's moral authority (see chapter 5 for more on these tweets). One of the most serious assertions made by @wikibaghdady is that a former Baathist colonel called Haji Samir, aka Haji Bakr, was the driving force behind ISIS until rival Islamists killed him in Aleppo in January 2014; Baghdadi is only a figurehead, contends @wikibaghdady.[34]

In a similar vein, a 2015 report by the German magazine *Der Spiegel* revealed the discovery of documents from Haji Bakr's household after his death. The documents that were found in Aleppo by Syrian rebels purportedly show that former Baathist officers of Hussein's army hijacked ISIS and instituted a Baathist system of control and domination from behind the scenes, though dressing it in religious garb.[35] Advancing a similar line of argument about Baathists' hegemony within ISIS, the writer of the *Der Spiegel* article, Christoph Reuter, published a book in German titled *The Black Power: The "Islamic State" and the Strategies of Terror*. Pointing to the hidden hand of the Baathists behind ISIS, this hypothesis has received widespread global media coverage and is now taken for granted by Western and Arab reporters and writers as well. For example, Haytham Manna, a Syrian activist, wrote a book in which he argued that the former army officers "occupied top positions within ISIS" and "controlled its military apparatus."[36]

The underlying assertion that the Baathists have taken over ISIS helps to explain the viciousness of this group, its military success, and its effective, centralized control of the population. This claim deserves critical scrutiny because it had been propagated by ISIS's Islamist rivals, particularly al-Nusra and top radical ideologues of Al Qaeda Central, including Abu Mohammed al-Maqdisi. While there is a natural temptation to buy this assertion because of its simplification of a complex social reality, offering a neat and elegant explanation, the hypothesis also exaggerates the role of one man: Haji Bakr. Furthermore, it conflates the presence in ISIS of former officers of Hussein's army and police, who joined Al Qaeda in Iraq after the fall of the regime with a Baathist plot to regain power by climbing on ISIS's shoulder. The unearthing of connections between the Baathist military and ISIS can offer a more credible and convincing explanation, one that shows how former Baathists who joined ISIS had already been Islamized and converted to Salafi-jihadism. The conversion from Baathism to Islamism occurred gradually in the midst of the violent social and political turmoil that engulfed Iraq in the 1990s. The ideological transformation intensified after the US-led invasion of the country and the subsequent armed resistance and socialization in US-run prisons.[37] In other words, ISIS converted Baathists en masse to its Salafi-jihadist cause, not the other way around (more on this point in chapter 5). This implies that there is no Baathist plot undermining Baghdadi's authority. Far from it. There is increasing evidence pointing to Baghdadi playing a pivotal role in the recruitment of hundreds of Baathist military and police officers to ISIS, as well as in the restructuring of the group's military wing. Notwithstanding Baghdadi's contested biography, his contemporaries and acquaintances note that his ascension to the helm marked a turning point in the military reorganization of the group. He professionalized the armed apparatus and put skilled officers in charge of strategizing and war planning.

What matters in the end is not Baghdadi's checkered history but that he had the strategic foresight to transform a fragile organization on the brink of collapse into a mini-professional army, an army capable of waging urban and guerrilla warfare as well as conventional warfare. In this sense, Baghdadi has surpassed his two mentors, Osama bin Laden and Abu Musab al-Zarqawi, in strategic cunning, organizational skills, and mobilizational outreach. Regardless of whether Baghdadi lives or dies, his declaration of an Islamic State in the Fertile Crescent has already upended the Arab state system in a fundamental way and brought a realignment of regional and international politics.

5

BAATHISTS AND ISIS JIHADISTS: WHO CONVERTED WHOM?

THE IRAQIZATION OF ISIS

Baghdadi's journey from emir of the Islamic State of Iraq in May 2010 to his anointment as the new caliph of ISIS and the Arabic-Islamic world in June 2014 is a narrative fraught with complexities and even contradictions. These contradictions may account for the "mystery" that surrounds the rise of Baghdadi from an anonymous student of the faith to global stardom as the foremost Salafi-jihadist alive. Despite the lack of a rich and credible narrative on Baghdadi's background, one thing is for certain: he is a product of his environment. Ideologically and temperamentally, Baghdadi represents more continuity than change in relation to his predecessors, Abu Musab al-Zarqawi and Abu Omar al-Baghdadi. ISIS is an extension of Al Qaeda in Iraq and the Islamic State of Iraq and has inherited its worldview and bloody legacy. Like Zarqawi and Abu Omar al-Baghdadi, from the beginning, Abu Bakr al-Baghdadi used excessive violence and brutality against both Shia and Sunni enemies to project an image of ruthlessness and robustness and show the resilience of his group after it had suffered hard blows. His preferred method of attack was to send suicide bombers to mosques, markets, police stations, and pilgrimage sites, where explosions would cause maximum casualties and bring much-needed publicity. A former mentor of Zarqawi and Baghdadi, Abu Abdullah Mohamed al-Mansour al-Issawi, compares them to each other and unequivocally states that Baghdadi is much more extreme than the founder of Al Qaeda in Iraq; Baghdadi has killed many more Sunnis, including likeminded Salafi-jihadists, who opposed his blanket takfiri ideology. From the onset Baghdadi imitated his predecessors and excommunicated ordinary Shias and also those Sunnis who did not convert to his cause, earning the label of a "super-*takfiri*" by a prominent former jihadist.[1] According to Issawi, who is highly regarded by Zarqawi's and Baghdadi's followers, Zarqawi did not go as far as his successor and perpetrate a killing spree, although he acknowledges that Zarqawi was ruthless and theologically misguided. Issawi reserves his harshest criticism for Baghdadi, whose actions, in his estimate, observe no limits. His bloodletting is typical of the early *kawarij* (an extremist sect that excommuniciated Muslims at will), argues Issawi, while, in his opinion, Zarqawi does not fit the bill, even though he was in error.[2] It is worth noting that Issawi's distinction between Zarqawi and Baghdadi is more technical than philosophical. He faults Baghdadi for being more bloodthirsty than his predecessor, though he concedes that the difference was a matter of degree, and states that Zarqawi was as super-takfiri as Baghdadi (liberally excommunicating Muslims). Both possess a similar worldview and stand on the far right of the Salafi-jihadist movement. There is no daylight between Baghdadi and Zarqawi, and the former and his followers revere Zarqawi as the progenitor of ISIS.

Baghdadi followed in the footsteps of his predecessors, and a partial mapping of his attacks in Iraq between 2010 and 2011 shows large-scale operations, all initiated under his "command" and "authority," designed to convince both supporters and detractors that he was faithful to the Zarqawi legacy—that he had what it took to terrorize the kuffar (infidels), which included anyone who disagreed with ISI. Long before Baghdadi gained notoriety as the powerful leader of ISIS in June 2014, he had established a reputation for brutality and viciousness in Iraq by carrying out devastating suicide attacks. Like Zarqawi and Abu Omar al-Baghdadi, his rise to power was drenched in blood, overwhelmingly relying on terror to silence dissent among Sunnis. As emir of ISI, Baghdadi was responsible for masterminding spectacular attacks, such as the suicide bombing at the Umm al-Qura Mosque in Baghdad on August 28, 2011, an attack that killed twenty-eight people, including Khalid al-Fahdawi, a member of the Sunni Iraqi Islamic Party (IIP). According to the Islamic Party, ISI launched a four-week terror campaign against moderate Sunni leaders that killed seven IIP personalities.[3] "Al Qaeda has been distributing a lot of leaflets which say that there is no repentance for IIP members anymore, and killing them is allowed everywhere," said Rasheed al-Azawi, an IIP leader. "They want to silence the moderate voices in order to give the extremists more space inside Sunni areas," he added.[4] Between March and April 2011, ISI claimed more than twenty attacks in south Baghdad alone.

Following the killing of bin Laden on May 2, 2011, Baghdadi released his first written statement, a eulogy to the Al Qaeda leader in which he threatened to avenge his death by carrying out bloodier attacks: "I tell our brothers in Al Qaeda organization and on the top of them Sheikh Mujahid Ayman al-Zawahiri . . . be merry, you have faithful men in the Islamic State of Iraq who are following the right path and will not quit or be forced out. . . . I swear by God, blood for blood and destruction for destruction."[5] On May 5, Baghdadi took responsibility for an attack on police headquarters in Hila, south of the Iraqi capital, that killed twenty-five police officers and wounded seventy-two others.[6] On August 15, a wave of suicide bombings beginning in Mosul claimed by ISI killed seventy people, with the organization pledging on its website to carry out more than one hundred attacks across the country. On December 22, the

organization launched a series of coordinated attacks, including car bombings and IED explosions, in more than a dozen
Baghdad neighborhoods, killing at least 68 people and injuring 185.[7] Four days later ISI claimed responsibility for the attacks and warned that "the series of special invasions [was]
launched ... to support the weak Sunnis in the prisons of the
apostates and to retaliate for the captives who were executed."[8]

Beyond their flamboyant brutality, Baghdadi's operations
clearly showed that despite suffering major setbacks at the
hands of the United States and Iraqi security forces and the
Sunni Sahwa or Awakening, ISI was still capable of carrying
out devastating, simultaneous attacks against multiple targets
throughout Iraq. Far from paralyzed, the organization still had
plenty of willing suicide bombers and a functioning centralized operational infrastructure. This military structure allowed
ISI to survive a relentless onslaught by the US and Iraqi forces
and then ride the shifting political winds inside Iraq and Syria
in 2011 and 2012 and rebuild its ranks. ISI's speedy recovery and
subsequent revival were also enabled by its ideological cohe-
siveness and certainty. Believing in the righteousness of their
cause and ultimate victory, Salafi-jihadists have a different take
on time and do not measure success in months or years but
rather in decades. Loss and suffering are seen as God's will to
test the faith, endurance, and conviction of the mujahideen.
The road to salvation runs through trial, sweat, blood, and pain.
The greater the sacrifice, the greater God's rewards would be.
One of the lessons learned about the Salafi-jihadist movement
over the past few decades is its capacity for self-renewal, regeneration, and the conceptualization of new crusading missions.
From the late 1950s until the present, the Arab regimes, together
with their superpower patrons, had prematurely written the
obituary of the Salafi-jihadist movement. Yet, time and again,
Salafi-jihadists have reinvented themselves under a new banner
and gone on to fight another losing battle. Armed with an absolute, totalitarian ideology, ISI was able to sustain significant
losses between 2006 and 2011 and then rebound, a testament to

the resilience of Salafi-jihadists and a lesson worth bearing in mind. At the height of ISI's crisis in May 2010, when Baghdadi assumed leadership, he and the inner circle did not give up or lose sight of their strategic goal—consolidation of the Islamic State of Iraq. They redoubled their efforts and patiently rebuilt their weakened networks.

Participants in the group and contemporaries of Baghdadi point to two developments that structurally transformed the organization. First, while Arab lieutenants and fighters dominated the senior echelons of Zarqawi's Al Qaeda in Iraq, by 2010 Iraqis had taken over the decision making, and their imprint has been on it ever since. The Iraqization of ISI's network was one of necessity, not choice, prompted by the decrease in foreign recruits, a product of Syria's closing down the jihadist pipeline to Iraq as well as the Sunnis' armed opposition to the presence of foreign fighters in their neighborhood. As a result, ISI turned its focus further inward, thus implicitly distancing itself more from its transitional parent organization—Al Qaeda Central—and becoming more localized, more parochial, and hypersectarian. Although Baghdadi pledged allegiance to bin Laden and AQC after his selection as emir of ISI, he did not commit to bin Laden's fight against the far enemy (the US-led coalition) because his core concern was the near enemy (the Shia and the central authority in Baghdad and those affiliated with it). Zarqawi and Baghdadi belong to the same generation and hold the same worldview, but Baghdadi actively pursued an "Iraq first" track and formalized the separation from Al Qaeda Central. In practice, the Iraqization of ISI meant deepening the sectarian divide in Iraq through the promulgation of increased viciousness as well as the pinning of the group's future on internal developments inside the polarized country, a risk that paid off handsomely. It is worth stressing that the Iraqization of ISI did not usher in an ideological shift. Baghdadi has been faithful to Zarqawi's sectarian legacy of targeting the Shia as the primary enemy and establishing an Islamic state in Iraq as a bridgehead in the Arab heartland. While Baghdadi and his inner council reorganized their network to make it militarily more potent and effective, they have not shed their Salafi-jihadist colors or lost sight of the strategic goal: cleansing the Sunni lands of the Shia and building an Islamic state.

Second, the Iraqization of ISI went hand in hand with a fundamental restructuring of power within the group. The weight of evidence indicates that a significant role was played by former officers of Saddam Hussein's army and police in transforming a mafia-like network into a skilled and professionalized army.[9] The skills and expertise of former military and police officers of Hussein's army were pivotal. It is estimated that 30 percent of senior figures in ISIS's military command are former army and police officers from the disbanded Iraqi security forces. The military expertise contributed by former officers, together with the skills of the veterans of Al Qaeda in Iraq, transformed ISIS into an effective fighting machine, combining urban guerrilla warfare and conventional combat to deadly effect. The organization pierced the defensive lines of the Syrian and Iraqi armies and captured major urban centers and rural provinces, including Mosul in Iraq and al-Raqqa province on the north bank of the Euphrates River, ISIS's current de facto capital.

The question is not whether these former officers have renovated ISIS's military apparatus, but rather the extent of their political influence and control of the network,[10] as well as the durability of their Baathist affiliation. Posting more than a thousand tweets in Arabic from December 2013 to January 2015 by either a disgruntled former member of ISIS or a rival Islamist, the mysterious Twitter account of a whistle-blower (or whistleblowers) going by the name @wikibaghdady asserts that former Baathist officers dominate the decision making within ISIS. The leaker offers some information about the ways and means by which they exercise influence. For example, he asserts that a former colonel who goes by the pseudonym Haji Bakr, together with two officers from Hussein's army, commanded the military council (Shura), the highest executive decision-making equivalent to a cabinet, whose membership is about eight to thirteen people. "All of al-Baghdadi's inner circle is 100 percent Iraqi and he does not accept any other nationality because he does not trust anyone else," @wikibaghdady charges.[11] The leaks provide valuable insights into and details about the internal workings of this shadowy universe that can be corroborated with other sources. However, the whistle-blower makes big, unsubstantiated claims, implying that former Baathist officers of Hussein's army and police have taken over the organization and are reconstructing the late regime. In particular, the claim of an unholy alliance between former Baathists and ISIS jihadists, which is now taken at face value by observers inside and outside the region, must be treated cautiously and skeptically and subjected to critical scrutiny because of its implications for understanding ISIS as a social movement and determining its durability.

A close reading and analysis of the 1,196 tweets indicates that the leaker was privy to deliberation within ISIS from the moment Baghdadi assumed reign in May 2010 until very recently; obviously he decided to spill sensitive secrets after the violent rupture between Baghdadi and Abu Mohammed al-Joulani, the head of Jabhat al-Nusra, at the end of 2013. Although the whistle-blower has provided some information on the organization and makeup of ISIS, he seems to be motivated by a desire to smear Baghdadi's reputation, together with that of his associates, in the eyes of the Islamist base. The leaks are designed to expose the cynicism and impurity of ISIS's top echelon and tie them to the discredited ex-Baathists, unraveling their image and revealing the falsehood of their religious beliefs and their treacherous betrayal of fellow jihadists, particularly members of al-Nusra. The whistle-blower's strategic goal is to shatter ISIS's self-portrait as an Islamic movement whose behavior, objectives, and engines of growth pertain to the genuinely and consciously held belief of its members and leaders that they are working to fulfill the will of Allah on earth. Instead, the leaks depict ISIS as an organization that uses Islamic rhetoric and categories as a veil to obscure the true nature of its top leaders as a kind of Stasi or Gestapo junta, bred in Hussein's architecture of internal terror and committed, energized by personal and sectarian ambitions, to ruling as predatory and ruthless exploiters of resources and populations.

Although attractive and containing elements of truth, this hypothesis is misleading and reductionist, conflating the rebirth of ISIS with the enlistment of ex-Baathist officers in the organization and overlooking internal and external, structural conditions in Iraq and Syria that fueled the group's revival. The hypothesis also takes for granted that these former officers have always been committed Baathists, as if Baathism is a coherent and monolithic ideological frame of reference; that officers in the former Iraqi army were more ideologically oriented than professional; and that ex-Baathist officers have not undergone transformation as a result of recurrent wars that climaxed with the US-led invasion of Iraq and the subsequent dissolution of the army and armed resistance.

Regardless of the motivation of the individual(s) behind the @wikibaghdady Twitter account, and his implicit alignment with Joulani in the intra-jihadist civil war, the leaker reveals strategic information that helps us, together with other sources, to unpack the journey of ISIS and its twists and mutations. In particular, the snippets of information provided by the whistleblower throw further light on the important role that former officers of Hussein's army and police play within ISIS.[12] Although it is difficult to corroborate all the specific details provided by @wikibaghdady, there is increasing evidence that ISIS would not have expanded so swiftly without the military and internal security skills of these professional men, who joined Baghdadi's organization following the second round of the de-Baathification of Iraq in 2010.

Christoph Reuter's article in the German magazine *Der Spiegel* and @wikibaghdady focus overwhelmingly on a former Iraqi army colonel called Haji Samir, aka Haji Bakr (his real name is Samir Abed Hamad al-Obeidi al-Dulaimi), who was killed in a clash with rival Syrian rebels in Aleppo in January 2014. Bakr, one of Baghdadi's closest advisers until his assassination, was reportedly instrumental in Baghdadi's selection as emir. Another former officer in Hussein's military, Adnan Ismail Najm, also known as Osama al-Bilawi but better known by the nom de guerre Abdul Rahman al-Bilawi, was head of ISIS's military council until he was killed by the Iraqi security forces a few days before the fall of Mosul in June 2014. Bilawi was a notable military aide to Baghdadi, who named the operation for the invasion of Mosul after him. While Bakr and Bilawi are discussed at length by Reuter and @wikibaghdady, there are other former officers, notable members of ISIS's military council, who hail from Hussein's ruling Baath Party. For example, Baghdadi appointed two deputies to be second in command, one in Iraq and one in Syria. Fadel al-Hayali (also known as Abu Muslim al-Turkmani and Haji Mutazz) was Baghdadi's deputy in charge of Iraq until he was killed by a US military strike in August 2015. A former special forces officer from the town of Tal Afar, near Mosul, Hayali effectively governed Islamic State territory in Iraq for Baghdadi. Like Hayali in Iraq, Abu Ali al-Anbari, a former major general in the Iraqi army and currently Baghdadi's top military commander and envoy in Syria, directs the group's operations there and oversees its governors, who manage ISIS's finances, weaponry, and legal issues. Another top aide to Baghdadi was Abu Ayman al-Iraqi or Suedawi (also known as Abdul Nasser al-Janabi), a former colonel in air force intelligence and a senior member of the military council who served in both Syria and Iraq until he was killed in late 2014. Baghdadi also relies on other important former officers, such as Waleed Jassem al-Alwani, known by his nom de guerre, Abu Ahmad al-Alwani, a member of the military council who was killed in late 2014; Abdullah Ahmad al-Mishhadani, who is in charge of suicide bombers and guesthouses for foreign fighters; and Abd Nayef al-Jabouri, known by his nom de guerre, Abu Fatima al-Jaheishi, who is in charge of ISIS's operations in the northern city of Kirkuk.[13]

What these former officers have in common is that they were all incarcerated in the US-run prison at Camp Bucca, known as the "Al Qaeda School" by former detainees, where Baghdadi spent time as well. This partial list shows clearly the important role these officers play in ISIS's military council. It also indicates that the US-led coalition has had success in killing Baghdadi's top military aides, though many feign their own deaths in order to evade detection. Nevertheless, given the attrition in ISIS's command and control, it has become more difficult to discern the group's current shadowy leadership structure. This constant bleeding is bound to degrade the group's capacity to go on the offensive or even keep control of its extensive territory in Syria and Iraq in the meantime. Although Baghdadi and his inner circle have been able to restaff the top posts in the military structure, the deaths of these experienced and skilled commanders will ultimately make ISIS more militarily vulnerable and less resilient. Nevertheless, it would be too soon to assert, as some US officials do, that the killing of ISIS's senior operatives by airstrikes has decimated the group's leadership networks.[14] At the time of writing, at the beginning of 2016, the leadership hemorrhage within ISIS has not caused diminishment of its operational potency, though it has stopped the group's march forward.

THE CONSTRUCTION OF IDEOLOGY IN THE QUEST FOR POWER

While there are apparent links between ISIS and former officers of Hussein's Baathist regime, both the whistle-blower and Reuter, along with other writers, go further and claim that these former Baathist officers control the group from behind the scenes and are the real power brokers. Taken for granted by many observers inside and outside the Middle East, the hypothesis propounded by the whistle-blower and Reuter is that ISIS is controlled more by ex-Baathists from Iraq than by Salafi-jihadists of the Al Qaeda variety. As Reuter noted, "IS has little

in common with predecessors like al-Qaida aside from its jihadist label. There is essentially nothing religious in its actions,
its strategic planning, its unscrupulous changing of alliances
and its precisely implemented propaganda narratives. Faith,
even in its most extreme form, is just one of many means to an
end. Islamic State's only constant maxim is the expansion of
power at any price."[15] Similarly, @wikibaghdady claims that
Baghdadi himself was no more than a front man for the Baathist
officers who engineered his rise to power. Before the blood
dried on Baghdadi's predecessor, Abu Omar al-Baghdadi, in
April 2010, the leaker asserts that Bakr met with Baghdadi and
offered him the leadership position on a silver platter. When
Baghdadi expressed fear about the new responsibility, Bakr re-
assured him that he would guarantee his personal security and
the survival of the organization as well. Both Reuter and the
whistle-blower argue further that the Baathists led by Bakr have
taken over the organization. This hypothesis is based on a fal-
lacy in which Iraq is seen as frozen in time and space and the
Baathists are unchanging nationalist ideologues who infiltrated
ISIS and used it as a vehicle to recapture power.

A more complex argument should take into account the effects of the cost of wars, particularly the US-led invasion and occupation of Iraq, on state and society, including elite formation
and worldviews. As a result of these wars, an important segment
of the Sunni and Shiite elite have been radicalized and Islamized,
with some former officers of the disbanded Iraqi army joining
Al Qaeda–affiliated groups. A gradual process of ideological and
identity conversion occurred within both Sunni and Shia communities, fueled particularly by armed resistance to the US occupation since 2003. Al Qaeda in Iraq, together with sectarian
militias, was a direct beneficiary of the sectarianization and fragmentation of Iraqi identity and the fraying of social cohesion.
The former officers of Hussein's army and police who joined
either Al Qaeda in Iraq or Shia militias had already shed their
Baathist colors and fully embraced their new parochial identity.
Therefore, it behooves us to be cautious about seeing a Baathist
takeover bid behind the decision of former Baathist officers to

join ISIS. This could not be further from the truth. Bakr and his associates wage all-out war against the very ideas and symbols that Baathism championed, such as secular local nationalism, Arabism, and the national state. They have little in common with the Baath Party except its totalitarian mind-set and its tools of repression. Far from hijacking ISIS, many Baathists migrated en masse to Islamist groups, including Al Qaeda in Iraq and then ISIS. The founder of AQI, Zarqawi, was suspicious of former Baathist officers and kept them at arm's length. His first successor, Abu Omar al-Baghdadi, who replaced him in 2006, was allegedly an ex-officer of the Iraqi army and opened up the group to former members of the armed forces. The co-option of former officers was a gradual process that began in 2006 and intensified with Abu Bakr al-Baghdadi's selection as emir of AQI in 2010 after the death of Abu Omar al-Baghdadi.

For these former officers, the Baath Party did not provide a satisfying ideological frame of reference or answers to the existential challenges that confronted them after the occupation of their country, the dissolution of their institutions, and the loss of their jobs, rank, and income. Instead, they, together with many aggrieved Sunnis, found ideological solace and an anchor in Islamist references. As the armed resistance against the US-led coalition escalated, former army and police officers split along two differing ideological poles—Islamist and nationalist. On one side, a small group of religiously minded officers joined jihadist insurgents, including Al Qaeda in Iraq. On the other, General Izzat Ibrahim al-Douri, former Iraqi vice president, head of Hussein's Revolutionary Command Council, and one of his few confidants, was pivotal in trying to resurrect the banned Baath Party by bringing thousands of former Iraqi army and police officers and soldiers into the burgeoning Sunni resistance soon after the US-led invasion in 2003. After Hussein's execution in 2007, Douri became the leader of the banned Baath Party and a coalition of insurgent groups known as the Naqsha-bandi Army, a Sufi group of ex-Baathists and their supporters.

This nationalist-Islamist divide among former officers debunks a widespread assertion that former Baathist officers have taken over ISIS. Unlike their nationalist counterparts, who joined Douri's banned Baath Party, the former officers recruited by ISIS had already undergone a gradual conversion to Islamism, a conversion that has substantive meaning and is not mere playacting. Ever since, they have lent ISIS operational and battlefield skills learned in Hussein's architecture of terror, internal security control, and foreign wars. While strengthening the organization's military apparatus, these former officers have not dented its ideological vision or worldview. Baghdadi has been too faithful to Zarqawi, the founder's bloody legacy, and his hypersectarianism, and might have only surpassed him in the use of flamboyant violence, though Zarqawi pioneered many of ISIS's vicious tactics, including beheading. Ideologically, there is little daylight between Al Qaeda in Iraq and ISIS. So far, the influx of former officers into the group has not brought any marked shift in the construction of its Salafi-jihadist identity or its worldview. As discussed previously, it is essential not to confuse the operational and military input of the former officers with any sinister Baathist plot to either hijack ISIS or pull the strings from behind. This would be a simplification, even a distortion, of a complex reality. There is nothing surprising about ISIS's recruitment of skilled military and police officers of Hussein's security services, a strategic decision that allowed it to control a third of Iraq and almost half of Syrian territory. As sociologist Charles Tilly notes, "Even when they organize in opposition to existing governments, specialists in coercion typically adopt forms of organization, external connections and sources of supply resembling those of government-employed specialists."[16] For example, although initially Douri's Baathists and ISIS's jihadists cooperated against the Iraqi security forces, particularly in Mosul, once ISIS consolidated its control of the city, it persecuted the Baathists and forced them to repent or be killed (more on this later).

More importantly, the hypothesis of an unholy Baathist-ISIS union hardly touches on internal and local conditions in Iraq and the social transformation that the country had undergone after Hussein was forced to withdraw his occupying forces from Kuwait following the 1991 Gulf War. The Iraqi invasion of Kuwait in 1990 and the subsequent defeat motivated a sizable segment of the Shia community, who felt marginalized and persecuted, to revolt against the Baghdad regime in 1991, a rebellion that was brutally suppressed but left deep scars on state and society. As discussed in the previous chapter, after 1991 Iraq became increasingly plagued by divisive identity politics and sectarianism along Sunni-Shia lines.[17] The subsequent punishing UN-led sanctions exacted a heavy toll on Iraqis and led to increased religiosity in society. Trying to pacify Sunni and Shia opinion and counterbalance US efforts, Hussein instrumentalized religious references and symbols and announced in 1993 his Faith Campaign, which involved a more socially conservative agenda. Hussein was not a born-again Muslim, however, and his Faith Campaign was merely a propaganda stunt designed to project the image of a pious president. Hussein continued to brutally suppress radical Islamists, showing tolerance only toward his deputy, Douri, who turned into a Salafi and established close relations with Salafi groups.[18]

Long before the US-led invasion and occupation of Iraq, a marked shift to communal identity occurred in a country weighed down by war, social turmoil, and economic sanctions. Religious and other parochial identities began to be asserted alongside Iraqi identity, but not as a replacement for it, except in the case of the Kurds.[19] These shifting forms of identification cemented with the removal of the Baathist regime in Baghdad in 2003, the culmination of a decade-old social trend in which many junior police and army officers shed their nationalist uniforms for more sectarian affiliations. While in the army, some junior officers had had Salafi-Islamist leanings and were under surveillance by Hussein's security forces. When these officers began to show signs that they could pose a threat to the inner workings of the regime, they were either arrested or expelled from the military. For example, people who knew Bakr say he was a Salafi before the fall of Baghdad in 2003, and, soon after, he and like-minded officers joined Al Qaeda in Iraq and other conservative Salafi insurgent groups, holding positions of leadership within these organizations. Like other Sunni families, Bakr's split into Salafi and Baathist wings, a trend that sheds further light on the social transformation that has occurred within the Sunni community from the 1980s until the present. The Sunni Arab identity has been reconstructed due to wars, social turmoil and, ultimately, the destruction of the state in 2003. After the US-led invasion of Iraq and the onset of the armed resistance, more and more Sunnis, including former officers, migrated from Baathism to Salafism and Salafi-jihadism. Iraqi academic Saad Jawad argues that there was no clear indication of deep sectarian divisions in the country before 2003. But after the US-led invasion, social conditions rapidly changed and deteriorated. As the old regime was branded Sunni, Sunnis were marginalized and excluded from the nascent political process. Sectarian-based Shia parties and militias dominated the political space and abused power by flagrantly violating the human rights of Iraqis. The most important factor, in Jawad's estimate, was the dismantling of state institutions, particularly the summary dissolution of the armed forces, without any compensation or regard for nationalist sentiments. In the absence of cross-sectarian civil society organizations, the majority of officers had no alternative but to join their own communities, sowing the seeds of communal polarization and segmentation. As the Iranian-led, -trained, and -protected militias hunted down pilots and army officers, a sectarian divide began to take shape and solidify into what it is today. As was the case with the Baath Party, Shia-led militias and parties are seen to function as a social ladder, providing protection and economic profits for former Shia officers of Hussein's army and police. In contrast, Jawad asserts that, with the exception of hard-core ideologues who have joined Al Qaeda in Iraq and now ISIS, the majority of former Sunni officers regard the group as a powerful instrument to exact revenge against the sectarian-dominated central government in Baghdad and its Iranian patron.[20]

In my conversations with former Iraqi officers, they caution against the generalization and simplification of a complex phenomenon. These officers tell me that a small but important segment of their comrades joined ISIS and other Salafi-jihadist groups because of either ideological conviction or disillusionment with nationalist Baathist ideology. But they hasten to add that the value of former officers who joined ISIS lies more in their talents for command and control, battle plans, organization, intelligence gathering, and internal security than in their ideology and theology. The story is familiar: America's invasion and occupation of Iraq and its swift disbanding of the military turned patriotic and proud army officers to armed resistance and underground subversion. Years of prolonged fighting and incarceration in US-run prisons radicalized some of these officers and led them either to ISIS or to other insurgent groups. Particularly abhorrent to Sunni officers was the fact that they were not only disfranchised but also hunted down by the nascent post-Hussein regime in their homes in the so-called Sunni Triangle. Adding insult to injury, the US-led coalition used Iraqi officers to pursue their former Sunni comrades, a ruinous experience, and authorized the Shia-dominated police to arrest suspects accused of resistance to the occupation. Thousands of Sunnis were arrested by the US-led coalition and many were brutally tortured and humiliated, leaving a bitter legacy that still haunts post-Hussein Iraq.[21] As discussed in chapter 3, Sunnis believed that the Shia-dominated government used and abused de-Baathification to victimize their community and exclude them from decision making and power. Abu Mutlak, a staff lieutenant general under Hussein, is a case in point. He said that he has been reduced to driving a taxi to support his family, and that the bitterness over their treatment drove some former colleagues to fight the US coalition and the Shia-led government in Baghdad. "How do you want me to take part in building a new political system that dismissed me from everything and robbed me of everything?" he asked.[22]

Iraqi sociologist Walid al-Saad notes that after the fall of Baghdad in 2003, a religious tide gradually swept Iraq, including

Baathists who discovered religiosity and piety—not all out of genuine belief, as for some it was simply to protect themselves against the clampdown by post-Hussein authorities: "Many shifted from nationalism and secularism to Salafism and fundamentalism."[23] The migration of these officers from Baathism to Salafism and jihadism is a testimony to the breakdown of Iraq's state institutions and the transformation of the new ruling elite and social classes.[24] If ISIS is a product of the US-led invasion of Iraq, it is not then surprising that scores of officers from Hussein's army joined the jihadist caravan. Hussein's officer corps was a microcosm of Sunni and Shia society in general, which fragmented along communal, ideological, and social lines. As mentioned above, Baathism was less of a coherent ideology than a *hizb al-Sulta*, a ruling party that distributed rewards to stakeholders based on loyalty to the head of the party. In a way, Baathism in Iraq and Syria degenerated into a cult of personality of Hussein and Hafez al-Assad, former Syrian president and father of the current president Bashar, a label devoid of ideological meaning.[25] Therefore, the transition by some former officers of Hussein's army from Baathism to Salafi-jihadism is not that transformative.

Shia members of the security establishment also experienced changes. The majority of the armed forces were young Shia draftees. Following the US-led invasion, they found themselves in a situation that allowed them to either remain part of the newly formed armed forces or join one of the many autonomous Shia militia groups that functioned independently of the post-2003 Iraqi state. Many of them were, in fact, sympathetic to Shia opposition movements, both before and after the 2003 invasion.[26] This included the Sadrist movement, which mobilized Iraq's Shia underclass and gained such prominence during the brutal sanctions era of the 1990s that its founder, Mohammed Mohammed Sadiq al-Sadr, Muqtada al-Sadr's father, was assassinated by the Baath regime.

The extent to which Shia members of the armed forces joined militia groups like the Sadrist movement's Jayish

al-Mahdi (Mahdi Army) or the Badr Brigade—established in
Iran in the 1980s as the armed wing of ISCI—is difficult to ascer-
tain precisely. Although the picture is initially somewhat blurry,
it becomes clearer when some of the realities of the post-2003
security environment are considered. Iraq's armed forces were
reorganized after 2003 in a fundamental way to ensure that its
members were loyal or sympathetic to the post-2003 political
order. There was considerable political pressure to do so, not
least because of the army's role in oppressing and persecuting
Iraq's population, in particular its Kurdish and Shia communities, whose leaders became the most dominant actors after 2003.
Iraq's Shia ruling elite also directly controlled or had influence
over the country's Shia militia groups, just as they dominated
the judiciary and other institutions. In other words, whether or
not Shia members of the armed forces joined militia groups
after 2003 becomes irrelevant. There was and remains considerable overlap between these militias and the Iraqi state.[27] It is a
widely established fact, for example, that Shia members of the
Iraqi army and police force sometimes doubled as militia members, as already alluded to above. The Interior Ministry was run
by a senior member of the Badr Brigade and still is today. The
overlap between these institutions and militias like the Mahdi
Army and Badr Brigade provided a crucial strategic advantage
during the sectarian civil war of 2006.[28] It is, at the same time,
worth pointing out that the nature of the relationship between
the Sadrists and the Shia-controlled and -dominated post-2003
Iraqi army is contentious and at times strained. The Sadrist
movement and the Mahdi Army have traditionally challenged
the power and legitimacy of the Shia establishment that reorganized and controlled the armed forces and that came to dominate the Iraqi state after 2003, having spent decades in exile. At
some points, as has already been noted, the Sadrists fought the
Iraqi army, as well as other militia groups like the Badr Brigade.

These circumstances were not lost on Iraq's Sunni population. The considerable overlap between the security forces and
Shia militia groups not only delegitimized the Iraqi state in

their eyes but significantly helped create an environment conducive to the aims and objectives of Salafi-jihadists and the Sunni armed resistance at large.

As discussed previously, Baghdadi maintained continuity with his two predecessors and their blood-drenched legacy. His ritualized violence is based on their template, though on a bigger scale. As vicious psychopaths, Zarqawi and his two successors, Abu Omar al-Bahdadi and Abu Bakr al-Baghdadi, used violence systematically and strategically to instill fear and terror in their enemies and awe and adoration in the eyes of their followers. There is nothing unique or mysterious about ISIS's savagery, which would be a false measure by which to draw conclusions about the nature and structure of the group.

In this respect, context is important. After the violent confrontation between Jabhat al-Nusra, the official arm of Al Qaeda Central, and ISIS at the end of 2013, each camp tried to discredit the other by claiming it was Baathist. Each has waged a fierce struggle for the soul of the global jihadist movement. Each has aspired to inherit the jihadist torch and depict itself as a theologically pure custodian of the faith while accusing its rival of being morally contaminated and polluted. As discussed above, for more than a year, the mysterious Twitter account of the whistle-blower(s) who goes by the name @wikibaghdady posted more than a thousand tweets claiming that ISIS is led by former Baathist officers and that Baghdadi is just a figurehead. Similarly, Reuter's article in *Der Spiegel* asserts that ISIS is more of a Baathist-like organization than a Salafi-jihadist one.[29] An influential scholar of Salafi-jihadism and a mentor to the late Zarqawi, Abu Mohammed al-Maqdisi, blamed ISIS's viciousness on former Baathists who dominate its ranks, an indictment of the group's jihadist credentials.[30] This hypothesis has gained wide traction in the global press and media. In a similar vein, ISIS accused al-Nusra's senior commander, Abu Marya al-Qahtani, of having been a member of Fida'iu Saddam (Saddam's Martyrs), in an effort to delegitimize its rival. This disparaging remark elicited a response by Qahtani in which he called ISIS's chiefs "Baathists-Saddamists."[31]

Obviously, the claims and counterclaims by the two warring jihadist camps are politically motivated. More importantly, despite the bitter and bloody rivalry between Baghdadi and Joulani, the latter never accused his former boss of either having Baathist sympathies or being a figurehead leader controlled by Baathist officers. Joulani was a junior commander in ISI under Baghdadi, who sent him to Syria at the end of 2011 to establish a jihadist base. Joulani served closely under Baghdadi in Iraq between 2010 and 2011, and he would have publicly exposed any links or ties that Baghdadi might have had with former Baathist officers. In a widely watched TV interview on Al Jazeera's satellite station, Joulani, while challenging ISIS's authority in Syria, praised the group's success against the Shia-led government in Baghdad. He said he refuses to excommunicate his current rival even though ISIS excommunicated al-Nusra, a decision that puts to rest claims of an unholy Baathist-ISIS union.[32] In another interview with several Arab journalists at his headquarters in Idlib, Syria, Joulani refused to indict Baghdadi and said that both of them wage a war against the enemies of Islam in Syria and Iraq.[33] Similarly, if there is anyone with a score to settle against Baghdadi, it would be Ayman al-Zawahiri, the leader of Al Qaeda Central, whose leadership of the global jihadist movement has been seriously contested by the Iraqi upstart. Zawahiri has never questioned Baghdadi's Islamist or jihadist credentials while disputing the legitimacy of his caliphate and accusing him of sedition for encouraging Al Qaeda members to abandon their pledges and switch their allegiance to ISIS. Despite Zawahiri's blistering criticism of Baghdadi's "big mistakes," he has called on his followers and ISIS's to cooperate against the US-led coalition: "If I were in Iraq and Syria I would cooperate with them [ISIS] in killing the crusaders and secularists and Shias even though I don't recognize the legitimacy of their state, because the matter is bigger than that," he said in an audiotape statement in 2015.[34] Zawahiri repeatedly insisted that the conflict between ISIS and Al Qaeda Central has more to do with Baghdadi's political ambitions and unwillingness to confine his authority to Iraq than with any

ideological disagreements. He has never uttered an accusatory
word alluding to a Baathist-ISIS conspiracy or suggesting that
Baghdadi was not the real power behind the organization.

Instead of reducing the cause of the rebirth of ISIS to a
fallen Baathist Party, the influence of one great man, or conspiracy theories, any explanation calls for a complex examination of the power structures in Iraq and Syria and beyond. The
Sunni community now in Iraq (and in Syria, to a lesser extent)
is torn mainly between two ideological poles—religious nationalism and Salafi-jihadism. An important Sunni segment
has adopted a purely sectarian identity. There also exists a hard-
core Baathist segment that acts independently (more on this
below), though most Sunnis want to get on with their lives and
find a place within the new order.[35] Of all the Iraqi communities, the Sunnis have suffered the most, and ISIS's resurgence
has aggravated their predicament, pressed between the extremist organization and the central government and its Shia militias. The durability of ISIS will depend on the struggle within
the Sunni community and shifting loyalties and political reconciliation at home. Still, in almost four decades in power, the
Baath Party failed to supplant Iraq's traditional religious and
ethnic loyalties with an inclusive national identity.[36]

Complicating matters is the fact that repression, tyranny, and
foreign wars created a rift within Iraqi society, one that is difficult to bridge. Many Iraqis find more solace and security in
local, provincial loyalties than in a greater national identity. The
postindependence, postcolonial state in the Arab world, particularly Iraq, has nourished traditional institutions at the expense of a nationalist project around which citizens could
unite. Hussein is a case in point, although his forced ouster
by the United States neither healed the deep wounds caused
by his repressive rule nor ushered in a new social pact. The
destruction of the Iraqi state by the US-led invasion has had
more everlasting consequences on the country than any other
internal cleavage or mutation. The result is that Sunnis and
Shias feel entrapped in narrow communal identities, and battles
over identity rage not only between communities but also

within them. The fights within communities are real and very
serious. As stressed throughout the book, there is a civil war raging within the Sunni community, which ISIS fully exploited,
depicting itself as its sole defender against the "other" Shias and
the "apostate" Sunnis who sold their souls to the devil. The
Shia community is deeply splintered along social and ideological lines, with a fierce power struggle among leading stakeholders. Although united on the surface, the Kurds are divided
over the future direction of their community. The war within
the Salafi-jihadist camps, especially ISIS and al-Nusra, is ugly
and vicious, dwarfing those of the three major communities.
The difficult questions to answer are, when will these internal
struggles break outside, and what form will they take? As a
hypersectarian, identity-driven organization, ISIS effectively
tapped into the clash of identities and internal cleavages that
have almost wrecked the social fabric in Iraq and now Syria.

BAATHISTS AND JIHADISTS: ACCOMMODATION TO CONFRONTATION

Another point regarding the role of former officers of Hussein's army and police in ISIS deserves critical scrutiny. ISIS not
only co-opted a sizable segment of former army and police
officers to its ranks but also briefly collaborated with other officers, a majority of whom have not shed their Baathist nationalist skin. General Douri, one of Hussein's few confidants, is a
case in point. As mentioned above briefly, Douri tried to resurrect the banned Baath Party soon after the 2003 US-led invasion by organizing army and police officers and soldiers into a
coalition of insurgent groups known as the Naqshabandi Army.
The United States linked him to Ansar al-Islam, a militant Iraqi
group with ties to Al Qaeda, and accused him of being a major
financier of armed groups. Despite repeated claims of his death
by the Iraqi authorities and Shia militias and continual attempts to capture him, with the authorities even listing him as
the sixth most wanted of fifty-five Iraqis after the US-led invasion, he has survived and emerged as the leader of the banned

Baath Party. Douri is one of the most prominent fugitives to have evaded capture by American and Iraqi forces and battled the US coalition and the Iraqi government while in hiding. Composed mainly of former Baathist military and police officers and hard-core nationalist supporters, the Naqshabandi Army established important social networks in major Sunni-dominated cities like Mosul and Tikrit, according to local residents, and collaborated briefly and intermittently with Salafi-jihadists, including Al Qaeda in Iraq and then ISIS. Arguably, neither city would have fallen like ripened fruit to ISIS in summer 2014 without ISIS's collaboration with the Naqshabandi Army's Baathist followers. For example, when Tikrit was overrun in June 2014, local residents said fighters raised posters of Hussein and Douri. Units loyal to the Naqshabandi Army as well as former members of Hussein's Baath Party were the dominant forces in Tikrit at the time of its capture, according to local residents.[37] In an audiotape that was released a month after the fall of Mosul, Douri praised the "heroes and knights of Al Qaeda and the Islamic State" as well as other groups fighting the "Persian, Safavid colonialization" of Iraq, a reference to the Shia-led government of Nuri al-Maliki. Douri called on all Iraqis to overcome their differences, hinting at increasingly evident divisions among various armed groups fighting Maliki's forces, and to join efforts to "liberate" the country.[38] There is also tentative evidence that indicates that the Baathists had a role in infiltrating and exploiting the mass rallies and social mobilization throughout 2013 and early 2014 that corresponded with the Arab Spring. These social protests quickly became more militant and uncompromising as a result of the brutal tactics used by the central government in Baghdad as well as the militarization of these rallies by the Baathists and other radicalized elements. In a way, the Baathists and their allies played a dangerous game by handing the area to ISIS on a silver platter. The protesters included many in the local governments and tribal leaders who were erstwhile allies of Maliki, but they succumbed to the mood and gradually fell by the wayside until ISIS took over completely. Between the takeover of Fallujah and the fall of Mosul, there were explicit local declarations of war by the so-called revolutionary military councils, which clearly had a Baathist tinge. Douri's first audiotape message after the fall of Mosul alluded to this unholy alliance among ISIS, the Baathists, and like-minded factions.[39]

Unsurprisingly, within three weeks of taking over Mosul in June 2014, ISIS began arresting senior ex-military officers and members of the Baath Party, according to residents and relatives. The honeymoon period between the Baathists and ISIS's Salafi-jihadists was short-lived, with initial accommodation turning to confrontation. Douri's Baathists and Islamic State jihadists clashed with one another as their initial tactical cooperation did not withstand a deep ideological gulf and a power struggle as well. Despite assertions to the contrary, there exists an unbridgeable doctrinal divide between ISIS's Salafi-jihadists and the Baathists of the Naqshabandi Army. The confrontation between the two groups was inevitable because ISIS would never accept any challenge to its authority in areas under its control. ISIS derogatively refers to its nationalist rival as "the devious Baath" and similarly calls Douri a "scheming infidel."[40] A tribal Sunni sheikh, Uns al-Jabarra, from Salah al-din province, says that after government forces retreated from Mosul and Tikrit in summer 2014, Douri attempted to manage the cities by placing his Baathist men in governorships and other key positions of authority. ISIS immediately removed Douri's appointees and gave them an ultimatum: either pledge allegiance to Baghdadi or face persecution. In two audio recordings that were released in April and May 2015 (one on social media and the other broadcast by Iraq's al-Taghyeer television station after yet another premature report of his death), Douri verbally assaulted ISIS for holding about a third of the top Iraqi leaders of the Baath Party captive, including Seif al-din al-Mashdani and Fadel al-Mashhadani. He noted that takfiri groups like ISIS pose an existential threat to the Arab nation because they do not recognize its existence, and reiterated his commitment to Arab nationalism. This was the same fugitive who, nine months earlier, had praised Islamic State extremists as "heroes." Douri went on to criticize ISIS for the massacre in June 2014 of hundreds (more than a thousand, according to some reports) of mainly Shia cadets at Camp Speicher, a former US military base near Tikrit. Moreover, the Naqshabandi Army censured ISIS's persecution of religious minorities and the burning of a Jordanian coalition pilot in Syria.[41] Some Baathists have gone to the other extreme by cooperating with the Iraqi government and the Americans in an effort to organize resistance to ISIS in Mosul along the Awakening movement lines.[42] The divisions among the Baathists mirror those of Iraq Sunnis in general, a development often overlooked by writers who analyze the role of former Baathist officers who joined ISIS. Leaderless and fragmented, the Sunni community is pulled and pushed in multiple directions and suffers from a severe identity crisis. In the past two decades the fierce social struggle in Iraq has led to the reconfiguration of the Sunni Arab identity there. Exploiting the leadership vacuum and the sense of victimhood felt by Sunnis, ISIS offers a utopian vision for Sunnis, the caliphate, around which to unite, as well as protection—a triple feat of salvation, security, and empowerment. As discussed previously, there is no evidence that shows ISIS's ideology of Sunni pan-Islamism to be the adopted identity in Sunni areas in Iraq and Syria. Many Sunnis fight under the ISIS banner because they see the group as a protector against the Shia-led government in Baghdad and the Shia militias as well as a defender of their interests. ISIS's dark cloud has a silver lining. Salafi-jihadists have not colonized Sunni minds or lands yet. In Syria and Iraq, there is a convergence of interests between rebellious Sunnis and ISIS's Salafi-jihadists, a marriage of convenience as opposed to an ideological affinity. This gulf between ISIS's hard-core ideologues and its ordinary fighters spells trouble for the group in the midterm and the long term, especially if and when its military fortunes decline.

There was nothing surprising about ISIS brutally suppressing the Baathists in Mosul and Tikrit after the cities had fallen. Time and again ISIS had shown tactical toleration and acceptance of like-minded armed groups in Iraq and Syria, only to crush them when they did not submit to its dictate. Fallujah is a case in point. As the first major Iraqi city seized by ISIS in January 2014, local witnesses testify that initially the group worked with and co-opted prominent Sunni clerics and tribal leaders and fellow jihadists and displayed flexibility and teamwork, a radical departure from the conduct of its predecessors, AQI and ISI. But after ISIS consolidated power in Fallujah, it purged the city of all potential rivals and imposed a reign of terror against its former allies. Credible evidence shows that ISIS used deceptive tactics to win over Iraqi and Syrian communities under its control and then systematically purge these areas of dissidents and independent activists. In Syria, activists widely reported on ISIS's arbitrary arrests, kidnappings, and summary executions of journalists, dissidents, students, and other political suspects (see chapter 6, on Syria). Far from concealing its vicious deeds, the organization has produced massive incriminating evidence designed to terrorize the public and deter the formation of any institutionalized opposition. Although it is misleading to assert that the Baathists have stealthily taken over the organization, ISIS seems to have adopted the Baathists' system of repression and control of the population. On the one hand, ISIS excommunicated the Baathists and ordered them to repent and pledge allegiance to its caliph, Baghdadi. On the other hand, it imitates the Baathists' vicious methods while dressing them in Islamic garb, though this dichotomy is easily explained by the fact that the group inherited the bloody legacy of Al Qaeda in Iraq.

6

HOW THE SYRIAN WAR EMPOWERED ISIS

Two of the key driving forces behind the resurgence of ISIS were the dysfunctional political system in Iraq that developed after the US-led invasion and occupation of the country, and the exclusionary policies of Prime Minister Nuri al-Maliki. But Syria's descent into all-out war is a significant variable in explaining ISIS's expansion. Maliki's second term in office coincided with a political earthquake in the region: the Arab Spring. Beginning in December 2010, millions of Arabs took to the streets to protest decades of political authoritarianism and developmental failure and to call for justice, dignity, and freedom. The phenomenon, which had gradually materialized during decades of economic, social, and political hardship, reached its climax in Tunisia when the self-immolation of a street vendor named Mohamed Bouazizi provided motivation and inspiration for millions of Arab citizens to rise up against their dictators. In a concerted effort, the people mobilized to remove their leaders from power, including in Egypt, Libya, Yemen, Syria, and Bahrain. The subsequent derailment of the aspirations of Arab protesters established a contentious environment that proved to be the catalyst for ISIS's subsequent success and expansion into Syria after the country's uprising in 2011.

THE SOCIOPOLITICAL ORIGINS OF THE SYRIAN REVOLUTION

Initially, the large-scale popular uprising in Syria was socially and politically driven, originating in rural areas—like Dara'a—that were hit hard by years of drought and a decade of neoliberal policies that siphoned resources away from the pressed agrarian sector toward the tertiary sector. Former Syrian president Hafez al-Assad (1930–2000) and his son and successor Bashar restructured the country's socioeconomic landscape, distributing social, political, and economic power strategically in a manner meant to divide Syrians along both socioeconomic and sectarian lines. Although seen as a Shia minority in Syria, the Alawites often dominated key military and security posts, and Assad was able to co-opt and cultivate urban Sunni elites from the middle and upper classes of society, specifically the business and merchant classes of the leading cities of Aleppo and Damascus. From the late 1980s until the outbreak of the revolutionary uprising in 2011, the Syrian regime forged capital networks that allied business elites from the country's large cities with state officials, thus transforming the country, in a twenty-year period, from a state-controlled to a capitalist economy characterized by cronyism.[1] The liberalization policies of the 1990s led to private sector growth but were accompanied by the gradual decline of public jobs, subsidies, and other welfare-enhancing economic measures that for millions of Syria's citizens had been a real safety net.[2] Such regressive policies inherently led to a widening of the conspicuous gap between the rich and the poor. While regime loyalists, businessmen, and politicians harvested the rewards of economic liberalization and greatly profited from new economic opportunities, people in rural areas and small cities faced accrued poverty and displacement, fostering social polarization.[3] Accelerated neoliberal reforms during the Bashar regime (2000–2010) neglected the agricultural sector, leaving rural people ostracized and increasingly forced to rely on communal solidarity networks and the informal market. According to the Food and Agriculture Organization of the United Nations (FAO), by 2009, 18.2 percent of the Syrian population had fallen below the poverty line, with the rural Damascus, Idlib, Homs, Dara'a, al-Sweida, and Hama governorates among the most affected.[4] Additionally, the rural areas had to cope with devastating droughts from 2006 to 2010 and increasing food insecurity, with farmers being severely deprived of the resources of their livelihoods.

It is no wonder, then, that protests and social restiveness originated in rural areas and on the fringes of large cities and commercial hubs. Unlike Bashar al-Assad's close circle of businessmen and the urban elite in general, the rural population had gained few benefits from the regime's economic opening and liberalization. Having previously been economically prioritized by the Baath regime in the 1970s and early 1980s,[5] this ironic turnaround was heavily felt by the rural population. The tragic irony is that initially the large-scale popular uprising in Syria was neither sectarian-driven nor violent. Protesters in Syria braved bullets in order to send a message to the authorities and dared to call for legitimate political and social reforms, not even regime change. It was not until six months later that the uprising became militarized, taking on a sectarian façade. However, that development should not blind us to the universal aspirations of the protesters and their struggle to bring about change.

I vividly recall many conversations with Syrian activists of all ideological colors inside and outside Syria at the onset of the revolt; they talked about taking ownership of their country and building an open and tolerant society in which ethnic and religious communities peacefully coexist under the rule of law. Despite early warnings of a massive clampdown by Assad's security forces against protesters, activists said they did not lose hope that Syria could be rescued and that Assad, like his Tunisian and Egyptian counterparts, would ultimately submit to the will of the people. Sadly, Assad's desire for power and domination triumphed over this hope. As mentioned in the introduction, civil-military relations in Syria are radically different from those in Tunisia and Egypt, and the Syrian military sided with the Assad regime against the protesters. This was partly due to the sectarian makeup of the senior echelons of the military, and partly due to the fear of Islamist extremism that found receptive ears among many Syrians. In fact, the Syrian armed and security forces' loyalty to the Assad regime and their involvement in its crimes have been extensively documented by human rights groups and international organizations. In 2012, the United Nations stated that gross violations committed against the civilian population in Syria "have been committed in line with State policy, with indications of the involvement at the highest levels of the Government, as well as security and armed forces."[6] As the security forces brutally clamped down on peaceful protesters and accused antiregime dissidents of being sectarian-inspired and -motivated, the uprising rapidly turned violent and eventually radicalized. Protesters increasingly adopted religious symbols and references, with armed Islamist factions and gangs in rural villages exploiting the tumult to advance their ultraconservative Salafi-jihadist worldview and agenda. By May 2012, the UN estimated that ten thousand people, mostly civilians, had been killed in incidents related to the uprising,[7] and by July 2012, the fighting in Syria had officially become an internal armed conflict, according to the International Committee of the Red Cross (ICRC).[8] At the same time, human rights organizations such as Amnesty International charged the Assad regime with committing state-sanctioned war crimes and crimes against humanity.[9] A number of human rights and humanitarian organizations pressed hard for the international community to step in and put an end to the "increasingly widespread attacks against the civilian population, including crimes against humanity and war crimes, committed by government forces and militias with utter impunity."[10]

The Syrian uprising quickly mutated into war of all against all—along the lines of the Lebanese civil war in 1975, a confrontation that lasted for fifteen years. As the Syrian conflict escalated, scores of armed groups proliferated and professed Islamist ideologies, ranging from the moderate to the Salafi-jihadists. Even nationalist rebels such as the Free Syrian Army (FSA) used Islamic symbols in their rhetoric as a way to gain legitimization in the eyes of the public and to compete with emerging Islamist groups for funding from donors in the Gulf States. In an interview with France24 in November 2013, an FSA fighter confirmed that funders mostly donate to groups that are aligned with their religious affiliations and interpretations, asserting, "That's why, in the videos made by our brigade, we like to recite verses from the Koran and to include Islamic symbols in the background.... We are all salesmen, in a way: we must bend in any direction to fit our potential donors, whatever our actual beliefs, and the donor is always right."[11] In turn, Islamist armed groups and the Islamist rhetoric of jihad were empowered, their existence becoming somewhat justified in the eyes of a significant proportion of Syrians due to the regime's violent crackdown on civilians. In a replay of the strategy of militant Islamists in Iraq since 2003, Islamist groups in Syria positioned themselves, and were often seen, as the tormentors of the Alawite-dominated and Shia-backed Assad regime.

As the conflict in Syria spiraled out of control, the country's socioeconomic fabric and fragile institutions were inevitably destroyed. Calls for jihad against Assad and his Shia supporters resonated among many Syrian rebels and their foreign sponsors, who contributed to the sectarian overtones and religious fervor of the political struggle. In a similar vein, Assad and his supporters at home and in neighboring countries invoked an existential struggle, depicting themselves as the protectors of cultural diversity and a secular way of life. "We are engaged in an existential war which knows no compromise or concession" is a refrain frequently uttered by Assad.[12] Similarly, the leader of Lebanon's Shia-dominated Hezbollah, Hassan

Nasrallah, a pivotal supporter of Assad, defined the fight in Syria in stark terms: "Today we are facing a kind of danger that is unprecedented in history, which targets humanity itself," he stated, speaking before the anniversary of the withdrawal of Israeli troops from Lebanon in 2000.[13]

THE ISLAMIC STATE OF IRAQ ESTABLISHES AL-NUSRA IN SYRIA

Feeding upon each other, the conflicts in Syria and Iraq provided Abu Bakr al-Baghdadi and his inner circle with a golden opportunity to build new social networks—and revive old ones—in both countries that championed the grievances of disaffected Sunnis. What seemed like an impossible mission in 2010 was accomplished two years later: a mafia-like network transformed into a powerful, lethal insurgency that captured huge swathes of eastern Syria and western Iraq, with the exception of only the Kurdish region. This feat did not come about haphazardly or accidentally. Credible evidence points to Baghdadi and his top commanders, many of whom were former Sunni military leaders under Saddam Hussein's regime, meticulously planning to appeal to Sunni communities in both Iraq and Syria and gain their trust in a systematic effort to build a solid foothold and to expand their influence. ISIS's chiefs boast that long before the Syrian crisis escalated into a full-blown confrontation, they had already plotted to expand their operations there. Taking advantage of the jihadi power vacuum that followed Osama bin Laden's death in May 2011, Baghdadi and his inner circle sent two trusted lieutenants, Abu Mohammed al-Joulani and Mullah Fawzi al-Dulaimi, to Syria in late 2011 to set up a jihadist operative cell there and battle the Assad regime.[14]

For more than a year ISIS did not promote its participation in the Syrian conflict. Instead, it provided al-Nusra with a few skilled former Iraqi army officers, money, and arms, thus allowing the jihadists to insert themselves among the armed rebels in 2012 and partner with local groups. In fact, in a confession to his supporters, Ayman al-Zawahiri, emir of Al Qaeda Central, admitted that he and Baghdadi had indeed agreed "to not announce an official presence in Syria."[15] In an audio recording released by Al Qaeda's As-Sahab Media in May 2014, Zawahiri asserted that from the onset a decision was made to blend in with the local population in a bid to avoid alerting the Americans to Al Qaeda's presence in Syria—a move that subsequently allowed al-Nusra to grow, expand, and build coalitions with various Islamist factions. In a statement announcing the formation of al-Nusra in January 2012, Joulani stated that "the appeals for the people of Jihad have risen, and we could only respond to the call and to return to our people and land from the first months of the outbreak of the revolution."[16] Joulani presented his group as an extension of the Syrian mujahideen rather than that of AQC or ISI. In the first year of its existence, al-Nusra in Syria practiced a form of *taqqiya* (a religious lie, permitted in circumstances where there is a fear of persecution), hiding its real jihadist identity and portraying itself as part of the legitimate Syrian opposition. During this early phase Baghdadi and his cohorts avoided flooding Syria with Iraqi fighters and relied instead on Syrian Sunni recruits and local and tribal coalitions, together with foreign volunteers and a few skilled and trusted Iraqi lieutenants. Even the name chosen by Joulani (Jawlan or Golan) indicated the desire to situate al-Nusra as a Syrian nationalist group.

As they did in their operations in Iraq, the jihadist organization appealed to the Sunni community and acted as a vanguard for Sunnis who felt persecuted and victimized by the sectarian regime in Damascus. Its strategy was to "break the barriers" and get rid of the "colonialist" borders separating the two neighboring countries by assembling Sunni coalitions across Syria and Iraq. This coalition of Sunni forces was assembled as a counterweight to Iran's expanding influence in the region, specifically its backing of the regimes in Baghdad and Damascus. A close look at the map of armed groups in Syria clearly shows that the rise and expansion of the Salafi-jihadist group was fueled by local social and tribal networks painstakingly built all over Syria from one province to another. In addition to these networks, many of the jihadist organizations' commanders and field lieutenants were former members of the Free Syrian Army and other armed factions who switched sides, either because of financial incentives or following the success of the more radical armed groups who appeared to be better funded and more highly trained and organized. Other rebel factions flocked to join al-Nusra, and included members from the al-Tawhid Brigade in Aleppo and Liwa' Daoud in Qalamoun and Idlib, while jihadists released from Assad's prisons also became key players.[17] A number of prominent members of al-Nusra, and later ISIS, had been imprisoned by Assad until a general amnesty in May 2011, including Awwad al-Mahklaf, who later became an ISIS emir in al-Raqqah, and Abu al-Athir al-Absi, a member of ISIS's Shura Council and the head of ISIS's media council.[18] Some argue that the amnesty, which was intended to cover political prisoners but instead led to the release of a number of prominent Islamists, was a deliberate and strategic calculation on behalf of the Assad regime in an attempt to transform the protest movement from a legitimate political and nonmilitarized uprising into a radicalized extremist attack on the "secular" state of which Assad saw himself as a guardian.[19]

THE RURAL AND URBAN POOR

From the start, al-Nusra found a receptive constituency in rural districts and provinces, such as Deir al-Zour, al-Hasakah, and al-Raqqah, where high unemployment and abject poverty were aggravated by a devastating war. Unemployment in opposition-held areas increased from 60 percent to 90 percent[20] following the outbreak of the armed conflict, and inflation increased drastically, with areas such as Idlib reaching 400 percent.[21] Losing their sources of income and property, eleven million people—half of the country's population—became destitute, and many were forced to join armed groups, particularly those that paid them salaries and took care of their families.[22] Deir al-Zour, historically Syria's poorest province, was a particularly fertile ground for Islamist groups such as al-Nusra, having been a prominent base for jihadist networks operating in Iraq in the years following the 2003 Iraqi invasion.[23] Of all the armed factions in Syria, al-Nusra and subsequently ISIS recruited the most fighters, hundreds of poor Sunnis who lacked the means to feed their families, and whose grievances allowed them to become somewhat politically disposed to the groups' sectarian narrative, if not their jihadist ideology. According to Syrian sources, ISIS pays its fighters $400 a month and, if married, a fighter received an additional $50 per child and $100 for every wife, as some fighters had more than one wife.[24] In addition to a regular salary, the jihadist organization also provided housing for homeless fighters, with heating oil and fuel for their cars covered through their control of oil fields in Deir al-Zour.[25] By the end of 2015 there exists increasing evidence that the group can no longer sustain its current spending as a result of the decline in its financial resources and has been forced to tighten its belt. In January 2016 a leaked internal memo by the group said that "it has been decided to reduce the salaries that are paid to all mujahideen by half without exception and regardless of one's rank" from $400 to $200.[26]

Nevertheless, for poor Sunnis who feel hopeless and desperate, the ISIS project reflects their hopes and fears and provides answers to their existential queries triggered by all-out civil war. They view the Islamic State as a viable alternative to the corrupt armed factions that butchered each other over the spoils of war and developed a reputation for thuggery, thievery, and moral corruption.[27] In Iraq and Syria, ISIS invested heavily in poor Sunnis and tried to co-opt them through employment and empowerment, putting many in charge of policing, security, surveillance, and field command, an investment that has secured the organization's control of its newly captured territories in Deir al-Zour, al-Raqqah, Mosul, Fallujah, and elsewhere. For example, many ISIS and al-Nusra field command-ers come from manual labor and blue-collar backgrounds such as street vendors, farmers, construction workers, shopkeepers, and mechanics.[28] This tactic also played a key role in empow-ering Sunnis and adding to the image that ISIS was trying to create for itself as the only force willing to stand up to Shia ex-pansion and allow Sunnis to take control of their own lives. As one opposition fighter put it, "I have heard my voice for the first time," implying that even under the exceptionally difficult circumstances of war, he celebrated the voice that was once stifled by the ruling regime.[29]

Following years of drought, economic decline, and the grow-ing gap between cities and rural areas,[30] farmers had been forced to move from the countryside to the suburbs in search of economic opportunities, leaving behind their established support networks. Religion provided a communitarian narra-tive for the disenfranchised, anchoring them in a community and providing a bridge between tradition and modernity. Bolstered by donations from wealthy Arab Gulf donors, ultra-conservative Salafi movements, which until then represented a fraction of the Islamist opposition, stepped up their rhetoric and took advantage of the social cleavage that had been grow-ing in Syria. As the country descended into all-out war and chaos, Salafi groups held an appeal comparable to that of the Taliban in Afghanistan in the early 1990s by providing simple answers anchored in identity, which attracted members of disadvantaged and poor rural and urban communities. They proposed a system of government that was justified in religious terms and rooted in a traditional interpretation of shariah. The conflict's increasingly sectarian dimensions also bolstered the Salafists' claim. While Salafi religious scholars such as Adnan al-Aroor, Salim al-Rafei, and Ahmad Assir had long accused Assad of sectarianism and decried his subservience to Iran, the support given to the Syrian regime by Iranian, Lebanese, and Iraqi Shia groups only further reinforced the Salafi rhetoric. Other developments that converged to empower Salafists and Salafi-jihadists who depicted the conflict in Syria in sectarian terms included the escalation of armed hostilities in Iraq and the Syrian regime's use of the Alawite-dominated security forces and the so-called *Shabiha* (paramilitary groups) to crush demonstrators and attack villages. The Shabiha led by the president's brother, Maher al-Assad, were often deeply imbedded with Syrian armed forces during ground offensives and are believed to have been responsible for a number of massacres against Sunni civilians, including the Houla massacre in May 2012, in which one hundred people were killed, mostly women and children.[31] Furthermore, the persistent regime propaganda that claimed that Alawites and other minorities would be massacred by armed opposition groups only worked to solidify the divide. In Syria, ISIS, together with al-Nusra, was able to take advantage of feelings of desperation that engulfed the country following the Assad regime's savage response to peaceful demonstrations. With a fragmented opposition and a regime that was willing to crush peaceful protesters and activists on a daily basis, hopes for a quick resolution or for regime change rapidly receded. As many Syrians felt abandoned, the conflict became a regional war by proxy between Turkey, Qatar, and Saudi Arabia on the one hand and Iran, Iraq, and Hezbollah on the other. Arms, money, and foreign fighters flowed freely to Syria, and soon a plethora of rebel groups emerged, including al-Nusra and then ISIS, as well as scores of Islamist factions.

THE IRAQ AND SYRIA CONFLICTS FEED UPON EACH OTHER

The first phase of the ISI–al-Nusra connection, from 2012 until April/May 2013, should not be overlooked. The connection proved to be pivotal in establishing an important jihadist base as well as a durable and resilient infrastructure, even though it subsequently fractured into two warring camps. There is a tendency among observers of ISIS to focus exclusively on the period following the violent breakup between ISIS and al-Nusra in summer 2013, to the detriment of a more encompassing approach. Before the split, Baghdadi and his lieutenants invested heavily in strengthening al-Nusra and received massive financial and logistical returns on their investment. These resources, coupled with the disintegration of Syria's social fabric and governance, provided motivation and inspiration for ISIS jihadists to embark on the offensive and conquer Mosul and other Sunni provinces. For example, in late 2012 Haji Bakr, a top ISIS commander and a former officer in Hussein's army, reportedly traveled to northern Syria as part of a small advance party to help al-Nusra, which was, until late 2013 and early 2014, ISIS's front in Syria.[32] The strategy at this time was to consolidate its power and secure as much territory as possible.

As discussed in chapter 5, Christoph Reuter's report in the German magazine *Der Spiegel*, based on documents uncovered by Syrian rebels opposed to ISIS in Tal Riffat, a small city in the province of Aleppo, details Haji Bakr's meticulous planning and brutal tactics to recruit followers and silence dissenters. By focusing too much on Bakr's previous Baathist background during Hussein's rule and his obsession with espionage and intelligence gathering, Reuter overlooked a significant point in the files: ISIS went to great lengths to back al-Nusra's expansion in many towns in northern Syria, particularly in rural areas in the provinces of al-Raqqah, Idlib, Deir al-Zour, and Aleppo. The documents show that ISIS used a number of techniques to help al-Nusra establish itself in the war-torn country. These tactics included the gradual infiltration of villages and towns; the mapping of social, regional, and tribal groups (heads of clans, influential personalities, businessmen, activists, clerics, and dissidents); and Islamist indoctrination camouflaged as the opening of al Dawa (the call to religion) offices.[33] ISI–al-Nusra spared no effort to secure areas under their control, using methods including assassination, terror, and instilling fear among inhabitants. The files obtained by *Der Spiegel* focus almost exclusively on ISI–al-Nusra's use of coercive means to spread their influence and terrorize their real and imagined enemies in Syria.

However, there is a missing link in this narrative: from late 2011 until late 2013, ISI–al-Nusra was not distinguished from other rebels and armed factions that proliferated in Syria's chaotic environment except by its fierceness and hypersectarianism. During the summer of 2012, Salafi and Salafi-jihadist organizations intensified their presence on the battlefield and participated in large-scale attacks against the Syrian army. Al-Nusra was a case in point. From November 2011 to December 2012, it carried out more than six hundred attacks across the country, targeting security branches, the army, and the Shabiha.[34] The group positioned its military assets in rural areas, an environment hospitable to Salafi ideology and difficult for hostile forces to storm, while concentrating its guerrilla tactics and suicide bombings in urban areas.

Part of al-Nusra's "paced global"[35] strategy was to promote itself as the defender of Syrians against the Assad regime and to gain as much support from local communities as possible. Heeding Ayman al-Zawahiri's warning from 2005 that "in the absence of [this] popular support, the Islamic mujahid movement would be crushed in the shadows,"[36] Joulani showed great sensitivity to public sentiment in Syria and positioned his organization and its foot soldiers as a local group rather than a transnational jihadist movement. Al-Nusra's active efforts to recruit Syrian fighters during this time worked to improve this public image and gained them significant support from local communities that now had men fighting with the group. From the beginning, al-Nusra successfully infused itself with indigenous Syrian insurgents and groups, masking its jihadist identity. In fact, it did this so well that when in December 2012 the United States declared al-Nusra a terrorist organization, protests erupted within Syria's moderate opposition groups, with twenty-nine of these signing a petition condemning the United States for this decision.[37] The extent to which al-Nusra was able to co-opt local communities in Syria is astonishing, and it contrasts significantly with how these same communities viewed ISIS. Time and again, intellectuals in Syria opposed to Assad have defended al-Nusra as moderate and locally rooted, which they contrast with ISIS's borderless, extraterritorial ambitions and extremism. Syrians tell me that al-Nusra will ultimately shed its jihadist skin and become Syrianized, reflecting a blind faith in Joulani's wisdom. After spending six hours interviewing Joulani, together with three other colleagues, a Syrian broadcast journalist came out convinced that the man was redeemable. Moussa al-Omar, who works for an Arab-based television station called *al-Ghad al-Arabi*, told me that Joulani is moderate and does not share Al Qaeda's extremist ideology. I reminded Moussa that Joulani fought with Abu Musab al-Zarqawi, the founder of AQI, and served as a loyal commander under his successor, Abu Bakr al-Baghdadi, and swore baiya to Ayman al-Zawahiri, head of Al Qaeda Central. Moussa retorted by saying that Joulani came across as rational and cognizant of the complexity of regional and global politics. He is clear-headed and a realist, Moussa assured.[38] As recently as March 2015, following the significant gains made by ISIS, a *Financial Times* article explored the potential of al-Nusra to unite Syrian opposition forces in an effort to defeat both the Assad regime and ISIS in Syria, stressing that "the group's core force is made up primarily of local Syrian fighters rather than foreign militants and it has shown a willingness to ally with groups that do not share its ideology."[39] Indeed, al-Nusra itself has attempted to explain and justify Joulani's previous relationship with ISIS by claiming that the baiya that Joulani had given Baghdadi was a war baiya, rather than a *Khilafah* one, meaning that it was a temporary military alliance rather than a long-term, ideological one.[40]

After his cover was exposed by Baghdadi in April 2013, Joulani not only publicly swore baiya to Zawahiri, emir of Al Qaeda, but also reiterated his pledge of allegiance in May 2015 in an Al Jazeera TV interview, watched by millions of Syrians and Arabs, in which he stated that he receives "instructions" from Zawahiri.[41] The interview itself was an attempt by Joulani to better define what al-Nusra stood for and to differentiate it from Baghdadi's ISIS, a move that may have helped al-Nusra to appear somewhat more moderate and obtain future funds from certain donors in the Gulf.[42] Joulani, however, has yet to express how he plans to balance his group's transnational jihadist identity with the imperative of Syrian sovereignty. The two projects are mutually exclusive, yet many in the Syrian opposition give him the benefit of the doubt and have teamed up with al-Nusra on the battlefield against Assad's forces. Joulani's local strategy seemed to have allayed the fears of many in the Syrian opposition, despite the fact that al-Nusra has a Salafi-jihadist worldview that is similar to that of ISIS, with the two only differing tactically and operationally.

From the beginning of its operations in Syria and before it was revealed that al-Nusra was an extension of ISI, al-Nusra's spokespeople sought to convey a different image from that of their parent organization and repeatedly indicated that they wanted to avoid its past mistakes. In an interview with *Time* magazine in December 2012, one of al-Nusra's chiefs, Abu Adnan, even denied any links with ISI, saying, "We are not like al-Qaeda in Iraq, we are not of them."[43] Al-Nusra's pronouncements emphasized this strategic message. For example, in January 2012 al-Nusra posted a statement claiming that it did not intend to enforce shariah in Syria, but rather wanted to bring "the law of Allah back to His land," essentially meaning the same thing. The statement also portrayed the jihadist group as the protector of the Sunni community against the *al-Nusayrin* (a derogative term for Alawites) enemy.[44] In March 2012, al-Nusra carried out a double car bombing of an air force intelligence building that killed forty-four people in Damascus. The targeted area was primarily residential and contained many Christian families. Soon after news of the attack and the civilian casualties surfaced, al-Nusra released a statement noting that its sole target was the intelligence base, not the Christian residents, saying, "We notify the *Nasaraa* [the Christians] that they had not been targeted in the bombing of the Air Force Security building [in their district]. Whatever damage the district incurred was an effect caused by the aftermath of the explosion. We appeal for all to avoid living near security buildings and hotbeds of the regime."[45]

Moreover, al-Nusra has been willing to cooperate with other Islamist factions as well as the FSA in the fight against Assad's forces.[46] A report by the International Crisis Group points out that al-Nusra and the FSA shared bomb-making facilities in Deir al-Zour and Idlib, citing an al-Nusra leader in Deir al-Zour as saying, "We meet almost daily. We have clear instructions from our leadership that if the FSA needs our help we should give it. We help them with IEDs and car bombs. Our main talent lies in bombing operations."[47] But al-Nusra kept its strategic cards close to its chest and positioned its battalions along strategic supply lines leading from east Aleppo to Turkey and from Aleppo and al-Hasakah to Iraq. Al-Nusra also infiltrated significant parts of the eastern and northern countryside, which offer access to the oil-producing governorates of al-Raqqah, al-Hasakah, and Deir al-Zour and considerable economic resources.[48]

At first al-Nusra mainly attacked the Syrian government's military infrastructure and avoided civilian targets in order to avoid alienating the population. By doing so, al-Nusra amassed a vast military arsenal, including equipment and ammunition. In December 2012, for instance, al-Nusra, together with other Islamist factions, captured the Sheikh Suleiman army base, about twenty-five kilometers (fifteen miles) northwest of the city of Aleppo.[49] These military gains provided the jihadist organization with a critical advantage over other antiregime factions, such as the FSA, which relied on foreign support for arms and finance. Al-Nusra's military advantage on the battlefront brought it notoriety and more Syrian recruits, including fighters who defected from FSA brigades. As an FSA commander in Aleppo told the *Guardian* in May 2013, "Fighters feel proud to join al-Nusra because that means power and influence. . . . Al-Nusra fighters rarely withdraw for shortage of ammunition or fighters and they leave their target only after liberating it." He added, "They compete to carry out martyrdom [suicide] operations."[50] Other brigades in Hama, Idlib, Deir al-Zour, the Damascus region, and al-Raqqah also made similar moves.[51] According to a commander of the FSA brigade called al-Tawhid Lions, al-Nusra had infiltrated FSA with undercover members in order to target potential recruits.[52]

What distinguished ISI–al-Nusra from armed competitors was its impressive military performance on the battlefield against Assad's forces, which brought it notoriety, helping it attract local and foreign recruits. Carrying out hundreds of attacks in major cities, al-Nusra deployed suicide bombings to great effect and impressed friends and foes through its muscular, offensive posture, with its Chechen fighters earning a legendary reputation. Less than a year after its appearance, al-Nusra established itself as one of the most powerful anti-Assad armed groups and controlled an important segment of the population. The jihadist group also set up religious courts, usually run jointly with other armed opposition groups, to arbitrate disputes in the towns and cities where it held influence or control, as well as to try to administer punishment to captured prisoners, alleged collaborators, and those accused of criminal acts. By attempting to create an administrative system that competed with the Assad regime, al-Nusra presented a picture of order and legitimacy while filling the vacuum that was left behind by the devastating tide of war. The strategy of al-Nusra and then ISIS has consistently been one of "first build and then later leverage influence,"[53] establishing state-like institutions, providing essential services, and delivering order. For instance, in a Vice News documentary following ISIS in al-Raqqa, members are seen operating a day nursery where they take care of children.[54] Moreover, al-Nusra has organized "fun days" aimed at entertaining children affiliated with its organization.[55] In Aleppo, activities included "tug of war, hands-free ice-cream-eating competitions for boys and Qur'an readings for girls." Another video, released in August 2013, shows a family fair that was organized in Aleppo as part of Eid celebrations, where, after listening to Islamic sermons, children were handed out toys, including Teletubbies and Spider-Man dolls.[56]

Similar to publicity methods previously used by groups such as the Muslim Brotherhood and Hezbollah, al-Nusra's use of a media network called al-Manara al-Bayda (the White Minaret) to publicize its charitable acts clearly shows strategic messaging designed to court Sunni favor and blend in with local communities. The group established its own relief department, Qism al-Ighatha, aimed at providing food and aid to the poorest, a hearts-and-minds initiative. In December 2012, al-Nusra posted a video where members are shown preparing bread rations to be distributed to residents in Deir al-Zour.[57] In addition to distributing bread, the group also set up a free clinic in Shahadi, giving health care to residents, and ensured a free and constant electricity supply across the city.[58] Another video posted online contains footage of a fire truck recently acquired by al-Nusra and shows the group involved in garbage collection in the city of Dara'a, demonstrating its capability to run the city.[59] In Hama, the group reportedly opened a "modesty charity shop" that provides free Islamic clothing for women.[60]

Al-Nusra won Syrian hearts and minds by acting more as a defender of the locals than as a criminal gang like other armed factions. In approximately one year, al-Nusra managed to establish itself as one of the most powerful rebel groups; its leader, Joulani, gained popularity and emerged as a key player within the armed opposition, earning the distinguished title *Al Sheikh Al Fateh* (the conqueror sheikh). By 2013, al-Nusra was active in eleven of Syria's thirteen provinces.[61]

POWER STRUGGLE BETWEEN BAGHDADI AND JOULANI: THE RISE OF ISIS

Al-Nusra's surge, coupled with Joulani's rise to stardom, threatened the ambitions of Baghdadi and his inner circle, who swiftly acted to assert control over what they perceived as their men and their project in Syria. In an audio recording in April 2013, Baghdadi publicly divulged the connection between the Islamic State of Iraq and al-Nusra, stating that al-Nusra was an extension of ISI and that al-Nusra's strategic goal was to establish an Islamic state in Syria. Unilaterally dissolving the Islamic State of Iraq and al-Nusra, Baghdadi announced a merger, a new entity, called the Islamic State of Iraq and Syria (ISIS) in April 2013.[62] Baghdadi's declaration threatened not only Joulani's leadership of al-Nusra but also other armed Islamist groups in Syria. In his proclamation of the Islamic State of Iraq and Syria, Baghdadi had warned that Islamist groups who refused to swear allegiance to ISIS would be considered enemies. Less than twenty-four hours after Baghdadi's ultimatum, Joulani fired the first shot in an internal jihadist civil war that is still raging today by strategically involving AQC as a way of circumventing Baghdadi's order.[63]

In a response to his Iraqi nemesis's statement, Joulani insisted he had only learnt about the merger announcement through the media, before adding, "If the attributed speech is true, then we weren't consulted or issued requests."[64] Trying to reassure his local Syrian allies, Joulani noted that his alliance with Al Qaeda would not shift the group's policies or priorities, which remained focused on toppling the Assad regime. While this claim rings true in the short term, it is untenable in the long term. For instance, in his interview with Al Jazeera in May 2015, Joulani was asked how al-Nusra might react if the United States and its Western allies continued to target his group in Syria, to which he answered, "The guidelines we received until now were to refrain from attacking the West and America from Syria. And we abide by the guidelines of Dr. Ayman [al-Zawahiri] ... but if this situation continues like this I believe that there will be outcomes which will not be in the benefit of the West and not in the benefit of America."[65]

Joulani's response left out two important points, the absence of which shed further light on the relationship between al-Nusra and AQC on the one hand and al-Nusra and Baghdadi's ISI on the other. As mentioned before, from the beginning al-Nusra was conceived as a jihadist outfit by Baghdadi and his inner circle, although its identity was kept secret until Baghdadi exposed the link in April 2013. Zawahiri revealed that Baghdadi's declaration of ISIS "was a clear violation of the orders of the Al-Qaeda leadership . . . to not announce an official presence in Syria." He also called Baghdadi's decision catastrophic because it triggered *fitna* (sedition) within the jihadist camps: "The announcement caused a sharp split within the same group which led to infighting . . . and a stream of blood."⁶⁶ Therefore, Joulani's pledge of allegiance to Zawahiri was more the product of an internal jihadist rivalry, a ploy to avoid subordination to Baghdadi, than a radical ideological shift. Nevertheless, seasoned Islamists said they were surprised by the al-Nusra–ISI connection and feared that Joulani's pledge of allegiance to Zawahiri might have negative reverberations for the unity and ranks of rebels in Syria, an important development that will be discussed in further detail later.⁶⁷

Additionally, contrary to Joulani's claim that he learned of Baghdadi's announcement from the media, the mysterious Twitter account that goes by the name @wikibaghdady, discussed in depth in chapter 5, has posted over a thousand tweets, starting in 2013, documenting a sinister struggle between the two ambitious emirs. According to the whistle-blower(s), who had access to Baghdadi's inner circle long before the formal announcement of ISIS, Baghdadi and top associates, particularly Bakr, had pressured Joulani to annex al-Nusra to the Islamic State of Iraq. Baghdadi and Bakr even allegedly conspired to assassinate Joulani because he procrastinated. Fearing for his life, al-Nusra's leader went underground and plotted his next move.⁶⁸

Two months after Baghdadi's announcement of ISIS and Joulani's pledge of allegiance to Zawahiri, the latter attempted to mediate between his two warring emirs and end the military escalation. Both camps, together with their respective followers, had written to Zawahiri imploring him to take sides and stop the spread of fitna. Zawahiri subsequently revealed that Baghdadi had contacted him and warned against supporting "what this traitor has done [Joulani's refusal to merge with ISIS]," cautioning that "even hinting [at] support will cause greater *fitna*." Zawahiri added that Baghdadi had bluntly

threatened "that any support towards al-Nusra or delaying what
he sees to be the 'Right Position', will lead to a stream of blood."[69]
Zawahiri said that Joulani's spokesman, Abu Mohammed al-
Adnani, had written to him pleading that he intervene before
more harm was done to the radical Islamist project in Syria.
Zawahiri stated that he had sent a letter to Baghdadi and Joulani in which he "confirmed that this verdict was from a leader
about a problem between his soldiers and not a verdict from a
judge," signaling his desire to maintain leadership of the global
jihadist project.[70] Zawahiri's "verdict" called for the cancellation
of the merger and for Baghdadi and Joulani to preserve their
independent emirates in Iraq and Syria, respectively, effectively
siding with al-Nusra against ISIS.[71] Putting his authority on the
line, Zawahiri later noted that Baghdadi's declaration of ISIS
did "more damage than good" because "the elements of a state
are now not available in Syria." He acknowledged that he had
written to Baghdadi highlighting for him the fact that "if you
had asked our opinion before announcing the state, we would
not have agreed."[72] Zawahiri's decision put him in direct confrontation with Baghdadi and his inner circle, and the die had
now been cast for a bloody struggle for leadership of the global
jihadist movement.

Baghdadi had a two-pronged response to Zawahiri's verdict that defied and challenged his superior's authority and
unequivocally stated that ISIS would continue to exist and
expand. Baghdadi sent a letter to an official of AQC, not to
Zawahiri, in which he stated that after consultation with ISIS's
Majlis al-Shura (consultative council), it was decided that
"obeying our leader would be disobeying God and destruction for our Mujahideen. Especially the Mujahideen, so we
sought the pleasure of our Lord over the pleasure of the
leader."[73] Baghdadi's statement coincided with a massive attack launched by ISIS against al-Nusra and its Islamist allies in
Syria, a response to al-Nusra's decision to go on the offensive
against Baghdadi's men in Syria in an effort to neutralize the
newly declared entity.

ISIS EXPANDS AT THE EXPENSE OF AL-NUSRA AND ISLAMIST RIVALS

Joulani's insistence on al-Nusra's independence posed a serious operational problem for ISIS. In Syria, al-Nusra had adopted a different strategy from that of the Islamic State in Iraq. By allying with other antiregime organizations during battles and co-opting rather than alienating the communities that fell under its control, by 2013, al-Nusra had become the leader of the Islamist organizations fighting the Assad regime. Joulani's defiance meant that ISIS had to reestablish itself as one of the key players in the Syrian conflict. As a result, the Joulani-Baghdadi power struggle turned into a bloody mini-war in Syria, killing thousands of skilled fighters and culminating with ISIS inflicting a hard blow against al-Nusra and its Islamist partners and consolidating its territorial conquests. ISIS started to rebuild an independent base in Syria with the help of former al-Nusra foreign fighters who, following the ISI–al-Nusra split, had decided to side with Baghdadi. To expand its control, ISIS first had to impose itself on the nucleus of forces that battled the Assad regime, and it targeted zones that had fallen under al-Nusra's command in northern and eastern Syria. Interestingly, ISIS first prioritized the fight against al-Nusra and other opposition militias rather than against Assad's forces. Although ISIS's move was met by retaliation from Islamist factions that shared power and governance with al-Nusra, the group, with the help of former al-Nusra fighters, was able to infiltrate the city of al-Raqqah soon after it came under the control of the rebel opposition.

In March 2013, rebel groups, mainly al-Nusra and the Ahrar al-Sham Brigade, an ultraconservative Islamist militia, had captured al-Raqqah, a city in northeastern Syria with approximately one million inhabitants that was once the capital of the Abbasid caliphate, from the Syrian government. As the first major city to be seized by the opposition, al-Raqqah earned the label "icon of the revolution," though this honor was short lived. Soon, however, al-Nusra retreated from the city and moved the bulk of its forces to the town of al-Tabaqa, west of al-Raqqah. Ahrar al-Sham followed suit by moving many of its foot soldiers to the city of Tal Abiyad, north of al-Raqqah. In May 2013, with the FSA focusing its effort on fighting the Syrian regime's Seventeenth Battalion and with most of the al-Nusra and Ahrar al-Sham forces out of the way, ISIS marshaled its forces and asserted control over al-Raqqah. Under al-Nusra and Ahrar's command, activist and youth groups in al-Raqqah had been allowed to operate in the city, as long as they focused on humanitarian rather than political work, but the arrival of ISIS marked a distinct and drastic change.

Soon after seizing control of al-Raqqah, the group publicly executed three men in the city center, one of whom was wearing a military uniform. This action set the tone of its governance of the city: obey us or die by us.[74] By the end of the summer, the group was also able to drive other Islamist factions out of the city. In August, for example, it targeted a train station that was used as the headquarters for the Ahfad al-Rasul (Grandsons of the Prophet) Brigade, a Sunni armed opposition group affiliated with the FSA. The move was efficient, and the Ahfad al-Rasul Brigade, which had until then been very active on the front in battling ISIS, fled the city.[75] In September, al-Nusra, bolstered by an alliance with some of the FSA brigades, made a return to al-Raqqah,[76] but within days some of its leaders were targeted, including one of its top commanders, Abu Saad al-Hadrami,[77] who was executed in January 2014, and ISIS remained in control of the city.[78]

In the meantime, Baghdadi's group also expanded its control to other parts of the country and made advances in eastern Syria. In February 2014, al-Nusra and Ahrar al-Sham intensified fighting operations to stop ISIS's advances in Deir al-Zour and killed a top ISIS commander.[79] ISIS was able to consolidate its position by bringing fighters in from al-Raqqah, and in April it launched a two-month-long offensive against al-Nusra and Ahrar to take control of Deir al-Zour, a battle that significantly contributed to the forced displacement of many residents.[80]

Despite fierce fighting by its opponents, by the summer ISIS had been able to seize control of 95 percent of the resource-rich Deir al-Zour province.[81] The capture of Deir al-Zour, with its fertile agricultural land and crude petroleum, provided ISIS with critical resources to finance its war and governance and buy the loyalty of hard-pressed tribes and local communities. Indeed, ISIS's seizure of more than 80 percent of Syria's oil fields allowed it to recruit more local and foreign fighters and secure areas under its control.[82] Its monopoly on resource-rich areas in Syria has also forced other actors and armed groups to concede to ISIS's demands in return for fuel and other everyday necessities. For instance, even groups like al-Nusra in rural Aleppo and Idlib depend on crude oil from ISIS-controlled areas in northern Syria, and in turn they allow ISIS fighters to use the strategic Bab al-Hawa crossing on the Turkish border with Aleppo.[83]

In Syria, where ISIS had consolidated its conquests and shattered rival rebels, it earned a reputation for boldness, military prowess, fanaticism, and organizational efficacy. As an exclusionary organization, it is uncompromising and unwilling to tolerate dissent or rivalry by even like-minded Islamist factions. Like most monarchs and sultans before them, Baghdadi and his top commanders have chosen the sword to impose their political will, regardless of the costs. This strategy of blood and demolition impressed both friends and foes and convinced many wavering Syrian rebels, together with foreign activists, that ISIS is a winning horse. In turn, the rise and success of ISIS generated more recruits, often from other Islamist groups, who joined Baghdadi and his army. New converts to ISIS say they were impressed by its military might, resilience, and financial solvency; in contrast, their own groups did not regularly pay their petty salaries, despite obtaining plenty of foreign assistance, and did not build a sustainable organization or potent identity.[84] These personal testimonies point to structural defects, such as factionalism, parochialism, and warlordism, that hindered the ability of Syrian rebels to offer a viable ideational alternative to the Assad regime, as well as to provide for the material needs of its fighters.

What turned the tide in ISIS's favor was its ability to learn and adapt in the face of fierce internal and external opposition. Specifically, it drew lessons from the experience it acquired in the decade-long battle against the US-led coalition in Iraq, and, as a result, it succeeded in forming a solid military command and control in both Syria and Iraq. More importantly, ISIS defined the struggle in Syria and Iraq through the framework of identity rather than ideology, developing a distinct pan-Sunni identity, a deliberate contrast to the pan-Shia identity represented by the sectarian-dominated, Iran-backed regimes in Damascus and Baghdad. In the case of ISIS, there is a synergy between ideology and praxis. Of all the Sunni armed groups in Syria, ISIS's brutal clarity allowed it to monopolize the identity narrative (deliverance of the Sunnis from Shia domination) and appeal to downtrodden and marginalized Syrians.[85] Ideologically and militarily, ISIS was seen as a powerful force that could deliver Syrians from bondage by toppling Assad and establishing a centralized Sunni rule in Damascus and Baghdad, a feat that none of its Islamist rivals could accomplish.

BREAKING DOWN THE BORDERS BETWEEN IRAQ AND SYRIA

Making large advances on the Syrian front, ISIS was then able to turn its attention back to Iraq, where, in January 2014, it carried out strategic attacks in the Anbar province. The Anbar tribal leaders had become increasingly resentful of the Iraqi government, which, they insisted, had not followed through on many of its promises related to Sunni grievances. In an interview given in a bid to calm their anger, then prime minister Maliki assured these tribal forces of his willingness to reward them and recognize their help in working for the security of the country. Maliki said he had personally asked the Council of Ministers to agree to give the long-neglected Sahwa forces[86] a salary of up to $430 per month as well as more weapons and equipment.[87]

A huge turning point came in June 2014, when ISIS seized Mosul, cementing its control across parts of Aleppo, through the Syrian desert, and into Iraq's Anbar and Nineveh provinces. ISIS would not have been able to achieve this had it not quickly learnt to exploit the growing tensions between the government and the Sahwa forces and the impact of such tensions on the Sunni communities in Iraq. In an interview just after the fall of Mosul, the then governor of Nineveh province, Atheel al-Nujaifi, attempted to explain why the atmosphere in Mosul was conducive for a group like ISIS: "People were under the heavy pressure of the army and the regime. They didn't like the army and they needed someone to protect them from the army. Also, the police and the army resorted to sectarian attitudes when doing their duties."[88]

In Mosul, in a bid to co-opt members of the security forces that now fell within its territory, ISIS reportedly offered them a "repentance card," which promised pardon to those who would not defy its authority.[89] ISIS also reportedly entered into negotiations with Jayish Rijal al-Tariq al-Naqshbandi, or the Naqshbandi Army, a Sunni group led by ex-Baathists that remained opposed to the Iraqi government. In an interview, Ghanim Al-Abed, a former spokesman for protesters against the central government in the city, said, "There are discussions between the Naqshbandi Army and ISIS regarding their [ISIS's] withdrawal via the left side [of the city], in preparation for their [complete] withdrawal from Mosul. . . . The presence of the Naqshbandi is the strongest on the ground and among the people, because they are peaceful and do not have a culture of violence and revenge."[90]

By allying with other Sunni armed groups, ISIS showed a new willingness to co-opt Sunni communities. Initially it also allowed local forces to control their territories and made its own forces less apparent in the streets; importantly, ISIS showed it had learnt from al-Nusra's tactics in Syria. It also created its own "moral police," known as *hisbah*, whose role is to make sure that shariah is respected across the cities under ISIS control. The hisbah has a wide range of tasks, from making sure both men and women abide by the strict dress code, to ensuring that the prices in local shops correspond to imposed market regulations.

ISIS's successful comeback in Iraq was greatly bolstered by its victory over al-Nusra in Syria. Following its takeover of important Syrian cities, the group was able to dissolve the international border that separated the two countries, making the Islamic State of Iraq and Syria a reality. By doing so, it showed that its tactic of *kasr al-hudud* (breaking down borders) had worked. ISIS used its breakthrough in Iraq and Syria as a bridgehead to expand to neighboring countries and beyond. In Iraq the group was able to reap the benefits of the deteriorating relationship between the central government and the Sunni community. Maliki's failure to co-opt the Sahwa members led many to switch sides and turn against Baghdad. In an interview, the fugitive Iraqi vice president, Tariq al-Hashimi, warned, "We have many groups beside ISIS. I am not going to deny that ISIS exists, that ISIS is not influential. No, they are influential, very strong, they could be a vanguard even in the whole operation in Mosul and other provinces, but they are not representing the whole spectrum of the groups.... If we leave things developing on the ground there will be a possibility for wide-scale sectarian warfare."[91]

Syria's descent into all-out war led to the criminalization of its war economy, in which armed factions and warlords began to acquire funds from a variety of sources such as kidnapping, smuggling, looting, drug trading, trafficking in cultural artifacts, corruption at border controls and checkpoints, and, of course, oil, which provides a significant percentage of ISIS's budget.[92] The funds generated through this war economy, as well as through external sources, were used wisely by al-Nusra and then ISIS, as they recognized that their swift military expansion depended on their ability not only to terrorize enemies but also to co-opt Sunnis, including the poor and the tribes, using economic incentives and networks of patronage and privilege, such as the protection of contraband trafficking activity and the provision of a share of the oil trade and smuggling in eastern Syria. Tribal leaders backed ISIS because they shared common interests and a realpolitik political culture. For instance, driven by material interests, the prominent Albu Ezzedine tribe of Deir al-Zour decided to ally itself with ISIS after it engaged in a dispute with al-Nusra over revenue generated from oil smuggling.[93] In exchange for their oath of allegiance, ISIS also allowed tribes in al-Hasakah to trade in crude oil and refine it in ISIS-controlled areas in al-Raqqah, Deir al-Zour, and Iraq.[94] Many of these tribes had also previously aligned themselves with Assad's rule and constantly sought protection and economic advantage. ISIS recognized the role of the tribes and the importance of their backing in cementing the geographical gains made by the jihadist group. In fact, ISIS took tribal issues so seriously that it set up its own tribal affairs department in order to liaise with tribal leaders and mediate intertribal disputes.[95] As mentioned previously, initially ISIS tried to gain the support of local communities for its cause and utilized various tactics, not just coercion, to consolidate its power. It would be misleading to argue that ISIS could have secured allegiance by sheer domination, even though fear and terror are frequently used. ISIS's capture of al-Raqqah from al-Nusra in 2013 is a case in point.

Similar to the Taliban in Afghanistan in the 1990s, ISIS developed a rudimentary infrastructure of administration and governance in captured territories. It aimed to provide the inhabitants of these territories with basic services, physical security, and daily subsistence, including bread, water, electricity, trash collection, policing, and shariah-based justice. Al-Raqqah's residents acknowledge that ISIS preserved the bureaucracy and relied on qualified foreign technocrats to deliver basic services, and most ordinary citizens have come to terms with the new political order. In order to ensure a continuing stream of external funding and to maintain a certain level of support from the local communities, ISIS had to strike a "critical balance between the reputation of rebel leaders as good providers for their communities and their reputations as effective warlords leading successful battles."[96] The organization has at times been extremely successful in achieving this. For instance, residents in Deir al-Zour reported a noticeable increase in services such as electricity following ISIS's takeover of their city, noting that before the jihadist group arrived, electricity was often cut off for several days at a time, but after the group arrived, residents would get electricity for at least ten hours a day. ISIS even managed to fix water pipes and provide water to rural villages that had not had this service for years, though by the end of 2015, residents in the areas under the group's control reported that they were being financially squeezed by ISIS as it is pressed financially.[97]

The jihadist organization instituted a division of labor between its military and civilian operations, appointing competent civilian deputies to local sectors, including those of education, health, economy, electricity, and telecommunications.[98] According to a resident opposed to ISIS, Baghdadi selected a Tunisian with a doctorate in communications who joined the militant organization to manage that sector and develop it further.[99] The civilian arm of ISIS includes several administrative departments, such as a religious and proselytization bureau, an education bureau, a judiciary system, and a security apparatus. The religious (al Dawa) bureau is in charge of establishing shariah institutes and Qur'anic study groups as well as organizing religious outreach events where pamphlets are distributed,[100] often along with food and beverages. The education outreach program is in charge of restructuring the educational curriculum by placing Qur'anic and religious sciences at its core to, according to Baghdadi, "eradicate ignorance and disseminate Shari'a sciences."[101]

These "guidelines" seem to borrow heavily from Saudi Arabia's ultraconservative Salafi curriculum, especially that taught in public middle and high schools, which is strict and puri-

tanical. According to an al-Raqqah activist, after capturing the
city, ISIS withdrew several modules from the education curriculum, including music, arts, history, and philosophy, and imposed a weekly shariah course for teachers.[102] It enforced a
similar education program in Mosul and other areas under its
control and segregated males and females in the classrooms,
including teachers and faculty. In September 2013, ISIS posted
a video of around fifty children attending an Islamic class in
al-Raqqah, and held Qur'an memorization workshops in
Mosul for children and teenagers between the ages of ten and
eighteen. After graduation, children would receive prizes and
attend military training camps, thus indoctrinating young
minds and supplying ISIS with the next generation of fighters.[103] Similar to what al-Nusra had enacted, ISIS has extended
the authority of its court system to civilian affairs, such as di-
vorces, inheritance, and family disputes. In al-Raqqah, residents
can allegedly use the courts to file a complaint against ISIS
members or even local emirs,[104] and *hudud* (religious punishments)[105] that include public executions are regularly carried
out. As noted previously, ISIS has a police force tasked with
maintaining security in the streets and ensuring that court
orders are executed. Much of the organization's administrative and educational strategy in the cities it controls depends
to some extent on support from the local populations.

The key point to highlight is that ISIS established a hadanah sha'biyya (a social base)[106] in Syria, as well as in Iraq, among
poor Sunnis and tribes, and several factors lie behind this popular support for the jihadist organization. The ISIS narrative
found acceptance in socially traumatized rural areas and urban
poverty belts devastated by drought and war. Baghdadi and his
cohorts benefited considerably from the severe social contradictions that exist in Syrian and Iraqi society, particularly the
abject poverty and abandonment of the rural areas that led to
a vacuum of legitimate authority. As stressed throughout this
book, ISIS exploited Sunni *madhloumiya* (a sense of victimiza-
tion and injustice that many Sunnis felt in relation to the Shia

ruling elite) and used the revolt of the poor, particularly agrarian, populations against authority as an integral part of its ideological project. In this sense, ISIS differs fundamentally from Al Qaeda Central by nourishing a social constituency rooted in a pan-Sunni identity that provides it with a plentiful source of potential recruits.

ISIS has also instituted strict rules and punishments in a bid to prevent mass mobilization against its rule and to ensure absolute loyalty. According to Amnesty International, in al-Raqqah and Aleppo provinces ISIS has several detention facilities where torture and extrajudicial killings are conducted indiscriminately.[107] In a testimony in an Islamist newspaper, a member of ISIS who spent several months in an ISIS jail in Aleppo recounts horror stories of summary execution and torture by a security clique without regard to any religious, legal, or moral code. According to the Yemeni fighter who says he escaped from captivity, most of the detainees are ISIS members who were arrested because they had lodged complaints about corruption or misuse of authority by fellow commanders. His final verdict is damning: "ISIS excommunicates anyone who disagrees with it." Anyone who enters ISIS's prisons is kafir until he proves otherwise, as his jailers bluntly put it.[108] Other accounts corroborate his testimony. For instance, Amnesty International documented the case of a married man in his forties who was initially detained by ISIS because he was accused of dealing with forged currency; however, when searching his home, ISIS fighters found a memory card containing images that led ISIS to accuse the man of *zina* (unlawful sexual relations). The man was then tortured and sentenced to death by a shariah court judge in al-Raqqah. The man had protested that he had recorded the images in 2006 or 2007, years before ISIS was established in Syria.[109]

ISIS also forces residents in the areas under its control to abide by its strict implementation of shariah, including a strict dress code, closure of shops during prayer times, and a ban on smoking.[110] Its hisbah, initially made up of only men, announced in February 2014 the creation of an all-women division, the al-Khansa force. At first, the aim of al-Khansa, whose female members are said to be paid just over $200 a month, was to prevent male dissidents and subversives from infiltrating ISIS-controlled territories by verifying the identities of women entering ISIS territory. Now the role of al-Khansa has expanded to encompass the policing of morality and public behavior, including ensuring that women abide by ISIS's strict dress code and that they are accompanied by a male relative when they leave their homes.[111] ISIS also has set up its own system of taxation in al-Raqqah, which extracts 2.5 percent of shopkeepers' revenues as a form of *Zakat* or alms, and a monthly fee of just over $8.00.[112] Christians are allowed to live in the city, but only if they agree to pay jizya twice a year. Even those held in ISIS detention reported being forced to adhere to strict religious rules. According to Human Rights Watch, a number of the released Kurdish students who were detained in Kobane in 2014 said that those who performed badly in compulsory religious lessons were beaten.[113]

7

MISAPPROPRIATING THE ARAB
SPRING UPRISINGS

Social and political circumstances in Syria and Iraq presented ISIS with a fertile opportunity to exploit legitimate Sunni grievances in both countries. ISIS could not have expanded without the breakdown of state institutions and the deepening communal rift, which has been wearing down the social fabric of Arab countries in the Fertile Crescent for decades. Although only a minority adheres to ISIS's ideology of Salafi-jihadism, by depicting itself as the sole defender of authentic Islam and the sole representative of persecuted Sunnis, the group has filled a governance and ideational void created by the absence of solid national identity and security.[1] While it is imperative to unpack ISIS's ideology, worldview, recruitment tactics, and sources of finance, the driving forces behind its surge stem from the accumulated failures of Arab political authoritarianism over the past four decades that span both the political and the economic spheres. On one level, the tyranny of the political regimes suffocated society and sowed the seeds of nonstate, identity-driven radical movements. On another level, autocratic Arab regimes failed to develop their economies and meet the rising expectations of their growing and increasingly youthful populations, causing a severe social crisis of abject poverty and double-digit unemployment rates among the young. This convergence between political authoritarianism and economic developmental failure was the fuel that powered the uprisings of the Arab Spring.

A REVISIONIST INTERPRETATION OF THE ARAB SPRING

In early 2011, millions of Arabs across the Middle East and North Africa burst out onto the streets and called for social justice, freedom, and a life of dignity. On the whole, these large-scale protests were peaceful, including people from all social classes, men, women, and children. The world watched with romanticism and astonishment as the "veiled Arab" became visible and broke his or her chains. Al Qaeda's black flags remained notably absent[2] as the Arab revolts gathered steam in Tunisia, Egypt, Libya, Yemen, Bahrain, and Syria. The calls echoing from various mayadeen revolved around human rights, respect, and other universal aspirations, not identity politics or parochial interests.

Contrary to what Al Qaeda's proponents claim, Osama bin Laden and Ayman al-Zawahiri, together with their supporters, did not—and do not—have their finger on the pulse of the Arab masses. Salafi-jihadists and even Islamists in general did not play a prominent role in the large-scale popular uprisings, although mainstream religious activists did eventually join the protesters and raise similar banners. Despite claims by both Al Qaeda's supporters and its detractors that attempt to establish a link between the revolutionary moment that erupted in 2011 and the contentious and violent transition that has since unfolded in post–Arab Spring countries, the uprisings were neither religiously driven nor Islamist based. For example, in a book published in 2015, the former deputy director of the CIA, Michael Morell, asserts that "the Arab Spring was a boon to Islamic extremists across the Middle East and North Africa. . . .

From a counterterrorism perspective, the Arab Spring had turned to winter."[3] Morell points out that the US intelligence establishment failed to anticipate the Arab revolutions when it offered optimistic assessments that these uprisings would undermine Al Qaeda's ideology and worldview: "We thought and told policy-makers that this outburst of popular revolt would damage al-Qaeda by undermining the group's narrative."[4]

In a similar vein, bin Laden and Zawahiri, together with their cohorts, were stunned by the political earthquake that rocked the Middle East and North Africa. After recovering from the shock, Al Qaeda's leaders fully embraced the Arab uprisings and welcomed the downfall of their ideological rivals, the arguably secular and often Western-backed Arab rulers in Tunisia, Egypt, Libya, Yemen, and Syria. More importantly, they hoped to ride the Arab revolts and take ownership of them. Bin Laden, a month before he was killed in a US Navy SEAL team raid on his compound in May 2011, described the Arab Spring uprisings as a "tremendous event," according to a cache of letters and documents seized from the Al Qaeda leader's hideaway and recently released by American authorities, and he urged his deputies to seize the narrative of "revolution" and rally Muslim youth.[5] Bin Laden suggested launching a media campaign to incite "people who have not yet revolted and exhort them to rebel against the rulers" while hoping to guide them away from "half solutions" like nationalist democratic politics. In his posthumously revealed message, bin Laden expressed his "happiness" and "delight" with the demonstrators, saying that the umma had been waiting for this revolution for decades. He said he hoped the "the winds of change [would] spread over the entire Muslim world" and liberate it from "Western domination." In an undated letter released by US authorities after the raid on bin Laden's compound, he urges his followers to "make best use of this great opportunity" and to keep these revolutions "alive,"[6] reiterating his belief that these developments were opportunities that should not be missed. Bin Laden goes on to plead, "To the children of my Muslim *umma*, [I tell you] this is a crossroads and a historic moment to get out of the chains of slavery. So, make best use of it and break the shackles of Zionism. It is ignorant as well as sinful to waste this long-awaited opportunity." In another letter, which was also seized in the raid, bin Laden repeats this rhetoric: "When revolutions erupt, they must be supported, or else the opportunity will pass."[7] In a letter to Egyptians, he said that "your revolution is a definitive one between *Al-kufr al-'alami* [world atheism] on one hand and the Islamic nation on the other hand."[8] In other statements, bin Laden was clear about what he meant by this "opportunity," linking it to the existential conflict that he had long portrayed between Islam and the West, the far enemy.

Bin Laden's successor, Zawahiri, celebrated "the fall of corrupt and corrupting agents of America in Tunisia and Egypt, and the shaking of their thrones in Libya, Yemen, and Syria." In his eulogy for his predecessor, Zawahiri affirmed his support for the uprisings in Yemen and Libya and called upon the people not to be "tricked" by American and Western support for the uprisings, particularly the NATO mission in Libya. Trying to jump on the bandwagon of the Arab Spring and appeal to the protesters, Zawahiri, Al Qaeda's current emir, reminded Egyptians that before he escaped from the country, he "had participated in many popular protests and demonstrations," including one "in Tahrir Square in 1971."[9] Strategically, Zawahiri avoided any mention of an ideological difference during the 1970s protest movements, which had been led by Marxists and leftists. As Anwar Sadat had used Islamists to demolish these leftist movements in the 1970s, Zawahiri heaped praise on "those honourable brothers" who took part in them.[10] The overlooking of such ideological differences demonstrates Zawahiri's opportunism in the aftermath of the Arab Spring. Several of Zawahiri's contemporary associates told me in the 1990s that he never believed in political activism as a means to overthrow the secular Egyptian regime and did not even use the mosque for recruitment or mobilization. From a very young age, growing up during a period of profound socioeconomic and political change in Egypt in the 1950s and 1960s, Zawahiri rejected the political process and waged a crusade against the Egyptian government, a crusade that took him from a high school in an upper-middle-class neighborhood in Egypt to the killing fields of Afghanistan and Pakistan. The truth is that mass protesters in Egypt succeeded in toppling an autocrat by peaceful means, whereas Zawahiri, who dedicated his life to such a task, failed to do so by violent means.

Aware of inherent contradictions between Al Qaeda's ideology and that of the protesters, Abu Yahya al-Libi, Zawahiri's right-hand lieutenant, described the uprisings as an extension of Al Qaeda's prolonged struggle to expel Western influence from the Muslim world. To Libi it was simply "a step of many efforts to reach the goal." In a 2011 videotape, Libi hailed the revolutions in Egypt, Tunisia, and Libya as a considerable step on the path toward fighting "*taghut al-asr* [the despot of the age], America, the source of terrorism and the destruction."[11] He argued that the mujahideen's fight created a weaker United States, which was incapable of stopping the flow of the revolutions toppling tyrants such as Hosni Mubarak of Egypt.[12] In a similar vein, Anwar al-Awlaki, the infamous American-Yemeni militant preacher killed by a US drone strike in 2011, was candid and realistic, conceding that Al Qaeda had nothing to do with the historical developments remaking the region. In an article titled "Tsunami of Change," which appeared in his *Inspire* magazine in May 2011, Awlaki said, "We do not know yet what the outcome would be, and we do not have to. The outcome doesn't have to be an Islamic government for us to consider what is occurring to be a step in the right direction."[13]

What all these statements show is that bin Laden, Zawahiri, Libi, and Awlaki were caught off guard by the storm that was the Arab Spring, and labored to understand its impact. They celebrated the downfall of Arab rulers, hoping to capitalize on a subsequent power struggle and security vacuum to advance the jihadist cause. Today Al Qaeda chiefs attempt to rewrite the history of the Arab Spring by claiming that the organization backed it and even encouraged Al Qaeda members to be actively involved. In a widely watched satellite television interview with Al Jazeera in May 2015, the emir of Jabhat al-Nusra, the official arm of Al Qaeda Central in Syria, Abu Mohammed al-Joulani, openly stated that Zawahiri, his superior, counseled members to support the Arab Spring uprisings, which, he asserted, they did.

Al Qaeda's new Arab Spring narrative is part of its attempt to rewrite Arab-Islamic history from the birth of Islam to the present day. If the organization has tried so hard to convince the public of its support and involvement in the uprisings, it is first and foremost because they constitute one of the greatest movements of civil resistance the region has known since decolonization. By overthrowing long-seated autocratic regimes, the people proved that together and without being united by a common political or religious ideology, they could achieve what Islamist and opposition movements had been trying to do without success for decades. In doing so, they not only defied prevalent conceptions of the region as being "dormant," but also debunked Salafi-jihadists' depictions of acts of civil resistance as weak, ineffective, and hopeless. They undercut Al Qaeda's claim that only an Islamist vanguard would spearhead revolutionary change in Muslim societies, thereby directly challenging the standard jihadist narrative on political change in the Arab and Islamic world. The millions of Arabs who took to the streets openly performed a political act par excellence and grounded their aspirations and interests in the earthly world, in contrast to Al Qaeda and other Salafi-jihadists, who have put rhetorical emphasis on the world beyond earth. They proved that oppression is a sign of weakness rather than strength, as regimes rapidly crumbled in the face of mass popular rebellion. In addition, the uprisings also defied prominent claims of Islam's incompatibility with democracy by showing that "the compatibility or incompatibility of Islam and Democracy is not a matter of philosophical speculation, but of political struggle; it is not as much a matter of texts as balance of power between those who want an authoritarian religion and those who desire a pluralistic, progressive version."[14] On the whole, the revolts were peaceful, nonideological, and inclusive, composed of a coalition of men and women of all ages and political persuasions: liberal-leaning centrists, democrats, leftists, nationalists, and mainstream Islamists who accept the rules of participatory politics. While the middle class remained an important component of the protests, these were multifaceted and also included laborers, peasants, factory workers, civil servants, intellectuals, unions, political parties, and, in some instances, members of the security services and police force. The social and political mosaic initiated an important political process and an opening up of the public space that included negotiations and re-modulations of the protesters' diverging societal visions, which had never been embraced by the security-dominated state. "Bread, Freedom and Social Justice" was the rallying cry, which echoed from the squares of Tunisia, Egypt, Yemen, Bahrain, Syria, and elsewhere. The large-scale popular uprisings defied al-istibdad (repression), fear, and bullets and called for effective citizenship and more representative and egalitarian political and economic systems.[15] Scholars drew links between these uprisings, revolts, and revolutions (using different labels) and the earlier "secular" waves of dynamic open debate in burgeoning civil societies in the 2000s.[16] Others took these Arab Spring actions out of their localities, claiming that they were part of a group of transnational movements that employ similar symbiosis.[17] Whether they have their origins in local circumstances or transnational circumstances or both, the Arab Spring uprisings have formally inscribed the people of the region in the global narrative of resistance through civil movements. Indeed, in their analysis of the lead-up to the uprisings, what some political scientists and all Salafists had in common was their propensity to overlook the history and role of contentious politics and civil resistance in the region. In particular, Salafi-jihadists of all persuasions insisted that political change would only come about by revolutionary means, not through civil resistance or the ballot box.

Al Qaeda's chiefs, including bin Laden, Zawahiri, Abu Musab al-Zarqawi, Abu Bakr al-Baghdadi, and Joulani, preached that only violence, armed struggle could bring about their heavenly utopia—Qur'an-based states and a caliphate. Their subsequent attempt to take credit and even ownership of the 2011 uprisings is a preposterous, political act. One of the key terms that emerged out of the uprisings' discourse was not caliphate but *al-dawla al-madaniyya* (the civil state). Although the term has various meanings and is used by nationalists, secularists, and mainstream Islamists, it clashes fundamentally with the utopian religious vision of the state articulated by Al Qaeda Central and ISIS. Moreover, the struggle by both nationalist and Islamist movements over the appropriation and ownership of the civil state shows that the concept of the civil state resonates much more powerfully with the majority of the Arab-Islamic masses than does the concept of the caliphate. Indeed, central to the discourse of the protesters was their call for a new political, progressive vision and a political restructuring of the state along inclusive and transparent lines. The protesters' emphasis on social justice rather than individual rewards indicates that while they wanted to break away from autocracy, their demands did not fit a neoliberal agenda. The subtext of the uprisings, therefore, should be interpreted as that of a struggle against the oppression, whether secularist or religious, that had stripped citizens of their political identity, and a fight for civil rights and citizenship.

TRANSITION ABORTED

Despite the exaggerated claims from Al Qaeda's leaders, they did not spearhead the Arab uprisings. However, Salafi-jihadists did benefit from the post–Arab Spring chaos that erupted as a result of the collusion between counterrevolutionary forces at home and abroad, a chaos that led to the abortion of the transition from authoritarianism to pluralism. Writing in 2012, I warned that if the "transition is aborted in Arab countries, Al Qaeda local branches might exploit the ensuing turmoil and spread their tentacles near and far."[18] As a subversive social movement, Al Qaeda feeds on mayhem and breeds in conflict zones. Instead of addressing the legitimate demands of the Arab masses for social justice, freedom, and effective citizenship, Arab rulers, together with their foreign patrons, used delaying tactics; violence; the divisive policies of sectarianism, regionalism, and tribalism; and financial bribery to preserve the authoritarian status quo. They squandered a precious opportunity to structurally reform and rebuild dysfunctional institutions and give their citizens a stake in the new order. The rallying cries of the Arab Spring uprisings fell on deaf ears and in many cases were met with more repression, rather than political restructuring and real change. In Libya, Yemen, and Syria, and to a lesser extent in Iraq, the brutal suppression of protesters militarized the largely peaceful uprisings and caused a breakdown of state institutions, particularly in the security sector. Al Qaeda Central and like-minded local factions found a receptive home in disaffected local Sunni communities in Iraq, Syria, and Yemen gradually replacing peaceful collective action with an armed collective insurgency. The failure of formal opposition movements to unify, engage, and work with the popular groupings behind the protests also benefited armed and violent factions. In Iraq, for instance, a decade of political turmoil, state-sanctioned sectarian policies, and Sunni political alienation played a significant role in the rise of a plethora of smaller groups (ranging from Salafi-jihadists to Sunni nationalists) in Sunni provinces, which in turn paved the way for ISIS.[19] In this sense, what the uprisings showed is the inability of political opposition parties to break away from politics based on state sovereignty and move toward popular sovereignty. Therefore, it is misleading and disingenuous to attribute the surge of ISIS solely to the Arab Spring uprisings, as both Al Qaeda's advocates and its detractors do.

In fact, Al Qaeda's chiefs have tried to hijack and claim popular agency. After the large-scale peaceful uprisings of the Arab Spring became militarized in Syria, Iraq, and Libya, Al

Qaeda made a concerted effort to infiltrate the armed revolts and dominate them militarily as well as to appeal to and win the hearts and minds of local Sunni populations. In concert with their military campaign, Al Qaeda leaders have exploited the violent upheaval and social turmoil that followed the Arab Spring to promote their ideological narrative, a narrative that dismisses nonviolent political activism as useless and stresses that violence is the only means to oust authoritarian rulers. For example, at the beginning of the uprisings in 2011, Al Qaeda's powerful deputy, Libi, cautioned the protesters against "wasting the fruits of liberation" by pursuing democracy, describing it as a "road to hell," calling instead for the establishment of an Islamic emirate based on Qur'anic laws. In another speech, in 2012, he urged support for overthrowing the Assad regime not only because of its oppressive nature, but also because of the need to "establish the rule of [Islamic] law" in Syria.[20] A few years later, the leader of al-Nusra reiterated the same message live on Al Jazeera's satellite television station. Joulani took credit for backing the Arab uprisings and dismissed politics and peaceful protests as futile. Only armed militias formed by the people (jihadist groups) would topple the rulers, he stated.[21] Another Salafi-jihadist radical, Abu Qatada, whom successive British home secretaries tried to deport to Jordan on terror-related charges, ascribed the Arab Spring revolts to divine will and depicted the struggle in binary terms, as one between Islam and its enemies—albeit an interpretation of Islam as defined by the jihadists.[22]

Jihadist leaders from various factions have all savagely criticized mainstream Islamists, mainly the *Ikhwan* (Muslim Brotherhood) in Egypt and al-Nahda in Tunisia, for playing by the rules of the democratic game and for participating in elections and joining parliaments. The ouster of Mohamed Morsi, the first democratically elected president in Egypt's contemporary history and a prominent member of the Ikhwan, provided Salafi-jihadists with a perfect opportunity to attack mainstream Islamists as unauthentic and portray their commitment

to electoral politics as un-Islamic. According to Baghdadi, Joulani, Zawahiri, and Abu Qatada, political change could only
come about through the barrel of a gun, not through the electoral box. Al Qaeda leaders point toward events in Egypt as a
warning to religious activists and the public at large against
political engagement and democratic participation. Joulani is
a case in point. He is considered a "moderate" Salafi-jihadist,
and he borrows from similar theological sources to those of
the Muslim Brothers. Yet, while acknowledging doctrinal ties
with the Ikhwan, Joulani accused them of forfeiting jihad and
putting their faith in democracy and parliament, which are, in
his opinion, un-Islamic. Neither the military nor its superpower patron, the United States, would allow the Islamists to
rule, stated Joulani. He claimed that then defense minister Abd
al-Fatah al-Sissi would not have carried out his coup against
the Muslim Brothers without a green light from the Americans.[23] In contrast to Joulani and his emir, Zawahiri, who limit
their disagreement with the Muslim Brothers to public criticism, ISIS excommunicates fellow Islamists and consider their
participation in electoral politics in Iraq, Egypt, and Tunisia as
blasphemy, thus sanctioning the killing of Ikhwan members.
In April 2015, a statement by Beit al-Maqds (now known as
Wilayet Sinai or "Sinai Province"), a Sinai-based Salafi-jihadist
group that pledged allegiance to ISIS, stated that the Muslim
Brothers "were dragged into humiliation and shame as they
had diverted from obeying the rules of Allah and as they had
adopted democracy instead of Jihad."[24] The clampdown on
the Muslim Brotherhood by the Egyptian authorities is divine will, assert ISIS's advocates, because the Muslim Brothers
worship "democracy" over God's laws.[25] In a new twist nine
months later, "Sinai Province" called on the Muslim Brotherhood and the Salafi movement, to abandon "peaceful means"
and do jihad. "We call upon Egyptians to fight for the sake of
god. We invite you to take arms against tyranny," says a militant in a video, wearing a Jalabyia and gun holster and speaking in colloquial Arabic. The "soldiers of the Caliphate" have
proven loyal in countering "tyrants," added the speaker.[26]

Criticism of the Muslim Brotherhood by Salafi-jihadists is designed to show the utter failure of fellow Islamists who participated in democratic politics while highlighting the success of their own violent path. As Syria and Iraq plunged into civil strife and social turmoil, Baghdadi, Joulani, and Zawahiri commanded Muslims worldwide to join their jihad, and, indeed, recruitment swelled. At the zenith of its power in 2001, the membership of bin Laden's Al Qaeda was between two thousand and three thousand fighters. In contrast, Baghdadi now has a growing mini-army of between thirty thousand and one hundred thousand members. By becoming the major beneficiary of the breakdown of state institutions in the Fertile Crescent, ISIS, together with like-minded Al Qaeda factions, was able to hijack the people's calls for freedom, justice, and dignity and turn popular as well as intellectual opinions against the Arab Spring uprisings.

In the eyes of people from across the political spectrum, the Arab Spring has become synonymous with ISIS and the unleashing of a sectarian war that threatens state and society alike. Arab commentators and civil society leaders, along with many in the West, now refer to the Arab Spring as the Arab Winter, comparing this moment in history to a virus and a curse that has afflicted the region and poisoned it socially, destroying its fragile institutions and undermining its political stability. For example, Adonis, a prominent secular Arab poet and public intellectual, dismisses the Arab uprisings as vacuous, lacking a vision or a plan to structurally transform Arab society. "What is important are the results, not the beginnings," argued Adonis, accusing reactionary regional powers, such as Turkey, Saudi Arabia, and Qatar, together with the Islamists, of driving and subverting the Arab revolts. Adonis has been relentless in his criticism of the Arab Spring, offering a conspiratorial interpretation of its violent aftermath.[27] He is in good company on the left and the right of the political spectrum in the Arab world. Such critics do not recognize that the failure to structurally transform society and politics in the Arab countries resulted not from the lack of political cohesion at the popular level, but from the lack of real engagement among the popular, intellectual, and political elites.

Moreover, hoping to turn back the wheels of history, supporters of the old regime portray the large-scale popular uprisings as a conspiracy hatched by the Western powers, together with their Islamist cronies at home, to divide the Arab peoples into warring tribes and factions.[28] Noticeably, conspiracy advocates include historians, cultural critics, and public intellectuals, such as Egyptian historian Assem Desouki, who contended that the "Arab revolutions are a clear-cut American industry."[29] Other writers called the Arab Spring the "second Sykes-Picot,"[30] referring to the secret British-French agreement that defined their spheres of influence and control in the Middle East after the demise of the Ottoman Empire during the First World War. This conspiratorial view of the Arab Spring not only dismisses agency altogether but also implicitly absolves the old regime of responsibility for pauperizing Arab societies and sowing the seeds of extremism. For example, in his book, *Islam and the Arab Awakening*, Tariq Ramadan, a Muslim philosopher and academic, comes dangerously close to suggesting that these uprisings were a foreign conspiracy instigated from the outside to facilitate Western control of the Arab world. This is disappointing coming from the pen of an influential Muslim writer, who sadly contributes to a preponderant tendency in the political culture of the Arab-Islamic world, a tendency that seeks to explain the politics in the region as result of ongoing foreign conspiracies, thus denying moral and political agency to local actors.[31] Despite differences among these voices on the left and right, they share a common tendency: a lack of confidence in popular movements. These narratives of differing ideological persuasions show that whether the Arab peoples challenge authoritarianism or not, they are rarely conceived of as a potentially powerful force for change, a viewpoint reminiscent of the discourse propagated by the colonial narrative framework that aimed to maintain an autocratic conception of power. The European Enlightenment, in contrast, is pregnant with writers and texts that praise popular will and agency as a vehicle for change.

The Arab Spring uprisings did not occur in a vacuum. Millions of Arabs reached a breaking point after decades of political tyranny and developmental failure, and rebelled against oppressive conditions. The Arab state system had broken down long before the uprisings. Thus, it would be false to blame foreign conspiracies for the ruptures that have shaken the old regimes to their foundations, because that would overlook the real struggles the people faced and the valid demands they made. Equally important, these narratives confuse cause and effect; they entangle an emancipatory moment with still-unfolding contentious and violent transition. They project a vision of change as linear and straightforward, excluding constitutive elements of change such as violence, chaos, and digressions. It is too early to pass an indictment on the Arab Spring because such historical developments cannot be measured in a short time span. In reality, the Arab Spring was sabotaged by a multitude of actors, including autocratic rulers and their regional allies, the military-security apparatus in each of the countries, *al-fulul* (elements of the old regime), and Salafi-jihadists of the ISIS variety. All of these actors had a common interest in blocking peaceful political change. Despite their various pronouncements to the contrary, Al Qaeda and ISIS, along with Salafi-jihadist groups, are counterrevolutionary movements par excellence. From Zarqawi to Baghdadi, leaders of jihadist organizations such as AQI and ISIS have been quick to show that they have no qualms about resorting to terror and unabated brutality to discourage, prevent, and stop popular dissent against their rule. ISIS's self-declared caliphate is a utopia rooted in seventh-century Arabia that is divorced from the realities and complexities of fourteen centuries of Muslim history and society. In fact, ISIS's caliphate is a mythology masquerading as law and imposing the past on the present wholesale. Baghdadi and his cohorts' new Islamic mythology is used to reflect an ontological cultural and historical unity that binds a community together; they also assert their absolute power by rejecting modernity while using its logistical and propaganda techniques.

ISIS tolerates no dissent or diversity in the areas under its control and has systematically engaged in cultural cleansing in both Iraq and Syria. It enforces political and social uniformity and rigidity and viciously punishes dissent. It asserts its power through various coercive and disciplinary methods, which involve not only a rewriting of history but also socio-territorial remodulations that are accomplished by creating rudimentary institutions, jobs, and hierarchies. Its territorial advances are spearheaded by calculated and meticulous war planning; it uses various propaganda means, including social media, radio, television or Internet channels, forums, and leaflets to portray itself as a civilizational force whose aim is to "educate" and uncover and reclaim the true meanings of Islam. ISIS's strategic goal is to establish a totalitarian system or hegemony that is rooted in a reactionary interpretation of shariah. It considers anyone who disagrees with its interpretation of shariah a *murtad* (apostate), a sin punishable by death. Mincing no words, ISIS's spokespeople and proponents explicitly acknowledge that military might, the sword, gives them the right to dictate the umma's covenant.[32] In turn, this very same interpretation of shariah gives ISIS the perfect impetus for the justification of its establishment of a new monocratic regime in the name of change, making religion the perfect tool to obtain and maintain power.

In his explication of the reasons for the declaration of the Islamic State of Iraq, one of ISIS's key theological mentors, Othman bin Abdel Rahman Al-Tamimi, said that battle-hardened jihadists have the final say because they exercise military control and are better acquainted with the circumstances on the ground, mimicking a Manichean-Hobbesian worldview.[33] Tamimi's philosophy, which not only cancels agency but also eliminates the popular will, sheds light on the mentality of ISIS. Baghdadi and his top lieutenants invest their authority with religious legitimation and anoint themselves as the guardians of the Muslim community worldwide. Thus the barrel of the gun matters more than the will of the people, a violation of the spirit of the Arab Spring. Moreover, ISIS, al-Nusra, and like-minded groups seem to have revived a controversial and contested notion about *Hakimiyya* (God's sovereignty or rule) made popular by Abul Ala Mawdudi, an Indian-Pakistani theologian, and Sayyid Qutb, an Egyptian master theorist of revolutionary Islamism. Hakimiyya means that God alone is sovereign, not human rulers; laws or nations and political power in this world exist in order to apply the divinely ordained principles of the shariah. In his seminal manifesto, *Milestones*, Qutb said that the whole world, even Muslims, "live in *Jahiliyya* [ignorance of the true path]," similar to the world of the pre-Islamic age.[34] According to Qutb, "Islam . . . is in battle with *Jahiliyya* and its surroundings."[35] Therefore, he emphasized the need to fight this Jahiliyya for "Islam to end up the supreme singular rule," a concept which he called Hakimiyya.[36] As had been the case in the pre-Islam era, Qutb said, such a goal would be realized with the use of force. Indeed, Qutb was preceded by another scholar who proposed the same conceptualization of confronting the *jahili* society. Mawdudi, who founded the Jamaat-e-Islami in 1941, said that the teachings of the Qur'an or Sunna should not be overrun by any laws or constitutions. Mawdudi said that "no single individual, a family, a class, a party or any individual living in the state has the right to *Hakimiyya*, as Allah is the true ruler and holder of real power."[37] Mawdudi was against dividing up powers, as he believed that they all should be concentrated within the prerogatives of God. Qutb compared and contrasted God's rule, an ideal type, with Jahiliyya, which, in his opinion, includes all systems of governance based on man's laws. While in prison in Egypt in the 1950s and 1960s, Qutb called for the replacement of Jahiliyya with Hakimiyya by force if necessary, and led a jihadist vanguard whose mission was to lay out the foundation of an Islamic state. His call resonated near and far and marked the beginning of the global jihadist movement. In spite of differences among jihadists, all share in common a profound commitment to reconstituting Hakimiyya as a governing principle and getting rid of man-made laws and institutions, such as elections, parliaments, and democracy in general.[38] Of all jihadist groups, ISIS is the only one to have declared an Islamic state and then a caliphate, an ambitious imperial project that is supported by its control of a wide swathe of territory in Iraq and Syria that is roughly the size of the United Kingdom, with an estimated population of between five million and eight million people. While many argue that the Arab Spring's aftermath gave rise to ISIS, it is more accurate to state that the jihadist organization took advantage of an opportunity and conspired to infiltrate and militarize a rocky and contentious transition by trying to hijack the popular will.

Moreover, the new regional cold war between the leader of Arabian Sunni Islam, Saudi Arabia, and the leader of Shia Islam, (Persian) Iran, provided ammunition to nonstate actors like Al Qaeda and ISIS by diverting the path of the struggle away from social and political emancipation toward geostrategic and sectarian rivalry. Syria, Iraq, Libya, and Yemen have become proxy theaters for regional and global wars in which Saudi Arabia and Iran, together with Turkey, Qatar, Egypt, and others, vie for dominance by financing and arming warring groups, including Salafi-jihadists. As elaborated in the introduction, neither ISIS nor al-Nusra could have expanded without the existence of an unholy alliance between authoritarian Arab rulers and their regional and global patrons to preserve the old regime. In particular, Saudi Arabia and Iran acted as counterrevolutionary powers and tried to stem the tide of political change at home and in the neighborhood. In a similar vein, although US policymakers belatedly backed regulated change in Tunisia, Egypt, Libya, Yemen, and Syria, they were more reluctant to do so in Bahrain lest they lose the support of Gulf allies. The unfolding of regional and global wars by proxies, together with the derailment of the Arab Spring by counterrevolutionary powers, provided fuel that powered al-Nusra, ISIS, and other Al Qaeda local factions in general. These nonstate actors exploited the chaos and armed clashes that followed the dislocation of the Arab Spring in the Fertile Crescent to indirectly gain finances, arms, and a religious cover from neighboring Sunni states.[39] This precious social and material capital has been decisive in the growth and success of these Salafi-jihadists.

ISIS AND THE CLASH OF IDENTITIES

Of all variables empowering ISIS and like-minded Salafi-jihadi groups in Iraq and Syria, the anti-Shia, anti-Iranian factor tops the list. ISIS has successfully developed a narrative rooted in a pan-Sunni identity that is intrinsically opposed to what it portrays as an aggressive and expansionist Shia ideology that has infiltrated and is engulfing the Islamic world. ISIS's anti-Shia, anti-Iranian program is the most powerful card it has played in Iraq and Syria, and it has so far proved to be a potent recruiting tool. Salafi-jihadists have exploited a creeping communal rift that deepened and widened after the US-led invasion of Iraq in 2003. This dispute spiraled out of control after the Arab Spring was aborted and after Syria and Iraq descended into war and chaos. It is this clash of sub-Islamic identities, a mini intra-Islamic war, that has fueled ISIS's spectacular growth. After the fall of Mosul in June 2014 and the declaration of the Islamic State, time and again the organization's spokespeople asserted their leadership of the umma and Ahl al-Sunna (the global Muslim community) and dismissed existing and potential rivals to this honor as pretenders. Baghdadi and his inner circle are severely critical for the leadership of Saudi Arabia, the historic birthplace of Islam and a bastion and leader of Sunni Islam. In his few pronouncements after his appointment as the newly anointed caliph in the summer of 2014, Baghdadi presented ISIS as the sole guardian of Sunni interests worldwide, not just in Iraq and Syria. He went on to accuse Saudi leaders of forfeiting their responsibility to defend Sunni Islam. "The Arabian Peninsula's rulers have been exposed and disgraced and have lost their supposed 'legitimacy,'" said Baghdadi in a thirty-four-minute audio recording in May 2015. He has consistently called on Saudis to rally around the Islamic State against their "apostate tyrannical rulers," who fail to defend the Sunni faith and community against the *Rafidah* (a pejorative term for the Shia meaning "rejecters"). Only the caliphate will bring back to Muslims "glory, honor, rights and leadership," Baghdadi preached.[40] Bringing down Saudi Arabia would provide an opportunity for Baghdadi to try to assert his authority over the Sunni community by ruling over one of the most important places of Sunni Islam, solidifying his pan-Sunni caliphate. For ISIS, the politics of identity is a ladder that has enabled the group to climb to new heights.

Conceptually and operationally, there exist important differences between Al Qaeda Central and ISIS, even though they belong to the same Salafi-jihadist family. Bin Laden and Zawahiri never wavered from viewing America as the real enemy and consistently reminded their followers that "the focus should be on killing and fighting the American people and their representatives." According to another cache of letters and documents seized from the Al Qaeda leader's hideaway and released by American authorities in May 2015, bin Laden urged his deputies and lieutenants to avoid diverting jihad away from the far enemy (the United States) to the near enemy (Middle Eastern rulers or the Shia). "We should stop operations against the army and the police in all regions, especially Yemen," bin Laden wrote in one of the newly revealed documents, imploring Al Qaeda affiliates to only defend themselves if they are attacked. He argued that the most effective means to defeat Arab and Muslim rulers is to alter US foreign policy and level the playing field in the region. This could not be achieved, in bin Laden's view, without systematically "striking America to force it to abandon these rulers and leave the Muslims alone." It is clear that bin Laden, Zawahiri, and other top deputies preferred to attack America and its European allies and avoid Muslim infighting. "Uproot the obnoxious tree by concentrating on its American trunk," bin Laden wrote in a letter urging Al Qaeda affiliates in North Africa to follow his advice.[41] There was a strategic logic to bin Laden and Zawahiri's focus on the United States, which, in their opinion, maintains the political status quo in the Middle East and North Africa. For them, the road to Cairo, Riyadh, Algiers, and Jerusalem will be open after the expulsion of US influence from the region.

Zawahiri's correspondence with Zarqawi, the founder of Al Qaeda in Iraq, illustrated a conceptual dissonance in their worldview. While Zawahiri urged his subordinate Zarqawi to attack the US coalition and desist from attacking the Shia and Iranian interests, Zarqawi doubled down on the Shia and by 2006, just before his death, had embroiled Iraq in civil war. In contrast to bin Laden and Zawahiri, who prioritized the struggle against America, Zarqawi and his successors, particularly Abu Bakr al-Baghdadi, view the Shia and Iran as the primary enemy. In an interview on Al Jazeera, Joulani revealed that Zarqawi was the godfather of ISIS and had pioneered the shift in focus from the far enemy to the near enemy. According to Joulani, Zarqawi consciously sucked Iran into Iraq's killing fields by repeatedly attacking the Shia. Ironically, Joulani, who fought alongside Zarqawi in Iraq and became part of his inner circle, compared Zarqawi's strategy toward Iran to that of bin Laden's toward the United States. According to Joulani, while Zarqawi sucked Iran into the shifting sands of Iraq, bin Laden sucked the United States into the killing fields of Afghanistan and Iraq, a statement that perfectly contrasts the two jihadists' worldviews. Zarqawi and Baghdadi (ISIS) are driven by a clash of identities between Sunni and Shia Islam, a conflict that fuels their movement and provides them with recognition and acceptance among aggrieved Sunnis. Ethnically and religiously diverse countries such as Syria and Iraq were particularly vulnerable to this kind of identity-driven conflict due to decades of dictatorship and failed governance, a fact that was not lost on ISIS's planners. Therefore, the derailment of the Arab Spring, not the Arab Spring itself, was a godsend to Salafi-jihadists, particularly ISIS.

8

ISIS VERSUS AL QAEDA: REDEFINING JIHAD AND THE TRANSITION FROM THE GLOBAL TO THE LOCAL

There is a common tendency among supporters and detractors of ISIS to impose the framework of the present on the past in order to make sense of the recent spectacular resurgence of this organization in Iraq and Syria. While this is a standard narrative, it overlooks the structural constraints and different social conditions that its predecessor, the Islamic State of Iraq, faced between 2006 and 2011. The constraints included the hostile Sunni Iraqi opinion and the co-option of leading Sunni tribes by the United States, centrifugal fault lines among Sunni armed groups that clashed with one another, and the shrinking pool of foreign recruits. As discussed, by 2010 the attacks by the Sahwa councils, composed of Sunni tribes and backed financially and militarily by the United States, had forced ISI to retreat from many Sunni areas and pushed it to the brink of collapse. When the last American soldiers exited Iraq in December 2011, they left behind a fairly battered ISI, which was only to reemerge as the most powerful Salafi-jihadist group on the planet within the span of three years.

Therefore, one of this book's aims is to explain the social and political forces and causes behind the resurgence of ISI and its final metamorphosis into ISIS. The previous chapters contextualized ISIS's surge within Iraq's dysfunctional political system and deepening sectarianism following the US-led invasion and occupation of the country in 2003 and the dismantling of state institutions, the militarization of the largely peaceful Syrian uprising, and the regional wars by proxies that poured gasoline on raging fires in Syria, Iraq, Libya, Yemen, and elsewhere.

Arguably, the spectacular rise of ISIS, and other armed Islamist nonstate actors in general, is linked to the organic crisis of the Arab state, a crisis of failed political and economic governance decades in the making. However, it is important to focus on the similarities and dissimilarities between ISIS and Al Qaeda Central. Doing so will shine light on how ISIS has made a break from traditional approaches to the Salafi-jihadist movement, turning into the most powerful and wealthiest nonstate actor with potent and active affiliates in the greater Middle East and beyond.

One point must be made crystal clear: Al Qaeda and ISIS belong to the same family—Salafi-jihadism—and share a similar worldview. The idea of an Islamic utopia lies at the heart of this Salafi-jihadist ideology, which aims to replace state sovereignty with God's rule. A common thread that runs through the Salafi-jihadist universe, which includes Al Qaeda and ISIS, is a belief in the establishment of Qur'anic-based states and a rejection of human-made laws. This is central to the worldview of all Salafi-jihadists. While Al Qaeda is characterized as an underground, transnational, borderless organization, ISIS managed to blend in with local Sunni communities, functioning within the concept of statehood. Additionally, ISIS is a group firmly rooted in the Sunni-Shia divide, sometimes referred to as *geosectarianism*, a fierce rivalry between Sunni-dominated Saudi Arabia and Shia-dominated Iran.[1] However, Al Qaeda, despite being an organization steeped in Salafi-jihadist doctrine, cautioned its members and divisions against targeting the Shia. In contrast, ISIS is not a mere terrorist or even an insurgent organization; rather, it is a quasi-state entity, that aspires to build a pan-Islamic state, a caliphate, and to tear down the "colonialist" borders erected by the European powers after the collapse of the Ottoman Empire at the end of World War I. Moreover, Abu Bakr al-Baghdadi offers an alternative to the discredited, "over-stated" Arab state and taps into a reservoir of bitterness created by the "ruling castes" over the last four decades.[2] More than a terrorist threat, ISIS challenges the foundation of the postcolonial order and distinguishes itself from other jihadist groups by its territorial and statist ambitions.[3]

AL QAEDA CENTRAL VERSUS ISIS: CHANGE AND CONTINUITY

Comparison between Al Qaeda Central and ISIS will help us understand the poignant similarities and differences between these two jihadist organizations, which will illuminate ISIS's worldview and conduct. The comparison highlights the tactics and strategies used by ISIS that allowed it to seize the ideological narrative from Al Qaeda Central and make a serious bid for leadership of the global jihadist movement. Examining the operational, structural, and ideological differences between the two organizations and the resulting split within the Salafi-jihadi movement will also help us assess the potential durability and resilience of ISIS in the long term. My contention is that ISIS represents a post–Al Qaeda generation whose obsession with the politics of identity differs dramatically from that of its parent organization, Al Qaeda Central, which targets the far enemy. There are considerable differences in tactics, amounting to a huge variance in regard to geopolitical threats and opportunities that consequently alters the environment and context in which the two groups operate. For example, as ISIS faced punishing military pressure in Iraq and Syria at the end of 2015, it had begun to increasingly attack foreign targets, including spectacular operations against Western homelands and Russian interests.

OPERATION CALIPHATE

Operationally, Osama bin Laden and Ayman al-Zawahiri mainly targeted the United States and its European allies (the far enemy) and never controlled territory and population, dispersing their cells underground in many theaters after the United States invaded and occupied Afghanistan in 2001. Carrying out hit-and-run attacks against American and European interests, Al Qaeda Central was, until recently, an underground transnational movement. In contrast, from the beginning, ISIS and its forerunner, ISI, aimed to capture territory and establish a protostate in the Sunni areas under their nominal control in Iraq and then in Syria. Although Al Qaeda Central and ISIS share the strategic goal of establishing a caliphate, bin Laden and Zawahiri advised patience and argued against hastily declaring either an Islamic state or a caliphate. The West would strangle such a baby before it grew up and could defend itself, bin Laden and Zawahiri told their supporters.[4] Moreover, after the United States expelled Al Qaeda Central from its home base in Afghanistan, the idea of establishing a caliphate became a distant goal because Al Qaeda's operators were scattered in small groups far away from the Arab core of the Muslim world. The jihadist organization prioritized the physical safety of its leaders over the operational leadership of the movement as a whole, thus relinquishing direct control over local divisions like Al Qaeda in Iraq and then ISI.

In contrast to Al Qaeda Central, AQI and ISI were located at home in Iraq and put down roots by exploiting the geosectarian conflict between Iran and Saudi Arabia. Despite serious opposition from within the jihadist community to the establishment of an Islamic State of Iraq, including by bin Laden and Zawahiri, Baghdadi's predecessors overruled dissenters and declared a state in 2006, forcing critics to accept their decision as a fait accompli (for background and context, see chapter 2). Moreover, facing armed resistance from within and without, Baghdadi and his cohorts formally declared the establishment of the caliphate worldwide, not just in Iraq and Syria, in June 2014.[5] As mentioned previously, more than a year after the declaration of the caliphate, ISIS still controls a wide swathe of territory in Iraq and Syria that is as large as the United Kingdom, with a population estimated at over five million people.[6]

Although the resurrection of the lost caliphate is Al Qaeda's ultimate goal, bin Laden and Zawahiri wanted to take a gradualist approach. Both leaders of Al Qaeda argued that the establishment of a caliphate had to be timed correctly, following the elimination of global enemies and the construction of a secure and prosperous Islamic state. Bin Laden and Zawahiri believe that the establishment of the caliphate would be the last stage in the development of Islamic rule or governance, not the first. In a letter to his supporters in 2010, less than a year before his death, bin Laden warned them against repeating the error of establishing Islamic emirates before conditions are ripe, lest the United States should crush them; he cited the Taliban, Hamas, and Islamic State of Iraq as examples.[7] Al Qaeda believed that the presence of the caliphate could not be virtual and that it required territorial authority for its establishment and continued existence. The bottom line is that AQC failed to conquer and retain territory and declare a caliphate, whereas ISIS succeeded in both goals. One could cynically argue that Al Qaeda's gradual approach toward declaring a caliphate was driven by its inability to capture and hold territory as ISIS did in Syria and Iraq. Capacity, not ideology, lies behind Al Qaeda's reluctance to proclaim an Islamic state.

The allure of the caliphate has taken hold of the imagination of some Sunni Islamists who see it as redemptive, a means to salvation, and a worthy cause for which to do jihad. The establishment of the caliphate has brought ISIS thousands of local and foreign recruits as well as pledges of allegiance from Al Qaeda affiliates in Egypt, Libya, Somalia, Nigeria, and elsewhere.[8] ISIS has even made inroads in Yemen, home to Al Qaeda's stron-

gest affiliate, Al Qaeda in the Arabian Peninsula (AQAP), in
the Hamas-ruled Gaza Strip, and it is beginning to challenge
the Taliban in Afghanistan and several prominent figures
among the Al Qaeda–linked Pakistani Taliban factions have
pledged allegiance to Baghdadi. It announced in January 2015
the creation of a council for the province of Khorasan—the
historic name of the territory covering modern-day Afghanistan, Pakistan, and surrounding areas.

Although it appears that ISIS has gained much support from
the Sunni Muslim community in Iraq, and Syria to a lesser extent, many of its separate Salafi-jihadist counterparts have been
anxious about rifts opening up within their ranks. In response
to the move into Afghanistan, Pakistan, and the surrounding
areas, the Taliban published a rare open letter to ISIS, warning
the jihadist organization to "stay out of Afghanistan" and for
the first time indirectly acknowledging the threat ISIS posed to
its control of the insurgency in Afghanistan, which has spanned
fifteen years. Signed by the second in command, Mullah
Akhtar Mohammad Mansour, the letter said the group's unity
was its biggest success and warned, "If there are attempts to
create separate jihad fronts, it will become the cause of in fighting and division within the ranks of Mujahedin."[9] In April
2015 the Taliban released a biography of their reclusive leader,
Mullah Muhammad Omar, who had been in hiding for thirteen years. The move was reportedly designed to sway the attitudes of commanders in Afghanistan and Pakistan who
were beginning to look to ISIS for inspiration and leadership.[10]
But with the subsequent announcement of Omar's death in
July 2015, a unifying historical figure and the glue that kept the
movement together for almost twenty years, the Taliban faces
a serious threat of poaching by ISIS. There was reportedly a
fierce opposition by military and political heavyweights among
the Taliban to the selection of Mansour as Omar's successor.
Mansour, Omar's longtime deputy, is seen as subservient to
Pakistan and favors peace talks with the Afghan government.
A key challenge facing the new supreme leader is whether
he will be able to unify the ranks of the Taliban and stop the

defection of field lieutenants to ISIS. If Mansour fails to fill the shoes of Omar—who in 1996 draped himself in a cloak believed to have belonged to the Prophet Mohammad, giving him religious legitimacy—and to consolidate his authority, the current trickle of defections to ISIS might turn into a flood.[11]

Similarly, Hamas faces a problem in the Gaza Strip from ISIS's followers, who, feeding off the miserable social conditions, have grown in number. Although Hamas tried to downplay the ISIS challenge, there have been reports of armed clashes and arrests of ISIS's members.[12] The challenge to Hamas in Gaza is further aggravated by the fact that post-Morsi Egypt is experiencing a Salafi-jihadist surge in the Sinai and even in the mainland. In an effort to silence dissent by clerics sympathetic to Al Qaeda Central, ISIS also sent feelers to about a dozen top-ranking Islamic scholars, inviting them to relocate to the caliphate, where they could live in peace and prosperity with generous financial rewards.[13]

The creation of the so-called "Caliphate" occurred at a critical moment for the state system in the Arab Middle East, which faced internal and external trials. As long as ISIS controls territory and people, the group will continue to attract a small segment of Muslims worldwide, and not just radical religious activists who imagine that the establishment of the caliphate heralds a golden age that could bring about cultural renewal and an Islamic renaissance. ISIS appeals to members of constituencies that idealize a past that has not been contextualized and explained in reference to its particular history and that, in their eyes, must be resurrected wholesale. In all their pronouncements since the declaration of the caliphate, Baghdadi and his chief propagandist, Abu Mohammed al-Adnani, repeatedly exhort Muslims, particularly those with prized technical skills, such as doctors and engineers, to travel to the caliphate and help defend it and rebuild it. In the second issue of ISIS's English-language magazine *Dabiq*, the group called on Muslims to migrate to the lands of caliphate lest they face the consequences on Judgment Day: "Rush to the shade of the

Islamic State with your parents, your siblings, your spouses and children."[14] These calls have found receptive ears among thousands of men and women in dozens of countries who have left everything behind, including their families, and migrated to Syria and Iraq to build an Islamist utopia. Fundamentally, ISIS is a youth movement. It is difficult for a Westerner to understand why a person who lives in relative comfort and safety abroad would join an extremist group like ISIS and risk his or her life. The lure of the caliphate is that it imbues these recruits with a greater purpose in life: to be part of a historical mission to restore Islamic unity and help bring about redemption and salvation. It provides them with a strong sense of collective identity, a transformative experience, particularly young Muslims who do not feel integrated or who feel excluded in Western societies.[15]

After the terrorist attacks in Paris in January and November 2015 in which hundreds of civilians were killed and injured, a key analytic question repeatedly raised is: Why are some Western youth attracted to ISIS's ideology and willing to revolt against their nations and kill their own countrymen? Although there is no "one-fits-all" explanation of this phenomenon, it is possible to argue that the personal experiences of a young person in a specific Western country tend to underpin that person's emotive response to ISIS's propaganda, particularly through social media, or, rather, a media war room. The ISIS social media recruiting propaganda—videos, Facebook postings, YouTube videos, Instagram photos, and so on—is high quality, slick, chatty, and youth friendly. While not preaching, the ISIS message offers youth, especially unemployed, alienated, disfranchised, and religiously confused Muslims, a higher cause to fight for and a more promising life under the self-proclaimed caliphate. Of course, the response varies from one Western country to the next. For example, US analysts say the United States does not have a so-called Muslim problem, as some European countries do, and thus relatively few young Americans have responded to ISIS's call for jihad. The reality is much more complex, as was made clear when in July 2015 James B. Comey, the FBI director, said at the Aspen Security Forum in Colorado that of all militant groups, ISIS poses the greatest danger to the homeland. Comey revealed that the group was focusing on how to "crowdsource" terrorism, by having thousands of its promoters reach out and screen potential adherents on Twitter and other open social media. "They're just pushy," Comey said. "They're like a devil on somebody's shoulders saying, 'Kill, kill kill,' all day long." A few days later, the attorney general, Loretta E. Lynch, reiterated a similar message on ABC News, saying of ISIS, "It's as serious—if not more serious a threat—than Al Qaeda."[16]

Nevertheless, Europe faces a greater challenge than does the United States. More European youth from Belgium, France, the United Kingdom, Germany, and Sweden, for example, have gone to Syria to do jihad. Of all European countries, Belgium and France have the largest contingent of young combatants within ISIS as well as limited networks of radicalized youth or stay-at-home groupies. ISIS would not have succeeded in allegedly carrying out a massively complex operation in Paris, which included seven suicide bombers, without having a foothold in France and Belgium. The attacks in Paris, in which young Belgian and French radicals were involved, show clearly the vulnerability of some European youth to ISIS's new pointed message to kill those around them. As ISIS came under sustained military pressure by the Western-led coalition, its leaders began to devote more resources to the battle abroad by inciting supporters to take action into their own hands. For example, after the United States started airstrikes against ISIS in fall 2014, the group spokesperson and Baghdadi's right-hand man, Adnani, called for Muslims in the West to kill their countrymen. "If you can kill a disbelieving American or European—especially the spiteful and filthy French—or an Australian, or a Canadian, then rely upon Allah and kill him in any manner or way however it may be."[17]

Western countries' attempts to counter the ISIS message through "Countering Violent Extremism" (CVE) strategies have not resonated with Muslim communities in the West, especially in Europe and Australia. In order to respond positively to the "See Something, Say Something" message, Muslim communities will have to feel they are an integral part of the societies in which they live. This requires a sustained effort at the integration of marginalized Muslim communities in Europe. While this might have been partially accomplished in the United States, unfortunately it's not so easy in other Western countries. Another reason why Muslim youths in the West join ISIS might be that some of them feel betrayed by their adopted countries' support of Muslim autocrats across the Islamic world. Some disgruntled youth perceive Western leaders' advocacy of human rights while supporting Muslim dictators as hypocritical, and they use it as a justification for embracing the jihadist message. The danger these potential Salafi-jihadists pose to the societies in which they live primarily hinges on whether they are willing to commit violence at home rather than in faraway Syria or Iraq. The so-called lone wolf is a potential jihadist who for whatever reason cannot travel to the Levant and therefore opts to accept ISIS's call to "kill wherever you are." In addition, stay-at-home groupies or a tightly knit cell have carried out spectacular operations worldwide, such as the two attacks in Paris in January and November 2015; the two attacks in Tunisia in 2015 that together killed more than sixty people, many of them foreign tourists, at the National Bardo Museum in Tunis and at a resort hotel in Sousse, about eighty miles south of Tunis; and the attack by a couple in San Bernardino, California, who went on a rampage in December 2015, leaving fourteen people dead.[18] These cells, whose operators are either related by blood or close friends, allow ISIS and divisions of Al Qaeda to strike in the heart of Europe and beyond with far-reaching political and social consequences. Although disconcerting and serious, the menace that ISIS represents to Western security must not be exaggerated and blown out of proportion, as some pundits and politicians do. A limited danger has been depicted as an "existential" threat, sowing panic and fear among the public.

THE COERCION PARADOX

By establishing a caliphate and displaying spectacular violence, ISIS's brand has eclipsed that of Al Qaeda Central. Seen as invincible and unstoppable, both hardened and wannabe jihadists now flock to Baghdadi's caliphate. The organization has nurtured a mythological narrative concerning its military prowess in which actions speak louder than words and ISIS is portrayed as a powerful vanguard that honors the umma and humbles its enemies. Its exhibition and celebration of brutality and savagery are designed not only to terrorize enemies but to appeal to a core Sunni constituency and inspire young recruits who long for an identity, adventure, blood, and, most importantly, justice for aggrieved Sunnis in Iraq and Syria and across the Arab-Islamic world. ISIS's viciousness is thus transformed into benign and divine justice against the real and imagined enemies of Islam. It is worth mentioning that all jihadist groups sanction spectacular violence for its political and psychological effects on foes and friends alike. For example, until his dying days, bin Laden urged his commanders to carry out large-scale attacks against America along the lines of those carried out on September 11, 2001. According to the cache of letters and documents seized from the Al Qaeda leader's hideaway and recently released by American authorities, notwithstanding his encouragement, bin Laden's deputies were finding it difficult to organize massive operations due to constant pressure by US drone strikes and eavesdropping.[19]

Although bin Laden wrought the most damaging attacks on American soil, ISIS's spectacle of ritualized violence and its display of viciousness and savagery differ qualitatively from those of Al Qaeda Central, as it revels in sadistic war crimes and builds a totalitarian reign of terror. For Baghdadi and his lieutenants, persuasion (hegemony) and domination are two sides of the same coin, extracting loyalty and submission through fear and naked power. ISIS adheres to a doctrine of total war, with no constraints. For example, the group metes out brutal punishment to Sunnis who show signs of dissent and disloyalty. Punishment has ranged from the immolation of the captured Jordanian pilot Muath al-Kasasbeh to the crucifixion of rival Islamists. The group is in a state of perpetual war, incorporating the rules of seventh-century Arabia into its use of modern technology and social media. It appears that its spectacular staging of violence is a means to cleanse the land and purify it, bringing about a rupture or the "final days," when, after battling the "antichrist," the Mahdi and Islam will emerge victorious. This millenarian thinking is at the heart of the ideology of Baghdadi's caliphate. It was central to bin Laden's concept of perpetual jihad against the "enemies" of Islam, though not on the same grand scale.

Making ISIS even more distinct is its disdain for arbitration or compromise, even with Sunni Islamist rivals like the Syrian-based Jabhat al-Nusra. Unlike Al Qaeda Central, ISIS does not agonize over "Islamic pretext" to justify its violent actions; its propagandists even dismiss opinions by prominent radical scholars like Abu Mohammed al-Maqdisi, the Jordan-based mentor to Zarqawi, as "misleading" and deceptive.[20] In issue six of its magazine, *Dabiq*, ISIS published a picture of Maqdisi and Abu Qatada, another senior Salafi-jihadist preacher, with the caption "misleading scholars." The magazine cites a *hadith* (a punishment specifically for a crime considered to be against the rights of God) in which the Prophet warned against those "misleading imams."[21] In May 2014 Maqdisi issued a *fatwa* (edict) against ISIS in which he stated that Baghdadi, his commanders, and their religious officials were "deviants" who had "disobeyed the orders of their leaders and head scholars." He instructed ISIS's soldiers to defect to al-Nusra.[22] In an audio statement released on June 23, 2015, ISIS's chief spokesperson and a confidante of Baghdadi, Adnani, warned Islamist soldiers against taking seriously "the fatwa of the donkeys of knowledge," a reference to prominent Salafi-jihadist theorists like Maqdisi who support Al Qaeda Central.[23] In his audio statement, Adnani poured scorn and abuse on Maqdisi and his entourage of radical Islamist scholars. It is worth citing at length to show the disdain felt by ISIS's propagandists and commanders for any notion of theological pluralism:

> Do not let their famous reputations deceive you, even if they have a long history of writing and authorship, for they neither left the laps of the tawaghit [tyrants], nor marched forth to jihad. They spent their entire lives remaining behind with the women in their rooms, hunting the slips-ups and mistakes of the mujahideen. If they perform ribat [doing jihad in defense of Islam], their ribat is on the frontiers of Twitter, and if they take part in battle, their battle is in the form of an interview on satellite TV. They have never fired a single bullet for the cause of Allah, nor have they witnessed a single scene or episode on the battlefield with the mujahideen.[24]

The significance of Adnani's statement lies in prioritizing action (violent jihad) over theory (theology), a distinctive characteristic of ISIS. "The only law I subscribe to is the law of the jungle," retorted Adnani, in response to a request in 2013 by rival Islamists in Syria who called for ISIS to submit to a shariah court so that a dispute with other Islamist factions could be properly adjudicated. For the top ideologues of Salafi-jihadism, such statements and actions are sacrilegious, "smearing the reputation" of the global jihadist movement, in the words of Maqdisi.

Maqdisi and other senior clerics of the Salafi-jihadist movement find ISIS's actions excessive and counterproductive, harming the reputation of radical Islamism. Instead of examining the motivation and inspiration behind ISIS's brutality, Maqdisi and Abu Qatada accuse the ISIS leaders of being khawarij and newcomers to Islam, having recently been part of the Baathist struggle and killing Muslims.[25] On the other hand, Zawahiri insinuates that the fault might lie with Baghdadi's character, a defect that Zawahiri says had led Osama bin Laden to have reservations about his selection of Baghdadi as top dog of the Islamic State of Iraq in 2010.[26] In either case, the violence used by ISIS and its total rejection of theological diversity and pluralism produced a growing chasm between ISIS and other Salafi-jihadist groups.

THE DEVELOPING SALAFI-JIHADIST SPLIT

Preoccupied with the future of the global jihadist movement, the old theoreticians like Maqdisi and Abu Qatada have waged an aggressive counteroffensive against ISIS; they belittle Baghdadi and his cohorts as theologically and religiously ignorant and dismiss them as upstarts, pretenders, and perpetual liars. Instead of coming to terms with the mutation and fragmentation that has afflicted the movement as a whole, giving rise to ISIS, Zawahiri, Maqdisi, Abu Qatada, and others bury their heads in the sand and absolve themselves of the mass murders committed in their name. Top Al Qaeda preachers are silent about the decline of their own narrative and the shattering mutiny by this post–Al Qaeda generation, a revolt that originated with Zarqawi in 2004 and strengthened with his successor, Baghdadi, who inherited his bitter legacy.

Al Qaeda Central's hegemony and monopoly on transnational jihadism has come to an end. Yet the old jihadist elite refuses to come to terms with the new reality and hopes that Al Qaeda movement as conceptualized by bin Laden and his inner circle two decades ago can still be revived and revitalized. For example, dismissing the ISIS revolt as a "bubble," Abu Qatada, a colorful character known for his bombastic language, accused the Western intelligence establishment and the media of exaggerating the importance of ISIS and building it into a more prominent organization than it actually is. The ISIS phenomenon is all part of a Western design, Abu Qatada told Al Jazeera, to eliminate "the jihadist project that has found public acceptance." According to this reasoning, after al-Nusra had gained momentum, the West intervened and shone a light on Baghdadi's ISIS in order to sideline and undermine the jihadist project in Syria. "We have fallen into a Western trap that inflates ISIS's prowess, a strategy known as building enemies as part of manufacturing victory," stated Abu Qatada, whom the British authorities deported to Jordan on terror-related charges in 2013.[27] The summation of Abu Qatada's argument, and Maqdisi's to a lesser extent, is that ISIS is more of a media phenomenon, a public relations exercise meant to dupe fellow Muslims, than a serious power to be reckoned with.

More than a year after the declaration of the caliphate, Maqdisi and Abu Qatada, two of the most visible and vocal symbols of the old jihadist vanguard, have slightly changed their tune; they now accuse ISIS of carrying out a "coup" against Al Qaeda Central to destroy it from within and subvert the "radical Islamist project" that they have long nurtured. No longer is ISIS seen as a media spectacle constructed by the West. In June 2015, on the first anniversary of the caliphate, the two radical Islamist scholars, together with some of their disciples, spoke at length with the *Guardian* and fumed about ISIS's treachery and "cancerous growth" within the jihadist movement. Both expressed shock at how ISIS uses their radical ideas to further its own separate interests at the expense of their own transnational brand of Al Qaeda Central. "ISIS took all our religious works," Maqdisi said. "They took it from us—it's all our writings. They are all our books, our thoughts." Now, Abu Qatada said, "they don't respect any one," sounding like a CEO executive demanding rights for his intellectual property and respect for his senior status within the jihadist establishment.[28] The two elderly jihadists bemoaned the passing of bin Laden because, in their opinion, no one would have dared to challenge his authority, saying that his successor, Zawahiri, does not command the respect or operational control to rebuff the internal threat from ISIS.

Maqdisi and Abu Qatada got the story partially right. ISIS threatened not only the failed Arab state system but also Al Qaeda Central and the old jihadist elite, including Zawahiri, Maqdisi, and Abu Qatada. As a subversive post–Al Qaeda organization, ISIS is waging a two-pronged offensive to demolish the post–World War I "colonialist" borders and gain leadership of the global jihadist movement. The rise of ISIS represents a generational and ideological rupture with previous iterations of Salafi-jihadism. It is not just a "coup" or a petty quarrel between Zawahiri and Baghdadi; this has been in the making for more than decade. The first shot in this raging civil war was fired by the founder of ISIS, Zarqawi, at Al Qaeda Central in 2004, during bin Laden's lifetime. Zarqawi not only defied bin Laden's command but also established a separate local grouping anchored in identity politics that revolve around Sunni-Shia sectarianism. Bin Laden and Zawahiri yielded to Zarqawi because Al Qaeda in Iraq had already surpassed the parent organization in power and captured world headlines. Although both sides avoided a public showdown and rupture, the writing was on the wall. As discussed in chapter 2, Zarqawi and his successors, Abu Omar al-Baghdadi and Abu Bakr al-Baghdadi, had the upper hand, using Al Qaeda's brand while pursuing their own agenda, an arrangement that did considerable harm to bin Laden's organization. Zarqawi and his followers benefited from the post-Baathist environment in Iraq, one that is often described as violently chaotic. On the other hand, bin Laden and his associates were trying to remain below the radar in Pakistan, hiding from the world's intelligence agencies, and were therefore unable to leave a heavy footprint in the soil. As a result, Arab and Muslim opinion turned increasingly against the radical Islamist project, forcing bin Laden to publicly apologize for the mass murders perpetrated by his subordinates. But neither his public apology nor his pleas had the desired effect on Al Qaeda in Iraq, which persisted in its separatist ways. Therefore, Maqdisi and Abu Qatada confuse rhetoric with reality when they lament bin Laden's death by saying, "No one used to speak against him."[29] In fact, Zarqawi and the two Baghdadis had indirectly rebuffed bin Laden, even though they paid lip service to his seniority in the global jihadist movement. The recently released documents seized during the raid on bin Laden's hideaway in Abbottabad, Pakistan, reveal that bin Laden and his deputies were anxious about the recklessness and insubordination of their junior partners in Iraq. Iraqi jihadist groups also pleaded with bin Laden and his deputies to intervene and put a stop to the destructive tactics used by the Islamic State of Iraq, which weakened the resistance against the US-led coalition, bin Laden concluded.[30]

Abu Abdullah Mohamed al-Mansour al-Issawi, the leader of Jayish al-Mujahedin (the Mujahedin Army), a Salafi-jihadist (Iraqi) armed group, is a case in point. In a recently published book, *Al-Dawla al-Islamiyya: Bayna al-Haqiqa wa al-Wahm* (The Islamic State: Disentangling Myth from Reality), Issawi, a highly respected commander among radical Salafis, faults Al Qaeda Central for sanctioning the conduct of ISI and providing it with legitimation. Issawi is particularly critical of Zawahiri's double-talk on ISI as well as his neglect of the views of Iraqi armed groups who had urged Al Qaeda Central to disown the organization.[31] Issawi's cohorts also pleaded with bin Laden and Zawahiri to disinherit ISI for sowing divisiveness within jihadist ranks. A May 2007 letter to bin Laden from the Jihad and Reform Front, an Iraqi jihadist faction, implores him to disavow "the ongoing catastrophes and disasters" committed by Al Qaeda in Iraq, the forerunner of today's ISIS, which strayed from Al Qaeda's orders with its attacks on fellow Muslims: "If you still can, then this is your last chance to remedy the jihad breakdown that is about to take place," the letter warns bin Laden.[32]

Bin Laden, however, viewed the disadvantages of taking a public stance against ISI as outweighing the advantages, thus the pleas for reform and the deconstruction of ISI fell on deaf ears. His decision not to actively engage in opposition to ISI was strategic, as Al Qaeda did not have the capabilities to do so. The relentless US drone attacks in Pakistan further hampered Al Qaeda Central, killing both commanders and operators, forcing its leadership underground, and severing communication. In fact, the central organization of Al Qaeda became dependent on local groups, such as ISI and Al Qaeda in the Arabian Peninsula in Yemen, for money and visibility. As chapter 2 discusses, Zawahiri pleaded with Zarqawi to send him $100,000 for expenses, a request that speaks volumes about the balance of power, which was tilting in favor of local commanders.

ISI leaders were able to draw most of the funds from the global jihadist financial pool, having skillfully positioned themselves as the sole defenders of the Sunnis against the Shia and their Persian masters. Similarly, AQAP in Yemen, which is still loyal to Al Qaeda Central, has evolved into a powerful organization thanks to its continual activities, which keep its base of support steady. In contrast to the new economic mobility experienced by ISI and the sociopolitical strength of AQAP, Al Qaeda Central barely had enough to sustain itself, much less run military operations. Although bin Laden and his deputies fumed privately about ISI's indiscriminate slaughter of Muslims in Iraq, they kept a tight lip publicly. In a revealing communiqué, Al Qaeda's frequent spokesperson, Adam Gadahn, known as "the American," voiced disgust with ISI's lack of respect and implicitly criticized Al Qaeda's passive reaction. In a letter to bin Laden in January 2011, Gadahn asked why ISI was allowed to sully Al Qaeda's reputation with its indiscriminate killing of Muslims when it could not even bother to keep in touch with the group's leadership. "Maybe," he suggested, "it is better for them not to be in the ranks of the mujahideen, as they are just like a polluted spot that should be removed and sanitised and cleaned from the ranks."[33]

Contrary to what Maqdisi and Abu Qatada would state, the ISI revolt against Al Qaeda Central occurred during bin Laden's lifetime, and ISIS subsequently eclipsed the parent organization in 2014. Bin Laden's death and his replacement by Zawahiri, a weaker and more divisive leader, facilitated ISIS's full-fledged rebellion in 2013–2014. But neither bin Laden nor Zawahiri had the foresight or courage to push back against their junior partners in Iraq lest they lose a major foothold in the heart of the Arab world. However, it is not solely a test of courage. Bin Laden and Zawahiri crucially lacked the means to oppose ISI due to their forced seclusion while ISI could act independently in Iraq, capturing territory and resources. Both continued to heap praise on ISI and defend it, even though it had rejected their commands and had committed atrocities against other Salafi-jihadists and Muslim civilians. In an online discussion with al-Sihab, Al Qaeda's propaganda arm, Zawahiri flatly denied the existence of any disagreement with ISI and deceptively praised its establishment as theologically legitimate, based on consultation with and baiya by most Iraqi mujahideen and tribes, a preposterous claim treated with derision by Issawi, the leader of Jayish al-Mujahideen. Adding insult to injury, Zawahiri called on ISI's jihadist rivals in Iraq to join ranks and merge with it, squarely siding with ISI in the internal war raging among Iraqi insurgent factions.[34] In an attempt to save face, bin Laden and Zawahiri hid the fact that they had lost control of ISI.

After ISIS launched its blitzkrieg against Zawahiri's partners in Syria in 2013–2014, Zawahiri fought back by saying that he and bin Laden were not in favor of the establishment of ISI and privately advised their junior Iraqi partners against it. He argued that Al Qaeda's top leaders were presented with a fait accompli and had little choice but to acquiesce. Zawahiri also revealed that he and bin Laden did not have a say in the selection of Baghdadi as emir of ISI and that, when they inquired about him, they were told that Baghdadi was a temporary choice selected hastily because of security risks.[35] Zawahiri's self-serving account does not shed light on why he and bin Laden persisted in publicly backing ISI, knowing full well its appalling record and irredentist agenda. From the beginning, Al Qaeda in Iraq had gone rogue, directly defying the authority of bin Laden and Zawahiri. The autonomy achieved under the AQI banner only increased as the group developed into ISI and later ISIS. Demonstrating their moral cowardice and cynicism, bin Laden and Zawahiri continued to reward their insubordinate junior partners by backing them against other Islamist insurgents in Iraq.

It would be mistaken to assume that bin Laden and Zawahiri were fooled by ISI's frequent rhetorical affirmation of fealty to them. The newly released documents found in bin Laden's hideaway show that bin Laden and his deputies privately fumed over ISI's defiance and imprudence. Yet their calculated decision not to confront ISI was driven by realistic, pressing considerations of survival and struggle against the far enemy—America. Facing a punishing offensive by the United States, bin Laden and Zawahiri were determined to maintain the unity of the global jihadist project at all costs and avoid dissension and fragmentation. They prioritized unity over ideological uniformity and absolute loyalty, even after ISI faced defeat by US and Iraqi forces between 2006 and 2010. The recently released documents show the fugitive leader voicing worries that infighting among jihadist factions would weaken the family further and could spell its demise.[36] Moreover, after fleeing Afghanistan in 2001–2002 and dispersing in different theaters, Al Qaeda ceased to exist as a tightly knit, centralized organization. The dispersal of Al Qaeda led to its devolution. No longer able to impose its will on its member parties, Al Qaeda's network became a decentralized network, from which ISIS emerged.[37]

Regional branches like Zarqawi's in Iraq gained world notoriety and power, overshadowing those of bin Laden and Zawahiri. Geographically isolated in the mountains on the Afghanistan-Pakistan border and hunted down by US drones and Special Operations forces, bin Laden and his deputies could no longer exercise operational control over a sprawling network. Their authority waned as the center of jihadist activities and financial resources moved from Afghanistan-Pakistan to the Arab heartland in Iraq, Yemen, and Syria. The execution of bin Laden's orders depended on the willingness and ability of regional commanders to do his bidding, a voluntary exercise. Starved financially and undermanned, bin Laden and Zawahiri's organization was at the mercy of a rising vanguard that did not play by the rules of the game and had grand ambitions of its own. As stressed previously, while Zarqawi paid lip service to bin Laden's leadership, he disobeyed his commands and pursued his own separatist agenda in Iraq, signaling the beginning of an insurrection against the parent organization. ISIS's revolt against Al Qaeda Central took place under bin Laden's watch.

THE DEEPENING INTERNAL WAR

The killing of bin Laden, a charismatic, historical leader, in 2011 was the straw that broke Al Qaeda's back. His exit fatally undermined the authority of the global jihadist movement in the eyes of ruthlessly ambitious commanders like Baghdadi, who were biding their time and waiting for an opportunity to strike a decisive blow. The moment could not have been better for Baghdadi, as bin Laden's death coincided with social and political turmoil in the Middle East, North Africa, and beyond, providing particularly fertile soil for ISI to grow beyond its original Iraqi home. Soon after, ISI's military expansion into Syria in 2012 considerably tilted the balance of power in its favor. Zawahiri's ascendance to the helm could not have come at a worst time for Al Qaeda, undermining its authority further. Unlike bin Laden, Zawahiri has never commanded the undivided loyalty of jihadists and is seen by many as divisive, weak, and quarrelsome, a reputation earned by waging theological and political battles with fellow jihadists over the past three decades. As mentioned previously, America's all-out war on Al Qaeda Central has dismantled the organization's military capabilities and forced Zawahiri to go deeper underground, becoming more isolated from regional commanders. Due to the changing environment, Zawahiri has become more of a figurehead than a commander in chief, and his "advice" is often perceived as voluntary, without the weight of executive authority. It would be misleading to argue, as Maqdisi and Abu Qatada do, that the change of leaders at the helm of Al Qaeda Central triggered ISIS's takeover bid. Instead, as the present book shows, there are structural causes behind ISIS's rebirth and Al Qaeda's decline.

The clash of approaches and variance of resources between ISIS and Al Qaeda Central are greater and deeper than in previous disputes within jihadist ranks. In addition to a fierce power struggle and a clash of personalities between Baghdadi and Zawahiri, there exists a deeper conceptual fault line regarding the future and identity of the Salafi-jihadist movement.

Although both groups belong to the Salafi-jihadist family and share a similar worldview, they have differing interpretations of this ideology. Zawahiri and the old jihadist elite oppose ISIS's genocidal stance against the Shia as well as its indiscriminate killing of Muslims. Bin Laden and Zawahiri repeatedly said they do not excommunicate ordinary Shias and cautioned against shedding Muslim blood. In contrast to ISIS, Al Qaeda Central takes a gradualist approach toward establishing Islamic states and sees the caliphate as a distant goal, not an immediate one. Since its creation more than two decades ago, Al Qaeda Central has evolved and softened its attitudes, urging its followers to blend with local communities and avoid offending Muslim opinion.[38] While ISIS excommunicates mainstream Islamist movements that participate in the formal politics of their societies, like the Muslim Brothers in Egypt, al-Nahda in Tunisia, and Hamas in Palestine, Zawahiri, in contrast, considers them to be misguided and even potential allies. Learning from past mistakes, particularly in Iraq, in September 2013 Zawahiri published a set of guidelines for jihadists that prioritizes the fight against "the global head of apostasy" (America) and its "local clients" and advises against indiscriminate attacks against noncombatants, including the Shia and minorities in general.[39] Placing limits on the use of violence, these guidelines signaled an attempt by the leadership of Al Qaeda Central to respond to widespread criticism and gain public trust, an effort by Zawahiri to reshape the image and standing of the jihadist organization and broaden its social constituency and base of support, a prerequisite for survival and revival.

In contrast, ISIS hardliners believe that Zawahiri betrayed Al Qaeda's legacy and the martyrs who have died along the way. They have demanded that he repent for his sins against the Salafi-jihadist community. This is exemplified in an angry letter to Zawahiri written by Adnani. The letter poured abuse on the elderly chief and accused him of causing *fitna* (sedition) among jihadists. Adnani, part of Baghdadi's inner circle, demanded that Zawahiri repent for the sins he had committed and apologize for his un-Islamic views. Insisting that Zawahiri excommunicate all the Shia, Arab armies, and Islamist groups that accept the political rules, Adnani went even further and questioned Zawahiri's commitment to bin Laden's Al Qaeda, implying that he may have renounced his jihadist identity. He concluded his diatribe by agreeing with Zarqawi that the conflict between ISIS and Al Qaeda Central is philosophical and ideological and not just a fight over territorial control and authority.[40] Zawahiri's jihadist guidelines and Adnani's letter succinctly display the depth of the differences between their two groups and highlight the gigantic struggle for supremacy of the global jihadist movement.

Never before has such a civil war raged among jihadists, on the Internet and on battlefields, exposing the existence of severe contradictions between ideology and action. While both sides voice their commitment to Islamic unity and eschew parochial and organization affiliation, in reality they act like tribes with flags. For example, ISIS and al-Nusra vowed to erase the "colonialist" borders erected by the European powers a century ago under the Sykes-Picot agreement in the Arab heartland and to unify the umma. Ironically, as soon as the two jihadist groups controlled territories in Iraq and Syria, they fought more bitterly with each other than the former Baathist regimes had in order to preserve the very same colonialist frontiers that they had pledged to demolish. The fight between Baghdadi and Joulani has become much bloodier than the conflict that raged between the late Saddam Hussein and Hafez al-Assad, of Iraq and Syria, respectively. When Baghdadi unilaterally declared the merger between the Islamic State of Iraq and al-Nusra in Syria in 2013, Joulani promptly rejected this takeover and insisted on maintaining the sovereignty of his Syrian fiefdom.

The subsequent civil war between ISIS and factions allied with Al Qaeda Central has been fought along regional, tribal, ethnic, and even nationalist lines. The current jihadist-jihadist rivalry mirrors the Baathist-Baathist clash of the 1970s and 1980s, with religious banners and references replacing secular-nationalist flags and slogans. In spite of the rhetoric of Islamic harmony and unity, Salafi-jihadists are as prone to bickering and infighting with one another as are their nationalist foes. A major difference is that Salafi-jihadists veil their struggle in religious terminology and existential overtones. For instance, Baghdadi and his commanders used the caliphate as an effective weapon of choice against fellow jihadist travelers. They attempt to silence opposition and dissent by claiming to be the guardians of the faith and the defenders of the umma, even though critics accuse Baghdadi and his inner circle of excluding non-Iraqis from the executive decision making.[41] Fighting within ISIS has also been reported in al-Raqqa, Deir al-Zour, and Mosul between al-Ansar (foreign fighters) and Syrians and Iraqis who feel that they should be put in charge of running the liberated areas of their countries, not foreigners.

With that in mind, we must also consider the following: historically, the global jihadist movement has suffered from ideological contradictions and social divisions, which structurally undermined its unity and resilience. One of the key arguments of my book *The Far Enemy: Why Jihad Went Global*, published in 2005,[42] was that Al Qaeda partly emerged as a direct result of the entropy of the jihadist movement in the 1990s and its military defeat at the hands of Arab regimes. Contrary to media and academic commentary, which treated jihadists as one undifferentiated constituency, *The Far Enemy* examined the simmering and hidden disagreements and contradictions within jihadist ranks that burst into the open in the late 1990s. For example, soon after Egyptian jihadists assassinated President Anwar Sadat in 1981, they split into two rival groups while in prison—al-Jama'a al-Islamiyya (Islamic Group) and Tanzim al-Jihad (Jihad Organization). Their differences over theological and operational matters were so great that they even disagreed over whether a blind cleric could be selected as the leader of the movement.

These deep divisions within the overarching jihadist movement and within specific groups have a long history of playing out in the open and behind closed doors. Throughout the 1990s and the first decade of the twenty-first century, Algerian militants led by Armed Islamic Group (GIA), later replaced by the

Salafist Group for Dawa and Combat, were notorious for in-fighting and bloodletting, a structural defect that allowed the Algerian government to crush them. Similarly, Zawahiri faced a revolt from within Tanzim al-Jihad when in 2001 he, as the emir, merged it with bin Laden's Al Qaeda as Qaeda al-Jihad. One of the issues that created internal dissent was the decision of which enemy to target. Many of Tanzim's lieutenants and members did not join the new holy alliance against the far enemy because they feared that striking America could spell the movement's demise. Al-Jama'a al-Islamiyya kept its distance from Qaeda al-Jihad and warned its followers not to enlist. Even the famed Al Qaeda under bin Laden's charismatic leadership was plagued with tensions and disagreements.

Bin Laden spent considerable effort and energy trying to soothe the feelings of combatants and bridge the divides among some of his lieutenants. Saudi and North African fight-ers resented the significant influence that Egyptians exercised over bin Laden. Although Egyptians were a minority within Al Qaeda, they dominated bin Laden's inner circle. Egyptians and others were critical of bin Laden's decision not to carry out big operations in Saudi Arabia, ascribing his resistance to his being a Saudi. There was no love lost between Arab fighters and the Taliban, and suspicion was mutual. Taliban leaders, with the exception of the emir, Mullah Omar, feared that Al Qaeda acted like a state within a state and damaged Afghanistan's international relations, especially with Saudi Arabia and the United States. Likewise, Arab fighters looked down on their Afghani counterparts because, in their opinion, they lacked an authentic understanding of puritanical (Arabian) Islam, and some of their practices, like revering shrines, offended the sen-sibilities of Salafi Arabs.[43]

Notwithstanding the ideological and political contradic-tions and disagreements that have plagued the modern global jihadist project since its emergence in the 1970s, the birth of Al Qaeda in Iraq after the US-led occupation of Iraq in 2003 has dramatically intensified the internal rivalries among Salafi-jihadists. Although ISIS's founder, Zarqawi, fired the first shot in this civil war in 2004 (see chapter 2), his successors have gone above and beyond by severing the umbilical cord with their jihadist elders and making a bid to inherit the spoils of bin Laden and Zawahiri's organization. In late 2013 ISIS launched a two-pronged war to take over the jihadist movement and transform its identity as well. There is no going back. Too much blood has been spilled and the stakes are too high. Lodged in their trenches, both camps view the conflict in existential terms. As Abu Qatada put it, "They [ISIS] are ruining the wider jihadi movement and are against the whole ummah [Muslim nation]."[44] Likewise, ISIS depicts the struggle in existential binary terms—Allah's laws versus man's laws—and portrays its Islamists rivals as traitors and sinners who sacrificed jihad at the altar of human ambitions and interests.[45]

Al Qaeda Central has ceased to exist as a federalized organization with worldwide affiliates that are loyal to the leadership. As the weakest link in the chain, the center has fallen and the movement has splintered into two warring factions—the remnants of old Al Qaeda and the rising ISIS. For the moment, ISIS has gained momentum at the expense of its parent organization as "the self-styled leader of a global movement in the face of [its] rapid expansion and proclamation of a Caliphate," concluded the State Department's annual report in June 2015.[46] Zawahiri has since struggled to weather the violent storm of ISIS, which threatens to sink his ship. He is anxiously watching the defections of his regional commanders to ISIS, powerless to stop the bleeding. In this sense, Baghdadi is finishing what the Americans started—dismantling Al Qaeda Central by subverting it from within. After Baghdadi delivered his hard blow, Zawahiri was reduced to pleading with his junior upstart to "stop [the] shedding of Haram [sacred] Muslim blood" and to sacrifice his right to the title of the caliphate and focus only on Iraq. He urged Baghdadi to follow in the footsteps of the Prophet's grandson, al-Hassan, who waived his right to the caliphate to save Muslim blood: "Is this glad tidings not enough?

Does it not make you happy to take a decision, which Allah will raise you higher in Dunya and Akhira [in this life and hereafter]? . . . O venerable Shaykh, follow your ancestor and be the best successor for the best predecessor and you will win in Dunya and Akhira."[47]

However, Zawahiri's plea fell on deaf ears. The ownership of the global jihadist movement is at stake; this is not just a petty dispute between Joulani and Baghdadi. Baghdadi's grand design is to be the undisputed leader, a caliph, of the whole Islamic world as well as the transnational movement. As mentioned previously, his spokesperson Adnani demanded that all jihadist groups (and Muslims worldwide), not just in Iraq and Syria, including Zawahiri's Al Qaeda, pledge allegiance to Baghdadi's Islamic state, because the "legality" of their organizations is now "null." Adnani told ISIS's fighters that "if anyone wants to break your ranks, split his head with bullets and empty his insides, whoever he may be," a direct threat that dissent or opposition to the Islamic State would be punishable by death.[48]

As to Zawahiri's command to ISIS to withdraw from Syria and focus solely on Iraq, Adnani dismissed the request as "impossible" because ISIS applies God's laws there, saying that handing Syria on a silver platter to the opposition might please Al Qaeda, but it would not please God, a direct insult to Zawahiri's religious authority. Adnani also reminded Zawahiri that ISIS had not intervened in Tunisia, Egypt, and Libya, and Al Qaeda did nothing to stop the march of these countries to electoral and parliamentary politics, seen by jihadists as unIslamic. Displaying contempt, Adnani questioned Zawahiri's suitability to be the leader of the global jihadist movement, citing some of Zawahiri's followers who had reportedly called the emir of Al Qaeda Central "senile." Adnani, speaking on behalf of ISIS, accused Zawahiri of subverting Al Qaeda Central and turning it into a quietist political group that has nothing in common with its charismatic founder, bin Laden.[49] His key points were that Zawahiri's Al Qaeda had lost its historical mandate, jihadist compass, and raison d'être and that ISIS has inherited the real legacy of bin Laden as the vanguard of transnational Salafi-jihadism. He turned the arguments of ISIS's detractors, like Maqdisi and Abu Qatada, on their heads. Adnani blamed Zawahiri for being unfaithful to Al Qaeda's original worldview and for traveling down a slippery slope rather than following bin Laden's resolute and unbending path, an accusation designed to discredit the elderly jihadist among his own soldiers and lieutenants. To justify their revolt, Baghdadi and Adnani argued that Al Qaeda Central, to which they had pledged fealty, had ceased to exist with the death of bin Laden.

ISIS COMING OUT ON TOP?

Zawahiri knows he is on the defensive. ISIS is ascendant and has gained the military upper hand in Iraq and Syria while threatening Al Qaeda's authority in Yemen, Egypt, Libya, the Maghreb, Afghanistan, Pakistan, and beyond. Equally important, ISIS has seized the ideological narrative from Zawahiri's Al Qaeda and won the hearts and minds of young, zealous Sunnis.[50] There is more ideological clarity, certainty, and potency in ISIS's strategic message to Sunni Arabs than in that of Al Qaeda Central and its local branches like al-Nusra in Syria, Al Qaeda in the Arabian Peninsula in Yemen, and Al Qaeda in the Islamic Maghreb (AQIM), which operates in the Sahara and Sahel. It depicts itself as the sole defender of Sunnis against the enemies of Islam and does not dilute or compromise its strategic message by overtly aligning itself with regional powers. For example, in Iraq and Syria, ISIS battles not only the minority-based central governments but also the Kurds, who are seen as encroaching on territories inhabited by Sunni Arabs and carving out land with the intent to establish a separate state of their own. ISIS's targeted message, in which it portrays itself as the defender of Sunni Arabs against the Shia and Kurds, allowed the organization to build a loyal social constituency in the areas under its control while excluding others.[51]

As mentioned previously, the declaration of a caliphate also appealed to both seasoned and wannabe jihadists, thus undermining the ability of Zawahiri's Al Qaeda to compete with ISIS and stop the defection of commanders and fighters to its rival. To date, far from crippling ISIS militarily, the US-led coalition has augmented the ideological narrative of the caliphate that it is the protector of the Sunnis against the near enemy and the far enemy alike.[52] Although ISIS is fundamentally an identity-driven movement, intrinsically anti-Shia, now Baghdadi and his commanders devote just as much propaganda, together with some military resources, to the fight against the far enemy—the Western powers and even Russia. On October 31, 2015, ISIS allegedly placed an explosive devise inside a Russian jet in Sinai and killed 224 people. On November 13, 2015, ISIS, together with local operators in Belgium and France, carried out seven suicide bombings in the heart of Paris, killing and injuring hundreds of civilians. A day earlier ISIS struck a shopping area in Beirut with two suicide bombings that also killed and injured hundreds. These attacks represent a tactical shift in ISIS's modus operandi, not a strategic change of priorities. The group still prioritizes the fight against the near enemy, and its key goal is to consolidate its territories in Syria and Iraq. Nevertheless, ISIS's planners no longer limit their attacks to Syria and Iraq, and the distinction in the group's rhetoric and actions between the near enemy and the far enemy has been erased. As ISIS loses ground in Iraq and Syria, the group will attempt to use spectacular attacks on foreign targets to divert attention from military setbacks and reinforce its narrative of invincibility. For example, at the end of January 2015, ISIS released a video in which a French-speaking fighter threatens to launch attacks that will "make the West forget" the 9/11 attacks and the Paris siege.[53]

Reports and surveys from Syria and Iraq suggest that more and more Sunnis believe that the airstrikes by the United States and its coalition partners target Muslims (Sunni Arabs), not just ISIS. In a May 2015 audio statement, Baghdadi reinforced this dominant perception among Sunnis: "And if the crusaders today claim to avoid the Muslim public and to confine themselves to targeting the armed amongst them, then soon you will see them targeting every Muslim everywhere," he said, adding, "This war is only against you and against your religion."[54] In a way, Baghdadi, together with ISIS's propagandists, tries to pull the rug from underneath Zawahiri's feet and take possession of his most important asset—the fight against the Western powers, including the United States. Young activists are attracted by the clarity of ISIS's strategic message, as well as its uncompromising overtones. As two seasoned Arab reporters in Syria and Iraq aptly pointed out, ISIS had already won the war of narratives before it won on the battlefields.[55]

In this clash of narratives, Zawahiri's Al Qaeda is at a disadvantage because its narrative is more nuanced, fluid, and uncertain. Young religious activists find ISIS's warmongering, vicious tactics, and belligerent discourse appealing; in contrast, Al Qaeda Central no longer satisfies their thirst for adventure, revenge, and blood. The major challenge facing Zawahiri has less to do with his physical proximity to the battlefields in Syria and Iraq, as his diehard supporters assert, and more with a lack of capacity and his narrative, which does not provide nourishment or mobilization in the wars of identity raging across the Arab-Islamic world. The ground has shifted under Zawahiri's feet, and he finds himself at the mercy of powerful forces beyond his control. Al Qaeda Central still battles the wars of yesterday, while today's wars are identity driven and local in character, though ISIS has recently begun to attack foreign targets, thus erasing the distinction between the near enemy and the far enemy. It would not be an exaggeration to say that Zawahiri's Al Qaeda suffers from an identity crisis. In the post–bin Laden environment, in an attempt to remain relevant, the organization is torn between offensive jihad and defensive jihad, as well as between focusing on the far enemy and the near enemy. As mentioned previously, in September 2013 Zawahiri offered a set of guidelines or instructions to his followers that showed tactical flexibility and maturity, an attempt to broaden Al Qaeda's social constituency.[56] However, the flexibility in Al Qaeda's guidelines has since been used against the organization, particularly to indict Zawahiri.

ISIS's propagandists portray Zawahiri's flexibility as weakness and retreat, offering instead scenes of slaughter of the perceived enemies of Islam—a more appealing alternative for the jihadist base, one that erased distinctions between offensive and defensive jihad and the far enemy and the near enemy, as seen in his May 2015 audio statement. Here, Baghdadi cites from Qur'anic scriptures to claim that offensive jihad is an obligation for all Muslims at all times: "O, Muslims, Islam was never for a day the religion of peace. Islam is the religion of war. Your prophet (peace be upon him) was dispatched by the sword."[57] Baghdadi makes the further claim that offensive Islam is perpetual, unstoppable, and eternal, an assertion that omits fourteen centuries of Islamic history and society. He reminds Muslims that the Prophet's companions and their followers tirelessly carried out offensive jihad: "They did not soften and abandon war, until they possessed the Earth, conquered the East and the West, the nations submitted to them, and the lands yielded to them, by the edge of the sword. And similarly, this will remain the condition of those who follow them until the Day of Recompense."[58] Baghdadi's inflammatory rhetoric seems to be effective as a mobilization tool, particularly for zealous religious activists and young recruits.

For instance, an important lesson I learned from interviewing radical religious activists over the last two decades is that the youths are socialized into a political culture of sacrifice, blood, and martyrdom—fitting nicely with ISIS's apocalyptic vision of war against all and for all time. It is no wonder then that increasing evidence shows a steady flow of young men to ISIS at the expense of Al Qaeda Central, thus augmenting its ranks with potential suicide bombers.

In the meantime, Zawahiri, together with senior backers like Maqdisi and Abu Qatada, try to discredit Baghdadi and his cohorts by claiming that they are "deviants" and "theologically illiterate." In making his case against his nemesis, Zawahiri reveals that until 2013, Baghdadi had pledged allegiance to him and referred to him as "our leader and esteemed Shaykh." Zawahiri also points out that after bin Laden's death in 2011,

Baghdadi sent him a letter reaffirming his oath and loyalty to him personally and Al Qaeda generally.[59] By revealing Baghdadi's violation of his oath, Zawahiri hopes to impress on Islamists that Baghdadi cannot be trusted, a difficult task due to the intoxication of the jihadist base by ISIS's dazzling military performance and expansion. Operationally, in a bid to motivate the base and vie with ISIS, Al Qaeda's affiliates have carried out big attacks against Westerners, targeting shopping centers and hotels in Mali and Burkina Faso and elsewhere. In his most recent audio statement released at the beginning of 2016, Zawahiri sounded as rejectionist as his nemesis, Baghdadi, disregarding his jihadist guidelines of 2013 and calling on his supporters to wage all-out jihad to establish Islamic states.[60]

The campaign led by Zawahiri to discredit Baghdadi is one that could prove fruitful. However, circumstances exogenous to the discursive rivalry may hamper Al Qaeda's position even further. The US military campaign against Al Qaeda over the past fifteen years has degraded the operational capabilities of Zawahiri's Al Qaeda, weakening it from the outside. ISIS is now subverting it from within, a deadlier menace that seeks to finalize America's operation of destroying Al Qaeda, though the US national security community insists that Al Qaeda still poses a potentially serious threat. Intelligence agencies warn that Al Qaeda operatives in Yemen and Syria use the turmoil in those countries to plot much larger "mass-casualty" attacks, including bringing down airliners carrying hundreds of passengers.[61]

Nevertheless, Al Qaeda Central has devolved into an ideological brand tailored to fit the interests of regional commanders. The debate in Western circles revolves around the degree of control that Al Qaeda Central exercises over its worldwide network of affiliates, such as Al Qaeda in the Arabian Peninsula in Yemen, al-Nusra Syria, Al Qaeda in the Islamic Maghreb, and al-Shabaab in Somalia. A more critical question is, To what extent does the survival of Al Qaeda Central depend on the willingness of local divisions, such as al-Nusra in Syria and Al Qaeda in the Arabian Peninsula, to heed Zawahiri's advice? A litany of reports in the Arab press in 2015 disclosed heated debates among jihadist preachers and ideologues regarding an amicable separation between Al Qaeda Central and local branches, particularly al-Nusra, as a means to change public perceptions toward the jihadist group in Syria.[62]

The idea of an amicable divorce between al-Nusra and Al Qaeda became a proxy war between regional states, giving it momentum and further tearing away Al Qaeda's legitimacy. Turkey and Qatar reportedly lobbied hard for a split between al-Nusra and Zawahiri's Al Qaeda, which would make al-Nusra palatable to regional powers and the West and thus eligible to receive foreign military aid. Turkey and Qatar have invested considerable resources in trying to build a broad coalition of opposition groups, including (indirectly) al-Nusra, which is listed by the United States as a terrorist organization, to topple the Assad government.[63] However, against the wishes of Turkey and Qatar, the head of al-Nusra, Joulani, did not sever ties with Al Qaeda. In a widely watched Al Jazeera interview, together with subsequent interviews, Joulani publicly acknowledged that his group is part of Al Qaeda and receives instructions from Zawahiri.[64] Joulani's decision to stick with Al Qaeda for now is based on calculations of gains and losses. Foremost in his mind is the struggle with ISIS and how al-Nusra's divorce with Al Qaeda could dilute its Salafi-jihadist identity and strengthen its nemesis, ISIS. Particularly alarming to Joulani would be the defection of skilled foreign fighters to ISIS, as al-Nusra's foreign fighters are a sizable, effective contingent, numbering around 40 percent of all combatants within the group, though Joulani publicly acknowledged only 20 percent. Al-Nusra is caught between nationalist and transnational forms of jihadism and is pulled and pushed in two different directions. In an off-record meeting with an Arab journalist, Moussa al-Omar, a presenter for an Arab-based television station called *al-Ghad al-Arabi*, Joulani told Omar that cutting ties with Al Qaeda would be costly to al-Nusra, making him dependent on regional powers.[65] The basic fault line within al-Nusra is between a religious-nationalist wing—led by Syrian members and backed by regional powers—that aspires to fully integrate with the Syrian Islamist opposition, and a transnational bloc—led by foreign fighters, particularly senior Jordanian commanders—that wages battle in Syria, though its fighters' hearts and minds are far away. Although for now Joulani has put an end to the internal debates and infighting, the struggle is far from resolved. In the past year al-Nusra dismissed several senior leaders for insubordination and going rogue or supporting ISIS, including one of its first seven founders, Abu Mohammed Saleh al-Hamwi, Iraqi national Abu Marya al-Qahtani, a chief propagandist, and a senior military commander, Abu Samir al-Urdoni.[66]

Nevertheless, while the world obsesses over ISIS's savagery, a viciousness that has already alienated average Arab and Muslim opinion, al-Nusra depicts itself as a "rational" wing of the global jihadist movement and blends itself with mainstream rebel groups and local Syrians. Joulani summons top Arab media to his headquarters in Idlib, Syria, where he is given hours of prime time television to propagate his worldview. Al-Nusra is seen as moderate in comparison to ISIS, even though it belongs to the same Salafi-jihadist family and has a similar worldview, a fact that testifies to its effectiveness and its potential to inherit its rival's spoils in Syria. In making such a comparison, Abu Qatada, a prominent preacher of Salafi-jihadism, dismisses ISIS as "a bubble" and its leaders as "misguided." He pins his hopes on al-Nusra in Syria; its sister group in Yemen, Al Qaeda in the Arabian Peninsula; and jihadists in North Africa to deliver victory to the umma. Abu Qatada and Maqdisi, together with the Salafi-jihadist old guard, are still faithful to Al Qaeda Central, led by Zawahiri, who has recently shown flexibility toward moderate Islamist groups and advised his followers to avoid alienating local communities. "Despite all the contradictions that exist in the 'umma, I believe that victory is within our reach," Abu Qatada told his Arabic interlocutor after his release from prison in Jordan in 2014, adding that he has never been as optimistic about the future of the jihadist movement as he is today.[67] Abu Qatada's winning horse, Al Qaeda Central, does not differ dramatically from ISIS, except in the degree to which ISIS had flamboyantly used ritualized violence to subdue and terrorize its enemies and inspire potential young recruits.

In addition to support from some regional states, Salafi-jihadist supporters called on Zawahiri to dissolve Al Qaeda Central and allow local divisions to go their separate ways, a request that reflects the gravity of the crisis faced by the parent organization.[68] Even within al-Nusra, there have been vocal members who proclaimed their desire to sever ties with Zawahiri's Al Qaeda. According to Maqdisi, who says he is a friend of Zawahiri, Al Qaeda's leader would not object if al-Nusra decides to go its separate way, but it is feared that ISIS would be the main beneficiary. That is why Zawahiri accepted the renewal of Joulani's oath to him and to Al Qaeda Central, Maqdisi told *Al Hayat*, a London-based Arab newspaper. At this stage, a majority within al-Nusra feels that the Syrian-based organization "would have committed suicide if it had severed ties with Al Qaeda, even though Zawahiri would not have objected."[69]

The strategic arrangement between al-Nusra and Al Qaeda against ISIS reveals that Al Qaeda Central has become a liability. Joulani's decision to maintain ties with Zawahiri was voluntary, not obligatory, a fact that shows the erosion of the authority of the most senior leader of the global jihadist movement. In the jihadist culture, an oath of allegiance is sacred, and once it is sworn, it is religiously enforced. There is nothing voluntary about it. Moreover, Al Qaeda Central no longer exercises control over the scattered regional commanders who use the brand to advance their own agendas. As stressed before, although Zarqawi, the progenitor of ISIS, pledged allegiance to bin Laden in 2004, he pursued a unilateral path against the expressed wishes of bin Laden and almost succeeded in embroiling Iraq in all-out communal Sunni-Shia war. His successors in Iraq not only preserved his bloody legacy but also launched a full-fledged bid to take over the Salafi-jihadist tribe. Baghdadi, who swore baiya to bin Laden in 2010 and then to Zawahiri in 2011, made a mockery of Zawahiri by subverting

Al Qaeda from within and going as far as to give his propagandists instructions to publicly humiliate this jihadist elder. For the moment, Zawahiri's Al Qaeda seems to be swimming against the tide, struggling in rocky waters. With the wind at its back, from late 2013 until mid-2015 ISIS was on a winning streak, spreading near and far. Its utopian project resonates with young converts to its cause from Russia to China and beyond, though at the time of writing in late 2015 ISIS's momentum is blunted, facing a reckoning on nearly every front.

While the political and social conditions of the Arab world in recent years have not been favorable to Zawahiri's Al Qaeda, it would be misleading to pen its obituary. In fact, the struggle is far from over. Time has a different meaning for jihadists of Zawahiri's variety; it is measured in decades, not years or months. Zawahiri is biding his time, hoping that Baghdadi's recklessness will be his downfall. In comparison to Zawahiri's careful approach, ISIS is overextended and fights simultaneously on several fronts, a condition that it cannot sustain indefinitely. The weight of evidence suggests that ISIS is squeezed and on the defensive in both Syria and Iraq, losing as much as 40 percent of the Iraqi territory it conquered in 2014 and between 5 percent and 20 percent in Syria, including Kobani and key towns on the Syrian-Turkish border, which threatens to cut off its last direct access to the Turkish border, hampering its ability to attract new foreign recruits. Significant losses have also occurred in Tikrit and Baiji in the "Sunni Triangle" north of Baghdad, and in Ramadi, the capital and the largest city in Anbar, Western Iraq. The territorial losses have shattered the group's aura of invincibility and exposed the fragility of its "Caliphate."[70] ISIS's message of triumphalism and empowerment resonates less and less with Sunnis as the wheels of fortune turn against the group. Its finances are faltering at a fast rate, forcing the organization to cut its expenditures and heavily tax and fine the population under its control. By attacking Western, Russian, and Middle Eastern targets, Baghdadi united the world against ISIS. The skies of Syria and Iraq are crowded with Western and Russian jet fighters hunting down ISIS's senior and middle-level operators and destroying its oilfields and economic assets. Intensifying its airstrikes against ISIS in Iraq and Syria, the US-led coalition carried out more than 3,000 sorties in November 2015 alone and has carried out more than 10,000 in total.[71] The coalition has set up a local grouping called the Democratic Forces of Syria, which is made up of Syrian Kurds and Arab rebels with the aim of dislodging ISIS from Raqqa, its self-proclaimed capital, which would be the beginning of the end of the group. There is no tipping point, but ISIS is bleeding and faces increasing pressure in both Syria and Iraq. As the military tide turns against ISIS, it is forced to reduce its expenses and tighten its belt and struggle to survive. Although it is early to pen the obituary of ISIS, it can no longer live up to its slogan "to remain and expand." The writing is already on the wall with the group losing its popular appeal.

Clearly, there is a causal link between ISIS's impressive military achievements on the battlefield and the attractiveness of its utopian project. Nothing succeeds like success, a cliché aptly applied to ISIS. The durability and resilience of the ISIS narrative are organically tied to its continued ability to hold onto the territories and peoples under its control in Iraq and Syria. The caliphate will eventually disintegrate if ISIS loses its grip on these areas, an important point that must be kept in mind, especially when the organization is at the height of its influence. To think the unthinkable, a collapse of the "Islamic State" might not be imminent but it is conceivable in the near future.

A cunning survivor who has outfoxed the world's security services since the 1970s, Zawahiri ironically might be pinning his hopes on the US coalition to roll back ISIS before it devours the remnants of his organization. In the meantime, he plays the long game, showing that his local divisions are actively attacking Westerners and expanding their control over territory in war-torn Syria, Yemen, and beyond. Trying to outbid its bitter rival, ISIS, Al Qaeda's affiliates took responsibility for an assault in Paris in January 2015 that killed twelve people, including journalists from a French satirical newspaper, and another attack in November 2015 at the Radisson Blu hotel in Mali's capital of Bamako, in which militants took 170 hostages, twenty of whom were killed. Al Qaeda's North African affiliate, Al Qaeda in the Islamic Maghreb, together with allied militants, targeted a Western symbol in Mali days after ISIS claimed an attack in Paris that killed 130 people. AQIM also took responsibility for an assault in January 2016 on a luxury hotel in Burkina Faso that killed 29 people. Preempting any attempt by ISIS to seize territory, AQAP captured much of Hadramaut, Yemen's largest province, and also seized key towns in the southern Abyan province, where it briefly established an Islamic emirate in 2011 and has a strong following.[72]

Declaring all-out war against his nemesis, Zawahiri dismissed Baghdadi as illegitimate while expressing his willingness to cooperate with his rival in their fight against the Western-led coalition. "We don't recognize the caliphate of Abu Bakr al-Baghdadi," he said in an audiotape recorded in spring 2015 and released by al Qaeda's official media wing in September 2010. In an appeal to the Salafi-jihadist base, Zawahiri pointed out that Baghdadi caused *fitna*, or sedition within the ranks. "We have endured a lot of harm from Abu Bakr al-Baghdadi and his brothers, and we preferred to respond with as little as possible, out of our concern to extinguish the fire of sedition," Zawahiri said in only his second public message in 2015. "But Abu Bakr al-Baghdadi and his brothers did not leave us a choice, for they have demanded that all the mujahedeen reject their confirmed pledges of allegiance, and to pledge allegiance to them for what they claim of a caliphate," he added. Showing magnanimity and pretending to rise above the painful history and forget and forgive, Zawahiri called for unity against the common enemy. "Despite the big mistakes [of the Islamic State], if I were in Iraq or Syria I would cooperate with them in killing the crusaders and secularists and Shiites even though I don't recognize the legitimacy of their state, because the matter is bigger than that."[73] Barring Zawahiri's premature death, he may yet have the last word in his struggle with Baghdadi.

CONCLUSION:

THE FUTURE OF ISIS

For the moment, ISIS is ascendant. As this book has argued, the organization is both a symptom of the breakdown of state institutions in the heart of the Arab world and a clash of identities between Sunni and Shia Muslims. This two-pronged social and sectarian crisis has allowed ISIS to step forward and fill a governance void, depicting itself as the sole defender of aggrieved Sunnis. ISIS is a product of the social and political chaos that has engulfed the Arab Middle East, as well as of the subsequent decline of public goods and services, particularly employment, and the expanding Salafi-jihadist ideology that underpins its view of the caliphate and of Islam. In this sense, ISIS's umbilical cord is tied to raging civil wars in Iraq, Syria, Libya, Yemen, and beyond and the criminalized war economy that has emerged a result. This war economy enables the group to act as a protostate and to gain the acquiescence of poor local communities. If this reading is correct, the most effective way to delegitimize ISIS depends on the ability of Arab societies, together with the regional and great powers, to politically resolve spiraling communal conflicts and to support state-building structures along transparent and legitimate lines.

In addition, there is an urgent need to resolve the Israel-Palestine conflict, which has provided ideological nourishment to non-state actors, including Salafi-jihadists. The prolonged tragedy of the Palestinians is a constant source of motivation and re-cruitment for Al Qaeda groups of all varieties, including ISIS. Time and again, Salafi-jihadists refer to Palestine as the final stage or culmination of their jihad, promising to come to the aid of the Palestinians after they topple renegade Arab rulers at home. For example, as the US-led coalition ramped up air-strikes against ISIS and backed offensives by local forces at the end of 2015, Baghdadi purportedly released an audio statement in which he reaffirmed his commitment to extend the Islamic State to Palestine. "The Jews thought we forgot Palestine and that they had distracted us from it," he says in the recording. "Not at all, Jews. We did not forget Palestine for a moment. With the help of Allah, we will not forget it.... The pioneers of the jihadist fighters will surround you on a day that you think is distant and we know is close. We are getting closer every day."[1] This suggests that there is no quick fix to the ISIS crisis. A proper response necessitates a complex and prolonged political strategy that will take an enormous amount of time, reconciliation, compromise, and credible leadership at the local, national, regional, and international levels—all of which are commodities in short supply today.

A SOCIAL BASE

Instead of offering a policy menu, a more useful approach is to draw a balance sheet about ISIS's structural strengths and weak-nesses. The dynamic relationship between this group and its target audience allows a more nuanced and complex under-standing of ISIS's long-term durability and fragility.[2] To start with, of all existing fault lines in the Arab world, the deepen-ing and widening Sunni-Shia divide has provided ISIS with hadanah sha'biyya (a social base) among aggrieved Sunnis, es-pecially agrarian and urban poor. Sectarianism is the fuel that has powered the ISIS surge. Fundamentally, ISIS utilizes identity as the driving force for the movement and its expansion, expressed through a narrow-minded and intolerant Salafi-jihadist (Islamist) ideology. The group's rebirth in Iraq and its emergence in Syria are organically linked to communal polarization and a widespread perception among Sunnis that the central government in Baghdad has willfully disfranchised them. The outbreak of the civil war in Syria also provided ISIS with a golden opportunity to expand its influence to a neighboring Arab country and gain strategic depth there. By exploiting the Sunni-Shia rift in Iraq and the increasingly sectarian strife in Syria, Baghdadi and his cohorts succeeded in appealing to many rebellious Sunnis who felt persecuted, marginalized, and excluded by the Shia- and Alawite-dominated regimes in Baghdad and Damascus. Iran's role in backing both regimes further entrenched this view. From 2011 until the pronouncement of the Islamic State Caliphate in June 2014, Baghdadi blended his group with local communities and built a popular constituency.

This hadanah sha'biyya largely helps explain the staying power and endurance of ISIS in the face of attacks from within and without. Although it is difficult to precisely measure the extent of the Sunni backing for Baghdadi's combatants (there are no credible studies), it is substantial, dynamic, and fluid in Iraq and much weaker in Syria. ISIS's roots run deeper in Iraq, having previously engulfed a preexisting Sunni insurgency in the aftermath of the 2003 US-led invasion. Other than the somewhat frail attempts by the ill-equipped and under-sourced Awakening movement[3] in parts of Anbar, there has been almost no organized armed resistance against ISIS in the territories under its control in Iraq, though this might change if the group loses its military edge.[4] Residents are reluctant to fight the group, because many do not see governance by what they view as a sectarian authority in Baghdad as something worth fighting for.[5] It is unsurprising, then, that ISIS has not yet collapsed like a house of cards under the punishing weight of the US air campaign and ground offensives carried out by an increasing litany of enemies. With few exceptions, Sunni-dominated areas under ISIS's rule successfully resisted repeated assaults by more powerful military forces. For example, in the battle for Ramadi in May 2015, tribes reportedly provided cash, weapons, and intelligence to ISIS, which tilted the balance of power against the Iraqi security forces. Similarly, Sunni support for ISIS in Fallujah has allowed it so far to weather the violent storm of attacks by the Iraqi government and its allies. But where ISIS has tried to make inroads outside its core Sunni territory—against the Kurds in Syria and Iraq and among other rebel groups—it has been beaten back.[6]

A pattern has emerged that points to ISIS's being somewhat tolerated, if not completely supported in Iraq, among Sunnis, who see it as the enemy of their enemies, particularly the Shia-led government in Baghdad. While there has been some Sunni resistance to ISIS, notably the estimated seven hundred to one thousand Sunni tribal members fighting alongside the Iraqi security forces and the Hash'd al-Sha'bi (Popular Mobilization Force)[7] against ISIS in Tikrit,[8] revenge attacks carried out by Shia militias following ISIS's defeat and withdrawal from the city worked only to cement Sunni fears and suspicions, reinforcing an existing Sunni reluctance to confront ISIS more systematically.[9] Despite efforts by the US-led coalition to co-opt Sunnis into the anti-ISIS coalition in Iraq and Syria, the rift between the two communities has not been healed yet. There exists no coherent policy to bridge the divides among Iraqi ethnic and religious constituencies, divides aggravated by poor governance and intracommunal rivalries. More than a year after the declaration of an Islamic state, some of the most prominent and influential Sunni tribal leaders in Ramadi, Mosul, and Fallujah for the first time formally pledged allegiance to Baghdadi in summer 2015.[10] Complicating matters is the development of an intra-Sunni civil war in Iraq that has greatly benefited ISIS and like-minded groups and splintered the community further. ISIS exploits this Sunni-Sunni schism by presenting itself as a savior of the inhabitants of Anbar from the corruption of the ruling elite and the power struggle of tribal leaders. For example, in Anbar province, members of the same extended Sunni family battle each other on opposing front lines, with many fighting under the ISIS banner even though they may not believe in its Salafi-jihadist ideology.[11] On balance, Sunnis are still deeply suspicious of the new central authority in Baghdad, notwithstanding the change in head of state from Nuri al-Maliki to Haider Al-Ababdi, and view it as sectarian and beholden to Tehran.[12] Sunnis in Iraq and Syria also voice resentment against the US-led coalition targeting ISIS, while turning a blind eye to the crimes of the Assad regime as well as the Shia-led militias in Iraq. The United States' actions in Iraq in 2003 and the following years helped create and reinforce resentment and a feeling of persecution among many Sunnis in Iraq and Syria, sentiments that are now being resurrected against the US-led coalition's airstrikes targeting ISIS. Sheikh Abu Sleiman al-Hassan, an early leader of the Syrian revolt, notes that "the US-led coalition in Syria and Iraq targets only the Sunnis, and this generates public support for ISIS because popular opinion automatically sides with whoever America fights."[13] Explicit and implicit Sunni support supplies ISIS with social oxygen that prolongs its life span. As an Iraqi activist, Omar Fawwaz, who lives in Anbar and who does not back the group, put it, "For ordinary Sunnis ISIS is the last line of defence of their existence, identity, and property."[14] The only way to prevent further expansion and beat ISIS back is to deny it hadanah sha'biyya. This entails addressing legitimate Sunni grievances through the reconstruction of the state based on the rule of law, citizenship, and inclusiveness, not sect, ethnicity, and tribe. By the end of 2015, more Sunni tribes in both Iraq and Syria had begun to join anti-ISIS coalitions, a shift that shows pragmatism and a willingness to reengage in the political process.

GOVERNANCE

In addition to tapping into Sunni grievances and winning hearts and minds, ISIS has increasingly co-opted local communities under its control by partially filling a governance void and providing public services and good salaries.[15] While the world is captivated by ISIS's brutality and its institution of a modern sex trade, the group built its capacity to govern, embedding itself deeper into the fabric of life in war-torn Iraq and Syria. By increasingly acting like a rudimentary state, ISIS makes the inhabitants dependent on its services, planting the idea in their minds that they are in control. As long as ISIS delivers public goods and services, it will continue to enjoy the acquiescence of the public, making it harder to dislodge. According to local residents in al-Raqqah, Deir al-Zour, Mosul, Fallujah, and other cities, ISIS has set up a rudimentary functioning bureaucracy, administration, and institutions; it improved security and law and order—though harsh—and provided jobs in decimated economies. Residents report that ISIS delivers important services, such as bakeries, policing, a swift, shariah-based justice system, identity cards and birth certificates, consumer protection, garbage collection, day-care centers, and clean and well-run hospitals, and it has procured teachers to work in its schools, even though the quality of these services is neither stellar nor free.[16] The infamous pattern of behavior has been that each time ISIS captures new territory in Syria and Iraq, it begins by carrying out a wave of killings of civilian suspects, police, and members of the security forces. Following this, ISIS commanders often seek to garner public support by lowering the price of bread and quickly repairing electricity and water lines and calling on bureaucrats to return to work.[17] After ISIS seized Mosul in June 2014, the group began a campaign to clean, pave, and light the city, an impressive achievement, according to some residents, because successive Iraq governments had failed repeatedly to complete the job.[18] Baghdadi's planners have also used former Syrian and Iraqi government employees to keep the local government functioning. In al-Raqqah, a former Assad regime employee is now in charge of mills and the distribution of flour to bakeries.[19] Employees at the al-Raqqah dam, which provides the city with electricity and water, were kept in their posts when ISIS took over the city. Experts who have come from countries in North Africa and Europe have helped ISIS provide public services. For instance, Baghdadi appointed a Tunisian with a PhD in telecommunications to run and develop al-Raqqah's telecommunications.[20] As well as having the expertise of a number of former Baathist military officials in both Iraq and Syria,[21] Baghdadi and his associates have repeatedly called on Muslims worldwide with technical expertise to migrate to the Islamic State and serve it, including in his first sermon, which he delivered in Mosul after its capture in June 2014. To showcase their capacity to govern, ISIS's planners frequently advertise the launch of new ventures and projects, such as medical schools in Syria and Iraq, breakthroughs in artificial limb technology, and the reopening of a grand hotel in Mosul, with much public fanfare.[22]

For the inhabitants who have survived on the bare minimum and lived through decades of state-sponsored violence and repression, ISIS is not seen as the malevolent organization known to the outside world. They are left unbothered by the group so long as they avoid crossing ISIS's lines and obey its severe rules. Ultimately, within hard-pressed communities in conflict zones, what will matter most are bread and butter, security, governance, and fair salaries.[23] In order to support their families, destitute Syrian refugees in Turkey say they had to return to al-Raqqah and Deir al-Zour and swear baiya to ISIS in return for jobs as teachers and public service employees. According to personal testimonies, these jobs pay on average $100 per month, which is barely a subsistence living. Before they start work, the returnees have also to undergo religious reeducation to indoctrinate them with the group's radical theology, as well as military training.[24]

According to multiple reports by local activists who reside in the so-called caliphate, ISIS has built a lucrative and diverse criminalized war economy to finance its war making and state building, which includes oil sales, taxes, drug trafficking, kidnapping, theft, and sale of small religious and cultural artifacts. The group collected tens of millions of US dollars in ransom for Western and regional hostages.

According to a 2014 Thomson Reuters study, the terrorist group has more than $2 trillion in assets under its control, with an annual income of $2.9 billion. In January 2015 Abu Saad al-Ansar, an ISIS official in Mosul, told Arabic newspapers that the group's budget for that year was $2 billion, though UN monitors and independent observers now expect it to be half that.[25] In December 2015, Adam Szubin, the acting Treasury undersecretary for terrorism and financial intelligence, said containing ISIS has been difficult because only a tiny share of its money comes from foreign donors. According to Szubin, the group has generated more than $500 million from black market oil sales in Syria and Iraq and has looted between $500 million and $1 billion from bank vaults in territory under its control; it has extorted millions of dollars more from Syrians and Iraqis living under its domain, Szubin said.[26] By solidifying its rule over eastern Syria, especially in Deir al-Zour and al-Raqqah, along with its territory in neighboring Iraq, ISIS controls a significant percentage of Syria's oil and gas fields (160 fields), a hydroelectric dam, fertile lands, and a third of the wheat supply in each country. In Iraq, ISIS controls thirteen oil fields, three refineries, five cement plants, and a salt mine.[27] In the past year and a half the group has raised $500 million selling oil from the fields it controls in Syria and Iraq to Turkish and Iraqi businessmen and areas controlled by the Syrian government and the opposition.[28] Showing expediency, Baghdadi and his functionaries trade with their erstwhile enemies whenever it suits their interests. A 2015 report by the *New York Times*, supported with data from the Rand Corporation, estimated that oil generated only $100 million that year, though most experts valued oil-related revenues to be much higher.[29]

After poring through the intelligence for much of the summer in 2015, the US-led coalition, together with Russia, which does not coordinate with the coalition, escalated airstrikes against ISIS-run oil refineries and oil-trucking assets in eastern Syria and destroyed more than a thousand tanker trucks transporting oil to markets in Iraq and Turkey. Western governments have also taken initiatives in the UN Security Council and global financial institutions to prevent ISIS from moving money through the international financial system.[30] Although this double-barreled strategy has already exacted a heavy toll on ISIS's finances, it won't bankrupt it.

Indeed, there is increasing evidence that the bombing surge has significantly reduced ISIS's total oil production, leading fuel prices to soar and morale and salaries to decline. The group has recently reduced fighters' salaries from roughly $400 a month to about $300 and imposed additional taxes and fines on the inhabitants. Syrian activists and aid workers say that aid programs that benefit the needy appear to have been severely reduced, causing further poverty and acute shortages of medicine for chronic diseases, and there have also been prolonged electricity cuts. ISIS took a big hit in summer 2015 when Iraq's government stopped paying salaries to public employees in areas the militants had captured, particularly Mosul, which meant the group could no longer extort large sums from those civil servants.[31]

Despite the US-led coalition's efforts to prevent ISIS from cashing in on the vast crude oil and natural gas reserves within its domains, efforts that include hundreds of airstrikes on ISIS-controlled oil installations in Iraq and Syria, the group remains well funded.[32] As discussed throughout the book, ISIS has built a diverse criminalized economy that is not one-source-dependent. According to the study by IHS Global Strategies cited above, about 50 percent of ISIS's revenue comes from taxes and fines, a greater share of its budget than oil. Pervading nearly every aspect of life, ISIS has a total monopoly on economic activities for the five to eight million people under its control. As an Iraqi writer living in Mosul under a pseudonym eloquently put it, "Everything in the city is under the control of Daesh [the Arabic acronym for ISIS], without exception; if they had the ability to control the air that the population breathes, they would have done so."[33] ISIS's control of the population has allowed it to extract taxes, taking a share of profits or enforcing fines, a form of extortion. As the US-led coalition's airstrikes partially disrupted ISIS's oil and gas business, the group squeezed more revenues out of the households in the caliphate. "One of ISIS's biggest financial resources is the taxes it imposes on the citizens of al-Raqqah," according to a report from the antimilitant activist group al-Raqqah Is Being Slaughtered Silently.[34] A similar story is heard in Deir al-Zour and Mosul, where ISIS imposed heavy taxes on harvests, phone lines, water, electricity, and waste removal, bleeding the inhabitants and pauperizing them further. According to activists in the field, ISIS's goal is to make the population dependent on its administration for survival and force young men to join its ranks as fighters in order to feed their families, a strategy too familiar to the status quo under the Assad regime, and arguably a risky gamble that may backfire in the future.[35] More than a year after ISIS's takeover of almost a third of Syria and Iraq, oppressed communities under the control of ISIS complain that the cost of living is too high and that they are forced to finance its military operations. For instance, the cost of bread in al-Raqqah, an agricultural province where crops are plentiful, has risen fivefold and has reached a record, local sources report.[36]

As can be seen, shutting down ISIS's various financial channels has proven exceptionally difficult. As long as ISIS continues to diversify its criminalized war economy and replenish its coffers, it will strengthen its governance capacity. Paying the salaries and costs of combatants (which amount to 70 percent of its total annual budget), bureaucrats, and public services, even if inconsistently and at a reduced rate, would help the Islamic State to embed itself "deeper into the fabric of the communities it controls."[37] Therefore, the challenge for the international community is to deny ISIS social oxygen (or hadanah sha'biyya) and starve it financially, a complex task made more difficult by the fact that there are millions of people under its control. With its criminalized war economy and extortion, ISIS could extract enough resources to drive its military machine, though this option appears to have already alienated the inhabitants and thus could turn their acquiescence into opposition and resistance. As mentioned previously, there are credible reports of many defections of ISIS foreign fighters. Young men avoid attending Friday prayers for fear of being forcefully conscripted. Nevertheless, the most effective means to slow down the march of ISIS is to dislodge it from the towns and cities it controls and follow the trail of money and shut it down, a challenging task given that ISIS deals in cash and operates outside the legitimate channels that can be traced by Western governments. The US has begun to bomb the group's cash storage sites, depriving it of millions of US dollars. Unlike Al Qaeda Central, ISIS does not depend as much on foreign donors, making it more difficult to bankrupt it. Nevertheless, the group is extremely vulnerable because it is waging multiple battles on multiple fronts against powerful foes, while it attempts to build a proto-state, which requires "steady and renewable sources of funding," according to Adam Szubin, the acting Treasury undersecretary for terrorism and financial intelligence.[38]

"THE ISLAMIC RULE"

Although Baghdadi and his functionaries are mainly engaged in war making, they have also devoted resources to state building, or what they call "Islamic rule." A third of ISIS's annual budget is spent on propaganda and local and national government, including media, publishing pamphlets and books, building roads, running hospitals, and keeping schools open The group's planners recognize that domination and force can't guarantee compliance and consent in the long term; ISIS commanders use both violence and persuasion to establish the hegemony of the Islamic State.[39] ISIS's strategic goal is consolidate its political longevity. As hundreds of newly obtained, leaked ISIS documents show, the group has been actively engaged in a deliberate state-building exercise, from job creation and roads to nurseries, hotels, and marketplaces, from the Euphrates to the Tigris. One of the leaked ISIS documents obtained by the *Guardian* makes it clear that "The state requires an Islamic system of life, a Qur'anic constitution and a system to implement it," though this Islamic system should not come at the expense of rational planning and organization. "There must not be suppression of the role of qualifications, skills of expertise and the training of the current generation on administering the state," added ISIS's planners.[40] While the Western and Arab media widely report on how ISIS had set up a political structure similar to a modern government in the so-called form of a caliphate, there is little analysis of the revolutionary character of the group's governance. Three days after the fall of Mosul, ISIS published a manifesto called "Charter of the City" (Wathiqat al-Madina), which consists of sixteen articles in which the group lays the groundwork for political rule. "O people, you have tried all secular regimes, including the monarchical, republican, Baathist and then the Safavid [a reference to the Iranian state and Iranian-backed governments in Iraq and Syria], and now is the era of the Islamic State," notes article sixteen of ISIS's manifesto.[41] This citation sums up the group's social engineering project and clarifies what it means by "Islamic rule." The only way to fully grasp what ISIS means is to observe the organization's actions in Mosul, al-Raqqah, Deir al-Zour, Fallujah, and other cities. ISIS's leaders are trying to systemically eradicate the existing social order and replace it with a new moral and religious system that incorporates the legal rules of seventh-century Arabia into today's twenty-first-century society. In article sixteen, ISIS stipulates that the Qur'an is the only source of legislation, laws, and the constitution of the Islamic State. Although article sixteen states that the *al-Sunna* (the Prophet's life and sayings) is a secondary source of inspiration, the group relies exclusively on its harsh interpretations of Qur'anic scripture when issuing edicts and laws to regulate life in the caliphate.[42]

Less than a year after seizing Mosul, ISIS had created a system parallel to that of the secular nation-state and transformed social norms and laws that define state-society relations. Hundreds of leaked ISIS documents (mentioned previously) reveal an ambitious strategic road map to be self-sufficent in the future by "raising a knowledgeable Islamic generation capable of bearing the Ummah [Islamic Nation] and its future without needing the expertise of the West."[43] Writing under the pseudonym Morris Milton, a writer who lives in Mosul published a series of articles on the first anniversary of the fall of his city and painted a portrait of the changes that have occurred.[44] Isolating the indigenous population (Al-Moslawyin), Milton points out that ISIS's enforcers substituted "the sword" for consent, abolished the ideas of centrism and moderation, and deliberately staged atrocities in public. Although the physical scars of ISIS's brutality could be healed over time, he argues that the ethical and social rules that the group imposed on the city and the ways of life of its citizens will leave deeper scars. Article sixteen of the Charter of the City forbids the inhabitants from either publishing or broadcasting any news item that is not issued by the group or flying any flag except the banner of the Islamic State. From day one, ISIS labored hard to remake Mosul in its own image. According to the eyewitness, ISIS aimed to rid the city of its history, diversity, cosmopolitanism, and culture, and instead to enforce uniformity and obedience to a harsh set of rules—in short, it created a religious totalitarian system. This system essentially sought to change the political culture of Iraq and Syria so that the ISIS model would continue indefinitely. After closely observing the conduct of ISIS's planners for more than a year, the Mosul writer concludes that they must have read the German philosopher Friedrich Nietzsche, especially his treatises on values and ethics, for they have formulated new norms and values informed by their Salafi-jihadist ideology and imposed it wholesale on the community. ISIS's "Islamic rule" is being enforced by new social strata from rural areas, which serve as the moral police or revolutionary guards of the group. Increasing evidence indicates that ISIS's membership is predominantly composed of agrarian and urban poor, even though the top echelon is mainly middle class. Activists and residents living in the caliphate report that the organization has empowered villagers and rural elements and put them in charge in both Iraq and Syria, creating a social rift between ways of the city and those of the countryside.[45]

The "ruralization" of Iraqi and Syrian cities, particularly Mosul, which used to be a culturally diverse and cosmopolitan place, will have lasting social ramifications on both countries. More importantly, ISIS's rural vanguard is a potent tool of repression and control as well. By empowering villagers and agrarian elements, whose interests are organically linked to those of ISIS, the group has built a loyal constituency, willing and ready to do its bidding. While the world focuses on the operational and leadership roles of former Baathist officers of Saddam Hussein's army and police within ISIS, little attention is paid to the rural enforcers who terrorize communities and implement the group's severe laws. However, these recent rural converts to the jihadist cause represent a double-edged sword for ISIS because, on balance, they tend to be driven more by interests than by ideology. If and when ISIS retreats militarily, the agrarian and urban poor would not have qualms about shifting sides, as they have frequently done in the past.

IDEOLOGY AND POWER

Ideology and military capability are other major driving forces behind the strength of ISIS and its future durability. Armed with a messianic ideology and a belief that they are resurrecting the caliphate, ISIS's combatants are fearless.[46] One of ISIS's greatest strengths is an inner belief in the truth of its cause, a blind faith in the principles of Hakimiyya (God's rule on earth as opposed to the will of the peoples) and *al-wala' wa al-bara'* (allegiance to the faith and the Sunni community and denunciation of the other). Baghdadi's combatants believe that to die defending these principles would be "martyrdom for God's sake," a road to heaven.[47] Regardless of the veracity of this belief, it is a significant factor in building the battle spirit of ISIS's fighters, who shoulder the brunt of combat, and providing them with motivation and inspiration. This ideological conviction explains the abundance of suicide bombers within ISIS's ranks. In a sense, ISIS was able to operationalize the Salafi-jihadist concepts that have gained momentum among Islamists in the Middle East for the past two decades. This organization boasts of a long list of volunteers who await their turn to carry out suicide or "martyrdom" operations. Hundreds have already done so and facilitated the organization's offensive in Iraq and Syria.[48] While a form of existential struggle also drives the Iraqi, Syrian, and Kurdish forces, it is only the Shia militias' religious zeal, apocalyptic vision, and belief in the return of the Mahdi (a vanished descendant of the Prophet whom Shia believe will reemerge at a time of war to establish global Islamic rule and justice; it is believed he will return several years before judgment day) that compete with ISIS's determination and motivation.[49]

Time and again, Baghdadi and his propagandists have showered praise on ISIS's fighters for their sacrifice and steadfastness in the face of great odds. "Stay steadfast, I wish I could be sacrificed for you," Baghdadi told his soldiers in a recent audio recording.[50] ISIS's chiefs repeatedly remind their subordinates that they are following in the footsteps of the Prophet Mohammed and his righteous companions who erected the first Islamic state. ISIS's fighters are depicted as "the soldiers of the caliphate,"[51] who battle the enemies of Islam and bring honor, victory, and deliverance to the Sunni community. They are constantly fed an ideological diet, which transforms them into human robots. There are Syrian and Iraqi members of ISIS who are not ideologically committed to the Islamist cause and who joined the group either to gain economic advantage or for political reasons. But for many fighters, including foreigners and the jihadist veterans of Al Qaeda in Iraq, ideology is the superglue that cements their commitment to the group. These ideological combatants power ISIS's military machine and make a critical difference on the battlefields. Some foreign fighters move like shock troops around territory controlled by the group, according to Kurdish commanders.[52]

ISIS's planners train all combatants to be commanders and both fight side by side and die side by side, which explains a high rate of casualties among regional commanders who lead the charge in battles. Of all insurgent organizations in Iraq and Syria, ISIS alone practices what it preaches: "Believe in our call with the martyrdom of our commanders," a powerfully attractive slogan for religious, young activists. Faith, not rank and hierarchy, binds ISIS's fighting units. According to activists in the field, this ideological unity between fighters and commanders contributes to ISIS's resilience and durability and aids its expansion in the Sunni-dominated areas.[53]

One of the lessons learned over the past year and a half is that the organization has ideological cohesion and fraternity and operational agility. It is no wonder, then, that it has not collapsed under the hard blows of an endless litany of enemies. After more than ten thousand airstrikes by the US-led coalition, and more than twenty thousand ISIS combatants killed or wounded, according to official American figures, ISIS has shown tenacity and adaptability; while weakened by American airstrikes and repeated ground assaults in Syria and Iraq, the group remains a potent force, able to resist deadly offensives in both countries and to fight to the last man.[54] More than a year and half after its declaration of the Caliphate, ISIS continues to defend its territories in multiple theaters against multiple enemies, including the Iraqi security forces and powerful Shia militias as well as determined Kurdish fighters in Iraq and Syria and the Syrian army and its partners, especially Hezbollah. At the end of September 2015 Russia joined the fray against ISIS by intervening militarily in Syria and commencing airstrikes against the group and other opposition forces. By the end of 2015, Russia had carried out more than five thousand airstrikes in Syria, a third of them against ISIS. Moreover, in Syria, ISIS fights Islamist rivals such as Jabhat al-Nusra, Ahrar al-Sham, and Jayish al-Islam. It aims to convince both friend and foe that the Islamic State will "remain and expand" (as stated in its motto), and that it is invincible and undefeatable. The gap between the means and the objectives of America and Russia in Iraq and Syria has reinforced ISIS's narrative of invincibility so far. This narrative gained the group new adherents throughout the Middle East and beyond, due to its ability to deliver physically and militarily on what it claims in propaganda, though this is changing as ISIS loses territory in Syria and Iraq and retreats. The organization's unprecedented ability to recruit and radicalize followers through social media stems from its display and exhibition of military prowess and success on the battlefield. Ideology in isolation, important as it is, would not have empowered ISIS to such an extent and turned it into a power to be reckoned with.

An ironclad ideology, a blind faith, and an effective military apparatus fuel ISIS's armed strength. Its ability to outgrow and outperform groups with similar Salafi-jihadist ideologies, such as al-Nusra, is somewhat due to its deep and established roots. Its general staff in Iraq and Syria is made up of veterans of Al Qaeda in Iraq who survived the insurgency against US and Iraqi forces; former officers of Hussein's army and police with expertise in organization, intelligence, and internal security; and battle-hardened Chechen commanders with skills in guerrilla warfare. With this diverse and experienced military leadership pool, Baghdadi and his cabinet have fielded a mini army that wages both conventional and guerrilla warfare. Using psychological warfare and meticulous planning, ISIS's tacticians often outmaneuvered and outsmarted the organization's foes on the battlefield and displayed strategic cunning and tenacity. In particular, the influx of former officers of the Iraqi army into the ranks of ISIS propelled its early military victories in 2013 and 2014 in Iraq and Syria. As discussed previously, Baghdadi's momentous decision to surround himself with disbanded army and police officers from Hussein's era was decisive, probably the most decisive, in the group's military revival after the defeats inflicted on AQI's combatants by the Sunni Awakening councils between 2007 and 2010.[55] Regardless of their influence and weight in ISIS's decision making, the military role of former

Iraqi officers has been pivotal in drawing battle plans and strategically overseeing the wars. Baghdadi's reconstitution of ISIS's armed apparatus transformed a mafia-like network into a professionalized fighting force.

Despite gains made in Palmyra in 2015, ISIS has lost approximately 40 percent of the territory it once held in Iraq and between 5 percent and 20 percent in Syria since the declaration of the caliphate in June 2014.[56] Overextended and on the defensive, the group struggles to survive. Nevertheless, ISIS possesses organizational depth, agility, and dogged fanaticism and willpower.[57] Drawing lessons from the fates of likeminded groups in Pakistan and Yemen whose leaders have been systematically killed by repeated US drone strikes over the years, Baghdadi has empowered regional commanders in Iraq and Syria with wide-ranging authority, a plan designed to ensure the survival of ISIS if he and other top figures are killed. Given general operating guidelines, field lieutenants have significant autonomy and flexibility to run their own operations.[58] As a fallback option, Baghdadi and his planners have sent trusted commanders from Syria and Iraq to Libya and established a base in Surt, a port city on the Mediterranean about four hundred miles southeast of Sicily, according to UN and Western officials.[59] Although the group suffered serious setbacks in Syria and Iraq and incurred massive human losses, it fought to the bitter end and did not beat a hasty retreat. After almost every setback, ISIS's planners had been able to mount surge offensives, as they did in mid-2015 in northwest Syria and in Palmyra and Ramadi in Iraq, surprising adversaries and delighting its supporters, though by the end of 2015 the group's ability to go on the offensive had come to an end. ISIS's military planners have a system in place, effective networks that allow them to exercise operational control and sustain hard blows by the US-led coalition. The group is reportedly replacing its combatants in Iraq and Syria as fast as the United States and its allies are killing them there, due to a seemingly endless stream of recruits. In September 2015 American intelligence analysts released the findings of a confidential assessment that concludes that nearly thirty thousand foreign fighters have traveled to Iraq and Syria from more than one hundred countries since 2011, including about five thousand from the West. A year ago, the same officials estimated that flow to be about fifteen thousand combatants from eighty countries. Despite punishing airstrikes and concerted efforts to stem the flow of foreign fighters, the group continues to draw an average of about one thousand fighters a month, a stunning achievement that shows the existence of global networks for recruitment.[60]

Although American officials claim they have killed about 50 percent of ISIS's field lieutenants and regional commanders, they acknowledge that the group has quickly replaced them with other skilled operatives. Frustrated with the failure of conventional strikes to degrade the group's strength after more than a year of aerial bombings, the Obama administration authorized the CIA and US Special Operations forces to jointly launch a secret campaign to hunt senior ISIS operatives in Syria as part of a targeted killing program. This clandestine drone campaign is run separately from the broader US military offensive against ISIS, US officials said.[61] The administration is using lessons learned from its drone attacks against field lieutenants of Al Qaeda Central in the tribal region in Pakistan along the Afghan border, which have had devastating effects on the organization and operationally paralyzed it. Although US airstrikes against ISIS's leadership assets have exacted a heavy toll, they are unlikely to be as effective as those against AQC in Pakistan; the Islamic State has extensive territory, more than five million people under its watch, and a long roster of senior operatives, many of whom served in the military and police of Hussein. It has the capacity to replenish its depleted ranks for the foreseeable future, though significant leadership losses appear to have weakened the group. Moreover, firsthand reports from Iraq and Syria show that ISIS, along with other Islamist groups, has established camps to train children in al-Raqqah, Mosul, and other areas as the next generation of fighters, or, as ISIS calls them, *Ashbal al-Khilafa* ("caliphate cubs"). The leaked

ISIS documents discussed above specify that children should receive training in light arms and religious indoctrination, and that "outstanding individuals" will be given security assignments such as manning checkpoints.[62] The Syrian Observatory for Human Rights, a Britain-based advocacy organization with a wide network of contacts in Syria, said that it documented at least 1,100 children under sixteen who had joined ISIS by July 2015, many of whom were sent to fight in Syria and Iraq.[63] There is also credible evidence showing that ISIS goes to great lengths to indoctrinate children after they abduct them, forcing them to attend training camps and view footage of beheadings and other violent acts in an attempt to socially engineer the next generation of jihadists.[64] Activists in Mosul and al-Raqqah say that some parents have stopped sending their children to school lest ISIS kidnap them and indoctrinate them. The group frequently displays children, as young as ten years old, in its propaganda videos as executioners of victims, combatants, and members of a cheering, joyful audience during gruesome executions in public.[65] As long as ISIS controls territory and people, it will be able to recruit and coerce people to battle, using a strict and often brutal carrot-and-stick approach. For instance, desperate to feed their families, young Syrian men in Deir al-Zour and al-Raqqah say they were forced to pledge allegiance to ISIS and be prepared to fight in its ranks. Therefore, the key to denying ISIS its human supply chain is to dislodge it from the territories it occupies in Iraq and Syria and seal Turkey's border with Syria, through which most foreign recruits cross. While a difficult feat without a "boots on the ground" policy, this remains the most effective means to starve the group of fresh blood and treasure.

VULNERABILITIES

VACUUM OF IDEAS

Despite ISIS's impressive military prowess and achievements, it suffers from a structural defect: the absence of a positive blueprint for governance and a debilitating vacuum of ideas. Beyond ideological and moral rhetoric, the organization has not offered the Sunni communities in Iraq and Syria a positive program of action or a positive vision of governance. Although ISIS has managed to deliver bread and butter to the populations under its watch, it has not always invested social capital in the infrastructure of governance. This fundamental defect is common to all Salafi-jihadists who prioritize warfare over welfare. They obsess over physical and military power, disregarding soft power and political theory as an infringement on and violation of shariah or Qur'anic law. Any theorizing or philosophizing outside the confines of the shariah is forbidden and criminalized as un-Islamic. Time and again, Salafi-jihadists have not translated or operationalized their promises of salvation into a pragmatic material reality, a dichotomy that exposes the paucity and poverty of their ideas. More importantly, this handicap has not endeared Salafi-jihadists, including ISIS, to mainstream Muslim opinion, which, like publics elsewhere, craves stability, prosperity, and freedom. ISIS fails on all counts.

Much like it was for Al Qaeda before it, the world according to ISIS is characterized by a perpetual war against real and imagined enemies. Society is in constant mobilization, on a permanent war footing, to fend off enemies who lurk everywhere and hatch conspiracies against the Islamic State. According to this worldview, stability can only be attained when enemies are either subjugated or forced to recognize the group's sacred mandate. In the meantime, ISIS's planners see Muslim society as a wild jungle and define their mission as the "management of savagery." Conflict zones and chaos provide an ideal environment for Salafi-jihadists, who, according to one of their ideologues, Abu Bakr al-Najji (a pseudonym), have been called on to creatively manage this chaos and consolidate their authority. In this jungle of savagery, ISIS would manage Muslims like animals by providing them with the bare minimum of goods and services. Everything must take a backseat to the promotion of the extreme jihadist project.[66] As to freedom, ISIS substitutes religious tyranny for the political authoritarianism of the Syrian and Iraqi regimes and controls the minute details of peoples' lives, from how they dress to how they live. It is a totalitarian political system, one shared by Salafi-jihadists across the ideological spectrum. As mentioned above, ISIS, together with other Salafi-jihadists, claims to use the Qur'an as its constitution, a foundational document, and the only source of legislation. In addition to their narrow, harsh, and selective reading of the scripture, ISIS's ideologues overlook the fact that the Qur'an is a double-edged sword, at their own peril. On the one hand, they deploy it as a weapon of choice against foes. Yet this weapon also has the potential to be drawn over their own necks if they do not live up to the utopian Islamic state that they so confidently promise.

Although Sunnis in Iraq and Syria tolerate hardship and sacrifice during war, their mood is bound to change to active hostility if ISIS turns the extreme living conditions of an emergency into a permanent situation, which seems as if it will be the case. The writing is already on the wall. Activists in al-Raqqah, Deir al-Zour, and Mosul report widespread discontent and suppressed anger among local populations over dismal social conditions and the loss of individual freedoms, such as the rights of movement and smoking. Beyond anti-Shia and anti-Iranian rhetoric, ISIS does not offer Sunnis a positive program of action; only a bleak future. Laws and rules instituted by ISIS shed light on its goal for life under its watch, which is to return Arab-Islamic civilization to that of the seventh century. Reviving traditions that have been dormant for hundreds of years, "the Daesh model has no future because it is not only barbaric but also offers the worst of the past and seeks to destroy the present and the future," penned a well-known Islamist commentator, Fahmy Houeidi.[67] While many Sunnis implicitly and explicitly support ISIS's campaign against the Iranian-backed governments in Baghdad and Damascus, they do not condone its viciousness and harsh interpretation of shariah. Considerable evidence exists that the group's Salafi-jihadist ideology does not resonate with many Iraqis and Syrians, and that its utopia is more popular with young foreign recruits than with the indigenous population. Tensions over pay differentials have degenerated into skirmishes between local and foreign fighters in Tal Afar, Iraq, and clashes have also occurred between local and foreign combatants in Syria, more privileges having been granted to the latter.[68] In fact, senior ideologues and theorists of the jihadist movement, such as Abu Qatada and Abu Mohammed al-Maqdisi, fear that ISIS's severe rules and viciousness will drive ordinary Muslims away from the jihadist project. The ISIS project is cancerous, threatening the survival of the jihadist movement, according to Abu Qatada, who has thrown his lot in with Al Qaeda Central.[69] Both ideologues cautioned against taking ISIS's popularity among Muslims for granted, ascribing the group's attractiveness among the youth to its military prowess and victories on the battlefield. More than any other Salafi-jihadist group, ISIS is a youth movement. In other words, ISIS's claim to fame lies in war making, not hope or an opportunity for a better future, notwithstanding the rudimentary institutions it erected and its farfetched assertions of building an Islamic state. The group is more about negation than the construction of a rational and stable order, all sound and fury with no creative ideas about how to revive the collapsed economy and the educational system and give people hope in the future. An action-driven organization, ISIS's negativity is an inherent weakness that may work against the group if the military balance of power shifts against it in the future.

Unlike previous Salafi-jihadist waves, including that of Al Qaeda Central, ISIS has not come up with anything new in terms of a manifesto, preferring to borrow ideas from theorists who represent the most extreme thinking within the movement. In comparison with predecessors, ISIS's weakest link is its poverty of ideas. As discussed throughout the book, these Salafi-jihadist preachers and theorists, such as Najji, Abu Abdullah al-Muhajjer, and Abdel-Qader Ibn Abdel-Aziz (or Dr. Fadl), concentrate on extreme religious interpretations of day-to-day life and apocalyptic visions, rather than a detailed blueprint for actual governance or long-term plans. Maqdisi, whose writings are widely cited by militants, decries ISIS's misappropriation and misuse of his ideas and its failure to use recognized scholars for theological guidance. The group can maintain itself and thrive only in an environment of despair, communal polarization, state breakdown, and war. If these social conditions can be reversed, its appeal and potency will wither away, though its bloodletting will likely leave deep scars on the consciousness of Arab and Muslim youth. All jihadist groups without exception have failed to topple a functioning state and instead have only advanced under conditions of chaos. In contrast to previous waves, once ISIS is pushed back militarily, it will leave behind no ideas, no theories, and no intellectual legacy. It is theologically and intellectually vacuous, lacking a core, a repertoire of ideas to sustain it in the long term. This raises fundamental questions about its ability to legitimize itself and build a hegemony of its own as opposed to relying only on domination and force. To be durable, both social movements and states must construct a set of ideas and references that appeal to a broad constituency, and thus achieve acceptance more by persuasion than coercion. ISIS's anti-Shia genocidal ideology cannot serve as a basis for legitimation in the long term, especially if the Saudis and Iranians find common ground and stop disguising their geostrategic rivalry masked in communal garb; neither can the notion of a caliphate, a myth divorced from the harsh realities of the Syrian and Iraqi population that only Salafi-jihadist proponents take seriously. As discussed previously, historically, the institution of the caliphate carries significant resonance because it is seen as a means to salvation. But beyond empty rhetoric, ISIS's ideologues have not problematized the concept or invested it with positive meanings. No prominent Muslim scholar or figure has supported the idea. Even senior Salafi-jihadist preachers dismissed ISIS's caliphate as a "bubble," accusing Baghdadi and his inner circle of showmanship in their attempts to outbid Islamist rivals, bringing ruin to the concept and reputation of an Islamic state. While there may be some support for an Islamic caliphate in some shape or form from some sectors of Arab society, ISIS's declaration of a caliphate has elicited no serious engagement in the Arab-Islamic world or among Islamists specifically, a crushing vote of no confidence. A qualification is in order: while the worldview of ISIS's caliphate and the Islamic State will likely not endure, its legacy will be that these two concepts have been brought to center stage as far as Islamism is concerned. Islamists of all ideological colors are forced to address them.

MASTERING THE ART OF MAKING ENEMIES

Baghdadi and his inner circle have mastered the art of making enemies near and far. Although ISIS has done impressively on the battlefield so far, its political and strategic miscalculations and shortsightedness know no limits and do not bode well for the group in the long term. With ISIS, there are no blurred lines or gray areas, only followers and enemies: you either pledge allegiance to Baghdadi and his ideology or are labeled an enemy who could be killed. There is no neutral stance between good and evil; passivity is seen as apostasy. This binary black-and-white worldview pitted the organization against the world, including the godfathers of Salafi-jihadist thought. Although in 2013 and 2014 Baghdadi and his senior associates attempted to get endorsements from recognized Salafi sheikhs and theorists, their efforts came to naught. The radical Salafi-jihadist establishment repeatedly called on Baghdadi to exercise restraint and resolve his dispute with fellow Islamists in Syria in accordance with Islamic rules of jurisdiction. Their pleas fell on deaf ears. Baghdadi and his cabinet launched an all-out attack against al-Nusra, the official arm of Al Qaeda in Syria, and viciously suppressed the rival group and almost expelled it from two provinces. As the civil war among Salafi-jihadists intensified in early 2014, the radical Salafi-jihadist establishment turned against Baghdadi and his cohorts with vengeance. As discussed previously, top Salafi scholars dismissed ISIS as illegitimate, calling on its members to defect and warning of dire repercussions on the future of the jihadist movement. Alarmingly, ISIS turned all Salafi-jihadist heavyweights into bitter enemies, deepening its isolation and weakening its capacity to resist and survive once its military fortunes decay. If ISIS cannot gain the support of the custodians of the Salafi-jihadist temple, it will take a political miracle for the group to make inroads among both mainstream Islamists and religious clerics. Bereft of theological backing, the organization relies overwhelmingly on violence, which is no substitute for ideological legitimation. As the storm gathers force all around ISIS, the group is deeply vulnerable and will soon face its day of reckoning. Contrary to the received wisdom in and outside the region, ISIS may appear unbeatable in the current political and military context; but the cracks are undeniable, and its long-term future is far from certain.

Turkey is a prime example of the effects of ISIS's strategy of waging war on the entire world and turning neutral regional countries and potential friends into enemies. For more than a year, Turkish president Recep Erdoğan resisted repeated calls from the United States, its key global ally, to fully join the international coalition against ISIS. Dragging his feet, Erdoğan insisted that the fight against Assad is as important as the military campaign against the organization. Implicitly accusing Turkey of turning a blind eye to ISIS's recruitment efforts, supply, and logistics, the global media and some Western politicians lambasted Erdoğan for his ambivalence and demanded that Turkey better police its long border with Syria in order to prevent foreign recruits from joining the group. In fact, the Erdoğan government directly negotiated with ISIS and reached a settlement whereby the group released forty-six Turkish diplomats and their families who had been captured when ISIS stormed the Turkish consulate in Mosul after it seized the city in June 2014. Although the terms of Turkey's arrangement with ISIS were kept secret, the deal was a diplomatic breakthrough for Baghdadi's Islamic State. It could have signaled a turning point if Baghdadi and his planners had shown political shrewdness. Instead of building on the agreement with Turkey and keeping it neutral, ISIS allegedly carried out suicide bombings against Kurdish targets inside the country, thus violating Turkey's sovereignty and embarrassing Erdoğan. Recklessly, ISIS transformed a neutral regional power into an enemy and forced Erdoğan to finally agree to "coordinate operations" with the United States against the group. In response, the group released a propaganda video calling on the Turkish people to rise up and overthrow "Satan," a reference to Erdoğan, who had made his country "a slave to the crusaders."[70]

Of all regional powers, Turkey was the least hostile toward ISIS and could have encouraged the organization to demonstrate restraint and diplomatic awareness. At the end of 2015, ISIS allegedly carried out deadly attacks against foreign targets, including a Russian jet, and urban centers in Beirut and Paris, killing and injuring hundreds of civilians. These massive operations galvanized the great powers, particularly France and Russia, to coordinate and redouble their efforts to defeat ISIS. Instead of making an effort at diplomatic engagement that could have increased their claims of statehood, Baghdadi and his inner circle have united the world against them. In a way, ISIS has rejected the structure of the state system and is attempting to offer an alternative revolutionary model based on Islamic identity, not state sovereignty. ISIS's conduct seems suicidal, however. There is a disconnect between ISIS's limited military capabilities and the long list of regional and global powers pitted against the group, including the two most powerful militaries in the international system—those of the Americans, the Russians, and the Europeans. With too many enemies and shrinking resources, it is doubtful if ISIS could sustain its stranglehold on the major cities that it controls in a prolonged fight over several years. A more plausible scenario is that, as military pressure intensifies against ISIS in the near future, its core middle and senior leaders might melt into urban areas and wage a terrorist campaign along similar lines to that of Al Qaeda in Iraq (AQI) between 2007 and 2011. The "Islamic State" would mutate into its original type, an underground, paramilitary Salafi-jihadist organization. As explained previously, ISIS's success so far has mainly depended on the group's ability to exploit the deep communal divide in the region and the fragility of the state structures in Syria and Iraq as well as contradictions within the US-led coalition and the lack of effective local forces on the ground. More importantly, Baghdadi's armed apparatus and "state" require a constant resupply of men of fighting age, arms, ammunition, and money, all of which have become scarce. Although foreign recruits continue to travel to Syria to join ISIS, albeit at a much reduced rate, there are credible reports of fighters who are disillusioned and defecting from the organization. The flow of jihadists to Syria has also dried up due to the Americans and the Turks working closely together by the end of 2015 to close down Turkey's five-hundred-mile-long border with Syria, a border that until very recently provided a lifeline to ISIS.[71] Residents also report that ISIS is experiencing serious financial hardship and is squeezing the local population in order to extract resources and conscript young men. Hundreds of leaked ISIS documents show that since the start of October 2015, the group has taken a number of measures, including military mobilization, fearing traitors in their midst. Becoming increasing paranoid, ISIS issued an amnesty for military deserters because it presumably needs more soldiers.[72] Fundamentally, in the coming future, it may prove to be a significant challenge for ISIS to keep its overextended armada oiled and stocked within an increasingly hostile regional and international environment.

With many enemies and very few friends, Baghdadi and his armed contingents stand naked and alone in the eye of a gathering storm, much weaker than ISIS's propagandists would like us to believe. The Islamic State is built on shaky foundations, and the foolishness and recklessness of its planners aggravate its predicament. Baghdadi and his inner circle are their own worst enemies. While it is essential not to underestimate ISIS's military strength, its ideological fervor, and the *asabiya* (social solidarity) of its hard-core operators, it is also important not to buy into the group's narrative of itself as invincible, undefeatable, and expandable. In comparative historical terms, ISIS is more like the Taliban in Afghanistan than the great revolutionary movements such as the Bolshevik Revolution and the Chinese Communist Revolution. The notion of ISIS's invincibility is a myth. As mentioned previously, supported by the US-led coalition airstrikes, the Kurds in Syria and Iraq have bloodied the nose of Baghdadi and his cohorts, delivering ISIS a hard blow. The Iraqi security forces, backed by Sunni and Shia allies and US airpower, have recaptured major cities and towns from ISIS in 2015, including Tikrit, Baiji, Sinjar, and Ramadi. Supported by coalition planes, the American-backed anti-ISIS alliance of Syrian Kurds and Arab rebel groups, known as the Democratic Forces of Syria, made important gains against the group in the latter half of 2015, threatening to cut off its last direct access to the Turkish border and hampering its ability to attract foreign recruits. In addition, the introduction of Russian airstrikes on ISIS targets in Syria in 2015 has allowed the Syrian army to regain territories from the group, though most of the Russian attacks focused on other rebels opposed to the Assad regime. And after the Paris attacks in November 2015, the French, together with other European powers, have become more active in the fight against ISIS, providing logistical and military assistance to local forces in Iraq and Syria.

A few days before the Iraqi security forces expelled ISIS from the center of Ramadi in December 2015, Baghdadi released an audio tape, his first public message in seven months, in which he conceded that his group faces a dangerous moment, calling on his soldiers to be patient and steadfast. Trying to shore up the morale of his followers in a rare public message, his first in seven months, Baghdadi said that "Crusaders and Jews" did not dare to fight on his turf and portrayed the military setbacks as a trial by Allah to test the faith of his men. "Be confident that

God will grant victory to those who worship him, and hear the good news that our state is doing well. The more intense the war against it, the purer it becomes and the tougher it gets," he preached.[73] Baghdadi's unusual acknowledgment of hardship and tribulation is not only related to recent military setbacks in Iraq and Syria but also to dissension within the group's own ranks. For the first time, Baghdadi disclosed that some "mujahideen brethren" turned against ISIS, which reflects, in the opinion of a jihadist leader, the beginning of the fragmentation and dissolution of the Islamic State. As the organization suffers more military setbacks, Abu Qatada claims that more members will defect, opening a floodgate.[74] Although Abu Qatada's hopes for a collapse remain just that, the lesson is that ISIS can be defeated militarily if resisted by determined and organized local communities; whether this is an achievable goal in marginalized Sunni-majority areas in Iraq and Syria is another matter. In the meantime, the organization will endure as long as the factors and circumstances that have fueled its rise remain in place in Iraq and Syria and beyond, as previously elaborated in this book.

THE PRIMACY OF POLITICS

The end of ISIS, however, is a more complex task that requires political and social strategies that deny the group the oxygen that sustains it. As emphasized throughout the book, ISIS would not have done as well as it has if it were not for the breakdown of state institutions in Syria and Iraq and rising sectarianism. It is a result of decades of dictatorship, failed governance and development, and abject poverty, made worse by ongoing foreign intervention and the Palestinian tragedy. With the exception of the nascent pluralistic experiment in Tunisia, political authoritarianism and sectarianism are on the rise in the Arab world. The rule of law is frail, and the human rights of citizens are violated with impunity. Although the Arab Spring uprisings shook the roots of Arab authoritarianism, they have not ushered in new social and political contracts that enshrine the rule of law and empower the individual. Far from it. Counterrevolutionary forces, backed by Gulf money and the "deep state," fought hard to preserve the autocratic order; one of the beneficiaries of this development has been the Salafi-jihadist movement. ISIS is repressive, regressive, and nihilistic. Beyond sound and fury and a cult of death, it has nothing positive to offer Arabs and Muslims. But in the eyes of many people, the dysfunctional Arab regimes are hardly an oasis of freedom, delivering neither democracy nor prosperity. These trends go together. In short, the rise of radical Islamism is directly proportional to the deepening political authoritarianism in the Arab world.

ISIS is a product of an organic crisis in Arab politics. Therefore, the decline and demise of the group will depend on the reconstruction of fragile state institutions and genuine political reconciliation among warring ethnic and religious communities, a complex and difficult process that will take years to materialize. In the meantime, Salafi-jihadists of the ISIS variety will continue to exist. Even if ISIS is pushed back militarily, it will mutate and go underground—as its predecessor, Al Qaeda in Iraq, did from 2007 until 2010—and bide its time until the next round. Therefore, the challenge is to deny the group its hadanah sha'biyya and restore a healthy political life that has been suspended for decades. This is easier said than done, given that autocratic regimes remain as entrenched as ever. There can be no eradication of ISIS and other Salafi-jihadist groups like al-Nusra without a rejuvenation of the political system and the establishment of a legitimate authority. Authority must be transparent and inclusive, based on the rule of law and citizenship, not clientelism, sectarianism, or domination. The key to delegitimizing Salafi-jihadists is politics, not religion and theology. Although ISIS promises deliverance and salvation through the resurrection of the caliphate, the group's religious ideology is important inasmuch as it allows ISIS to exploit a poisonous political and social environment, and to offer an

alternative model (the Islamic State) to secular political authoritarianism. Syrians and Iraqis would not have embraced ISIS's
Islamist ideology if their legitimate political and social grievances had been addressed. Many who fight under ISIS's banner
do so more because of anger against the central governments
in Baghdad and Damascus than a belief in its Salafi-jihadist
ideology. Of course, Baghdadi and his ideologues would like us
to believe that their call to resurrect the caliphate resonates
among Muslims near and far, an enormously exaggerated claim.

Nonetheless, it would be shortsighted to downplay the significance of ISIS's Islamist ideology and that of Salafi-jihadists
in general. A traveling ideology, Salafi-jihadism has evolved into
a powerful social movement with a repertoire of ideas, iconic
leaders, worldwide supporters, theorists, preachers, and networks of recruiters and enablers. Regardless of what happens
to ISIS, this ideology is here to stay and will likely gain more
followers in politically and socially polarized Arab and Muslim societies. Despite a costly civil war unfolding between ISIS
and Al Qaeda Central, particularly in Syria, Salafi-jihadists continue to expand their influence and attract new recruits. It is a
popular, enduring brand. A sense of triumphalism permeates
the discourse and public pronouncements by Salafi-jihadist
ideologues who feel they are on the cusp of a historical breakthrough. Dismissing ISIS as a bump in the road, Salafi figures
like Ayman al-Zawahiri, Maqdisi, and Abu Qatada say the jihadist movement's progress in the Fertile Crescent, the heart
of the Arab world, is a regional game changer.[75] A tipping point,
they argue, was the derailment of the Arab Spring uprisings and
the breakout of civil wars in Syria, Iraq, Libya, and Yemen. As
Abu Qatada bluntly pointed out, Salafi-jihadists exploited the
security vacuum left by the weakening of authoritarian Arab
regimes and expanded their influence. Similarly, in private
deliberations, senior Al Qaeda chiefs, including Osama bin
Laden, belatedly called on their followers to back the large-
scale popular Arab protests as well as fill the vacuum of ideas
after the Arab Spring was aborted.

Broadly defined, these two variables—the security vacuum and the vacuum of ideas, and the collapse of the social contract between regimes and the populace—help explain the recent surge of Salafi-jihadists in the Arab world. Indeed, the vacuum of ideas is as important as the security vacuum in emboldening Salafi-jihadists and making them a power to be reckoned with. With the suppression of mainstream Islamists like the Muslim Brotherhood in Egypt and the return of the military to politics, Salafi-jihadists offered an alternative model based on identity and a harsh and selective reading of the scripture; a subversive alternative that has found receptive ears among some Muslims. Even if the security environment improves considerably, the vacuum of ideas provides Salafi-jihadists and other nonstate religious actors with a market and an audience. There is a fierce urgency to fill this vacuum of ideas and to counter Salafi-jihadists' religious interpretations that justify takfir of the "other." To do so, formal separation of mosque and state is essential in order to end the instrumentalization of religion for political purposes by both religious activists and secular politicians. The goal is to protect the sacred from political manipulation and to protect the state from religious manipulation. Although I am cognizant of the difficulty of separating mosque and state in Muslim-majority states, this is a historical process, a dynamic struggle that assigns a prominent role to agency. In the last few decades Arab intellectuals have called for cutting the umbilical cord between religion and politics. For example, Algerian writers Tahar Djaout and Youssef Sebti, who were killed for their views in 1993 along with other Algerian intellectuals, denounced totalitarianism in their work, whether of a military or a religious nature, as the ultimate evil.[76] Citizenship and the rule of law, not religious, ethnic, or tribal affiliation, should be the basis of membership in a nation-state. Toleration should also be enshrined as the foundation of the religious and educational curriculum.[77]

What this reformation entails is an intellectual revolution, a cognitive or epistemological rupture with the dominant religious and historical scripts and narratives about the past, as some Arab writers, like Abdullah al-'Arwi, George Tarabishi, and others, argue, a cultural revolution that transforms state and society. Arab intellectuals are fully aware of the derailed efforts by al-Nahda and renaissance pioneers who called for such "reformation" in the nineteenth and early twentieth centuries. While there is no assurance of success, this complex, generational struggle must be fought and won regardless of how long it will take.[78] Salafi-jihadists like ISIS must be denied the doctrinal and theological oxygen that nourishes their movement. Ideas are the first line of defense against the Salafi-jihadist nihilistic ideology and the final nail in its coffin. Without this revolution in ideas, the narrative and brand of Salafi-jihadism, of which ISIS is the most recent iteration, will continue to prevail in the Arab-Islamic world.

NOTES

INTRODUCTION: DOWN THE RABBIT HOLE AND INTO THE HISTORY OF ISIS

1. Precise figures are unknown as the total amount spent on training and equipping Iraqi security forces soared in a few short years. E. Schmitt and M. Gordon, "The Iraqi Army Was Crumbling Long before Collapse, U.S. Officials Say," *New York Times*, June 12, 2014, www.nytimes.com/2014/06/13/world/middleeast/american-intelligence -officials-said-iraqi-military-had-been-in-decline.html?_r=0; J. Keating, "The Fall of Mosul," *Slate*, June 10, 2014, www.slate.com/blogs/the _world_/2014/06/10/the_fall_of_mosul_the_u_s_spent_20_billion_on _iraqi_security_forces_who.html.

2. Rod Nordland, "U.S. Soldiers, Back in Iraq, Find Security Forces in Disrepair," *New York Times*, April 14, 2015.

3. D. Remnick, "Going the Distance," *New Yorker*, January 27, 2014, www.newyorker.com/magazine/2014/01/27/going-the-distance-2.

4. See a summary of an independent report compiled by the Parliamentary Committee for Security and Defense and approved by the parliament and the judicial branch in August 2015, which holds the country's former prime minister, Nuri al-Maliki, and other senior political and military officials accountable for the fall of the northern city: The report by the Parliamentary Committee regarding the fall of Mosul احتقيقية اخلاصة بسقوط الموصل لصوملا تفرير رير, قتنجلا, http://integrityuk.org/wp -content/uploads/2015/08/Arabic-Mosul-Report.pdf. See also Nordland, "U.S. Soldiers."

5. Joseph Rago, "Inside the War against Islamic State: The Weekend Interview: John Allen," *Wall Street Journal*, December 26, 2014, www.wsj.com/articles/joe-rago-inside-the-war-against-islamic-state-1419636790.

6. E. Schmitt and D. Kirkpatrick, "Islamic State Sprouting Limbs beyond Its Base," *New York Times*, February 14, 2015, www.nytimes.com/2015/02/15/world/middleeast/islamic-state-sprouting-limbs-beyond-mideast.html; Yezid Sayigh, "Are the Sykes-Picot Borders Being Redrawn?," Carnegies-mec.org, June 26, 2014, http://carnegie-mec.org/2014/06/26/are-sykes-picot-borders-being-redrawn/heq0 (the article originally appeared in *al-Hayat* in Arabic).

7. Neil MacFarquharov, "Russia Allies with France against ISIS, Saying Jet that Crashed in Sinai Was Bombed," *New York Times*, November 17, 2015.

8. See David D. Kirkpatrick, Ben Hubbard, and Eric Schmitt, "ISIS' Grip on Libyan City Gives It a Fallback Option," *New York Times*, November 28, 2015; Paul Cruickshank, "United Nations warns of ISIS expansion in Libya," CNN.com, December 2, 2015, www.cnn.com/2015/12/01/politics/isis-united-nations-libya-expansion; http://i2.cdn.turner.com/cnn/2015/images/12/01/mt.report.on.libya-.eng.pdf.

9. A. M. al-Maqdisi, interviewed by *Al-Quds al-Arabi*, October 21, 2014 [in Arabic].

10. M. Abu Rouman, interviewed by *Al Jazeera*, July 26, 2014 [in Arabic]; Y. al-Za'atirah, "From the 'Far Enemy' to the 'Near Enemy,'" *Al Jazeera*, January 22, 2014 [in Arabic].

11. See Ayman al-Zawahiri's memoirs: *Fursan tahta rayat al-nabi* [Knights under the prophet's banner], serialized in Arabic in *al-Sharq Awsat*, December 2001.

12. Fawaz A. Gerges, *The Rise and Fall of Al-Qaeda* (Oxford: Oxford University Press, 2011), chapter 1.

13. *Takfir* literally means "pronouncement of unbelief against someone"; *takfiri* refers to those who excommunicate and declare a person or group of people *kuffar* (infidels) or non-Muslims.

14. Benjamin Isakhan, ed., *The Legacy of Iraq: From the 2003 War to the "Islamic State"* (Edinburgh: Edinburgh University Press, 2015). For context, see M. Idrees Ahmad, *The Road to Iraq: The Making of a Neoconservative War* (Edinburgh: Edinburgh University Press, 2014), and Ali A. Allawi, *The Occupation of Iraq* (New Haven, CT: Yale University Press, 2007).

15. See Maytahm al-Jabani, *Falsafat al-Hawiyya al-Wataniyya (al-Iraqiyya)* (Baghdad: Dar Mezobo, 2011), and Khalil F. Osman, *Sectarianism in Iraq: The Making of State and Nation since 1920* (Abingdon, UK: Routledge, 2015). The division into Shia, Sunnis, and Kurds is assumed to be primary, and, more specifically, Kurds and Shia, are treated in the same vein. The Kurdish nationalist project has always had an element of separation, and this is at odds with any sense of Shia identity or political aspiration, past and present. Author's interview with Iraqi political economist Kamil Mahdi, August 8, 2015.

16. See *al-Quds al-Arabi*, February 6 and 8, 2015.

17. Hisham al-Hashimi, "ISIS between Survival and Fragmentation," Al Jazeera Center for Studies, August 10, 2015 [in Arabic]; see also "Bayana al-Fuqaraa wal-Muslemeen: al-Mughalatat al-Arab'a al-Sha'ia hawla Zaherat al-Irhab fil A'lam" [The phenomenon of poor Muslims: The four common misconceptions on the phenomenon of global terrorism], Rawabet Center for Research and Strategic Studies, January 18, 2015, http://rawabetcenter.com/archives/289; Ilyas al-Farahat, "Al-Taktik al-'Askari le Daesh" [Daesh's military tactic], *al-Nahar*, November 2014, http://newspaper.annahar.com/article/192432-%D8%A7%D9%84%D8%AA%D9%83%D8%AA%D9%8A%D9%83-%D8%A7%D9%84%D8%B9%D8%B3%D9%83%D8%B1%D9%8A-%D9%84%D8%AF%D8%A7%D8%B9%D8%B4.

18. Hashimi, "ISIS between Survival and Fragmentation."

19. Ibid.

20. The Alawites, while an offshoot of Shiism, are not *exactly* Shia, although in the ISIS worldview, this distinction is irrelevant—they are all apostates.

21. See the articles "Tikrit Tribes Protest Their Innocence of the Crime of Killing Soldiers at [Camp] Speicher," *al-Quds al-Arabi*, February 20, 2015 [in Arabic]; "Abu Qatada: Islamic State Will Vanish," *Al Jazeera*, November 12, 2014 [in Arabic]; Ahmed Haqqi, "Islamic State's Tactics Will Speed Up Clash with [Sunni Tribes]," *Al Jazeera*, July 26, 2014 [in Arabic]; and "Daesh . . . Illegal Child of Al Qaeda Commits Fast Suicide," *al-Quds al-Arabi*, August 18, 2014 [in Arabic].

22. See Abdullah Bin Mohamed, "Sen'at al-Qarar al-Jihadi," https://justpaste.it/kl2s; Nour Ayub, "Al Qaeda: Let Us Imitate the Saud Sheikhs," *al-Akhbar*, April 21, 2015 [in Arabic].

23. Syrian opposition figures contend that in its first several months of fighting in Syria, ISIS directed the overwhelming majority

of its firepower not at the Assad regime but at the Free Syrian Army (FSA) and its strongholds. According to this viewpoint, ISIS and the Assad regime largely ignored each other in that initial period, during which both attacked the FSA, thus reinforcing each other. In an audio statement in 2013, Baghdadi revealed that al-Nusra is "an extension of the Islamic State of Iraq," announcing a merger between ISI and al-Nusra and branding the new entity the Islamic State of Iraq and al-Sham (ISIS). See www.youtube.com/watch?v=K3U23JbBpIw.

24. A. al-Zawahiri, "Testimonial to Preserve the Blood of Mujahideen in al-Sham [Greater Syria]," *pietervanostaeyen* (blog), May 2014, https://pietervanostaeyen.wordpress.com/2014/05/03/dr-ayman-az-zawahiri-testimonial-to-preserve-the-blood-of-mujahideen-in-as-sham/.

25. Raqqa U.M.C, YouTube, April 10, 2013, www.youtube.com/watch?v=6FdTjm4-6Lo.

26. Ibid.

27. Ibid. See also the link to a voice recording by Abu Mohammed al-Joulani, announcing his pledge of allegiance to the leader of Al Qaeda Central, Ayman al-Zawahiri, posted on April 10, 2013: www.youtube.com/watch?v=6FdTjm4-6Lo.

28. Michael Slackman, "Bullets Stall Youthful Push for Arab Spring," *New York Times*, March 17, 2011.

29. Fawaz A. Gerges, *Obama and the Middle East: The End of America's Moment?* (New York: Palgrave Macmillan, 2012), 189–190.

30. Henner Furtig, "Iran and the Arab Spring: Between Expectations and Disillusion," *GIGA Research Programme: Violence and Security*, no. 241 (2013), 3, www.giga-hamburg.de/en/system/files/publications/wp241_fuertig.pdf.

31. The Pentagon says Baghdadi, after being arrested in Fallujah in early 2004, was released that December with a large group of other prisoners deemed to be low-level threats. Other accounts estimate that Baghdadi spent one to five years in Bucca. Tim Arango and Eric Schmitt, "U.S. Actions in Iraq Fuelled Rise of a Rebel," *New York Times*, August 10, 2014; Martin Chulov, "ISIS: The Inside Story," *Guardian*, December 11, 2014.

CHAPTER 1. THE WORLD ACCORDING TO ISIS

1. See, for example, Catarina. Kinnvall, "Globalization and Religious Nationalism: Self, Identity, and the Search for Ontological Security," *Political Psychology* 25 (2004): 741–767; J. K. Wellman and K. Tokuno,

"Is Religious Violence Inevitable?," *Journal for the Scientific Study of Religion* 43 (2004): 291–296; R. Ysseldyk, M. Kimberly, Matheson, and H. Anisman, "Religiosity as Identity: Toward an Understanding of Religion from a Social Identity Perspective," *Personality and Social Psychology Review* 14, no. 1 (2010): 60–71.

2. Ysseldyk et al., "Religiosity as Identity," 61.

3. Fethi Benslama, *La guerre des subjectivities en Islam* (Paris: Nouvelles Editions Lignes, 2014).

4. See the interview of Fathi al Makdisi: "The Modernity Promised by the Nation State Is No Longer Sufficient—There Is a Need for a New Affiliation," *al-Quds al-Arabi*, August 22, 2015 [in Arabic], www.alquds.co.uk/?p=391704&print=1#comments_controls.

5. See link to an audio message by Abu Mohammed al-Adnani, "Hazizahu Allah" (This is the promise of Allah) June 29, 2014, http://jihadology.net/2014/06/29/al-furqan-media-presents-a-new-audio-message-from-the-islamic-states-shaykh-abu-muḥammad-al-adnani-al-shami-this-is-the-promise-of-god/.

6. Ibid.

7. Ibid.

8. See link to a voice recording by Abu Mohammed al-Adnani, "Apologies, Leader of al-Qaeda," declaring the revocation of the pledge of allegiance to Al Qaeda and calling on it to reject the pledge of allegiance by Joulani: www.youtube.com/watch?v=CAB (posted on September 17, 2014).

9. Anne Barnard and Hwaida Saad, "ISIS Fighters Seize Control of Syrian City of Palmyra, and Ancient Ruins," *New York Times*, May 20, 2015. See also Anne Barnard, "ISIS Conquest of Palmyra Expands Militants' Hold on Syria," *New York Times*, May 21, 2015.

10. Jonathan Landay, Warren Strobel, and Phil Stewart, "Exclusive: Seized documents reveal Islamic State's Department of 'War Spoils,'" Reuters, December 28, 2015.

11. Rukmini Callimachi, "ISIS Enshrines a Theology of Rape," *New York Times*, August 13, 2015; see also Judit Neurink, "The ISIS Leader Abu Bakr al-Baghdadi Viewed Women Held Captive at a Syrian House as His Private Property, and Raped a Number of Them, Including the US Hostage Kayla Mueller," *Independent*, August 14, 2015.

12. Amnesty International, *Escape from Hell: Torture and Sexual Slavery in Islamic State Captivity in Iraq* (London: Amnesty International, 2014), www.amnesty.org.uk/sites/default/files/escape_from_hell_-_torture_and_sexual_slavery_in_islamic_state_captivity_in_iraq

_-_english_2.pdf; Rothna Begum and Samer Muscati, "Interview: These Yezidi Girls Escaped ISIS. Now What?," *Human Rights Watch*, April 15, 2015; Samer Muscati, "Raped by ISIS and Trying to Face the Future," *Human Rights Watch*, April 14, 2015.

13. Amnesty International, *Escape from Hell*.

14. The "price list" was first leaked by activists based in ISIS-controlled areas of Syria in November 2014, but it was unable to be verified and its authenticity was initially brought into question. Cormac Fitzgerald, "ISIS Executes 19 Female Prisoners for Refusing to Practice 'Sexual Jihad'—Kurdish Official," *Irish Independent*, August 6, 2015.

15. Fiker Center for Studies, "The Islamic State Organization: Drivers and Ideology" [in Arabic], www.fikercenter.com/, summarized in AlSouria.net, July 18 and 22, 2015.

16. Landy et al., "Exclusive: Seized documents."

17. ISIS, "The Revival of Slavery before the Hour," *Dabiq*, no. 4, October 2014.

18. For Baghdadi's audio statement in November 2014, see https://pietervanostaeyen.wordpress.com/2014/11/14/audio-message-by-abu-bakr-al-baghdadi-even-if-the-disbelievers-despise-such/.

19. Abu Bakr al-Najji, *Idaraat al-Tawahush: Akhtar Marhalaa Satamur Beha al-Umma* [Management of savagery: The most critical stage through which the Islamic nation will pass] (n.p.: Markaz al-Derasaat wal Buhuth al-Islamiyaa, n.d.), https://pietervanostaeyen.files.wordpress.com/2015/02/idarat_al-tawahhush_-_abu_bakr_naji.pdf; Abu Abdullah al-Muhajjer, *Masael fi Fiqh al-Jihad* [An introduction to the jurisprudence of jihad], https://archive.org/details/msael-mn; and Abdel-Qade Ibn Abdel-Aziz [Dr. Fadl], *Al-'Umda fi I'dad al-'Udda* [The essentials of making ready (for jihad)], www.m5zn.com/newuploads/2015/02/18/pdf/4f2fb076fd7d595.pdf.

20. Abdel-Aziz, *The Essentials of Making Ready*, 5.

21. Ibid. Moatez al-Khatib, "Daesh's Intellectual Origins: From Jurisprudence to Reality," January 2015, http://studies.aljazeera.net/en/dossiers/decipheringdaeshoriginsimpactandfuture/2014/12/2014123981882756.htm#a20.

22. Najji, *Management of Savagery*, 83.

23. Ibid., 20.

24. Ibid., 50.

25. Ibid., 75, 77.

26. Ibid., 15.

27. Abdel-Aziz, *The Essentials of Making Ready*, 340.

28. Ibid., 342.

29. Ibid., 313.

30. Ibid., 30, 344. *Fard Ayn* (an individual duty) is an act that is obligatory for Muslims individually. Each will be rewarded for performing it, or punished for failing to perform it. The five daily prayers, for which Muslims are individually responsible, is one example of this duty.

31. Ibid., 315.

32. Ibid., 293–295.

33. Ibid., 303.

34. Ibid., 304.

35. Ibid., 345.

36. Ibid., 30.

37. Ibid., 5.

38. Fawaz Gerges, *The Far Enemy: Why Jihad Went Global*, 2nd ed. (Cambridge, UK: Cambridge University Press, 2010), 14.

39. Muhajjer, *An Introduction to the Jurisprudence of Jihad*, 25.

40. Ibid., 32.

41. Ibid., 18.

42. See Najji, *Management of Savagery*, 4.

43. Ibid., 76.

44. Ibid., 32.

45. Ibid.

46. Muhajjer, *An Introduction to the Jurisprudence of Jihad*, 270, 288.

47. Ibid., 282.

48. Ibid., 187–188.

49. Ibid., 469.

50. Najji, *Management of Savagery*, 76–79.

51. Tim Arango, "ISIS Transforming into Functioning State That Uses Terror as Tool," *New York Times*, July 21, 2015.

52. Baghdadi's transcript and audio, "March Forth whether Light or Heavy," *Carol Anne Grayson (Radical Sister) Blog*, May 14, 2015, https://activist1.wordpress.com/2015/05/14/islamic-state-al-furqan-media-releases-new-audio-and-transcript-allegedly-of-baghdadi/; see also Fiker Center for Studies, "The Islamic State Organization."

53. K. Dilanian, "US Intel: IS Militants Drawing Steady Stream of Recruits," Associated Press, February 11, 2015, http://midco.net/news/read/category/Politics/article/the_associated_press-ap_exclusive_is_militants_drawing_steady_stream_of-ap; "Foreign Fighters Still Flowing

to Syria, U.S. Intelligence Says," Reuters, February 10, 2015, www
.reuters.com/article/2015/02/11/us-mideast-crisis-fighters-idUSKBN
0LE2YX20150211.

54. Ryan Browne, "Top intelligence official: ISIS to attempt U.S. attacks this year," CNN.com, February 9, 2016: http://edition.cnn.com
/2016/02/09/politics/james-clapper-isis-syrian-refugees/.

55. Shellie Nelson, "State Department Report: ISIS Breaking New
Ground as New Leader in Terror Groups," CNN.com, June 20, 2015,
http://edition.cnn.com/2015/06/19/politics/isis-report-state-department
-terror/.

56. Rukmini Callimachi, Katrin Benhold, and Laure Fourquet,
"How the Paris Attackers Honed Their Assault through Trial and
Error," New York Times, November 30, 2015.

57. "David Cameron: ISIS presents existential threat to UK—
audio," Guardian, June 29, 2015.

58. Liam Stack, "Qaeda Affiliate Uses Video of Donald Trump for
Recruiting," New York Times, January 1, 2016.

59. Scott Condon, "FBI Director Reveals Hidden Threat of ISIS at
Aspen Security Forum," Aspen Times, July 22, 2015.

60. Eric Schmitt, "ISIS or Al Qaeda? American Officials Split over
Biggest Threat," New York Times, August 4, 2015.

61. Ibid.

62. Anthony H. Cordesman, "New Year's Resolutions on Terrorism: Panic, Politics, and the Prospects for Honesty in 2016," Center for
Strategic and International Studies (CSIS), December 28, 2015, http://
csis.org/publication/new-years-resolutions-terrorism-panic-politics-and
-prospects-honesty-2016.

63. See Adnani, "This Is the Promise of Allah"; A. Al-Athari, "Mad
Al-Ayady La Baya'at Al-Baghdadi" [Extending hands to Al-Baghdadi's
Allegiance], Al-Tawhid and Al-Jihad Platform, July 2013 [in Arabic],
https://archive.org/details/baghdadi-001. See also A. Al-Azdari, "Mougbat Al-Andmam Lel Dawla Al-Islamya Fe Al-Eraq Wal Al-Sham,
A'atradat wa Gawabat" [Necessities for joining the Islamic State of Iraq
and Syria, objections and answers], Al-Ma'asadah Media Foundation, August 2013 [in Arabic], www.scribd.com/doc/184157776/الإ-في-العراق-والشام
سلامية-للدولة-الانضمام-موجبات

64. Helene Cooper, "Pentagon Officials Say They'll Bolster Special
Operations Force in Iraq," New York Times, December 1, 2015; Karen
DeYoung, "Despite the Critics, the White House Insists It Has a Plan to
Fight the Islamic State," Washington Post, December 6, 2015; and Rukmini

Callimachi, "U.S. Seeks to Avoid Ground War Welcomed by Islamic State," *New York Times*, December 7, 2015.

65. Gardiner Harris, "Deeper Mideast Aspirations Seen in Nuclear Deal with Iran," *New York Times*, July 31, 2015.

66. Chris Woods, "First Year of Coalition Airstrikes Helped Stall Islamic State—but at a Cost," *Airwars*, August 10, 2015; "Anti-IS coalition has killed 22,000 jihadists since mid-2014: France," *Agence France Presse*, January 2014.

67. "Daesh Lost 30 Percent of Its Territory," Associated Press, January 6, 2016. See also Columb Strack, "Islamic State Territory Shrinks by 9.4% in First Six Months of 2015," IHS, July 27, 2015, www.janes.com /article/53239/islamic-state-territory-shrinks-by-9-4-in-first-six-months-of -2015#.VbeipB_weRs.twitter.

68. Author's interview with Rami Abdel-Rahman, director of the Syrian Observatory for Human Rights, London, October 25, 2015.

69. Schmitt, "ISIS or Al Qaeda?"; Hermela Aregawi, "Operation Inherent Resolve: A Year of Fighting ISIL," *Al Jazeera America*, August 14, 2015.

70. Yaroslav Trofimov and Philip Shishkin, "Regional Discord Fuels Islamic State's Rise in Mideast," *Wall Street Journal*, October 16, 2015.

CHAPTER 2. WHERE ISIS CAME FROM: ZARQAWI TO BAGHDADI

1. See "Former Iraqi Intelligence Officer Reveals Secrets about the American Ministry of Defence to RT," *Russia Today*, March 20, 2013 [in Arabic], http://arabic.rt.com/prg/telecast/658078_اختراق_اسرار_اليوم /روسيا_ل_يكشف_سابق_عراقي_مخابرات_رجلالامريكية_الدفاع_لوزارة_جهازه; Walid Abdul-Malik al-Rawi, " Facts on the Relationship between Al-Qaeda and President Saddam Hussein's Regime," *Kitabat*, December 23, 2013, http://kitabat.com/ar/page/23/12/2013/20917/حسين-صدام-الرئيس-ونظام-القاعدة -تنظيم-بين-العلاقة-حقيقة/.html.

2. Jeffrey Record, "Threat, Confusion and Its Penalties," *Survival: Global Politics and Strategy* 46, no. 2 (2001): 51–71. See also "Sept. 11 Panel Deals Bush a Blow on Iraq; In Dismissing al Qaeda Link, Commission Undercuts President's Credibility on Going to War," *Wall Street Journal*, June 18, 2004; and Christopher Marquis, "Powell Admits No Hard Proof Linking Iraq to Al-Qaeda," *New York Times*, January 9, 2004, www.nytimes.com/2004/01/09/politics/09POWE.html.

3. See "President Obama Speaks with Vice News" (video), March 15, 2015, https://news.vice.com/video/president-obama-speaks-with-vice-news.

4. See full transcript of Collin L. Powell's Remarks to the United Nations Security Council on February 5, 2003, US Department of State Archive, http://2001-2009.state.gov/secretary/former/powell/remarks/2003/17300.htm.

5. Philip Shenon, "Final 9/11 Report Is Said to Dismiss Iraq-Qaeda Alliance," *New York Times*, July 12, 2004, www.nytimes.com/learning/students/pop/articles/12panel.html. See also the full 9/11 report by the National Commission on Terrorists Attacks, www.9-11commission.gov/report/.

6. Fu'ad Hussein, "Al-Zarqawi . . . : The Second Generation of Al Qaeda—Seif al-Adl's Testament," *al-Quds al-Arabi*, part 9, May 23, 2005 [in Arabic]. See also Fawaz A. Gerges, *The Far Enemy: Why Jihad Went Global*, 2nd ed. (Cambridge, UK: Cambridge University Press, 2009), chapter 6.

7. Loretta Napoleoni, "Profile of a Killer, Foreign Policy," *Foreign Policy*, November/December 2005, http://foreignpolicy.com/2009/10/20/profile-of-a-killer/. See also Joffe Laurence, "Abu Musab al-Zarqawi," *Guardian*, June 6, 2006, www.theguardian.com/news/2006/jun/09/guardian obituaries.alqaida.

8. In an article in the *Atlantic*, Marie Anne Weaver says that in December 1989, Huthaifa Azzam, the teenage son of the legendary Jordanian-Palestinian mujahideen leader Sheikh Abdullah Azzam, went to the airport in Peshawar and that Zarqawi was among the men who had traveled to fight in Afghanistan. In the article, Weaver interviews Azzam's son. See Marie Anne Weaver, "The Short, Violent Life of Abu Musab al-Zarqawi," *Atlantic*, July 1, 2006, www.theatlantic.com/magazine/archive/2006/07/the-short-violent-life-of-abu-musab-al-zarqawi/304983/.

9. For a full account of al-Hami's relationship with Zarqawi, see ibid. See also Loretta Napoleoni, *Insurgent Iraq: Al-Zarqawi and the New Generation* (London: Constable, 2005), 44–45; and Michael Weiss and Hassan Hassan, *ISIS: Inside the Army of Terror* (New York: Regan Arts, 2015), 16.

10. Nir Rosen, "Iraq's Jordanian Jihadis," *New York Times*, February 19, 2006, www.nytimes.com/2006/02/19/magazine/iraq.html?pagewanted=all &_r=0.

11. Hussein, "Al-Zarqawi," part 1, May 13, 2005.

12. *Zarqaoui: La question terroriste* [documentary], directed by Patrice Barrat, Najat Rizk, and Ranwa Stephan (France: HR Prod, 2007).

13. Hussein, "Al-Zarqawi," part 5, May 18, 2005.

14. Fu'ad Hussein, *Abu Musab al-Zarqawi, from Herat to Baghdad* [documentary] (Beirut: LBC TV, broadcast April 27 and 28, 2004) [in Arabic].

15. *Zarqaoui: La question terroriste.*

16. *Abu Musab al-Zarqawi, from Herat to Baghdad.*

17. Hussein, "Al-Zarqawi," parts 6 and 7, May 19 and 20, 2005.

18. Ibid.

19. See, for example, Napoleoni, *Insurgent Iraq*, 95. According to Napoleoni, bin Laden and Zarqawi met in Afghanistan, although the two did not then agree on a formal alliance. For more accounts of the alleged meeting, see also Weiss and Hassan, *ISIS*, 16, and Jessica Stern and J. M. Berger, *ISIS: The State of Terror* (London: HarperCollins, 2015), 27–28.

20. *Zarqaoui: La question terroriste.*

21. Ibid.

22. *Abu Musab al-Zarqawi, from Herat to Baghdad.*

23. Reuters, "Confrontation with the Gulf; Excerpts from Hussein's Statement Declaring a Holy War," *New York Times*, August 11, 1990.

24. Magdi Ahmed Hussein, "Growing Religious Tie in Iraq," *alarabnews*, July 20, 2001 [in Arabic], http://alarabnews.com/alshaab/GIF/20 -07-2001/MagdiHussien.htm.

25. Adeed Daweesha, "'Identity' and Political Survival in Saddam's Iraq," *Middle East Journal* 53, no. 4 (1999): 553–567; A. El-Affendi, "The Napoleonic-Saddam Syndrome and the Crisis of Arab Democracy: Beyond Political Culture and the Politics of Culture" (2008), in *Democracy and Development in the Arab World*, ed. Ibrahim Elbadawi and Samir A. Makdisi, International Development Research Centre (Canada) (London: Routledge, 2011).

26. Fanar Haddad, "Sectarian Relations in Arab Iraq: Contextualizing the Civil War of 2006–2007," *British Journal of Middle Eastern Studies* 40, no. 2 (2013): 115–138; *More than Shi'ites and Sunnis* (2009), report by Iraqi Academics and Professionals and the Norwegian Institute of International Affairs (NUPI), 1–32, www.historiae.org/documents /Post-sectarian.pdf; Jean-Pierre Luizard, "Islam as a Point of Reference for Political and Social Groups in Iraq," *International Review of the Red Cross* 89, no. 868 (2007): 843–855, especially 853.

27. Personal correspondence with Iraqi sociology professor Saad Jawad, August 4, 5, and 7, 2015, and with political economist Kamil Mahdi, July 31, August 3, and August 5, 2015.

28. Hussein, "Al-Zarqawi," parts 6 and 7, May 19 and 20, 2005.

29. *Zarqaoui: La question terroriste*.

30. Jean-Charles Brisard and Damien Martinez, *Zarqawi: The New Face of al-Qaeda* (Cambridge, UK: Polity Press, 2005), 130–135.

31. Ibid.

32. Ibid., 134–135.

33. Sami Moubayed, "Abu al-Ghadia to Build on al-Zarqawi's Legacy in Iraq," *Terrorism Focus* 3, no. 26 (July 9, 2006), www.jamestown.org /single/?tx_ttnews%5Btt_news%5D=827&no_cache=1#.Vm8hEzbVvzI.

34. Ali Hashem, "The Many Names of Abu Bakr al-Baghdadi," *Al Monitor*, March 23, 2015, www.al-monitor.com/pulse/originals/2015/03/isis -baghdadi-islamic-state-caliph-many-names-al-qaeda.html#.

35. Hussein, "Al-Zarqawi," part 3, May 16, 2005.

36. Maamoun Youssef, "Al-Qaida Announces Iraqi Suicide Squad," Associated Press, June 21, 2005.

37. Osama bin Laden, "To the Muslims in Iraq in Particular and the [Islamic] Nation [Umma] in General," Al-Sahab (Institute for Media Production), May 27, 2004. The full text of bin Laden's message was translated by FBIS Report FEA20041227000762, December 27, 2004. See also Hussein, "Al-Zarqawi," part 9, May 23, 2005; Gerges, *The Far Enemy*, 252.

38. Napoleoni, *Insurgent Iraq*, 137.

39. Dexter Filkins, "At Least 11 Die in Car Bombing at Jordan's Embassy in Baghdad," *New York Times*, August 7, 2003, www.nytimes.com /2003/08/07/international/worldspecial/07CND-IRAQ.html. For Zarqawi's involvement in the car bombing, see "Investigation of the Jordanian Embassy in Baghdad," *Asharq al-Awsat*, August 10, 2003 [in Arabic], http://archive.aawsat.com/details.asp?article=186448&issueno=9021#.VS -szVxN3zJ.

40. Kamil al-Taweel, "Al-Zarqawi: Islamic Government in Iraq as a Way Station to Overthrow Neighboring Regimes," *Al Hayat*, September 19, 2004 [in Arabic]; Kamil Taweel, "Al-Zarqawi Present and His Followers Everywhere," *Al Hayat*, September 5, 2004 [in Arabic]; Kamil Taweel, "Bin Laden Fails in Afghanistan . . . but 'Enters Iraq through the Zarqawi Gate,'" *Al Hayat*, October 19, 2004 [in Arabic]; "Emir of the Fallujah Fighters (Abu Osama) to Al Wasat: Every Mujahid in Iraq Is a Member of Al Qaeda," *Al Wasat*, May 3, 2004 [in Arabic].

41. Abu Musab al-Zarqawi, "Musab al-Zarqawi Letter Obtained by United States Government in Iraq," US Department of State Archive, 2004, http://2001-2009.state.gov/p/nea/rls/31694.htm.

42. Ibid.

43. Associated Press, "Al Zarqawi Group Vows Allegiance to Bin Laden," October 17, 2004; Dan Murphy, "In Iraq, a Clear-Cut Bin Laden-Zarqawi Alliance," *Christian Science Monitor*, December 31, 2004.

44. Bin Laden, "To the Muslims in Iraq."

45. "Islamic Figures, Scholars Worldwide Condemn 'US-Zionist' Crimes in Iraq, Palestine," *al-Quds al-Arabi*, August 23, 2003 [in Arabic].

46. Laura Jordan and Katherine Shrader, "Bin Laden Enlisting Al-Zarqawi for Attacks," Associated Press, April 1, 2005.

47. Hani al-Sibai, "Introduction," in *Ayman al-Zawahiri Kama Araftuhu* [Ayman al-Zawahiri as I knew him], ed. Montasser al-Zayat (Cairo: n.p., 2002); Mohammed al-Shafi'i, "Zawahiri Expelled Two Jihadi Leaders," *Asharq al-Awsat*, June 6, 2002 [in Arabic]; Shafi'i, "Zawahiri's Secret Papers," *Ashard al-Awsat*, part 1, December 13, 2002 [in Arabic].

48. Hussein, "Al-Zarqawi," part 3, May 16, 2005.

49. See Ayman al-Zawahiri, "Letter from al-Zawahiri to al-Zarqawi," Combating Terrorism Centre, 2005, www.ctc.usma.edu/v2/wp-content/uploads/2013/10/Zawahiris-Letter-to-Zarqawi-Translation.pdf.

50. Ibid.

51. Ibid.

52. Ibid.

53. Abu Musab al-Zarqawi, "Leader of Al-Qaeda in Iraq Al-Zarqawi Declares 'Total War' on Shi'ites," Middle East Media Research Institute, 2005, http://hdl.handle.net/10066/4810.

54. Ibid.

55. Al-Zarqawi, "Musab al-Zarqawi Letter."

56. Ibid.

57. Ibid.

58. Ibid.

59. Ibid.

60. Middle East Media Research Institute, "Abu Mus'ab Al-Zarqawi: Collateral Killing of Muslims Is Legitimate," www.memri.org/bin/opener.latest.cgi?ID=SD91705 (posted on June, 7, 2005).

61. A. Ibn Qassem, "Fataawa Shaykh al-Islam Ahmad Ibn Taymiyyah, Part 28: al-Jihad" (n.p.: King Fahd Printing Press, 2004), 482, http://d1.islamhouse.com/data/ar/ih_books/chain/Fatawa_Ibn_Taymiyyah/mfsiaitm28.pdf.

62. See Aula Hariri, "The Iraqi Independence Movement: A Case of Transgressive Contention," in *Contentious Politics in the Middle East: Popular Resistance and Marginalised Activism beyond the Arab Spring Uprisings*, ed. Fawaz Gerges (New York: Palgrave Macmillan, 2015).

63. Douglas Jehl, "Iraq May Be Prime Place for Training of Militants, C.I.A Report Concludes," *New York Times*, June 22, 2005; Dana Priest, "Iraq a New Terror Breeding Ground," *Washington Post*, January 13, 2005; Dana Priest and Josh White, "War Helps Recruit Terrorists, Hill Told," *Washington Post*, February 17, 2005; David Morgan, "Iraq Conflict Feeds International Threat—CIA," Reuters, February 16, 2005; "Iraq Warns Neighbors of Terror Threat," *Agence France Presse*, July 10, 2005.

64. "Iraq Now an Al-Qaeda Battleground, British Report Says," *Agence France Presse*, July 29, 2004.

65. Bob Herbert, "Iraq Then and Now," *New York Times*, February 21, 2005, www.nytimes.com/2005/02/21/opinion/21herbert.html?pagewanted=print&position.

66. Associated Press, "Rumsfeld Questions Terror War Progress," October 22, 2005, November 1, 2005, February 25, 2005, April 26, 2005, and May 25, 2004.

67. Abu Abdullah Mohamed al-Mansour al-Issawi, *Al-Dawla al-Islamiyya: Bayna al-Haqiqa wa al-Wahm* [The Islamic State: Disentangling myth from reality] (n.p., n.d.), 1–167. See also Abd al-Wahed al-Ansari, "The Principles of the Armed Islamist Groups Collapse with the Experience of the [Islamic] State," *Al Hayat*, November 19, 2014 [in Arabic].

68. Issawi, *The Islamic State*, 96–97.

69. Ibid., 7, 97.

70. Ibid., 96–154.

71. "Iraqi Death Squads 'Not Police,'" *BBC News*, April 12, 2006, http://news.bbc.co.uk/1/hi/world/middle_east/4901786.stm; see also Mona Mahmood, Maggie O'Kane, Chavala Madlena, and Teresa Smith, "Revealed: Pentagon Link to Iraqi Torture," *Guardian*, March 6, 2013, www.theguardian.com/world/2013/mar/06/pentagon-iraqi-torture-centres-link; Michael Schwartz, *War without End: The Iraq War in Context* (Chicago: Haymarket Books, 2008).

72. Al-Zawahiri, "Letter from al-Zawahiri to al-Zarqawi."

73. Hassan S. Fattah and Michael Slackman, "Three Hotels Bombed in Jordan; At Least 57 Die," *New York Times*, November 10, 2005, www.nytimes.com/2005/11/10/international/middleeast/10jordan.html?_r=0.

74. Fawaz Gerges, "Buried in Amman's Rubble: Zarqawi's Support," *Washington Post*, December 4, 2005, www.washingtonpost.com /wp-dyn/content/article/2005/12/02/AR2005120202370.html.

75. Ibid.

76. In another speech, Zawahiri also implied that Baghdadi is "the grandson of khawarij" after the killing of al-Qaeda representative in Syria Abu Khaled al-Surri reportedly assassinated by ISIS in February 2014. See "Al-Zawahiri Says that the Grandson of al-Khawarij and His Gang Who Killed Abu Khaled Al-Surri God Bless Him Would Be Doomed," YouTube, May 11, 2015, www.youtube.com/watch?v=VWdc -aZMCKU. In an interview with *al-Jazeera*, the leader of Al Qaeda– affiliated al-Nusra group Mohammed al-Joulani described members of the Islamic State as "Khwarij." "The Leader of al-Nusra Front Describes the 'Islamic State' Members of being Khwarij" [in Arabic], *France24*, June 4, 2015, http://goo.gl/IiJ0VT; Issawi, *The Islamic State*, 96–154; O. Abdel Rahman Al Tamimi, "A'alam Al-Anam Bmelad Dawlat Al-Islam" [Notifying (beings/people) with the birth of Islam], Al-Furqan Media Foundation, November 2008 [in Arabic], 24, 26, www.slideshare.net /yaken0/ss-5927504.

77. Abu Mohammed al-Adnani, "Apologies, Emir of Al Qaeda," Muasassat al-Furqan Tuqadem, July 5, 2014, https://justpaste.it/othran. See also Abu Mohammed al-Adnani, "Muasassat al-Furqan Tuqadem: Haza Wa'd Min Allah: Sheikh Abi Mohamed al-Adnani Hazizahu Allah," YouTube, July 5, 2014 [in Arabic], www.youtube.com/watch?v =Uen14MVYNqk; Abu Mohammed al-Adnani, "This Is the Promise of Allah," June 19, 2014, http://triceratops.brynmawr.edu/dspace/bitstream /handle/10066/14242/ADN20140629.pdf?sequence=1. See manifestos by ISIS chief propagandists: A. Al-Athari, "Mad Al-Ayady La Baya'at Al-Baghdadi" [Extending hands to Al-Baghdadi's allegiance], *Al-Tawhid and Al-Jihad Platform*, July 2013 [in Arabic], https://archive.org/details /baghdadi-001. See also A. Al-Azdari, "Mougbat Al-Andmam Lel Dawla Al-Islamya Fe Al-Eraq Wal Al-Sham, A'atradat wa Gawabat" [Necessities for joining the Islamic State of Iraq and Syria, objections and answers], Al-Ma'asadah Media Foundation, August 2013 [in Arabic], www.scribd .com/doc/184157776/موجبات-الانضمام-للدولة-الإسلامية-في-العراق-والشام.

78. Al-Adnani, "Apologies, Emir of Al Qaeda"; Al-Ansari, "The Principles of the Armed Islamist Groups."

79. Marwan Shahata, "The Zarqawi-Maqdisi Dispute," *Al Hayat*, July 5, 2005 [in Arabic]. See also Mahari al-Zaydi, "Abu Mohammed

al-Maqdisi: Al-Zarqawi's 'Spiritual Godfather,'" *al-Sharq al-Awsat*, July 26, 2005 [in Arabic].

80. See Zarqawi's response in Arabic: http://ak-ma.blogspot.co .uk/2013/03/blog-post_9.html.

81. Gerges, *The Far Enemy*, 298–299; see also Fawaz Gerges, "Osama bin Laden's Growing Anxiety," *Christian Science Monitor*, October 26, 2007.

82. Gerges, *The Far Enemy*, 298–299; see also Gerges, "Osama bin Laden's Growing Anxiety."

83. Gerges, "Osama bin Laden's Growing Anxiety."

84. Gerges, *The Far Enemy*, 298–299; see also Gerges, "Osama bin Laden's Growing Anxiety."

85. John F. Burns and Dexter Filkins, "A Jihadist Web Site Says Zarqawi's Group in Iraq Has a New Leader in Place," *New York Times*, June 13, 2006; Dexter Filkins and John F. Burns, "U.S. Portrayal Helps Flesh Out Zarqawi's Heir," *New York Times*, June 16, 2006.

86. Michael R. Gordon., "Leader of Al Qaeda Group in Iraq Was Fictional, U.S. Military Says." *New York Times*, July 18, 2007.

87. Tim Arango, "Top Qaeda Leaders in Iraq Reported Killed in Raid," *New York Times*, April 20, 2010, www.nytimes.com/2010/04/20 /world/middleeast/20baghdad.html?_r=0.

88. Al-Athari, "Extending Hands to Al-Baghdadi's Allegiance."

89. See an audiotape recording by Ayman al-Zawahiri explaining relations between Al Qaeda and ISIS: www.youtube.com/watch/v =oztWZfVU (posted on September 15, 2015). See also "Al-Nusra and Al-Qaeda: Repercussions of Revoking Pledge of Allegiance," Policy Brief, Omran for Strategic Studies, August 14, 2015, مركز عمران للدراسات الاستراتيجية 2015.

90. Abdel Rahman Al Tamimi, " Notifying [Beings/People] with the Birth of Islam," 36–38.

91. See "A Review of Events: As-Sahab's Fourth Interview with Shaykh Ayman al-Zawwhiri," November/December 2007, https:// archive.org/details/A-Review-of-Events2. See also Al-Azdari, "Necessities for Joining the Islamic State of Iraq and Syria."

92. See the audiotape recording by Zawahiri explaining relations between Al Qaeda and ISIS: www.youtube.com/watch/v=ozt WZfVU. See also the bin Laden documents in Office of the Director of National Intelligence, www.dni.gov/files/documents/ubl/arabic2 /Message%20for%20general%20Islamic%20nation%20-%20Arabic .pdf [in Arabic].

93. Issawi, *The Islamic State*, 154–159.

94. Ibid., 6.

95. Ibid.

96. Ibid., 102–103.

97. Sheikh Nabil Naeem, *Daesh: Al-Irhab al-Muqadas* [Daesh: The sacred terrorism] (Cairo: Al-Mahrousa, 2015), 14. This number only continued to grow, especially following the occupation of Mosul, Tikrit, parts of the Anbar province, and a third of the Syrian territories in the summer of 2014.

98. Khalid Al-Ansary, "Iraqis Say Qaeda Deaths Will Not Improve Their Lives," Reuters, April 20, 2010, www.reuters.com/article /2010/04/19/us-iraq-violence-alqaeda-idUSTRE63I3CL20100419; see also Arango, "Top Qaeda Leaders in Iraq Reported Killed in Raid."

99. Andrew England, "Al-Qaeda's Military Leaders in Iraq Killed," *Financial Times*, April 20, 2010, www.ft.com/cms/s/0/e3b88b42-4c13-11df -a217-00144feab49a.html#axzz3WWWD4Y9I.

100. "Iraqi al-Qaeda Leaders 'Killed,'" *BBC News*, April 19, 2010, http:// news.bbc.co.uk/1/hi/world/middle_east/8630213.stm.

CHAPTER 3. HOW BROKEN IRAQI POLITICS FUELED THE REVIVAL OF ISIS

1. For more on how the sanctions regime affected Iraqi society, including, specifically, its Shia community, see Nicholas Krohley, *The Death of the Mehdi Army: The Rise, Fall, and Revival of Iraq's Most Powerful Militia* (London: C. Hurst and Company, 2015).

2. Michael Eisenstadt and Jeffrey White, "Assessing Iraq's Sunni Arab Insurgency," *Policy Focus* no. 50, Washington Institute for Near East Policy, December 2005, www.washingtoninstitute.org/html/pdf /PolicyFocus50.pdf.

3. See Ellen Nickmeyer and Jonathan Finer, "Insurgents Assert Control over Town Near Syrian Border," *Washington Post*, September 6, 2005, www.washingtonpost.com/wp-dyn/content/article/2005/09/05 /AR2005090500313.html.

4. "Emir of the Islamic State of Iraq," *al-Faloja Forum*, February 25, 2007.

5. "Terror Tape Says 4,000 Foreign Fighters Killed in Iraq," *CNN*, September 28, 2006, http://edition.cnn.com/2006/WORLD/meast/09/28 /iraq.main/.

6. "Iraqi Tribal Leader Says Not 'Scared' by Abu-Hamzah's Message," *BBC Monitoring International Reports*, September 28, 2006.

7. "'Mujahidin Shura Council' Proclaims the Establishment of an Islamic State in Iraq—Expert Reveals Information about the Iraqi Dissident Osama Abu al-Qaeda," *Al Arabiya*, October 15, 2006 [in Arabic], www.alarabiya.net/articles/2006/10/15/28296.html. See also "The Nature of the Enemy," *U.S. Department of Defense* 1, no. 3 (October 24, 2006); Mohammad Ballout, "Details Emerge on Kidnapped Syrian Bishops," *al-Monitor*, August 15, 2013, www.al-monitor.com/pulse/tr /security/2013/08/bishops-kidnapped-syria-aleppo-details.html #ixzz3Z07MuRNL; Bill Roggio, "Divisions in al Qaeda in Iraq," *Long War Journal*, October 13, 2006, www.longwarjournal.org/archives/2006 /10/divisions_in_alqaeda.php.

8. Asharq al-Sawat, "Bin Laden Urged to Disown Iraq's Qaeda Chief-TV," *Asharq al-Sawat*, October 13, 2006, www.aawsat.net/2006/10 /article55264974/bin-laden-urged-to-disown-iraqs-qaeda-chief-tv.

9. "'Mujahidin Shura Council' Proclaims the Establishment of an Islamic State in Iraq." On Islam, see "Mujahideen Shura Declares 'Islamic Emirate' in Iraq," Onislam.net, October 15, 2006 [in Arabic], www.onislam.net/arabic/newsanalysis/3001-شيف أر/82233-2006-10 -15%2000-00-00.html.

10. See Maggie O'Kane and Ian Black, "Sunni Militia Strike Could Derail U.S. Strategy against al-Qaida," *Guardian*, March 21, 2008, www .theguardian.com/world/2008/mar/21/iraq.alqaida; Mark Kuki, "Turning Iraq's Tribes against Al-Qaeda," *Time*, December 26, 2006, http://content .time.com/time/world/article/0,8599,1572796,00.html. See also Cécile Hennion, "Irak: Des tribus sunnites se lèvent contre Al-Qaida, sans renoncer à la guerilla," *Le Monde*, June 12, 2007, www.lemonde.fr/proche -orient/article/2007/06/12/irak-des-tribus-sunnites-se-levent-contre-al -qaida-sans-renoncer-a-la-guerilla_922246_3218.html.

11. See the document published by the Combating Terrorism Center at West Point titled "Al Qaeda in Iraq, Situation Report" [in Arabic], www.ctc.usma.edu/v2/wp-content/uploads/2013/09/Al-Qaida -in-Iraq-Situation-Report-Original.pdf.

12. See O'Kane and Black, "Sunni Militia Strike."

13. Mark Wilbanks and Efraim Karsh, "How the 'Sons of Iraq' Stabilized Iraq," *Middle East Quarterly* 17, no. 4 (Fall 2010): 57–70.

14. Amit R. Paley, "Shift in Tactics Aims to Revive Struggling Insurgency," *Washington Post*, February 8, 2008, www.washingtonpost .com/wpdyn/content/article/2008/02/07/AR2008020703854.html?hpid =sec-world&sid=ST2008020801213.

15. Johan F. Burns and Alissa Rubin, "U.S. Arming Sunnis in Iraq to Battle Old Qaeda Allies," *New York Times*, June 11, 2007, www .nytimes.com/2007/06/11/world/middleeast/11iraq.html?pagewanted =all&_r=1&.

16. "Iraqi PM Says Ready to Tackle Militias," *Asharq al-Awsat*, October 25, 2006 [in Arabic], www.aawsat.net/2006/10/article55264854 /iraqi-pm-says-ready-to-tackle-militias.

17. "Le trouble des sunnites irakiens ralliés au pouvoir," *Le Monde and AFP*, April 1, 2009, www.lemonde.fr/proche-orient/article/2009/04/01 /le-trouble-des-sunnites-irakiens-rallies-au-pouvoir_1175208_3218 .html#Ee6uWrgvsoC3f7oR.99.

18. "PM Says Saddam Loyalists Infiltrated Iraq's Sahwa Militia," *Agence France Presse*, April 4, 2009, http://lebanonwire.com/0904MLN /09040417AF.asp.

19. Richard Spencer and Carol Malouf, "We Will Stand by ISIS until Maliki Steps Down, Says Leader of Iraq's Biggest Tribe," *Telegraph*, June 29, 2014, www.telegraph.co.uk/news/worldnews/middle east/iraq/10934438/We-will-stand-by-Isis-until-Maliki-steps-down-says -leader-of-Iraqs-biggest-tribe.html.

20. Ghaith Abdul-Ahad, "Meet Abu Abed: The US's New Ally against al-Qaida," *Guardian*, November 10, 2007, www.theguardian .com/world/2007/nov/10/usa-al-qaida; Al Itthad, "How Amiriya Turned into a Safe Area?," alitthad.com [in Arabic], www.alitthad.com/paper.ph p?name=News&file=article&sid=32667.

21. "Manifesto of the Political Council of the Iraqi Resistance," announced on Al Jazeera, October 12, 2007, and published in the Iraqi jihadist magazine *al-Furqan*, no. 15; Kirk Semple and Omar al-Neam, "Amnesty Plan for Insurgents Shows Divide in the Shiite Bloc," *New York Times*, July 4, 2006, http://query.nytimes.com/gst/fullpage.html?res=9E06E4DD1230F 937A35754C0A9609C8B63. See also interview with Ali al-Jabouri, secretary general of the PCIR, on *No Limits*, Al Jazeera, July 15, 2009, www .aljazeera.net/NR/exeres/C1561271-9BEB-470F-AA08-A88929A6C83C.htm.

22. See Ewan MacAskill, "Sunni Insurgents Form Alliance against US," *Guardian*, October 12, 2007, www.theguardian.com/world /2007/oct/12/usa.iraq.

23. Ibid.

24. "Iraqi Resistance Refuses al-Maliki's Offer for Dialogue," AlBawaba.com, November 15, 2010 [in Arabic], www.albawaba.com/ar/ للحوار-المالكي-عرض-ترفض-العراقية-المقاومة/الرئيسية-الأخبار.

25. Taheri Amir, "Iraq: Will Al-Maliki's Peace Plan Work?," *Aawasat*, June 30, 2006, www.aawsat.net/2006/06/article55266188/iraq-will-al-malikis-peace-plan-work.

26. "Le premier ministre irakien a présenté son plan de réconciliation nationale," *Le Monde*, June 25, 2006, www.lemonde.fr/proche-orient/article/2006/06/25/le-premier-ministre-irakien-a-presente-son-plan-de-reconciliation-nationale_787940_3218.html. See also "Iraqi Leader Outlines Plan for Reconciliation," *Washington Post*, June 25, 2006, www.washingtonpost.com/wp-dyn/content/article/2006/06/25/AR2006062500316.html.

27. Irk Semple and Omar al-Neami, "Amnesty Plan for Insurgents Shows Divide in Shiite Bloc," *New York Times*, July 4, 2006.

28. Damien Cave, "Baghdad Violence Declines in Security Push, Iraq Says," *New York Times*, March 15, 2007, www.nytimes.com/2007/03/15/world/middleeast/15iraq.html?pagewanted=all.

29. "Heavy Fighting between the Security Forces and the 'Mahdi Army,'" *Asharq al-awsat*, March 18, 2008 [in Arabic], http://archive.aawsat.com/details.asp?section=4&article=464255&issueno=10711#.VUUkm1xN3zJ. See also "Muqtada al-Sadr Calls for End to Operation 'Charge of the Knights' Supported by the Coalition," *Al Jazeera*, March 27, 2008 [in Arabic], www.aljazeera.net/news/arabic/2008/3/27/لوقف-يدعو-الصدر-مقتدى-دهاو-الائتلاف-الفرسان-صولة

30. For more on Saddam Hussein's relationship with Iraq's tribes, see Amatzia Baram, "Neo-Tribalism in Iraq: Saddam Hussein's Tribal Policies, 1991–96," *International Journal of Middle East Studies* 29, no. 1 (February 1997): 1–31.

31. Abdul-Ahad, "Meet Abu Abed."

32. Ned Parker, "Sunni Leader Hero to U.S., Outlaw in Iraq," *Chicago Tribune*, July 5, 2008, http://articles.chicagotribune.com/2008-07-05/news/0807040300_1_sunni-fighters-tahseen-sheikhly-shiite-dominated-government.

33. US Department of Defense, "Measuring Stability and Security in Iraq," March 2008, www.defense.gov/pubs/pdfs/Master%20%20Mar08%20-%20final%20signed.pdf.

34. Zaid al-Ali, *The Struggle for Iraq's Future: How Corruption, Incompetence, and Sectarianism Undermined Democracy* (New Haven, CT: Yale University Press, 2014).

35. Nada Bakri, "Iraq's Ex-Trade Minister, Abdul Falah al-Sudani, Detained in Graft Investigation," *Washington Post*, May 31, 2009, www

.washingtonpost.com/wp-dyn/content/article/2009/05/30/AR2009053001089
.html.

36. Steven Lee Myers and Anthony Shadid, "Leader Faulted on Using Army in Iraqi Politics," *New York Times*, February 10, 2010, www .nytimes.com/2010/02/11/world/middleeast/11iraq.html?_r=0.

37. Rod Norland, "Maliki Contest Results of Iraq Vote," *New York Times*, March 27, 2010, www.nytimes.com/2010/03/28/world/middleeast /28iraq.html?_r=0.

38. Judith S. Yaphe, "Maliki's Maneuvering in Iraq," *Foreign Policy*, June 6, 2012, http://foreignpolicy.com/2012/06/06/malikis-manuevering-in -iraq/?wp_login_redirect=0.

39. IISS, "Iraq: Maliki Power Grab Risks Fresh Civil War," IIS *Strategic Comments* 18, no. 3 (2012): 1–3.

40. Ali, *The Struggle for Iraq's Future*, 132.

41. Patrick Cockburn, "Iraq Regime Tries to Silence Whistleblowers," *Independent*, September 29, 2011, www.independent.co.uk /news/world/middle-east/iraq-regime-tries-to-silence-corruption -whistleblowers-2362637.html.

42. Ryan C. Cocker, "Maliki Reshapes the National Security System," *WikiLeaks*, May 15, 2007, www.wikileaks.org/plusd/cables/07 BAGHDAD1593_a.html.

43. Mohammed Taqi Jamal, "The Phenomenon of the State Military in Iraq," *al-Quds al-Arabi*, April 22, 2015 [in Arabic], www.alquds.co .uk/?p=330699&print=1#comments_controls.

44. "VP Arrest Warrant Plunges Iraq into Crisis," *Daily Star*, December 29, 2010, www.dailystar.com.lb/ArticlePrint.aspx?id=157339&mode =print.

45. Ayyad Allawi, "Iraq's Slide toward Renewed Violence," *Washington Times*, April 9, 2012, www.washingtontimes.com/news/2012/apr /9/iraqs-slide-toward-renewed-violence/.

46. Josh Rogin, "Kurdish Leader: No to Arming the Syrian Opposition," *Foreign Policy*, April 5, 2012, http://foreignpolicy.com/2012/04 /05/kurdish-leader-no-to-arming-the-syrian-opposition/.

47. Nour Malas and Ghassan Adnan, "Sunni Tribes in Iraq Divided over Battle against Islamic State," *Wall Street Journal*, May 22, 2015.

48. Established on February 1, 2011, and carries the slogan "The Grand Iraqi Revolution," www.facebook.com/Iraqe.Revolution.

49. Stephanie McCrummen "Iraq Protests: A Younger Generation Finds Its Voice," *Washington Post*, March 21, 2011, www.washingtonpost

.com/wp-dyn/content/article/2011/03/16/AR2011031602331.html?wprss
=rss_world.

50. Stephanie McCrummen, "23 Killed in Iraq's 'Day of Rage' Protests," *Washington Post*, February 25, 2011, www.washingtonpost.com/wp
-dyn/content/article/2011/02/25/AR2011022502781.html.

51. "Protesters Take to Iraq's Streets Despite Vehicle Ban," *Radio Free Europe Radio Liberty*, March 4, 2011, www.rferl.org/content/pro testers_iraq_streets_vehicle_ban/2327895.html.

52. Stephanie McCrummen, "After Iraq's Day of Rage, a Crackdown on Intellectuals," *Washington Post*, February 27, 2011, www.washingtonpost .com/wp-dyn/content/article/2011/02/26/AR2011022603345.html?wprss =rss_world.

53. Yasir Ghazi and Christine Hauser, "Moktada al-Sadr Encourages Demonstrations in Iraq," *New York Times*, January 1, 2013, www .nytimes.com/2013/01/02/world/middleeast/moktada-al-sadr -encourages-demonstrations-in-iraq.html. See also Adam Schrek, "Iraqi Shiite Cleric Lends Support to Sunni Protest," *Yahoo News*, January 1, 2013, http://news.yahoo.com/iraqi-shiite-cleric-lends-support-sunni-protest -112135871.html.

54. Jamal Al-Badrani, "Iraqis Rally against US Troops Presence," Reuters, April 24, 2011, www.reuters.com/article/2011/04/24/us-iraq -protests-idUSTRE73N21C20110424.

55. "Death Row Sentences and Executions 2012," Amnesty International, 2013.

56. "Pillay Condemns Execution of 34 Individuals in One Day in Iraq," Geneva Centre for Justice, January 24, 2012, www.gicj.org/index .php?option=com_content&task=view&id=124&Itemid=52.

57. "Iraq: Security Forces Abusing Women in Detention," Human Rights Watch, February 6, 2014, www.hrw.org/news/2014/02/06/iraq -security-forces-abusing-women-detention.

58. Alarfidan TV, "First Statement on the General Military Council for Iraqi Revolutionaries," YouTube, January 15, 2014 [in Arabic], www.youtube.com/watch?v=bV-y5B_Vbl0.

59. "Iraq MP Ahmed al-Alwani Arrested in Deadly Ramadi Raid," *BBC*, December 23, 2013, www.bbc.co.uk/news/world-middle-east-25534541.

60. "Thousands of Residents Displaced in Fallujah, amid Worsening Clashes and Shelling," *Moheet*, January 6, 2014 [in Arabic], http:// moheet.com/2014/01/06/1863786/تفاقن زوح-الآلاف-نم-ناكس لفالوة-طسو.html# .VaqCmGBN3zK.

61. Salman Raheem, "Fugitive Saddam Deputy Lends Support to Iraq Sunni Protests," Reuters, January 5, 2013, www.reuters.com/article /2013/01/05/us-iraq-protests-douri-idUSBRE9040BV20130105.

62. "Deadly Anti-government Violence Grips Iraq," *Al Jazeera*, April 27, 2013, www.aljazeera.com/news/middleeast/2013/04/201342 610411101447.html.

63. Iraqi Central Bureau of Statistics, "Social and Economic Survey of Households in Iraq," 2012 Report, Iraqi Ministry of Planning [in Arabic], http://cosit.gov.iq/documents/statistics_ar/living%20conditions/ survey/Full%20Report/المسح%20الاجتماعي%20والاقتصادي%20 202012.pdf.للأسرة%20في%20العراق

64. World Bank Group, "The Unfulfilled Promised of Oil and Growth—Poverty, Inclusion and Welfare in Iraq, 2007–2012," 2014, https:// openknowledge.worldbank.org/bitstream/handle/10986/21364/938580v 20WP0RE021B0102601500PUBLIC0.pdf?sequence=1.

65. Sam Jones and Borzou Daragahi, "Iraq's Security Forces Ill-Equipped to Face Militants," *Financial Times*, July 10, 2014, www.ft.com /cms/s/0/a089e41e-081c-11e4-9afc-00144feab7de.html#axzz3iW7JlpU9.

66. Ned Parker, Isabel Coles, and Salman Raheem, "Special Report: How Mosul Fell—An Iraqi General Disputes Baghdad's Story," Reuters, October 14, 2014, www.reuters.com/article/2014/10/14/us-mid east-crisis-gharawi-special-report-idUSKCN0I30Z820141014. See also Cocker, "Maliki Reshapes the National Security System."

67. "Iraq: Abusive Commander Linked to Mosul Killings," Human Rights Watch, June 11, 2013, www.hrw.org/news/2013/06/11/iraq-abusive -commander-linked-mosul-killings.

68. Ibid.

69. Christoph Reuter, "The Terror Strategist: Secret Files Reveal the Structure of Islamic State," *Der Spiegel*, April 18, 2015, www.spiegel .de/international/world/islamic-state-files-show-structure-of-islamist -terror-group-a-1029274.html.

CHAPTER 4. BAGHDADI'S EVOLUTION: FROM INVISIBLE TO INFAMOUS

1. Al-Furqan and al-I'tisam, two media arms of ISIS, released a video of Baghdadi leading the Friday prayers in July 2014 from the Iraqi city of Mosul, now under the control of ISIS. See the video of the first appearance of al-Baghdadi: "The Jum'a Prayer Speech in the

Big Mosque in Mosul by Abu Bakr al-Baghdadi," Al Jazeera Arabic YouTube channel, July 5, 2015 [in Arabic], www.youtube.com/watch?v =dIRf0EJuPak.

2. Cited by Janine Di Giovanni, "Who Is ISIS Leader Abu Bakr al-Baghdadi?," *Newsweek*, December 8, 2014.

3. "Abu Bakr al-Baghdadi," *Al Jazeera*, December 2, 2014 [in Arabic], www.aljazeera.net/encyclopedia/icons/2014/12/2/%D8%A3%D8%A 8%D9%88-%D8%A8%D9%83%D8%B1-%D8%A7%D9%84%D8%A8% D8%BA%D8%AF%D8%A7%D8%AF%D9%8A.

4. Tim Arango and Eric Schmitt, "U.S. Actions in Iraq Fueled Rise of a Rebel," *New York Times*, August 10, 2014; Martin Chulov, "ISIS: The Inside Story," *Guardian*, December 11, 2014.

5. Chulov, "ISIS: The Inside Story"; Trevor Royle, "The Mystery Man," *Sunday Herald*, December 28, 2014; Di Giovanni, "Who Is ISIS Leader?"; "Profile: Abu Bakr al-Baghdadi," *BBC*, July 5, 2014; Ruth Sherlock, "How a Talented Footballer Became World's Most Wanted Man, Abu Bakr al-Baghdadi," *Daily Telegraph*, November 11, 2014.

6. Abdel-Bari Atwan, *Al-Dawla al-Islamiyya: al-Guzour, al-Tawahush wal Mustaqbal* [Islamic State: The roots, savagery and the future] (London: Al Saqi, 2015), 46.

7. Wael Essam, "Baghdadi Left Bucca Prison More Extreme, Excommunicating the Ikhwan [the Muslim Brothers]," *al-Quds al-Arabi*, October 19, 2014 [in Arabic].

8. Di Giovanni, "Who Is ISIS Leader?"

9. Medyan Dairieh, "My Journey inside the Islamic State," *Vice News*, July 1, 2015, https://news.vice.com/article/my-journey-inside-the -islamic-state.

10. Chulov, "ISIS: The Inside Story."

11. Mohammed Mahmoud Mortada, "The Mysterious Link between the US Military Prison Camp Bucca and ISIS Leaders," *al-Akhbar*, September 13, 2014 [in Arabic and English].

12. Hisham al-Hashimi, *'Alam Da'esh: Min al-Nashaa ella I'lan al-Khilafa* [The Da'esh worldview: From birth to caliphate] (London: Dar al-Hekma, 2015), 168.

13. Abu Abdullah Mohamed al-Mansour al-Issawi, *Al-Dawla al-Islamiyya: Bayna al-Haqiqa wa al-Wahm* [The Islamic State: Disentangling myth from reality] (n.p., n.d.), 7–97.

14. Chulov, "ISIS: The Inside Story."

15. A. al-Zawahiri, "Testimonial to Preserve the Blood of Mujahideen in al-Sham [Greater Syria]," *pietervanostaeyen* (blog), May 3, 2014,

https://pietervanostaeyen.wordpress.com/2014/05/03/dr-ayman-az
-zawahiri-testimonial-to-preserve-the-blood-of-mujahideen-in-as-sham/.

16. Issawi, *The Islamic State*, 7–97.

17. In their rebuttal of Issawi's statements, ISIS's supporters of Baghdadi issued a manifesto in Arabic titled *Kashf al-Mastour an Akhbar Abdullah al-Mansour, the Emir of the Army of Mujahideen in Iraq*, exposing Issawi. In the pamphlet, Baghdadi's supporters conceded that Zarqawi and Baghdadi were among Issawi's "disciples," but they accused Issawi of contradictions and double-talk. Instead of responding to Issawi's specific charges, Baghdadi's followers focused on his motivation.

18. Rifa'at Said Ahmed, "American Da'esh," *al-Badeel*, November 24, 2014 [in Arabic], http://elbadil.com/2014/11/24/%.

19. Cited by Sherlock, "How a Talented Footballer."

20. Ibid.

21. Cited by Chulov, "ISIS: The Inside Story."

22. Atwan, *Al-Dawla al-Islamiyya*, 46.

23. Ibid.

24. Hashimi, *'Alam Da'esh*, 168.

25. In fact, after Baghdadi gave his famous *khutba* (sermon) from the main mosque in Mosul in summer 2014, many people, including Islamists, commented on how "uncharismatic" he sounded. See also Abu Mohammed al-Adnani, "Muasassat al-Furqan Tuqadem: Haza Wa'd Min Allah: Sheikh Abi Mohamed al-Adnani Hazizahu Allah" [This is the promise of Allah], YouTube, July 5, 2014 [in Arabic], www.youtube.com/watch?v=Uen14MVYNqk; Abu Mohammed al-Adnani, "This Is the Promise of Allah," June 19, 2014, http://triceratops.brynmawr.edu/dspace/bitstream/handle/10066/14242/ADN20140629.pdf?sequence=1.

26. A. Al-Athari, "Mad Al-Ayady La Baya'at Al-Baghdadi" [Extending hands to Al-Baghdadi's allegiance], *Al-Tawhid and Al-Jihad Platform*, July 2013 [in Arabic], https://archive.org/details/baghdadi-001. See also A. Al-Azdari, "Mougbat Al-Andmam Lel Dawla Al-Islamya Fe Al-Eraq Wal Al-Sham, A'atradat wa Gawabat" [Necessities for joining the Islamic State of Iraq and Syria, objections and answers], *Al-Ma'asadah Media Foundation*, August 2013 [in Arabic], www.scribd.com/doc/184157776/موجباتوالشام-العراق-في-الإسلامية-للدولة-الانضمام.

27. The report is cited by @wikibaghdady. For a complete list of the tweets in Arabic, see "'Wikileaks Baghdadi' Reveals the Truth about 'Daesh,'" *Zaman Al Wasl*, January 5, 2015 [in Arabic], https://zamanalwsl.net/news/45122.html.

28. Cited by Chulov, "ISIS: The Inside Story."

29. Issawi, *The Islamic State*, 7–97.

30. Essam,"Baghdadi Left Bucca Prison."

31. Baghdadi's transcript and audio: Abu Bakr al-Baghdadi,"March Forth Whether Light or Heavy," *Carol Ann Grayson (Radical Sister) Blog*, May 14, 2015, https://activist1.wordpress.com/2015/05/14/islamic-state-al -furqan-media-releases-new-audio-and-transcript-allegedly-of-baghdadi /. See also Rukmini Callimachi, "ISIS Releases Recording Said to Be by Its Reclusive Leader," *New York Times*, May 14, 2015.

32. See the link to Baghdadi's audio statement: A. al-Baghdadi, "Even If the Disbelievers Despise Such," *pietervanostaeyen* (blog), November 14, 2014 [audio transcript in Arabic], https://pietervanostaeyen .wordpress.com/2014/11/14/audio-message-by-abu-bakr-al-baghdadi -even-if-the-disbelievers-despise-such/.

33. 'Abdel-Sattar Hatitta, "Testimony by the Defectors from the Extremist Movement," *al-Sharq al Awsat*, May 16, 2015 [in Arabic], http:// aawsat.com/home/article/361546/%.

34. See "'Wikileaks Baghdadi' Reveals the Truth about 'Daesh.'"

35. Christoph Reuter, "The Terror Strategist: Secret Files Reveal the Structure of Islamic State," *Der Spiegel*, April 18, 2015.

36. Haytham Manna, *Khelafat Da'esh* [The Da'esh caliphate] (Geneva: Scandinavian Institute of Human Rights, 2014), 34–35.

37. Michael Weiss and Hassan Hassan, *ISIS: Inside the Army of Terror* (New York: Regan Arts, 2015).

CHAPTER 5. BAATHISTS AND ISIS JIHADISTS: WHO CONVERTED WHOM?

1. Najih Ibrahim and Hisham al-Najar, *Daesh: Al-Sikin alati Tazbah Al-Islam* [Daesh: The knife that butchers Islam] (Cairo: Dar al-Shorouk, 2014), 46.

2. Abu Abdullah Mohamed al-Mansour al-Issawi, *Al-Dawla al-Islamiyya: Bayna al-Haqiqa wa al-Wahm* [The Islamic State: Disentangling myth from reality] (n.p., n.d.), 97, 102–103.

3. Suadad Al-Sahly, "Iraq Mosque Bomb Targeted Moderate Sunnis, Say Officials," Reuters, August 29, 2011, www.alarabiya.net/articles /2011/08/29/164654.html.

4. Ibid.

5. "Iraq's Qaeda Pledges Support to Zawahri, Vows Attacks," Reuters, May 9, 2011, www.reuters.com/article/2011/05/09/us-iraq-qaeda -zawahri-idUSTRE74835A20110509.

6. Michael C. Schmidt, "Al Qaeda Affiliate Is Blamed in Iraq Suicide Bombing," *New York Times*, May 5, 2011, www.nytimes.com/2011/05/06/world/middleeast/06hilla.html?gwh=945C868984004CB0A90B94A4C7721C07&gwt=pay.

7. "Dozens Killed in Co-ordinated Baghdad Attacks," *BBC*, December 22, 2011, www.bbc.co.uk/news/world-middle-east-16297707.

8. "Al-Qaida in Iraq Claims Responsibility for Baghdad Blasts," *Guardian*, December 27, 2011, www.theguardian.com/world/2011/dec/27/al-qaida-in-iraq-baghdad.

9. For a near-complete list of Tweets in Arabic, see "'Wikileaks Baghdadi' Reveals the Truth about 'Daesh,'" *Zaman Al Wasl Newspaper*, January 5, 2015 [in Arabic], https://zamanalwsl.net/news/45122.html. See also Christoph Reuter, "The Terror Strategist: Secret Files Reveal the Structure of Islamic State," *Der Spiegel*, April 18, 2015.

10. The *Washington Post* has a diagram explaining the roles of former Baathist army members in ISIS: "Most of Islamic State's Leaders Were Officers in Saddam Hussein's Iraq," *Washington Post*, April 4, 2015, www.washingtonpost.com/world/most-of-islamic-states-leaders-were-officers-in-saddam-husseins-iraq/2015/04/04/f3d2da00-db24-11e4-b3f2-607bd612aeac_graphic.html.

11. "'Wikileaks Baghdadi' Reveals the Truth about 'Daesh'"; Reuter, "The Terror Strategist."

12. "'Wikileaks Baghdadi' Reveals the Truth about 'Daesh'"; Reuter, "The Terror Strategist"; Liz Sly, "The Hidden Hand behind the Islamic State Militants? Saddam Hussein's," *Washington Post*, April 4, 2015, www.washingtonpost.com/world/middle_east/the-hidden-hand-behind-the-islamic-state-militants-saddam-husseins/2015/04/04/aa97676c-cc32-11e4-8730-4f473416e759_story.html.

13. Mohammed Mahmoud Mortada, "The Mysterious Link between the US Military Prison Camp Bucca and ISIS Leaders," *Al-Akhbar*, September 13, 2014 [in Arabic and English]; Tim Arango and Eric Schmitt, "U.S. Actions in Iraq Fueled Rise of a Rebel," *New York Times*, August 10, 2014. See al-Anbari's profile information on the Counter Terrorism Project website, accessible from www.counterextremism.com/extremists/abu-ali-al-anbari#sthash.emvGAQJg.dpuf.

14. Rebecca Kheel, "ISIS Finance Minister, Other Leaders Killed in Airstrikes," *The Hill*, December 10, 2015.

15. Reuter, "The Terror Strategist."

16. Charles Tilly, "Terror, Terrorism, Terrorists," in Theories of Terrorism: A Symposium (special issue), *Sociological Theory* 22, no. 1 (March 2004): 6.

17. For more on the 1991 uprising, see Fanar Haddad, *Sectarianism in Iraq: Antagonistic Visions of Unity* (London: C. Hurst and Company, 2011); Dina Rizk Khoury, *Iraq in Wartime: Soldiering, Martyrdom, and Remembrance* (Cambridge, UK: Cambridge University Press, 2013); and Nicholas Krohley, *The Death of the Mehdi Army: The Rise, Fall, and Revival of Iraq's Most Powerful Militia* (London: C. Hurst and Company, 2015).

18. Amatzia Baram, "From Militant Secularism to Islamism: The Iraqi Ba'th Regime, 1968–2003," *Woodrow Wilson International Center for Scholars: History and Public Policy Program*, October 2011; Adeed Daweesha, "'Identity' and Political Survival in Saddam's Iraq," *Middle East Journal* 53, no. 4 (1999): 553–567; Magdi Ahmed Hussein, "Growing Religious Tide in Iraq with Increased Steadfastness in the Face of the Siege," *Al-Arab News*, July 20, 2001 [in Arabic], http://alarabnews.com /alshaab/GIF/20-07-2001/MagdiHussien.htm. In fact, Douri has evaded the US and Iraqi dragnet since 2003 due to the protection by the Naqshabandi group.

19. According to political economy scholar Kamil Mahdi, the Baath Party was never a unifying nationalist symbol. Hence, it adopted oil nationalization and development as its main symbols in the 1970s, perhaps more prominently than it did Arab unity. The pragmatism of Hussein's regime led it to adopt a kind of Mesopotamian Iraqi nationalism, especially during the Iraq-Iran war, and then a form of religious piety. Author's interview with Mahdi on April 8, 2015. For historical context, see Malik Mufti, *Sovereign Creations: Pan-Arabism and Political Order in Syria and Iraq* (Ithaca, NY: Cornell University Press, 1996).

20. Author's conversation with Professor Saad Jawad, April 3, 2015.

21. Ali Hashemi, "The Fall of Iraq," *Assafir*, May 12, 2015 [in Arabic].

22. Sabah Arar, "Shadow of Saddam Lives on in Iraq," *Agence France Presse*, May 3, 2015.

23. Walid al-Saad in Alaa Yussef, "Lieutenants of 'Iraq Baath' Lead the Islamic State," *Al Jazeera*, April 8, 2015 [in Arabic].

24. A similar process of ideological migration and mutation took place in Egypt after the Six-Day War in June 1967, when Israel defeated the most powerful army in the Middle East and humiliated Egyptian president Gamal Abdul Nasser, leader of the pan-Arab nationalist bloc. As a result of this sudden *naksa* (a setback seen as transformative), many Egyptian and Arab nationalists migrated en masse to

various Islamist groups, a hemorrhage that culminated in the resurgence of political Islam at the expense of secular nationalism.

25. Khoury, *Iraq in Wartime*. See also Joseph Sasson, *Saddam Hussein's Ba'th Party: Inside an Authoritarian Regime* (Cambridge, UK: Cambridge University Press, 2012).

26. For them, the Baath was a ruling party, a social ladder that allowed them to survive and prosper economically, although many of them did not maintain an ideological affinity toward the party.

27. This was recently exemplified by the rise of the Hash'd al-Sha'bi (Popular Mobilization Force), the largely Shia and autonomous militia force that was established after Grand Ayatollah Sistani called on Iraq's population to combat ISIS. Although it is a so-called civilian reaction to ISIS, it functions alongside the Iraqi army and is controlled by members of the Shia ruling elite within the current government.

28. For a critical and informative history of Shia mobilization in Iraq, including the history of the Islamic Da'wa Party and the Shia community's relationship with the Baath regime, see Ranj Alaaldin, "The Rise of the Shi'a: Mobilisation and Disconnect in Iraq, 1958–1980" (PhD diss., London School of Economics and Political Science, 2016).

29. "'Wikileaks Baghdadi' Reveals the Truth about 'Daesh'"; Reuter, "The Terror Strategist."

30. Bassam al-Badareen, "Makdisi's 'Joke' and the Baathists and How a Daesh Fighter 'Toys' with a Severed Head of a Kurdish Woman," *al-Quds al-Arabi*, February 8, 2015 [in Arabic].

31. "Prominent Leader of Jabhat al-Nusra Was a Member of 'Saddam Martyrs,'" *al-Quds al-Arabi*, November 8, 2014 [in Arabic].

32. See Al Jazeera's video on al-Joulani and al-Nusra: *Al Jazeera*, May 27, 2015, www.youtube.com/watch?v=-hwQT43vFZA; "Al-Nusra's Emir, Abu Mohammed al-Joulani: Hezbollah Will Vanish with the Downfall of the Bashar al-Assad Regime," *Al Jazeera*, May 27, 2015 [in Arabic]; see also "Al-Joulani Praises Daesh-Iraq," *al-Akhbar*, June 4, 2015 [in Arabic].

33. Author's conversation with Moussa al-Omar, a Syrian broadcast journalist who interviewed Joulani, London, UK, January 25, 2016.

34. Omar Fahmi, "Al Qaeda Calls Islamic State Illegitimate but Suggests Cooperation," Reuters, September 9, 2015, www.reuters.com/article/2015/09/09/us-mideast-zawahri-idUSKCN0R91LY20150909.

35. Tim Arango, "With the Fall of Ramadi, Plight of Iraq Sunnis Worsens," *New York Times*, May 19, 2015.

36. Khalil Osman's basic presumption of primordial identities
raises critical questions about the significance of the multiple identities that prevail in Iraq today. For example, who decides which identity is
the primordial one? Or are all identities primordial? If the latter, then
there is an urgent need to examine not only sectarian identities that are
strongly prevalent now, but also other identities as well. There is also an
emphasis on the state versus the primordial, as there are modern
emergent popular identities that are subaltern. His approach leaves the
subaltern to be the preserve of the primordial. Osman's work is substantive but seems predestined to confirm received wisdom and to ig-
nore powerful external roles and the political economy in tipping the
scale in favor of traditional identities. See Khalil F. Osman, *Sectarianism
in Iraq: The Making of State and Nation since 1920* (Abingdon, UK: Routledge, 2015). See also Maytahm al-Jabani, *Falsafat al-Hawiyya al-Wataniyya
(al-Iraqiyya)* (Baghdad: Dar Mezobo, 2011).

37. Ahmed al-Anbari, "Relations between Iraqi Resistance Groups
and Islamic State," *Al Jazeera*, December 31, 2014 [in Arabic]. See also "Iraqi
Officials Say Saddam Deputy Believed Killed," Associated Press, April 17,
2015; Dan Murphy, "Most Senior Baathist General to Evade US in Iraq
Reported Killed. Does It Matter?," *Christian Science Monitor*, April 17, 2015;
Suad Al Salhy, "Dancing with Daesh," *Newsweek*, December 23, 2015.

38. Mohamed Shafiq, "Al-Douri Killed Accidentally," *al-Akhbar*,
April 18, 2015 [in Arabic]. See also "Close Aide to Saddam Praises ISIS
Extremists and Calls for the Fall of Baghdad," Reuters, July 13, 2014, www
.businessinsider.com/close-aide-to-saddam-praises-isis-extremists-and
-calls-for-the-fall-of-baghdad-2014-7#ixzz3aUEJougf.

39. Author's conversation with Kamil Mahdi, July 30, 2015.

40. "Daesh in Iraq and the Sunnis," *Al Hayat*, November 20, 2014
[in Arabic]. See also *Hayat*, May 28, 2015, http://alhayat.com/Opinion
/Letters/; Osman Mukhtar, "Izat al-Douri praises the Al-Hazm Storm
and Attacks Daesh," *al-Araby al-Jadded*, May 15, 2015 [in Arabic], www
.alaraby.co.uk/politics/2015/5/15. See also Hamad Jassim Mohamed al-
Khazraji, "Al-Baath, Naqshabandiyya and Daesh after Douri," *Al Hayat*,
April 28, 2015 [in Arabic], www.alhayat.com/Opinion/Letters/8834399.

41. "Ezzat al-Douri Announces His Support for 'Decisive Storm'
[in Yemen] and Calls for Confronting the Islamic State," *al-Quds al-
Arabi*, April 5, 2015 [in Arabic]. See also "The Baath Station Broadcasts
an Audio Recording by Ezzat al-Douri," *Assafir*, May 15, 2015 [in Arabic];
Anbari, "Relations between Iraqi Resistance Groups and Islamic State";

and "Iraqi Officials Say Saddam Deputy Believed Killed," Associated Press, April 17, 2015.

42. Wael Essam, "Former Baathist Officers Cooperate with the Iraqi Government and the Americans to Form 'Sahawat in Mosul,'" *al-Quds al-Arabi*, May 20, 2015 [in Arabic].

CHAPTER 6. HOW THE SYRIAN WAR EMPOWERED ISIS

1. Bassam Haddad, "The Syrian Regime's Business Backbone," *Middle East Research and Information Project* 42 (Spring 2012), www.merip .org/mer/mer262/syrian-regimes-business-backbone; Haddad, "Business Networks in Syria: The Political Economy of Authoritarian Resilience," *Stanford Studies in Jewish History and Culture*, December 2011.

2. Bassam Haddad, "As Syria Free-Falls . . . A Return to the Basics: Some Structural Causes (Part 2)," *Jadaliyya*, October 30, 2012, www.jadaliyya.com/pages/index/8095/as-syria-free-falls-.-.-.-a-return-to -the-basics_s; Francesca de Chatel, "The Role of Drought and Climate Change in the Syrian Uprising: Untangling the Triggers of the Revolution," *Middle East Studies*, January 27, 2014, https://blogs.commons .georgetown.edu/rochelledavis/files/francesca-de-chatel-drought-in -syria.pdf. See also Raymond Hinnebusch, "Syria: From 'Authoritarian Upgrading' to Revolution?" *International Affairs*, vol. 88, no.1, 2012.

3. Mohammed Jamal Barout, "The Last Decade in Syrian History," Arab Centre for Research and Policy Studies, April 2011 [in Arabic].

4. "Crop and Food Security Assessment Mission to the Syrian Arab Republic," FAO/WFP, July 5, 2013, www.fao.org/docrep/018/aq113e /aq113e.pdf.

5. Suzanne Saleeby, "Sowing the Seeds of Dissent: Economic Grievances and the Syrian Social Contract's Unraveling," *Jadaliyya*, February 16, 2012, www.jadaliyya.com/pages/index/4383/sowing-the-seeds -of-dissent_economic-grievances-an.

6. "Syrian Government and Opposition Forces Responsible for War Crimes," *UN News Centre*, August 15, 2012, www.un.org/apps/news /story.asp?NewsID=42687#.VcdJPzBViko.

7. Figure provided by the United Nations: "UN Emergency Fund Provides over $9 Million to Boost Aid to Syrian Refugees," *UN News Centre*, June 13, 2012, www.un.org/apps/news/story.asp?NewsID=42224# .VYHfP2RViko.

8. "Syria in Civil War, Red Cross Says," *BBC*, July 15, 2012, www
.bbc.com/news/world-middle-east-18849362.

9. "Syria: Fresh Evidence of Armed Forces' Ongoing Crimes
against Humanity," Amnesty International, June 2012, www.amnesty
.org/en/latest/news/2012/06/syria-fresh-evidence-armed-forces-ongoing
-crimes-against-humanity/.

10. Ibid.

11. "'Islamist Posturing' Is a Strategy to Raise Funds, Says Syrian
Rebel," France24, November 21, 2013, http://observers.france24.com
/content/20131121-islamist-posturing-funds-syrian-rebel.

12. See the article published by the Syrian Arab News Agency
(SANA), which is run by the state: "President al-Assad in Army Festival
Speech: There Is No Place for Complacency or Appeasement in Our Battle
against Terrorism," SANA, July 31, 2014 [in Arabic], www.sana.sy/?p=31515.

13. "Nasrallah: Hezbollah to Increase Presence in Syria," *Al Jazeera*,
May 25, 2015, www.aljazeera.com/news/2015/05/nasrallah-hezbollah
-increase-presence-syria-150524233716453.html.

14. Hashem Ali, "The Many Names of Abu Bakr al-Baghdadi,"
Al-Monitor, March 23, 2015, www.al-monitor.com/pulse/originals/2015
/03/isis-baghdadi-islamic-state-caliph-many-names-al-qaeda.html.

15. Ayman al-Zawahiri, "Testimonial to Preserve the Blood of Mujahideen in al-Sham [Greater Syria]," *pietervanostaeyen* (blog), May 3,
2014, https://pietervanostaeyen.wordpress.com/2014/05/03/dr-ayman-az
-zawahiri-testimonial-to-preserve-the-blood-of-mujahideen-in-as-sham/.

16. "Al-Nusra Founding Statement," YouTube, May 25, 2012.

17. Wael Essam, "IS Islamic State an Extension of Armed Groups
in Syria," *al-Quds al-Arabi*, May 8, 2015 [in Arabic].

18. Michael Weiss and Hassan Hassan, *ISIS: Inside the Army of
Terror* (New York: Regan Arts, 2015). See also "Amru al-Absi: Executive
Summary," Counter Extremism Project, 2015, www.counterextremism
.com/extremists/amru-al-absi.

19. Weiss and Hassan, *ISIS*. See also Phil Sands, Justin Vela, and
Suha Maayeh, "Assad Regime Set Free Extremists from Prison to Fire
Up Trouble during Peaceful Uprising," *National*, January 2014, www
.thenational.ae/world/syria/assad-regime-set-free-extremists-from
-prison-to-fire-up-trouble-during-peaceful-uprising.

20. Rim Turkmani, "ISIL, JAN and the War Economy in Syria," *Security in Transition* (London School of Economics), July 30, 2015, www
.securityintransition.org/wp-content/uploads/2015/08/ISIL-JAN-and
-the-war-economy-in-Syria1.pdf.

21. Rim Turkmani, A.K. Ali, Mary Kaldor, and Vesna Bojicic-Dzelilovic, "Countering the Logic of the War Economy in Syria; Evidence from Three Local Areas," Security in Transition (London School of Economics), July 2015.

22. Sabr Darwish, "Syria's 'Daesh': Unemployment, Despair, and Violence," Bidayat, no. 10 (Winter 2015): 17–26 [in Arabic].

23. "U.S Cross-Border Raid Highlights Syria's Role in Islamist Militancy," CTC Sentinel, November 15, 2008, www.ctc.usma.edu/posts/u-s-cross-border-raid-highlights-syria%E2%80%99s-role-in-islamist-militancy.

24. Zvi Bar'el, "How the Islamic State Buys Power," Haaretz, September 1, 2014, www.haaretz.com/news/middle-east/.premium-1.613395.

25. Syrian Observatory for Human Rights, "More than 6000 Fighters Have Joined the Islamic State since Last July/2014," Facebook post, August 20, 2014, www.facebook.com/syriahroe/posts/571680432940299.

26. "ISIS Halves the Salaries of its Fighters in Syria and Iraq," al-Quds al-Arabi, January 20, 2016.

27. "A Grant from al-Caliphate to His Fighters Who Desire Marriage," Al-Arabiya.net, August 28, 2014 [in Arabic]. See also Darwish, "Syria's 'Daesh.'"

28. Uns Garks, who goes by the pseudonym Abu Ali al-Shishani, and Abu Mariya al-Qahtani are two cases in point. Before joining ISIS, al-Shishani said he used to work as a cook in a restaurant in Lebanon. When the Syrian conflict broke out, he returned home and swore allegiance to ISIS and was put in charge of a battalion on the Syrian-Lebanese border. In an interview with an Arabic journalist at the end of 2014, al-Shishani took pride in his background and noted that he is fighting to resurrect the Islamic caliphate. See Radwan Mortada, "Abu Ali al-Shishani: From a Cook to an Emir in Islamic State," al-Akhbar, October 10, 2014 [in Arabic].

29. David Lesch, Syria: The Fall of the House of Assad (New Haven, CT: Yale University Press, 2014), 4.

30. See United Nation Development Programme, Arab Human Development Report, 2009 (New York: United Nations Development Programme, 2009), www.arab-hdr.org/publications/other/ahdr/ahdr2009e.pdf.

31. "Houla Massacre: UN Blames Syria and Militia," Guardian, August 15, 2012, www.theguardian.com/world/interactive/2012/aug/15/un-inquiry-syrian-arab-republic.

32. Christoph Reuter, "The Terror Strategist: Secret Files Reveal the Structure of Islamic State," *Der Spiegel*, April 18, 2015, www.spiegel .de/international/world/islamic-state-files-show-structure-of-islamist -terror-group-a-1029274.html.

33. Al Dawa offices are religious proselytization offices used to propagate a particular sect or religious ideology.

34. Press statement by US Department of State, "Terrorist Designations of the al-Nusrah Front as an Alias for al-Qa'ida in Iraq," December 11, 2012, www.state.gov/r/pa/prs/ps/2012/12/201759.htm.

35. Jennifer Cafarella, "Jabhat al-Nusra in Syria," *Middle East Security Report* 25, Institute for the Study of War, December 2014, www .understandingwar.org/sites/default/files/JN%20Final.pdf.

36. Ibid.

37. Ibid.

38. Author's conversation with Moussa al-Omar.

39. Erika Solomon, "Fighters Flock Back to Resurgent Jabhat al-Nusra," *Financial Times*, March 30, 2014, www.ft.com/cms/s/0/b0cc7652 -d61b-11e4-b3e7-00144feab7de.html?siteedition=intl#axzz3dVahQMdz.

40. Turkmani, "ISIL, JAN and the War Economy in Syria."

41. See the Al Jazeera video on al-Joulani and al-Nusra, *Al Jazeera* Arabic, May 27, 2015 [in Arabic], www.youtube.com/watch?v=-hwQT 43vFZA. See also "Al-Nusra's Emir, Abu Mohammad al-Joulani: Hezbollah Will Vanish with the Downfall of the Bashar al-Assad Regime," *Al Jazeera*, May 27, 2015 [in Arabic].

42. David Roberts, "Is Qatar Bringing the Nusra Front in from the Cold?," *BBC*, March 6, 2015, www.bbc.com/news/world-middle-east -31764114.

43. Rania Abouzeid, "Interview with Official of Jabhat al-Nusra, Syria's Islamist Militia Group," *Time*, December 25, 2012, http://world .time.com/2012/12/25/interview-with-a-newly-designated-syrias-jabhat -al-nusra/. See also Yasir al-Za'atirah, "Islamic State in Iraq and al-Sham," *Al Jazeera*, April 11, 2013 [in Arabic].

44. "Al-Nusra Front for the People in Syria," *Al Jazeera*, May 8, 2012 [in Arabic], www.aljazeera.net/home/print/f6451603-4dff-4ca1-9c10 -122741d17432/24579ea8-bbf0-41d0-9ae5-5060f828db76. See also the discussion of Jabhat al-Nusra's first video release in January 2012: "Profile: Syria's al-Nusra Front," *BBC*, April 10, 2013, www.bbc.co.uk/news/world -middle-east-18048033.

45. Jabhat al-Nusra, "Al-Nusra Front—Statement N.1—Bombing of Air Force Intelligence Branch in Damascus," *nationalkuwait* (blog),

March 2012 [in Arabic], www.nationalkuwait.com/forum/index.php ?threads/229910/.

46. Sara.Elizabeth Williams, "A Rebel Rift Is Brewing on Syria's Southern Front," ViceNews.com, May 25, 2014, https://news.vice.com /article/a-rebel-rift-is-brewing-on-syrias-southern-front.

47. International Crisis Group, "Tentative Jihad: Syria's Fundamentalist Opposition," *Middle Eastern Report* 131, October 12, 2012.

48. Hussein Jemmo, "Jabhat al-Nusra's Goals Extend beyond Syria," *al-Monitor*, January 11, 2013, www.al-monitor.com/pulse/security /2013/01/jabhat-al-nusras-goals-extend-beyond-syria.html. See also "Islamic State Expels Rivals from Syria's Dei al-Zor—Activists," Reuters, July 14, 2014, http://uk.reuters.com/article/2014/07/14/uk-syria-crisis-east -idUKKBN0FJ1I020140714.

49. "Syria Rebels Overrun Aleppo Military Base," *BBC*, December 10, 2012, www.bbc.co.uk/news/world-middle-east-20666047. See also a video statement announcing the "liberation" of the base, "Statement Announcing Control of the Sheikh Suleiman Base," YouTube, December 10, 2012 [in Arabic], www.youtube.com/watch?v=362OUioPV_A &spfreload=10, and "Jabhat al-Nusra Seize Sheikh Suleiman Base, West of Aleppo," *Alkhaleej*, December 11, 2012 [in Arabic], www.alkhaleej .ae/alkhaleej/page/b985449c-f1bb-4c93-84ee-173e8b2b0785#.

50. Mona Mahmood and Ian Black, "Free Syrian Army Rebels Defect to Islamist Group Jabhat al-Nusra," *Guardian*, May 8, 2014, www .theguardian.com/world/2013/may/08/free-syrian-army-rebels-defect -islamist-group.

51. See "FSA Brigade 'Joins al-Qaeda Group' in Syria," *Al Jazeera*, September 21, 2013, www.aljazeera.com/news/middleeast/2013/09/20139 20164342453621.html.

52. Ibid.

53. Cafarella, "Jabhat al-Nusra in Syria."

54. See the Vice News documentary, "The Islamic State," ViceNews .com, December 26, 2014, https://news.vice.com/video/the-islamic-state -full-length.

55. "Syria: Al-Qaeda Arm 'Stages Fun Day,'" *BBC*, July 23, 2013, www.bbc.co.uk/news/blogs-news-from-elsewhere-23420018. See also the video, "Al-Qa'ida Holds Family Fun Day in War Torn Aleppo," *Liveleak*, July 24, 2013, www.liveleak.com/view?i=588_1374686964&com ments=1.

56. Max Fisher, "Al-Qaeda Faction in Syria Hands Out Teletubbies and Spiderman Dolls," *Washington Post*, August 13, 2013, www.washingtonpost

.com/blogs/worldviews/wp/2013/08/13/al-qaeda-faction-in-syria-hands-out
-teletubbies-and-spiderman-dolls/.

57. See "Al-Nusra Front—Commission Relief—Distribution of
Bread," YouTube, December 16, 2012 [in Arabic], www.youtube.com
/watch?v=lA1BKRyJLPI&feature=youtu.be.

58. Gaith Abdul-Ahad, "Syria's al-Nusra Front—Ruthless, Organ-
ised and Taking Control," *Guardian*, July 10, 2013, www.theguardian
.com/world/2013/jul/10/syria-al-nusra-front-jihadi?iframe=true&width
=100%25&height=100%25.

59. See "Report on Water and Sanitation Services Provided to
the People of Dara'a (Part 2)," YouTube [in Arabic], www.youtube.com
/watch?v=D-3roUVlAMk.

60. See "Al-Nusra Front Opened 'Modesty Charity,' Offers Free Islamic Clothing to the Women in Hama," SITE Intelligence Group,
https://ent.siteintelgroup.com/Jihadist-News/al-nusra-front-opened
-modesty-charity-offers-free-islamic-clothing-to-women-in-hama.html.

61. IHS Jane's Terrorism & Insurgency Center, "Analysis: Syria's
Insurgent Landscape," September 2013, www.ihs.com/ pdfs/Syrias
-Insurgent-Landscape-oct-2013.pdf.

62. Raqqa UMC, YouTube, April 10, 2013, www.youtube.com/watch?v
=6FdTjm4-6Lo.

63. Ibid. See also Thomas Joscelyn, "Al-Nusra Front Leader Re-
news Allegiance to al-Qaeda, Rejects New Name," *Long War Journal*,
April 10, 2013, www.longwarjournal.org/archives/2013/04/al_nusrah
_front_lead.php.

64. Raqqa UMC, YouTube, April 10, 2013.

65. See Al Jazeera's interview with al-Joulani, "Nusra Leader:
Our Mission Is to Defeat Syrian Regime," *Al Jazeera*, May 28, 2015, www
.aljazeera.com/news/2015/05/nusra-front-golani-assad-syria-hezbollah-isil
-150528044857528.html.

66. Zawahiri, "Testimonial."

67. Za'atirah, "Islamic State in Iraq and al-Sham."

68. For a near-complete list of the tweets by @wikibaghdady in
Arabic, see "'Wikileaks Baghdadi' Reveals the Truth about 'Daesh,'"
Zaman Al Wasl, January 5, 2015 [in Arabic], https://zamanalwsl.net/news
/45122.html.

69. Zawahiri, "Testimonial."

70. Ibid.

71. See Zawahiri's audio recording in which he cancels the merger
and calls on ISIS and al-Nusra to stop infighting, www.youtube.com/watch

?v=s9KL6h1oQJI. See also "Al-Zawahiri Abolishes the Merger of the 'Ji-hadists' of Syria and Iraq," *Al Jazeera*, June 9, 2013 [in Arabic], www.aljazeera .net/news/arabic/2013/6/9/ظل هاو يﺮ-ﻲﻐﻠﻳ-سورﺪﻳا-واﻊﻟرﺎﻗ ﺪﻤﺟ-ﺞﻫاﺪﻳﻲ-.

72. "Al-Zawahiri Abolishes the Merger of the 'Jihadists' of Syria and Iraq," *Al Jazeera*, June 9, 2013 [in Arabic], www.aljazeera.net/news/arabic /2013/6/9/ظلهاو يﺮ-ﻲﻐﻠﻳ-سورﻲا-واﻊﻟرﺎﻗﺪﻣ ﺞ-ﺞﻫاﺪﻳﻲ-.

73. Ibid.

74. "The ar-Raqqa Executions—Confirmation of the Islamic State in Iraq and as-Sham," *pietervanostayen* (blog), May 15, 2013, https:// pietervanostaeyen.wordpress.com/2013/05/15/the-ar-raqqa-executions -confirmation-of-the-islamic-state-in-iraq-and-as-sham/.

75. Firas al-Hakkar, "The Mysterious Fall of Raqqa, Syria's Kanda-har," *al-Akhbar*, November 8, 2013, http://english.alakhbar.com/node /17550. See also Asharq al-Awsat, "Syria: Islamist Infighting Sweeps Raqqa," *Asharq al-Awsat*, August 15, 2013, www.aawsat.net/2013/08/article 55313705.

76. Erika Solomon, "Hundreds of Syria Rebels Pledge Loyalty to Qaeda Groups: Activists," Reuters, September 20, 2013, www.reuters .com/article/2013/09/20/us-syria-crisis-qaeda-idUSBRE98J0DK20130920.

77. "An Opposition Source Tells Arabi Press: Al-Nusra Vows to Liq-uidate DAESH in Eastern Syria," *Arabi Press*, October 22, 2015 [in Ara-bic], http://arabi-press.com/article.php?id=841552.

78. ISIS's statement announcing the execution is available from http://pbs.twimg.com/media/BdzBSZiCQAADbWz.jpg:large.

79. "Activists Say ISIS Top Commander Killed in Syria," *al-Arabiya*, February 8, 2014, http://english.alarabiya.net/en/News/middle-east/2014 /02/08/Activists-say-ISIS-top-commander-killed-in-Syria-.html.

80. "Jabhat al-Nusra Losing Support among Rebels, Tribes in South Syria," *al-Monitor*, May 6, 2014, www.al-monitor.com/pulse/security/2014 /05/syria-isis-jabhat-nusra-south-deir-ez-zour.html.

81. "'Islamic State' Expels Rivals from Syria City," *Al Jazeera*, July 15, 2014, www.aljazeera.com/news/middleeast/2014/07/state-expels-rivals -from-syria-city-2014714134248239815.html. See also Associated Press, "ISIS Militants Seize Another Oil Field in Syria's Deir el-Zour," *al-Arabiya*, July 4, 2014, http://english.alarabiya.net/en/News/middle-east/2014/07/04 /Islamic-militants-seize-Syria-oil-field.html.

82. "The Syrian Opposition: Eighty Percent of Oil and Gas Fields Are under the Control of Islamic State and Less than Eight Percent under the [Syrian] Regime," *al-Quds al-Arabi*, May 31, 2015 [in Arabic]. See also Lauren Williams, "Islamist Militants Drive Free Syrian Army

Out of Raqqa," *Daily Star*, August 15, 2013, www.dailystar.com.lb/News /Middle-East/2013/.

83. Turkmani, Ali, Kaldor, and Bojicic-Dzelilovic, "Countering the Logic of the War Economy in Syria."

84. Wael Eassm, "Is Islamic State an Extension of the Syrian Armed Rebels?," *al-Quds al-Arabi*, May 8, 2015 [in Arabic].

85. Ibid.

86. The Sahwa forces are a coalition of tribal sheikhs and ex-Baathist military officers formed in Iraq in 2005 to rival al-Qaeda in Sunni-majority provinces such as al-Anbar.

87. "Maliki Seeks to Give Greater Role to the Tribal Leaders in the Fight against al-Qaeda," *Azzaman*, January 13, 2014 [in Arabic], www .azzaman.com/?p=57782.

88. Fehim Tastekin, "'Sunni Project' Needed to Fight ISIS, Says Mosul Governor," *Al-Monitor*, June 16, 2014, www.al-monitor.com /pulse/originals/2014/06/tastekin-isis-sunnis-mosul-iraq-turkey-syria -erbil-kirkuk.html#.

89. "DAESH Seizes Control of Tal Afar, Baiji Refineries, Distributes 'Repentance Cards' . . . and Saudi Warns of Civil War," *al-Quds al-Arabi*, June 18, 2014 [in Arabic], www.alquds.co.uk/?p=182210.

90. Ma'ad Fayad, "Mosul: One Month On," *al-Sharq al-Awsat*, July 14, 2014, www.aawsat.net/2014/07/article55334237/mosul-one -month-on.

91. Nick Tattersall, "Fugitive VP Says Iraq Violence Part of a Sunni Arab Revolt," Reuters, June 16, 2014, www.reuters.com/article/2014/06/16 /us-iraq-security-hashemi-idUSKBN0ER28620140616.

92. Omar Abdulaziz Hallaj, "The Balance-Sheet of Conflict: Criminal Revenues and Warlords in Syria," *NOREF, Norwegian Peacebuilding Resource Centre*, May 2015, www.clingendael.nl/sites/default/files/Hallaj _NOREF_Clingendael_The%20balance-sheet%20of%20conflict _criminal%20revenues%20and%20warlords%20in%20Syria_Apr%20 2015_FINAL.pdf.

93. Weiss and Hassan, *ISIS*.

94. Turkmani, "ISIL, JAN and the War Economy in Syria."

95. Ibid.

96. Abdulaziz Hallaj, "The Balance-Sheet of Conflict."

97. Turkmani, "ISIL, JAN and the War Economy in Syria."

98. Mariam Karouni, "Insight—In Northeast Syria, Islamic State Builds a Government," Reuters, September 4, 2014, http://uk.reuters

.com/article/2014/09/04/uk-syria-crisis-raqqa-insight-idUKKBN
0GZ0DD20140904.

99. "Al-Baghdadi Is Hands-On in Running al-Raqqa and Relies on
Regime Employees and Foreigners," *al-Sharq al-Awsat*, September 5, 2014
[in Arabic].

100. See a propaganda video showing ISIS members distributing pamphlets to a crowd in Syria, "The Thirst of the People of Syria
for [Islamic] Preaching and Advocacy Publications—ISIS," You-
Tube, July 27, 2013, www.youtube.com/watch?v=E3dRIu5qVBM&spfr
eload=10.

101. Ali Mamouri, "IS Imposes New Rules on Education in Syria,
Iraq," *al-Monitor*, October 21, 2014, www.al-monitor.com/pulse/originals
/2014/10/islamic-state-impose-education-program-iraq-syria.html#.
See also Emile Nakhleh, "The Islamic State's Ideology Is Grounded in
Saudi Education," Inter Press Service News, October 27, 2014, www
.ipsnews.net/2014/10/opinion-the-islamic-states-ideology-is-grounded
-in-saudi-education/.

102. "ISIS Imposes New Curriculum in Raqqa," *Al Jazeera*, August 31,
2014 [in Arabic], www.aljazeera.net/news/reportsandinterviews/2014/8/31
/تنظيم-الدولة-في-ضرم-جهاد-راسية-جديدة-في-الرقق.

103. See the video, "Al Furqaan Media Presents Messages from the
Land of Epic Battles #5," uploaded November 6, 2011, https://archive.org
/details/AlFurqaanMediaPresentsMessagesFromTheLandOfEpicBattles
5FromQuraanMemorisationLes_201311. See also Omar al-Jabouri, "ISIS
Hold Qur'anic Memorizing Workshops for Children in Mosul," *al-Quds
al-Arabi*, April 21, 2015 [in Arabic].

104. Aymen Jawad Al-Tamini, "Announcement from Islamic State
of Iraq and ash-Sham's Tel Abyad Islamic Court," aymennjawaad.org,
March 9, 2014, www.aymennjawad.org/2014/02/announcement-from
-islamic-state-of-iraq-and-ash. See also the Vice News documentary, "The
Islamic State," for court operations in al-Raqqa.

105. A *had* (pl. *hudud*) is a punishment fixed in the Qur'an, and *hadith* is a punishment specifically for a crime considered to be against
the rights of God.

106. *Hadanah sha'biyya* is to organize and mobilize popular support.

107. See the report by Amnesty International, "Syria: Harrowing
Torture, Summary Killings in Secret ISIS Detention Centres," December 19, 2013, www.amnesty.org/en/articles/news/2013/12/syria-harrowing
-torture-summary-killings-secret-isis-detention-centres/.

108. "Former Detainees Expose DAESH Secrets and Mysteries," *Islamion*, June 3, 2014 [in Arabic], http://islamion.com/post.php?post =15034.

109. See Amnesty International, "Syria: Harrowing Torture."

110. Karouni, "Insight—In Northeast Syria."

111. See "Al-Khansaa Brigade," *Terrorism Research and Analysis Consortium*, 2015, www.trackingterrorism.org/group/al-khansaa-brigade.

112. Sarah Burke, "How ISIS Rules," nybooks.com, February 5, 2015, www.nybooks.com/articles/archives/2015/feb/05/how-isis-rules/. See also R. Al-Ali, "ISIS Applies Its Own Laws in Raqqa," *Al-Monitor*, February 10, 2014, www.al-monitor.com/pulse/security/2014/02/isis-islamic-rule -raqqa-syria.html.

113. "Syria: ISIS Tortured Kobani Child Hostages," Human Rights Watch, November 4, 2014, www.hrw.org/news/2014/11/04/syria-isis-tor tured-kobani-child-hostages.

CHAPTER 7. MISAPPROPRIATING THE ARAB SPRING UPRISINGS

1. Anne Barnard and Tim Arango, "Using Violence and Persuasion, ISIS Makes Political Gains," *New York Times*, June 3, 2015, www .nytimes.com/2015/06/04/world/isis-making-political-gains.html ?_r=0.

2. Nelly Lahoud with Muhammad al-'Ubaydi, "Jihadi Discourse in the Wake of the Arab Spring," *Harmony Program Combatting Terrorism Center at West Point*, December 2013, www.ciaonet.org/attachments /24119/uploads.

3. Michael Morell, *The Great War of Our Time: The CIA's Fight against Terrorism—From Al Qa'ida to ISIS* (New York: Grand Central Publishing, 2015).

4. Ibid., 180.

5. See the bin Laden documents online: Office of the Director of National Intelligence, *Bin Ladin's Bookshelf*, May 20, 2015, http://1.usa .gov/1ScFGXh. See also Connie Cass and Robert Burns, "US Releases 100+ bin Laden Documents," Associated Press, May 20, 2015.

6. See Office of the Director of National Intelligence, "Message for General Islamic Nation (Arabic)," *Bin Ladin's Bookshelf*, May 20, 2015, www.dni.gov/files/documents/ubl/arabic2/Message%20for%20 general%20Islamic%20nation%20-%20Arabic.pdf.

7. See "Undated Statement (Arabic)," *Bin Ladin's Bookshelf*, www
.dni.gov/files/documents/ubl/arabic/Undated%20statement%20-%20
Arabic.pdf.

8. See "Undated Statement 2," *Bin Ladin's Bookshelf*, www.dni.gov
/files/documents/ubl/english/Undated%20statement%202.pdf.

9. Explanation of a speech by Zawahiri, April 28, 2014, http://
justpaste.it/f9jw.

10. Ibid.

11. "Sheikh Abu Yahya al-Libi Praising the Egyptian and Tunisian
Revolution," YouTube, June 12, 2011, www.youtube.com/watch?v
=aqXoizHpOvs.

12. Ibid.

13. Anwar al-Awlaki, "Tsunami of Change," *Inspire*, no. 5 (May 2011).

14. Asef Bayat, "No Silence, No Violence: A Post-Islamist Trajec-
tory," in *Civilian Jihad: Nonviolent Struggle, Democratization, and Governance in the Middle East*, ed. Maria J. Stephan (New York: Palgrave Macmillan, 2010), 14.

15. Fawaz A. Gerges, ed., *The New Middle East: Protest and Revolution
in the Arab World* (Cambridge, UK: Cambridge University Press, 2014), 3.

16. Dafna Hochman Rand, *Roots of the Arab Spring: Contested Authority and Political Change in the Middle East* (Philadelphia: University
of Pennsylvania Press, 2013), 20–25.

17. Anna M. Agathangelou and Nevzat Soguk, eds., *Arab Revolutions and World Transformations* (London: Routledge, 2013).

18. Fawaz Gerges, "How the Arab Spring Beat Al Qaeda," *Daily
Beast*, May 13, 2012, www.thedailybeast.com/articles/2012/05/13/fawaz-a
-gerges-on-how-the-arab-spring-beat-al-qaeda.html.

19. Sinan Adnan with Aaron Reese, "Beyond the Islamic State:
Iraq's Sunni Insurgency," *Middle East Security Report* 24, Institute for the
Study of War, October 2014, www.understandingwar.org/sites/default
/files/Sunni%20Insurgency%20in%20Iraq.pdf.

20. "Sheikh Abu Yahya al-Libi Calling for Support for the Syrian
Revolution with Money and Weapons," June 13, 2012, www.muslm.org
/vb/showthread.php?483215.

21. See Al Jazeera video on al-Joulani and al-Nusra: Al Jazeera Arabic, YouTube, May 27, 2015 [in Arabic], www.youtube.com/watch?v=
-hwQT43vFZA. See also Al Jazeera, "Al-Nusra's Emir, Abu Mohammad
al-Joulani: Hezbollah Will Vanish with the Downfall of the Bashar al-
Assad Regime," *Al Jazeera*, May 27, 2015 [in Arabic].

22. "Abu Qatada: Islamic State Will Vanish," *Al Jazeera*, November 12, 2014 [in Arabic].

23. "Al-Joulani: Egyptians Brothers Lost Their Way . . . and ISIS 'Kawarij,'" *Al Jazeera*, June 3, 2015 [in Arabic], http://goo.gl/N8mY2u.

24. "Daesh Attacking the Egyptian Muslim Brotherhood Following Morsi's Imprisonment," April 23, 2015 [in Arabic], www.alaraby .co.uk/politics/2015/4/23/داعش-مصر-تهاجم-سلمية-الإخوان-بعد-حبس-مرسي.

25. "ISIS Group in Egypt Criticizes the 'Ikhwan': Instead of Doing Jihad, They Pursued Democracy and God Punished Them," *al-Quds al-Arabi*, April 23, 2015 [in Arabic].

26. Adham Youssef, "'Sinai Province' denounces Brotherhood's 'peaceful methods' of applying Islamic Sharia," *Daily News* (Egypt), January 26, 2015.

27. "Adonis: Democracy Will Not Be Achieved as Long as Religion Is the Reference," *Assafir*, June 15, 2015 [in Arabic], www.assafir.com.

28. Hussein al-Awdat, "In Defense of the 'Arab Spring,'" *Al-Safir*, June 13, 2015 [in Arabic].

29. "Asim Sheikh Historians: Arab Spring a US Plot to Serve Israel," May 12, 2014 [in Arabic], http://alwafd .org /674321/حوارات-وملفات/الربيع-العربى-مؤامرة-أمريكية-لخدمة-إسرائيل-.

30. Leo Messi, "Nabil al-Awadi, International Conspiracy against Syria," YouTube, uploaded on August 21, 2011, www.youtube.com/watch ?v=um6eCDFpHlM.

31. Tariq Ramadan, *Islam and the Arab Awakening* (New York: Oxford University Press, 2012), 6–22.

32. "What Is 'Islamic State'?," *BBC*, October 8, 2015, www.bbc.co.uk /news/world-middle-east-29052144.

33. O. Abdel Rahman Al Tamimi, "The Birth Place of the Islamic State," Al-Furqan Media Foundation, 2008, 12–13, www.slideshare.net /yaken0/ss-5927504.

34. Sayyid Qutb, *Ma'lim fil Tariq* [Milestones], 6th ed. (Cairo: Dar al-Shuruq, 1979), 17.

35. Ibid., 38.

36. Ibid., 107.

37. Abu Al-A'la al-Mawdudi, *Nazareyat al-Islam al-Siyassi* (Damascus: Dar al-Fikr, 1967), 29.

38. In *Milestones*, Qutb cautioned Muslims to shun Western social sciences lest they be corrupted and tricked into jahili beliefs and traditions as he himself had been. It is worth citing Qutb at length to show how he explained his shift from secularism to religiosity and radical re-

ligious activism: "The person who is writing these lines has spent forty years of his life in reading books and in research in almost all aspects of human knowledge. He specialized in some branches of knowledge and he studied others due to personal interest. Then he turned to the fountainhead of his faith. He came to feel that whatever he had read so far was as nothing in comparison to what he found here. He does not regret spending forty years of his life in the pursuit of these sciences, because he came to know the nature of Jahiliyya, its deviations, its errors and its ignorance, as well as its pomp and noise, its arrogant and boastful claims. Finally, he was convinced that a Muslim cannot combine these two sciences—the source of Divine guidance and the source of Jahiliyya—for his education." Qutb, *Milestones*, 131.

39. O. Abdulaziz Hallaj, "The Balance-Sheet of Conflict: Criminal Revenues and Warlords in Syria," NOREF, Norwegian Peacebuilding Resource Centre, May 2015, www.clingendael.nl/sites/default/files /Hallaj_NOREF_Clingendael_The%20balance-sheet%20of%20conflict_criminal%20revenues%20and%20warlords%20in%20Syria _Apr%202015_FINAL.pdf.

40. See Baghdadi's transcript and audio recording: "Islamic State: Al-Furqan Media Releases New Audio and Transcript Allegedly of Baghdadi," *Carol Ann Grayson (Radical Sister) Blog*, May 14, 2015, https:// activist1.wordpress.com/2015/05/14/islamic-state-al-furqan-media -releases-new-audio-and-transcript-allegedly-of-baghdadi/.

41. *Bin Ladin's Bookshelf*, available from the Office of the Director of National Intelligence, http://www.dni.gov/index.php/resources /bin-laden-bookshelf; See also Cass and Burns, "US Releases 100+ bin Laden Documents."

CHAPTER 8. ISIS VERSUS AL QAEDA: REDEFINING JIHAD AND THE TRANSITION FROM THE GLOBAL TO THE LOCAL

1. Kamran Bokhari, "Sectarian Spill," *Tribune* (New York), October 12, 2013, http://tribune.com.pk/story/617156/sectarian-spill/.

2. For context, see Nizih N. Ayubi, *Over-Stating the Arab States: Politics and Society in the Middle East* (London: I. B. Tauris, 1995).

3. Emile Nakhleh, "Why Is the Islamic State So Resilient?," *LobeLog*, June 5, 2015, www.lobelog.com/why-is-the-islamic-state-so-resilient/.

4. See the Bin Laden documents online: Office of the Director of National Intelligence, "Message for General Islamic Nation (Arabic),"

Bin Ladin's Bookshelf, May 20, 2015, www.dni.gov/files/documents/ubl /arabic2/Message%20for%20general%20Islamic%20nation%20-%20Arabic.pdf. See also A. al-Zawahiri, "Testimonial to Preserve the Blood of Mujahideen in al-Sham [Greater Syria]," *pietervanostaeyen* (blog), May 3, 2014, https://pietervanostaeyen.wordpress.com/2014/05/03/dr-ayman-az -zawahiri-testimonial-to-preserve-the-blood-of-mujahideen-in-as-sham/.

5. Abu Mohammed al-Adnani, "Muasassat al-Furqan Tuqadem: Haza Wa'd Min Allah: Sheikh Abi Mohamed al-Adnani Hazizahu Allah," YouTube, July 5, 2014 [in Arabic], www.youtube.com/watch?v =Uen14MVYNqk; Abu Mohmmed al-Adnani, "This Is the Promise of Allah," June 19, 2014 [in Arabic], http://triceratops.brynmawr.edu/dspace /bitstream/handle/10066/14242/ADN20140629.pdf?sequence=1.

6. Patrick Cockburn, "War with Isis: Islamic Militants Have Army of 200,000, Claims Senior Kurdish Leader," *Independent,* November 16, 2014, www.independent.co.uk/news/world/middle-east/war -with-isis-islamic-militants-have-army-of-200000-claims-kurdish-leader -9863418.html.

7. See Office of the Director of National Intelligence, "Message for General Islamic Nation (Arabic)."

8. Shuaib Almosawa, Kareem Fahim, and Eric Schmitt, "Islamic State Gains Strength in Yemen, Challenging Al Qaeda," *New York Times,* December 14, 2015; Kevin Sieff, "2,000 Miles from Syria, ISIS Is Trying to Lure Recruits in Somalia," *Washington Post,* December 24, 2015.

9. Mujib Mashal, "Taliban Are Talking Peace, Though Not with Afghan Government," *New York Times,* June 21, 2015; Fazul Rahim, Mujeeb Ahmed, and Mushtaq Yusufzai, "Taliban Splinters as ISIS Makes Inroads in Afghanistan," *NBC News,* June 21, 2015, www.nbcnews.com /news/world/afghan-taliban-splits-isis-makes-inroads-n378456. See also Fazul Rahim and F. Brinley Bruton, "Taliban Warns ISIS to Stay Out of Afghanistan," *NBC News,* June 16, 2015, www.nbcnews.com/news/world /taliban-warns-isis-stay-out-afghanistan-n376311; Mushtaq Yusufzai, "ISIS in Pakistan and Afghanistan: Taliban Fighters Sign Up, Commanders Say," *NBC News,* January 31, 2015, www.nbcnews.com/news/world/isis -pakistan-afghanistan-taliban-fighters-sign-commanders-say-n296707.

10. "Taliban Publish Mullah Omar's Biography," *Pakistan Today,* April 2015.

11. The Prospect Team, "Does Mullah Omar's Death Spell the End for the Taliban?," *Prospect Magazine,* July 31, 2015; Matthew Rosenberg, "Mullah Muhammad Omar's Life Ends with Little Clarity," *New York Times,* July 30, 2015. See also "Split Emerged over Successor, as Son

Disclosed Mullah Omar's Death," *Daily Times*, August 1, 2015; "Internal Dispute over Taliban Succession Hints at Rifts," Associated Press, August 2, 2015.

12. "Hamas Dialogues with 'Militants' Who Support Islamic State," *al-Quds al-Arabi*, June 21, 2015 [in Arabic], www.alquds.co.uk.

13. Shiv Malik, Ali Younes, Spencer Ackerman, and Mustafa Khalili, "How ISIS Crippled al-Qaeda: The Inside Story of the Coup that Has Brought the World's Most Feared Terrorist Network to the Brink of Collapse," *Guardian*, June 10, 2015.

14. "The Flood," *Dabiq* (al Hayat Media Centre, 2014), 3, http://media.clarionproject.org/files/09-2014/isis-isil-islamic-state-magazine-Issue-2-the-flood.pdf.

15. See the *New York Times* debate: "Homegrown Terrorists and the West," with Ghaffar Hussein, Jocelyn Cesari, Raffaello Pantucci, Jamie Bartlett, and Patrick M. Skinner, August 29, 2014, www.nytimes.com/roomfordebate/2014/08/28/how-to-stop-radicalization-in-the-west/challenge-radicals-loudly-and-clearly; Shiraz Maher, "The Roots of Radicalisation? It's Identity, Stupid," *ICSR*, June 23, 2015, http://icsr.info/2015/06/icsr-insight-roots-radicalisation-identity-stupid/.

16. Eric Schmitt, "ISIS or Al Qaeda? American Officials Split over Biggest Threat," *New York Times*, August 4, 2015.

17. See Abu Mohammed Al-Adnani al-Shami, "Ina Rabaka la belmersad" [Thy Lord is on the watch-tower], September 21, 2015 [in Arabic], https://archive.org/details/bilmirssad. Cited also by David D. Kirkpatrick, Ben Hubbard, and Eric Schmitt, "ISIS' Grip on a Libyan City Gives It a Fallback Option," *New York Times*, November 28, 2015.

18. "Islamic State Unfriended," *The Economist*, December 12, 2015.

19. Some deputies, like Abu Musab al-Suri, an influential theorist, believed that smaller attacks are more effective in bleeding the West economically. See the Bin Laden documents (Online): http://1.usa.gov/1ScFGXh. See also "Bin Laden Bent on Spectacular US Attack until the End: Files," *Agence France Presse*, May 20, 2015.

20. Rabi' al-Awwal, "Al-Qa'ida of Waziristan: A Testimony from Within," *Dabiq*, no. 6, December 2014.

21. Ibid.

22. Cited by Malik et al., "How ISIS Crippled al-Qaeda."

23. See the YouTube link to Abu Mohammed al-Adnani's statement: www.youtube.com/watch?v=484gfZ2Yodw&spfreload=10. See also an English transcript of his audio statement: Abu Mohemmad al-Adnani, "O Our People Respond to the Caller of Allah," *pietervanostaeyen*

(blog), June 23, 2015, https://pietervanostaeyen.wordpress.com/2015/06/23/o-our-people-respond-to-the-caller-of-allah-audio-statement-by-shaykh-abu-muhammad-al-adnani-as-shami/.

24. YouTube link to Abu Mohammed al-Adnani's statement; Adnani, "O Our People."

25. "Queen Rania Leads a Protest that Threatens Daesh with Death ... and a Greater Role for al-Maqdisi in Confronting the Organization," *al-Quds al-Arabi*, February 6, 2015 [in Arabic]. See also "Al-Maqdisi Accuses Islamic State of 'Tarnishing Islam,'" *Al Jazeera*, August 16, 2014 [in Arabic].

26. Zawahiri, "Testimonial."

27. "Abu Qatada: Islamic State Will Vanish," *Al Jazeera*, November 12, 2014 [in Arabic].

28. Malik et al., "How ISIS Crippled al-Qaeda."

29. Ibid.

30. See Office of the Director of National Intelligence, "Message for General Islamic Nation (Arabic)." Hersh disputes the Obama administration's narrative about the killing of bin Laden and the documents the SEAL 6 team captured from bin Laden's house. See Seymour Hersh, "The Killing of Osama bin Laden," *London Review of Books* 37, no. 10 (May 21, 2015), www.lrb.co.uk/v37/n10/seymour-m-hersh/the-killing-of-osama-bin-laden.

31. Abu Abdullah Mohamed al-Mansour al-Issawi, *Al-Dawla al-Islamiyya: Bayna al-Haqiqa wa al-Wahm* [The Islamic State: Disentangling myth from reality] (n.p., n.d.), 154–160.

32. See Office of the Director of National Intelligence, "Message for General Islamic Nation (Arabic)." See also Corina Cass and Robert Burns, "US Releases 100+ bin Laden Documents," Associated Press, May 20, 2015.

33. Cited by Malik et al., "How ISIS Crippled al-Qaeda." See also Office of the Director of National Intelligence, "Message for General Islamic Nation (Arabic)."

34. For Zawahiri's views, see "The Open Meeting with Shaykh Ayman al Zawahiri, Part 4," [in Arabic] www.youtube.com/watch?v=2f2XLkCG3Ls. For Issawi's response, see *The Islamic State*, 154–160.

35. Zawahiri, "Testimonial."

36. See Office of the Director of National Intelligence, "Message for General Islamic Nation (Arabic)."

37. www.stratfor.com/analysis/al-qaeda-2007-continuing-devolution.

38. Yet when it had the upper hand in the 1990s and early 2000s, Al Qaeda did not act rationally or peacefully in Afghanistan and Paki-

stan in the areas in which it has been able to project power via local
allies.

39. Ayman al-Zawahiri, "Jihadist Guidelines" [in Arabic], www
.arrahmah.com/arabic/as-shab-tqdm-twjyhat-aamt-llml-al-jhady
-llshykh-al-amyr-aymn-az-zwahry.html.

40. Mohammed al-Adnani, "Apologies, Emir of Al Qaeda," Muasassat al-Furqan Tuqadem, July 5, 2014, https://justpaste.it/othran. See
also Adnani, "Muasassat al-Furqan Tuqadem"; Adnani, "This Is the
Promise of Allah."

41. See "'Wikileaks Baghdadi' Reveals the Truth about 'Daesh,'"
Zaman Al Wasl, January 5, 2015, https://zamanalwsl.net/news/45122.html.
See also Christoph Reuter, "The Terror Strategist: Secret Files Reveal
the Structure of Islamic State," Der Spiegel, April 18, 2015.

42. Fawaz Gerges, The Far Enemy: Why Jihad Went Global, 2nd ed.
(Cambridge, UK: Cambridge University Press, 2009).

43. Ibid., chapters 2 and 3.

44. Cited by Malik et al., "How ISIS Crippled al-Qaeda."

45. Adnani, "Apologies, Emir of Al Qaeda."

46. US Department of State Publication Bureau, Bureau of Counterterrorism, "Country Reports on Terrorism 2014," June 2015, www.state
.gov/documents/organization/239631.pdf.

47. Zawahiri, "Testimonial."

48. Adnani, "Apologies, Emir of Al Qaeda."

49. Ibid.

50. Wael Essam and Ra'id al-Hamed, "One Year after the Fall of
Mosul: ISIS Beats Its Rivals First in the Struggle for Hearts and Minds
before the Battlefields," al-Quds al-Arabi, July 4, 2015 [in Arabic].

51. Ubaida al-Dalimi and Abdallah al-Omri, "A Year after the Fall
of Mosul: Tribes Reject the Return of the Shia and Kurds [to Their
Areas]," al-Quds al-Arabi, July 4, 2015 [in Arabic].

52. Raid al-Hamed, "A Year after the Declaration of the Caliphate:
Airstrikes by the Coalition on ISIS Increase Its Popularity," al-Quds al-
Arabi, July 4, 2015 [in Arabic].

53. See "French-speaking militant executes 'apostates' in ISIS
video," Al Arabiya English, January 31, 2016, http://english.alarabiya.net
/en/News/middle-east/2016/01/31/French-speaking-militant-executes
-apostates-in-ISIS-video.html.

54. Baghdadi's transcript and audio: Abu Bakr al-Baghdadi,
"March Forth Whether Light or Heavy," Carol Ann Grayson (Radical
Sister) Blog, May 14, 2015, https://activist1.wordpress.com/2015/05/14

/islamic-state-al-furqan-media-releases-new-audio-and-transcript
-allegedly-of-baghdadi/. See also Rukmini Callimachi, "ISIS Releases Recording Said to Be by Its Reclusive Leader," *New York Times*, May 14, 2015.
    55. Essam and Hamed, "One Year after the Fall of Mosul."
    56. See Zawahiri, "Jihadist Guidelines."
    57. Baghdadi, "March Forth Whether Light or Heavy." See also
Callimachi, "ISIS Releases Recording."
    58. Baghdadi, "March Forth Whether Light or Heavy."
    59. Zawahiri, "Testimonial."
    60. "Ayman al-Zawahiri, Aal Sa'ud Qatalat al-Mujahiddeen (The
Saud Family: The killers of Mujahiddin)," Arrahmah website, January 15, 2016, http://www.arrahmah.com/news/2016/01/15/tfrygh-aal-swd
-qtlt-al-mjahdyn-llshykh-aymn-az-zwahry.html. See also Abdullah Sulei-
man Ali, "Zawahiri Threatens the Saudi Family . . ." *Assafir*, January 15,
2016 [in Arabic].
    61. Schmitt, "ISIS or Al Qaeda?"
    62. Hazem Amin, "'Al-Nusra' Would Commit Suicide If It Severs
Ties with 'Al Qaeda' . . . and Zawahiri Would Not Have Objected," *Al
Hayat*, July 23, 2015 [in Arabic]. See also Hazem Amin, "Turkey Pressured
'al-Nusra' to Split from 'Al Qaeda;'" *Al Hayat*, July 23, 2015 [in Arabic];
Hazem Amin, "Jordanian Commanders Sabotaged Turkey's Desire to
Merge 'al-Nusra' with 'Ahrar al-Sham;'" *Al Hayat*, July 24, 2015 [in Arabic];
Saheeb Anjarini, "Splitting from 'Al Qaeda': Today 'Abdullah Azzam
Brigades' and Tomorrow 'al-Nusra,'" *al-akhbar*, April 7, 2015 [in Arabic].
    63. Amin, "Turkey Pressured 'al-Nusra.'" See also Ben Hubbard, "Al
Qaeda's Branch in Syria Denies Planning Attacks Abroad," *New York
Times*, May 27, 2015.
    64. See Al Jazeera video on al-Joulani and al-Nusra: Al Jazeera,
YouTube, May 27, 2015 [in Arabic], www.youtube.com/watch?v=-hwQT
43vFZA. See also "Al-Nusra's Emir, Abu Mohammad al-Joulani: Hez-
bollah Will Vanish with the Downfall of the Bashar al-Assad Regime,"
Al Jazeera, May 27, 2015 [in Arabic]; Abdullah Suleiman Ali, "Al-Joulani
Maneuvers Faces between Isolationism, Being Isolated and Facing As-
sassination," *Assafir*, December 14, 2015 [in Arabic]; "Al-Joulani: Russia
Will Not Dare to Intervene Militarily [Boots on the Ground]," *Al
Jazeera*, December 13, 2015 [in Arabic].
    65. Author's conversation with Moussa al-Omar.
    66. Abdullah Suleiman Ali, "Internal Divisions Lead to 'Hemor-
rhaging' of Jabhat al-Nusra Leaders," *Assafir*, July 21, 2015 [in Arabic]. See

also "What Does the Separation between al-Nusra and Al Qaeda Entail?," AlSouria.net, July 8, 2015 [in Arabic]; Abdullah Suleiman Ali, "Al-Ansar Facing the Test of Fighting al-Kawarij [ISIS] in Syria," *Assafir*, July 20, 2015 [in Arabic].

67. "Abu Qatada: Islamic State Will Vanish."

68. Kamil al-Taweel, "Zawahiri Moves to Dissolve Al Qaeda," *Al Hayat*, April 3, 2015 [in Arabic].

69. Amin, "Turkey Pressured 'al-Nusra.'"

70. Falih Hassan and Sewell Chan, "Iraqi Victory over ISIS in Ramadi Could Prove Pivotal," *New York Times*, December 28, 2015.

71. Islamic State: Unfriended," *The Economist*, December 12, 2015.

72. Hugh Naylor, "Reclaiming the Title 'King of Jihad' Means Al-Qaeda Will Target the West," *Washington Post*, December 27, 2015. See also "IS-Claimed Bombing Kills Yemeni Governor, 6 Guards in Aden," Associated Press, December 6, 2015.

73. "Bel Video: Al-Zawahiri: La a'taref be "Da'esh" "wala Nara al-Baghdadi ahlan Leil Khelafa [In video; al-Zawahiri: I Do not recognize Daesh and we do not consider al-Baghdadi qualified to be the Caliph], *Moheet*, December 29, 2015, http://goo.gl/LldEjH. See also Missy Ryan, "Al-Qaida Says ISIS Is Poaching Militants," *Washington Post*, September 10, 2015.

CONCLUSION: THE FUTURE OF ISIS

1. Abu Bakr al-Baghdadi, "Isdarat al-Ikhalfa: Fa tarabasu enna ma'kum lamutarabusoon" [The Khilafa publications: Await then! We are awaiting with you], *Dawlet al-Khilfa al-Islamiyya* [an Islamic blog], December 26, 2015, https://goo.gl/kbS0N0. See also Josie Ensor, "Islamic State Leader Baghdadi Goads West in Rare Audio Statement," *Telegraph*, December 26, 2015.

2. Audrey Kurth Cronin, *How Terrorism Ends: Understanding the Decline and Demise of Terrorist Campaigns* (Princeton, NJ: Princeton University Press, 2010).

3. A coalition of tribal sheikhs and ex-Baathist military officers formed in Iraq in 2005 as a rival force to Al Qaeda in Sunni majority provinces such as al-Anbar.

4. Borzou Daragahi, "The Front-Line Fight against Isis," *Financial Times*, March 6, 2015, www.ft.com/cms/s/0/cfe12b08-c2ae-11e4-a59c-00144feab7de.html.

5. Anne Barnard and Tim Arango, "Using Violence and Persuasion, ISIS Makes Political Gains," *New York Times*, June 3, 2015; Tim Arango, "With Fall of Ramadi, Plight of Iraq Sunnis Worsens," *New York Times*, May 19, 2015.

6. Wael Essam, "Why Did ISIS Retreat in Kobani and Tal Abyad?," *al-Quds al-Arabi*, June 19, 2015 [in Arabic]; Wael Essam, "How Will America Defeat ISIS When Its Marines Failed to Do So a Decade Ago?," *al-Quds al-Arabi*, May 22, 2015 [in Arabic]; Ra'id al-Hamed, "A Year after the Declaration of the Caliphate: Airstrikes by the Coalition on ISIS Increase Its Popularity," *al-Quds al-Arabi*, July 4, 2015 [in Arabic]; Ubaida al-Dalimi, "Inhabitants' Support for ISIS in Fallujah Allowed It to Resist Attacks by the Government," *al-Quds al-Arabi*, July 25, 2015 [in Arabic]; E. Banco, "Iraqi Sunni Sheikhs in Anbar Pledge Allegiance to ISIS, Aid Militant Group," *International Business Times*, June 4, 2015; and R. Spencer, "What We Have Learned about Islamic State after Its Victories in Ramadi and Palmyra," *Telegraph*, May 21, 2015.

7. The Hashd al-Shabi (Popular Mobilization Force) is a coalition of Shia militias that came together in order to fight ISIS in Iraq. They support the Iraqi security forces.

8. Omar Al-Jawoshy, and Tim Arango, "Iraqi Offensive to Retake Tikrit from ISIS Begins," *New York Times*, March 2, 2015, www.nytimes .com/2015/03/03/world/middleeast/iraq-tikrit-isis.html?_r=0.

9. See the reports by the Human Rights Watch: "After Liberation Came Destruction: Iraqi Militias and the Aftermath of Amerli," *Human Rights Watch*, March 18, 2015, www.hrw.org/report/2015/03/18/after-libera tion-came-destruction/iraqi-militias-and-aftermath-amerli; "Ruinous Aftermath: Militias Abuses Following Iraq's Recapture of Tikrit," *Human Rights Watch*, September 20, 2015, www.hrw.org/report/2015/09/20/ruinous -aftermath/militias-abuses-following-iraqs-recapture-tikrit.

10. Editorial, "A Tribal Association in Anbar Pledges Allegiance to ISIS," *al-Quds al-Arabi*, June 4, 2015 [in Arabic], www.alquds.co.uk/?p =351858; M. al-Douri, "Why the Increase in Bay'at for ISIS by Anbar Tribes?," *al-Quds al-Arabi*, June 15, 2015 [in Arabic]; Banco, "Iraqi Sunni Sheikhs"; M. Bajis, "A Public Bay'a for Baghdadi by Leading Iraqi Tribes in Mosul," *Arabi21*, April 1, 2015 [in Arabic]; and Omar Al-Jabouri, "Wali Mosul Promises Tribal Sheikhs to Have People Who Had Been Arrested Released," al-Quds al-Arabi, April 3, 2015 [in Arabic].

11. S. Al-Rabi'i, "Iraq: Tribal Infighting in Anbar Delays Defeat of Daesh," *al-Akhbar*, July 1, 2015 [in Arabic].

12. Douri, "Why the Increase in Bay'at?"; Nour Malas and Ghassan Adnan, "Sunni Tribes in Iraq Divided over Battle against Islamic State," *Wall Street Journal*, May 22, 2015; Ben Hubbard, "Offering Services, ISIS Digs In Deeper in Seized Territories," *New York Times*, June 16, 2015. See also "Iraq Struggles with Sectarian Politics after Ramadi Fall," Associated Press, May 19, 2015.

13. Hamed, "A Year after the Declaration of the Caliphate"; Barnard and Arango, "Using Violence and Persuasion."

14. Wael Essam and Ra'id al-Hamed, "One Year after the Fall of Mosul: ISIS Beats Its Rivals First in the Struggle for Hearts and Minds before the Battlefields," *al-Quds al-Arabi*, July 4, 2015 [in Arabic]; Ubaida al-Dalimi and Abdallah al-Omri, "A Year after the Fall of Mosul: Tribes Reject the Return of the Shia and Kurds [to Their Areas]," *al-Quds al-Arabi*, July 4, 2015 [in Arabic].

15. See Reem Turkmani, "ISIL, JAN and the War Economy in Syria," *Security in Transition* (London School of Economics), July 30, 2015, www.securityintransition.org/wp-content/uploads/2015/08/ISIL-JAN-and-the-war-economy-in-Syria1.pdf.

16. Tim Arango, "ISIS Transforming into Functioning State that Uses Terror as Tool," *New York Times*, July 21, 2015; Hubbard, "Offering Services, ISIS Digs In Deeper"; "IS Offers a Mix of Brutality, Charity during Ramadan," Associated Press, July 10, 2015; A. Shubert, "How ISIS Controls Life, from Birth to Football," CNN.com, April 21, 2015, http://www.cnn.com/2015/04/21/middleeast/isis-documents/index.html; M. Karouny, "In Northeast Syria, Islamic State Builds a Government," Reuters, September 4, 2014, http://www.reuters.com/article/us-syria-crisis-raqqa-insight-idUSKBN0GZ0D120140904. See also two working papers: T. Turkmani, A. Ali, M. Kaldor, and V. Bojicic-Dzelilovic, "Countering the Logic of the War Economy in Syria; Evidence from Three Local Areas," *Security in Transition* (London School of Economics), July 2015, http://bit.ly/1NcvHgH; and Turkmani, "ISIL, JAN and the War Economy in Syria."

17. Charles C. Caris and Samuel Reynolds, "ISIS Governance in Syria," *Middle East Security Report* 22, Institute for the Study of War, July 2014.

18. Khales Joumah, "Mosul Is 'Safe, Clean' . . . and Run by ISIS," *Daily Beast*, June 15, 2015 (this article is adapted from *niqash*: www.niqash.org/en/article/security/5029/Extremists'-Mosul-Is-A-Safe-Clean-City-Full-Of-Bearded-Men-Veiled-Women.htm); Z. Karam, V. Salama, B. Janssen,

and L. Keath, "Inside Islamic State Group's Rule: Creating a Nation of Fear," Associated Press, June 18, 2015; Shubert, "How ISIS Controls Life."

19. Karouny, "In Northeast Syria, Islamic State Builds a Government."

20. Ibid.

21. Liz Sly, "How Saddam Hussein's Former Military Officers and Spies Are Controlling Isis," *Independent*, April 5, 2015.

22. "ISIS Opens First Institute for Islamic Studies in Mosul," *al-Quds al-Arabi*, May 7, 2015 [in Arabic]; "ISIS Builds a Huge Medical School and Pharmaceutical Factories in Mosul," *al-Quds al-Arabi*, September 1, 2015 [in Arabic]; "ISIS Announces the Printing of New Curricula in Mosul and Promises to Deliver Them before the Beginning of the New Academic Year," *al-Quds al-Arabi*, September 1, 2015 [in Arabic]; F. Al-Hakkar, "Two Medical Colleges and a Factory to Manufacture Limbs and Daesh for Achievers," *al-Akhbar*, August 31, 2015 [in Arabic]; and H. Saul, "ISIS Opens 262-Room Luxury Hotel in Mosul," *Independent*, May 6, 2015.

23. Essam and Hamed, "A Year after the Fall of Mosul."

24. Y. al-Issa, "In Syria . . . a Bay'a in Return for a Job," *Al Jazeera*, June 11, 2015 [in Arabic].

25. Sarah Almukhtar, "ISIS Finances Are Strong," *New York Times*, May 19, 2015, www.nytimes.com/interactive/2015/05/19/world/middleeast/isis-finances.html?_r=0. See also Jean-Charles Brisard and Damien Martinez, "Islamic State: The Economy-Based Terrorist Funding," Thomson Reuters Report, October 2014, https://risk.thomsonreuters.com/sites/default/files/GRC01815.pdf; "Islamic State: Unfriended," *The Economist*, December 12, 2015. See also Colum Lynch and David Francis, "The Islamic State Has Gotten Rich from Extortion, Heists, and Smuggling. But How Long Can the Extremist Group Continue to Bankroll Jihad?," *Foreign Policy*, December 15, 2015.

26. Lynch and Francis, "The Islamic State Has Gotten Rich."

27. "Islamic State: Unfriended."

28. Sam Jones, Piotr Zalewski, and Erika Solomon, "Isis Sells Smuggled Oil to Turkey and Iraqi Kurds, Says US Treasury," *Financial Times*, October 23, 2014; David Blair, "Oil Middleman between Syria and Isil Is New Target for EU Sanctions," *Telegraph*, March 7, 2015; Eric Schmitt, "ISIS or Al Qaeda? American Officials Split over Biggest Threat," *New York Times*, August 4, 2015; Hermela Aregawi, "Operation Inherent Resolve: A Year of Fighting ISIL," *Al Jazeera America*, August 14, 2015.

29. Almukhtar, "ISIS Finances Are Strong." For instance, in 2015, the US government appraised ISIS's monthly income from its oil opera-

tions at $40–$50 million, but independent analysts think that number has decreased since the start of stepped-up airstrikes by the US-led coalition at the end of 2015. A similar analysis by IHS Global Strategies found that ISIS brought in about $80 million per month in the latter part of 2015, a large chunk of which is oil, which represents around 43 percent of its total revenues. Jason Abbruzzese, "Here's How ISIS Makes—and Spends—Its Money," *Mashable*, December 8, 2015, http://mashable.com/2015/12/08/isis-makes-its-money-like/#HvksJ1koXEq6.

30. Lynch and Francis, "The Islamic State Has Gotten Rich."

31. "Islamic State: Unfriended"; "What It Will Take to Bankrupt ISIS," *New York Times* [editorial], December 3, 2015. See also Hugh Naylor, "Islamic State Money-Making Streams Take a Hit as It Loses Territory," *Washington Post*, December 4, 2015. See "ISIS Halves the Salaries of its Fighters."

32. Erika Solomon and S. Jones, "Isis Inc: How Oil Fuels the Jihadi Terrorists," *Financial Times*, October 14, 2015.

33. Morris. Milton, "A Year after the Occupation of Mosul: What Has Changed and How?," *Assafir*, June 25, 2015 [in Arabic].

34. See the group's website, www.raqqa-sl.com/; Erika Solomon, "The ISIS Economy: Meet the New Boss," *Financial Times*, January 5, 2015.

35. Joanna Paraszczuk, "The ISIS Economy: Crushing Taxes and High Unemployment," *Atlantic*, September 2, 2015. See also A. Masi, "Life for Residents of ISIS Caliphate Is So Expensive It Could Be Its Downfall," *International Business Times*, May 20, 2015.

36. Joumah, "Mosul Is 'Safe, Clean' . . . and Run by ISIS"; Hubbard, "Offering Services, ISIS Digs In Deeper"; Y. al-Issa, "Selling Electricity—A New ISIS Activity in Deir al-Zour," *Al Jazeera*, April 12, 2015 [in Arabic]; F. al-Hakkar, "ISIS Sells Electricity," *al-Akhbar*, April 24, 2015 [in Arabic]; Masi, "Life for Residents of ISIS Caliphate"; and Karam et al., "Inside Islamic State Group's Rule."

37. Hubbard, "Offering Services, ISIS Digs In Deeper."

38. Lynch and Francis, "The Islamic State Has Gotten Rich."

39. Barnard and Arango, "Using Violence and Persuasion"; Hubbard, "Offering Services, ISIS Digs In Deeper." See also Karouny, "In Northeast Syria, Islamic State Builds a Government."

40. Shiv Malik, "The ISIS Papers: Behind 'Death Cult` Image Lies a Methodical Bureaucracy," *The Guardian*, December 7, 2015.

41. Wathiqat al-Madina [Charter of the city], https://azelin.files.wordpress.com/2014/06/islamic-state-of-iraq-and-al-shc481m-charter-of-the-city.pdf. See also Milton, "A Year after the Occupation of Mosul: What Has Changed and How?"

42. Charter of the City. See also Milton, "A Year after the Occupation of Mosul: What Has Changed and How?"

43. Malik, "The ISIS Papers."

44. Milton, "A Year after the Occupation of Mosul: What Has Changed and How?"; Morris Milton, "A Year after the Occupation of Mosul: The Judicial and Hisba Systems," *Assafir*, July 1, 2015 [in Arabic].

45. "Between the Poor and Muslims: The Four Misconceptions on the Phenomenon of Terrorism in the World," *Al-Rawabet Center for Research and Strategic Studies*, January 18, 2015 [in Arabic], http://rawabet center.com/archives/2898; Ilyas al-Farahat, "Daesh's Military Tactic," *al-Nahar*, November 25, 2014 [in Arabic], http://newspaper.annahar.com /article/192432-%D8%A7%D9%84%D8%AA%D9%83%D8%AA%D9% 8A%D9%83; Hisham al-Hashimi, "ISIS between Survival and Fragmentation," *Al Jazeera Center for Studies*, August 10, 2015 [in Arabic]; Milton, "A Year after the Occupation of Mosul: What Has Changed and How?"; Milton, "A Year after the Occupation of Mosul: The Judicial and Hisba Systems"; Joumah, "Mosul Is 'Safe, Clean' . . . and Run by ISIS."

46. Graeme Wood, "What ISIS Really Wants," *Atlantic*, March 2015.

47. Ibid.

48. A. Suleiman Ali, "The Caliphate in Its Second Year: New States Are Targeted," *Assafir*, June 29, 2015 [in Arabic].

49. Mariam Karouni, "Apocalyptic Prophecies Drive Both Sides to Syrian Battle for End of Time," Reuters, April 1, 2014.

50. See Baghdadi's transcript and audio recording: Abu Bakr al-Baghdadi, "March Forth Whether Light or Heavy," *Carol Ann Grayson (Radical Sister) Blog*, May 14, 2015, https://activist1.wordpress.com/2015/05 /14/islamic-state-al-furqan-media-releases-new-audio-and-transcript -allegedly-of-baghdadi/.

51. A phrase often used in ISIS propaganda videos and publications to refer to ISIS fighters.

52. Eric Schmitt and Ben Hubbard, "Islamic State Leader Delegates His Powers in Case He Is Killed," *New York Times*, July 21, 2015.

53. For further discussion of this point, see Hamed, "A Year after the Declaration of the Caliphate."

54. Missy Ryan and Greg. Jaffe, "With Fight against the Islamic State in Iraq Stalled, U.S. Looks to Syria for Gains," *Washington Post*, September 21, 2015; and Liz Sly, "Russia's Move into Syria Upends U.S. Plans," *Washington Post*, September 26, 2015.

55. Liz Sly, "The Hidden Hand behind the Islamic State Militants? Saddam Hussein's," *Washington Post*, April 4, 2015; J. Rayburn, *Iraq after America: Strongmen, Sectarians, Resistance* (Stanford, CA: Hoover Institute Press, 2014); Christoph Reuter, "The Terror Strategist: Secret Files Reveal the Structure of Islamic State," *Der Spiegel*, April 18, 2015. The *Washington Post* has a diagram explaining the roles of former Baathist army members in ISIS in Iraq and Syria: "Most of Islamic State's Leaders Were Officers in Saddam Hussein's Iraq," *Washington Post*, April 4, 2015, www.washingtonpost.com/world/most-of-islamic-states-leaders-were-officers-in-saddam-husseins-iraq/2015/04/04/f3d2da00-db24-11e4-b3f2-607bd612aeac_graphic.html.

56. "Daesh Lost 30 Percent of Its Territory," Associated Press, January 6, 2016. See also Columb Strack, "Islamic State Territory Shrinks by 9.4% in First Six Months of 2015," *IHS*, July 27, 2015, www.janes.com/article/53239/islamic-state-territory-shrinks-by-9-4-in-first-six-months-of-2015#.VbeipB_weRs.twitter.

57. Joseph Rago, "Inside the War against Islamic State," *Wall Street Journal*, December 26, 2014, www.wsj.com/articles/joe-rago-inside-the-war-against-islamic-state-1419636790. See also Ryan and Jaffe, "Fight against the Islamic State in Iraq Stalled."

58. Schmitt and Hubbard, "Islamic State Leader Delegates His Powers."

59. David D. Kirkpatrick, Ben Hubbard, and Eric Schmitt, "ISIS' Grip on Libyan City Gives It a Fallback Option," *New York Times*, November 28, 2015. See also Kevin Sieff, "2,000 Miles from Syria, ISIS Is Trying to Lure Recruits in Somalia," *Washington Post*, December 24, 2015.

60. There are many credible reports in the Arabic press documenting ISIS's effective recruitment techniques in Syria and Iraq and its appeal among local Sunnis. There is no space to list them here. For a sample of the views of US officials and strategists, see Eric Schmitt and Somini Sengupta, "Thousands Enter Syria to Join ISIS Despite Global Efforts," *New York Times*, September 26, 2015; Schmitt, "ISIS or Al Qaeda?"; and Shellie Nelson, "State Dept. Says ISIS, Not al Qaeda, Is World's Leading Terrorist Group," CNN.com, June 20, 2015, http://edition.cnn.com/2015/06/19/politics/isis-report-state-department-terror/index.html.

61. Greg Miller, "U.S. Launches Secret Drone Campaign to Hunt Islamic State Leaders in Syria," *Washington Post*, September 1, 2015.

62. Malik, "The ISIS Papers."

63. "Behead the Doll, Children Told in ISIS Training Camp," *Syrian Observatory for Human Rights*, July 20, 2015, www.syriahr.com/en /2015/07/behead-the-doll-children-told-in-isis-training-camp/.

64. Chas Danner, "How ISIS Abducts, Recruits, and Trains Children to Become Jihadists," *New York Magazine*, July 19, 2015, http://nymag.com /daily/intelligencer/2015/07/how-isis-abducts-recruits-and-trains -children.html#.

65. For a sample of reports in Arabic and English, see "In IS Camp, Beheading Lessons Start with Doll and Sword," Associated Press, July 19, 2015; Danner, "How ISIS Abducts"; A. al-Sibai; "Executions by Islamic State … Children at the Forefront," *Al Jazeera*, August 4, 2015 [in Arabic]; Saheeb Anjarini, "'Ashbal' Camps: A Generation of [Local] Supporters and Foreigners Prepares to Invade the World," *al-Akhbar*, August 21, 2015 [in Arabic]; "A Human Rights Organization: ISIS Recruited between 500 and 800 Iraqi Children," *al-Quds al-Arabi*, June 21, 2015 [in Arabic]; and "ISIS Graduates 60 Children from a Theology Camp in Fallujah," *al-Quds al-Arabi*, June 13, 2015 [in Arabic].

66. Abu Bakr al-Najji, *Idaraat al-Tawahush: Akhtar Marhalaa Satamur Beha al-Umma* [Management of savagery: The most critical stage through which the Islamic nation will pass] (n.p.: Markaz al-Derasaat wal Buhuth al-Islamiyaa, n.d.), 83, https://pietervanostaeyen.files.wordpress .com/2015/02/idarat_al-tawahhush_-_abu_bakr_naji.pdf.

67. Fahmy Houeidi, "When Sinai Becomes a Headline for Terrorism in Egypt," *Assafir*, July 15, 2015 [in Arabic].

68. Jessica Stern and J. M. Berger, "Thugs Wanted—Bring Your Own Boots: How Isis Attracts Foreign Fighters to Its Twisted Utopia," *Guardian*, March 9, 2015; Liz Sly, "Islamic State Appears to Be Fraying from Within," *Washington Post*, March 8, 2015; and "Islamic State: Unfriended."

69. Shiv Malik, Ali Younes, Spencer Ackerman, and Mustafa Khalili, "How ISIS Crippled al-Qaida," *Guardian*, June 10, 2015, www.theguardian .com/world/2015/jun/10/how-isis-crippled-al-qaida.

70. See the link to a voice recording by ISIS, declaring war on Erdoğan and threating to attack Turkey, posted on August 17, 2015. https:// www.youtube.com/watch?v=mhHqz_QAUdA. See also Adam Withnall, "Isis Video Urges People of Turkey to Rise Up and Overthrow 'Satan' President Recep Erdogan," *Independent*, August 18, 2015.

71. Martin Williams, "Dozens of Fighters Are Defecting from the Islamic State. Here's Why," *Washington Post*, September 21, 2015; Schmitt

and Sengupta, "Thousands Enter Syria." See also J. Diamond, "Congressional Report: U.S. Has 'Failed' to Stop Flow of Foreign Fighters to ISIS," CNN.com, September 30, 2015, http://edition.cnn.com/2015/09/29/politics/foreign-fighters-isis-congressional-task-force-report/index.html; Erin Cunningham, "The Flow of Jihadists into Syria Dries Up as Turkey Cracks Down on the Border," *Washington Post*, August 1, 2015; David Brunnstrom, "U.S., Turkey Working to Finish Shutting Northern Syria Border: Kerry," Reuters, November 17, 2015.

72. Malik, "The ISIS Papers."

73. Baghdadi, "The Khilafa Publications." See also Ensor, "Islamic State leader Baghdadi Goads West."

74. "Abu Qatada Predicts the Dismantling of Baghdadi's Caliphate ...," *al-Quds al-Arabi*, December 29, 2015 [in Arabic]. See also Ra'id al-Hamed, "Changes in the Balance of Power in Iraq and Syria," *al-Quds al-Arabi*, January 2, 2016 [in Arabic].

75. If ISIS is only a bump in the road, as the old guard of Al Qaeda claim, why has the group succeeded where Al Qaeda failed?

76. Pierre Joris and Habib Tengour, *Poems for the Millennium*, vol. 4, *The University of California Book of North African Literature* (Berkeley: University of California Press, 2012).

77. Emile Nakhleh, "Islamic Reformation: The Antidote to Terrorism," *LobeLog*, January 13, 2015, http://lobelog.com/islamic-reformation-the-antidote-to-terrorism/.

78. See, for example, *Deliverance or Destruction? Syria at a Crossroads* (Cairo: Cairo Institute for Human Rights Studies, 2014). The book is edited by Syrian thinker Yassin al-Haj Saleh and contains a set of research papers written by prominent Syrian researchers and writers, including Ahmed Hasso, Akram al-Bunni, Anwar al-Bunni, and Radwan Ziadeh. Also see Abdallah Laroui, *The Crisis of the Arab Intellectual: Traditionalism or Historicism?*, translated from the French by Diarmid Cammell (Berkeley: University of California Press, 1976); Mohammed Abed Al Jabri, *Naqd al-`aql al-`Arabi* [Critique of Arab reason], 3 vols. (Beirut: Centre for Arab Unity Studies, 1984–1990); George Tarabishi, *Naqd Naqd al-aql al-Arabi* [A critique of the critique of the Arab reason], 4 vols. (Beirut: Dar al-Saqi, 1999–2004).

INDEX

dissolution of ISI by, 16; Islamic State of, 89; joining ISI, 132; al-Joulani and, power struggle with, 150, 187–90; murder of Sunnis, 145; as new head of ISI, 96; al-Nusra and, 29; recruitment of Baathist officers, 143; rise to power for, 130, 136–37; strategy of mystery, 138–43; suicide bombers used by, 144–45, 147; during Syrian conflict, 175; *tajweed* for, 131; takfiri ideology for, 132–35; violence and savagery of, 139, 144–47, 162; al-Zawahiri and, 90–91, 143, 253. *See also* Islamic State of Iraq and Syria
al-Baghdadi, Abu Omar, 85–86, 93–96, 144, 155, 237; assassination of, 96, 136–37; violence and savagery of, 162
Bahrain, Arab Spring protests in, 15, 18–19, 170, 203
Bakr, Haji, 130, 141–42, 181; in AQI, 157–58
Bangura, Zainab, 31
Barqawi, Issam Mohammed Taher, 54. *See also* al-Maqdisi, Abu Mohammed
Barzani, Massoud, 117
Battle of Tora Bora. *See* Tora Bora, Battle of
Bayat al-Imam, 54
beheadings, 40; under al-Zarqawi, 88
Beirut, ISIS in, 250
Beit al-Maqds, 212
Bekka Valley, Lebanon, 11
Belgium, radicalized youth from, 230
Berg, Nicholas, 68
Biden, Joe, 96
al-Bilawi, Osama, 152
bin Laden, Osama, 97, 129, 291; Abu Bakr al-Baghdadi and, 134–35, 143, 234; AQC power influenced by, 90–91, 241–42; Arab Spring protests and, 203–5, 209; declaration of war against U.S., 71, 74–75,

225; ISI supported by, 240; loss of public support for, 89; power vacuum after death of, 175; under Taliban protection, 4; al-Zarqawi and, 52, 73–76, 89, 256
Bin Mohamed, Abdullah, 14
The Black Power: The "Islamic" State and the Strategies of Terror (Reuter), 142
Bolshevik Revolution, 288
Bouaziz, Mohammed, 170
Breaking Down the Walls operation, 122–23
Brisard, Charles, 65
Bush, George H. W., 99
Bush, George W., 50, 52, 105, 108

caliphate: al-Adnani on, 28; AQC's declaration of, 226; establishment of, religious foundations for, 46; for ISIS, 7, 215, 225–31, 262; popular support for, 226–27; as transformative for Arab region, 228
caliphate cubs, 278–79
Camp Bucca: Abu Bakr al-Baghdadi at, 21, 85, 132–35, 298n31; al-Adnani at, 133; as Al Qaeda training camp, 133, 153
Camp Cropper, 133
Camp Speicher, 168
Chalabi, Ahmad, 111
Charlie Hebdo, 44
Christians: in Iraq, 30; ISIS treatment of, 32–33; rape of, by ISIS, 33; in al-Raqqa province, 201; taxation of, 32
coercion paradox, 232–35
Comey, James B., 45, 230
Communist Revolution, 288
Concerned Local Citizens coalition, 104
Coulibaly, Amedy, 44
Countering Violent Extremism (CVE) strategies, 230–31
court systems, 199
Crocker, Ryan, 115–16

DATE DUE

AUG 1 8 2017

MAR 0 0 2017

14
Day
Loan